D1234374

Management for Professionals

More information about this series at http://www.springer.com/series/10101

Mary J. Cronin • Tiziana C. Dearing
Editors

Managing for Social Impact

Innovations in Responsible Enterprise

 Springer

Editors
Mary J. Cronin
Carroll School of Management
Boston College
Chestnut Hill, MA, USA

Tiziana C. Dearing
School of Social Work
Boston College
Chestnut Hill, MA, USA

ISSN 2192-8096   ISSN 2192-810X   (electronic)
Management for Professionals
ISBN 978-3-319-46020-8   ISBN 978-3-319-46021-5   (eBook)
DOI 10.1007/978-3-319-46021-5

Library of Congress Control Number: 2017932622

Printed on acid-free paper

This Springer imprint is published by Springer Nature
The registered company is Springer International Publishing AG
The registered company address is: Gewerbestrasse 11, 6330 Cham, Switzerland

To Scott, for everything and more

To Carla, whose life was a quiet but persistent pursuit of social change

Preface

What do a Boston nonprofit with a 50-year history of serving the homeless, a global enterprise working to revive both its brand and its headquarters community, a public–private partnership to accelerate social change in urban America, and a venture-funded startup setting up preschools in rural India have in common? Although their resources, geographies, and governance structures are very different, all four organizations are publicly committed to prioritizing positive social impact. The social change initiatives pursued by Haley House in Boston, by Whirlpool in Benton Harbor, Michigan, by Living Cities across the USA, by Hippocampus Learning in India, and by many other leaders in managing for social impact are featured in the chapters of this book.

By design, *Managing for Social Impact: Innovations in Responsible Enterprise* analyzes the challenges of tackling systemic social problems through a multisector, interdisciplinary perspective. This book arose from the editors' conviction that long-term, sustainable social impact requires active management, cross-sector collaboration, social innovation, and a shared framework for engaging stakeholders and measuring impact across multiple sectors. Researchers, public thought leaders, and practitioners around the globe are grappling with these questions, but their insights are not typically available in a single publication.

To highlight the commonalities of strategy and practice across disparate social impact efforts, each chapter reflects on the social impact strategies employed, as well as best practices and lessons learned, over years of responsible enterprise management. Also by design, the responsible enterprise management of the book's title highlights the core definition of "enterprise" as a bold and complex undertaking, an intrinsically challenging and long-term endeavor, while "responsible" reflects commitment to, and accountability for, the outcomes. In this context, responsible enterprise characterizes the social impact work of nonprofit managers, venture investors, and leaders of public–private sector partnerships alike, as well as innovations within traditional corporate responsibility programs.

This juxtaposition of management, social impact, and enterprise reflects the growing importance of social enterprise models for scaling and sustaining change efforts. As described in the chapters that follow, social enterprise strategies have been adopted by nonprofit managers and impact investors as well as implemented by intentional long-term coalitions of elected officials, urban developers, foundations, and educational institutions working alongside companies of all sizes.

Multisector Perspectives

Managing for Social Impact is organized into six parts, with chapters representing the perspectives of nonprofit, corporate, public sector, investor, community activist, researcher, and analyst authors. In Part I, co-editor Tiziana C. Dearing, Professor of Macro Practice in the Boston College School of Social Work, describes a framework for social impact management that incorporates multisector strategies and best practices. The framework incorporates four foundational pillars: **Open Circles** that foster stakeholder inclusion and dynamic engagement; **Focused Purpose Sharing** that identifies the intersection of multiple stakeholder objectives within specific initiatives and points of time to motivate support for broad-based change efforts; **Mutuality of Success** that defines and shapes outcomes based on the understanding of multiple stakeholders that social impact benefits will be experienced at different levels over time, with milestones that mirror a variety of goals, needs, and expectations; and a **Persistent Change Perspective** that enables commitment to social change over timescales that extend beyond the typical planning cycles of individual managers or projects to create deep, persistent and stakeholder-driven community engagement.

These four pillars are essential for all types of organizations to make long-term impact on systemic social problems and in particular to develop their capacity for scaling, sustaining, and measuring change efforts begun at a local level or as a targeted program with time-limited objectives and funding. There are, however, many cross-sector lessons to be learned from the propensity of different organizational structures to prioritize particular pillars in their impact management strategies.

The chapters in Part II, "Social Justice and Sustainable Enterprise," illustrate the strengths of nonprofit organizations and change leaders in implementing Open Circles and Focused Purpose Sharing. Successful nonprofit managers must be keenly aware of the needs and objectives of stakeholders in the communities that they serve directly and welcome those stakeholders to play a part in the solution. They must also be skilled at articulating those needs to the broader community, including private and public funders, in order to convert sometime skeptics into volunteers, partners, and financial supporters who come to believe in the organization's purpose. These very strengths often create severe challenges in scaling and sustaining programs that rely on philanthropy and volunteer efforts to meet escalating social needs among community stakeholders. The contributors in Part II discuss how social enterprise models can be adapted to create diversified streams of revenue at the same time as enabling new types of scalable services that empower community stakeholders through training and employment opportunities.

The chapters in Part III, "Rethinking Corporate Social Responsibility From the Outside In," reveal the rapidly changing landscape of corporate social impact. Many public corporations are hard pressed to balance the escalating social impact expectations of consumers, community members, environmental activists, and employees, given global pressures on earnings and profitability. For corporate managers, opening the circle of stakeholders to encourage ever broader participation can be a daunting prospect, requiring a decisive shift away from decades of company-centric definitions of responsible enterprise. Some companies have focused on aligning their brand purpose with a social cause that resonates with consumers and employees, aiming to develop a sense of shared purpose that will build brand loyalty. There is a growing realization, however, that such alignment may not be enough to satisfy stakeholders, nor to address the complex social problems that are now seen as material to business success as well as stakeholder well-being.

Part IV explores the potential of "Public–Private Partnerships to Make Cities More Livable for All." Each chapter underscores the importance of cross-sector partnerships as the key to mutual success in addressing complex and multilayered urban problems including providing equal access to economic opportunity, housing, and quality education while mitigating urban environmental impacts and improving quality of life for residents. These issues become ever more urgent as urban centers house the majority of the world's population. There is widespread recognition that city government cannot solve these problems alone. In fact, no entity can do it alone; all residents share the built environment and have a stake in its policies and impact. This understanding supports the strategy of Open Circles to involve community members, corporations, foundations, and nonprofits working alongside elected officials and public sector employees. But the disparate needs of urban populations and the complexity of systemic social issues often hinder Focused Purpose Sharing and agreement on mutual definitions of success. Likewise, election cycles, budget fluctuations, and political considerations make it more difficult for city leaders to maintain a Persistent Change Perspective. Long-term, public–private partnerships help to address these challenges to sustaining social impact initiatives.

Scaling and sustaining social change initiatives take money, and lots of it. Social impact investors are a rapidly growing source of private capital for launching and growing responsible enterprise business models in the USA and globally. According to the Global Impact Investing Network (GIIN), an estimated $60 billion in private capital has been invested in socially responsible companies as of 2016. This amount is expected to grow dramatically over the next 20 years, propelled by the millennial generation's commitment to creating a positive impact. An investor practice leader at the World Economic Forum projects that in 10 years global investing for social impact will skyrocket to $2 trillion. By way of comparison, the Ford Foundation, which announced in 2015 that it would focus its grant making entirely on programs to address social inequality, expects to award $1 billion in grants over the next 5 years. It's clear that strategies for impact investing will be a critical factor in shaping responsible enterprise in the coming decades. The chapters in Part V, "Investing for

Scalable Social Change," make the point that scaling impact investing will require active investor involvement to mentor the founders of social enterprise portfolio companies and help them to manage rapid growth. This active management will enable strong financial returns on social investments over time, attracting more private capital for social impact.

Best practices for managing multisector social impact initiatives are evolving, so it is no surprise that the frameworks for impact measurement are also still in flux. Part VI, "Measuring and Reporting on Social Impact," highlights two areas where global measurement frameworks are particularly important, the Smart City movement and corporate sustainability reporting through the Global Reporting Initiative (GRI). The GRI and Smart City assessment frameworks are continually adapting to encompass the complexity and interconnected nature of the social issues being addressed. This indicates that such frameworks need to incorporate multisector perspectives as well as become more inclusive of all stakeholders over the long term.

The editors hope that this volume will contribute to the multisector sharing of strategies and best practices for developing and managing scalable and sustainable social impact solutions.

Chestnut Hill, MA   Mary J. Cronin
                                                                                                             Tiziana C. Dearing

Acknowledgements

First, we extend our appreciation to the chapter authors; without their generous contribution of time and expertise this book, quite literally, would not have been possible. Our appreciation comes with a humble acknowledgement that due to the unavoidable constraints of page limits and editorial timelines, this book cannot hope to present the full depth of the social impact insights and experience embodied in the authors themselves and in their organizations. That said, heartfelt thanks to Jessica Abensour, Bridget Akinc, Jen Anderson, Bing Broderick, Talia Champlin, Ruthbea Yesner Clarke, Matthew Combe, Gregg Croteau, Liz Delaney, Mark Feldman, Ed Frechette, Michael Gilligan, Dawn Grenier, Ben Hecht, Nikki Korn, Allison Kroner, Amanda Lankerd, Susan Musinsky, Anna Trieschmann, and Susan Wickwire, and to their organizations, colleagues, and all the stakeholders who inhabit and give meaning to their chapter contributions and their ongoing work.

In the process of developing the framework for this book and in writing our chapters, the editors have benefited from interactions, feedback, and resources provided by scores of generous colleagues—too many to name individually. We thank you all and hope that you are pleased with the outcome of so many fruitful discussions and thoughtful suggestions. In particular, thanks to Will Poole and the Unitus Seed Fund for access to the invaluable background materials, discussions, and time in reviewing drafts that made the "Impact Investing at the Base of the Pyramid" chapter possible. Thank you, too, to the Center for Social Innovation at Boston College, whose work first brought the two editors together. In addition, Tiziana Dearing would like to thank center co-director Dr. Stephanie Berzin, and Deans Alberto Godenzi and Gautam Yadama of the School of Social Work at Boston College. A special note of appreciation from Mary Cronin to Andy Boynton, Dean of the Carroll School of Management, for his ongoing support of research, teaching, and publication about managing for social impact.

Thanks to Neil Levine, our editor, and to all the Springer team for your help and encouragement in making the book a reality. We also thank Ben Horton at Boston College for his administrative and editorial help.

Finally, in the spirit of Open Circles and Mutuality of Success, the editors are proud to donate any and all proceeds from the publication of this book to nonprofit organizations that are working towards social impact on a daily basis.

Contents

Contributors

Jessica Abensour VOX Global, Washington, DC, USA

Bridget Akinc Carroll School of Management, Boston College, Chestnut Hill, MA, USA

Jen Anderson VOX Global, Washington, DC, USA

Bing Broderick Haley House, Boston, MA, USA

Talia Champlin Battle Creek, MI, USA

Ruthbea Yesner Clarke International Data Corporation, Framingham, MA, USA

Matthew Combe Seattle 2030 District, Seattle, WA, USA

Mary J. Cronin Carroll School of Management, Boston College, Chestnut Hill, MA, USA

Gregg Croteau UTEC, Lowell, MA, USA

Tiziana C. Dearing Boston College School of Social work, Chestnut Hill, MA, USA

Liz Delaney Environmental Defense Fund, Boston, MA, USA

Mark Feldman Cause Consulting, Boston, MA, USA

Ed Frechette UTEC, Lowell, MA, USA

Michael Gilligan Urban Catalyst, Boston, MA, USA

Dawn Grenier UTEC, Lowell, MA, USA

Ben Hecht Living Cities, New York, NY, USA

Nikki Korn Cause Consulting, Boston, MA, USA

Allison Kroner b.good, Boston, MA, USA

Amanda Lankerd Battle Creek, MI, USA

Susan Musinsky Social Innovation Forum, Boston, MA, USA

Anna Trieschmann Social Innovation Forum, Boston, MA, USA

Susan Wickwire Seattle 2030 District, Seattle, WA, USA

I

Managing for Return on Social Innovation (ROSI): Pillars for Sustainable Social Impact

Tiziana C. Dearing

Abstract As global focus on Corporate Social Responsibility, impact investing, and systems change increases, large-scale and cross-sector initiatives have emerged that attempt to create sustainable impact on some of the most intractable social problems. These efforts range in size—from local to global; in scope—from a few parties to massive collaborations; and in sector of origin—public, private, or non-governmental. As yet, however, it has been difficult to articulate a framework of best practice strategies for positive, sustainable success in such endeavors.

This chapter argues that emerging best practices do, however, suggest four common pillars for sustainable social impact. When employed from the beginning in social change strategies, they not only can increase the likelihood of creating positive social impact, but also can help overcome common challenges faced by long-term, systems change endeavors, including challenges of scaling, sustainability, and measurement.

The chapter then looks forward, to management and measurement practices required to support sustained implementation of these strategies. Persistent Change Perspective and an accompanying persistent change measurement approach become essential factors in the strategies used by collaborating parties, as well as in the cultures of teams, managers, and organizations involved.

Keywords Open Circles • Focused Purpose Sharing • Mutuality of Success • Persistent Change Perspective • Pillars of sustainable social impact

Introduction

Social impact has become a kind of watchword for corporations, nonprofits, governments, impact investors, and community organizations around the world. Whether it is expressed through Corporate Social Responsibility (CSR), strategic

T.C. Dearing (✉)
Boston College School of Social Work,
140 Commonwealth Avenue, McGuinn Hall 217, Chestnut Hill, MA 02467, USA
e-mail: dearing@bc.edu

© Springer International Publishing Switzerland 2017
M.J. Cronin, T.C. Dearing (eds.), *Managing for Social Impact*,
Management for Professionals, DOI 10.1007/978-3-319-46021-5_1

philanthropy, sustainability, socially responsible investing, social entrepreneurship, or other terms, a commitment to positive social impact is now included in the mission statements of tens of thousands of organizations in the private and public sectors. The United Nations Global Compact calls itself "the world's largest corporate sustainability effort," and lists over 12,000 signatories in 170 countries "representing nearly every sector and size," including over 8000 global corporations as participants. These Global Compact signatories have pledged "to align strategies and operations with universal principals ... and take actions that advance societal goals" (UN Global Compact 2016).

Increased attention to social impact has brought an increase in the dollars invested in its pursuit, as well as the diversity of those dollars. For example, in the emerging world of impact investing—"investments made into companies, organizations and funds with the intention to generate social and environmental impact alongside a financial return"—a 2015 Global Impact Investing Network (GIIN) survey identified $60 billion in impact investing capital under management (GIIN 2016c). Investors committed $15 billion to 7500 investments in 2015 alone (Mudaliar et al. 2016).

This interest carries over to philanthropic bodies as well. In a 2015 survey conducted by the Center for Effective Philanthropy, 41 % of foundation CEOs reported engaging in impact investing (Buchanan et al. 2015). Traditional giving also focuses on social impact for systems-level issues. The USA's 1000 top foundations gave away more than $22 billion in 2012, for example, with the top 50 giving nearly half of that. Fully 60 % of that money went to systems-change-oriented issues, including, among others, education, health, the environment, and international affairs and human rights (Foundation Center 2012, 2013).

This global attention and investment in social impact are reinforced at the local level by a multiplicity of community-based programs, and an outpouring of volunteer efforts and individual donations dedicated to social impact causes. In the USA alone, there are approximately 2.3 million nonprofit organizations (National Center for Charitable Statistics 2012), and 43,000 family and community foundations (Foundation Center 2012, 2013). In addition, Americans clock about 8 billion volunteer hours annually (Clolery 2014).

With such intense focus on social impact, it might seem that there would be a well-integrated, shared framework underpinning the multitude of initiatives by organizations that include managing for social impact as a significant component of their strategies. But the massive scale of today's multi-sector social impact activity comes with its own intrinsic challenges. One such challenge is discerning commonality in emerging best practices, social impact frameworks, and measurement models among change leaders working in different sectors, on diverse social issues, in programs that vary in scale from hyper-local to global. It's also a challenge to address the program timing and assessment needs of a wide variety of players across government, philanthropy, nonprofits, and for-profit entities. Structural incentives, acceptable return horizons, and attitudes toward risk all vary, often dramatically. Add to this mix the varying capacities for sustained collaboration, and the multisystem complexity of the issues themselves, and it becomes clear why creating standard, shared frameworks across the social impact landscape is an unmet challenge.

A multi-sector framework of best practices may not be necessary for a single organization to take on an ambitious social change project on a single issue. The most pressing social problems, however—income inequality, gentrification, equitable development, environmental degradation, and other system-level issues— require a deeper, more integrated commitment. For leaders and organizations ready to take on today's complex social challenges, a shared framework is essential to achieve economies of scale, to ensure buy-in from all relevant stakeholders and to sustain their efforts over extended timescales.

Examples and lessons do exist that suggest a framework for successful, sustained social impact strategies. Best practices are emerging in processes and approaches for creating sustainable social change, in measurement approaches with sufficient scope and breadth to capture the results, and in responding to the complex challenges that come along the way. These emergent best practices call for previously unprecedented collaboration, flexibility to allow for shifting roles and responsibilities, fierce tenacity in the face of what will sometimes be slow-moving change, ecumenical and process-oriented measurement that invites more than one definition of success, and the ability to scale by going big and/or going deep, depending on what the situation requires. This chapter seeks to describe a framework emerging from these best practices, some challenges to developing and maintaining strategies that employ the framework, and what those strategies suggest must come next in achieving return on social innovation.

Shared Social Impact Foundations

Understanding the commonalities in social impact strategies across organizations, and from different sectors, enables more effective cross-fertilization and learning. This is true even from seemingly unrelated, but relevant, programs that are initiated by different types of organizations or stakeholder groups. The pillars described below represent key shared characteristics of emerging best practices that are common across multiple sectors, types of organizations, and types of social change initiatives, though they are often expressed in different terminology and implemented in different ways depending on whether the entity is a global enterprise, a community organization, or a social venture.

These four characteristics comprise the foundational pillars of sustainable social impact. Together, they offer a basic framework for social change initiatives that are deployed across multiple sectors and stakeholders. They seek to solve for questions of scope, buy-in, sustainability, and systems-level change. They also begin to provide a blueprint for the management practices and strategies necessary to sustain them. Designing social innovations with these pillars in mind will create the best possible chance of long-term return on investments made by organizations in the public, nonprofit, and private sectors.

There have been numerous attempts to capture the art of successful social impact collaborations in the past. See, for example, "Collective Impact" by John Kania and

Mark Kramer (2011) and "Creating Shared Value" by Michael Porter and Mark Kramer (2011). The pillars described here are an attempt to move such efforts both into a new arena and into greater levels of dynamism. The new arena is a flexible one in which both the source of the enterprise—public, private, and nonprofit—and its scope—hyper-local to global—can vary. The dynamism is also a type of flexibility, this time in players and time horizon. The framework offered here specifically seeks to allow for (a) stakeholders to come in and out over extended periods of time; (b) shared definitions not only of agenda or the ultimate goal, but also resources, processes, and leadership along the way; (c) success as defined by each stakeholder, and as one in which parties not only benefit from the initiative's objectives being met, but also benefit in their own ways from the positive results of social change; and (d) mutuality of purpose and success without requiring equal distribution of either. The definitions of the pillars offered in the next section should help clarify these distinctions.

The four pillars are grounded in expanded stakeholder roles—defined here as the relationships between any and all interested parties engaged in or affected by an organization, company, collaborative, or initiative. They also are steeped in attitudes of openness, tenacity, constructive impatience, a willingness to share control, and an appetite for and ability to recognize success for the enterprise in larger social change successes. Once understood, commitment to employing these pillars can drive strategy, hiring, culture, and management practices across a wide variety of actors and initiatives.

Further, the four pillars, at least to some extent, cascade. As described below, the capacity to welcome new stakeholders via Open Circles leads to Focused Purpose Sharing. Focused Purpose Sharing supports stakeholder expectations for Mutuality of Success, and so on. The cascading is not linear, however. These are ongoing strategies, not steps in a process. Each must be actively sustained, and each will evolve as the others are pursued.

Four Common Pillars of Sustainable Social Impact

Open Circles: Open Circles refers to the capacity to welcome new stakeholders. It requires embracing broad and often shifting stakeholder engagement. Stakeholder identities become dynamic, and engaged stakeholders often evolve into different or multiple roles over time: employees become community activists; activists become managers or social entrepreneurs; CEOs become investors; public sector leaders become foundation heads; individual residents become public sector leaders, etc. The practice of Open Circles broadens considerably who might be a stakeholder, favoring self-identification. It also involves the extra effort required to engage and maintain this broader group, including their entrances and exits along the way, throughout a social change process. Open Circles must be actively cultivated and maintained, and not all parties in collaboration are equally suited to the role of cultivator. Building the trust, credibility, and neutrality necessary to help foster and sustain Open Circles is an act of cultivation in and of itself.

Focused Purpose Sharing: Focused Purpose Sharing requires a level of specific, shared definition of purpose and process among stakeholders. That's not the same as everyone having the same objectives all along the way. Just as stakeholders will come in and out of the work over a long-term systems change process, so their objectives will align more or less at different times, and different priorities will take precedence at different stages. Adopting Focused Purpose Sharing embraces these fluctuations, even with the challenges they represent. What is necessary is (a) solid agreement on what the overall social change objective is; (b) shared understanding of the roles needed to pursue the objective; (c) shared commitment to participate in the process; (d) a willingness among stakeholders to share their resources—and among other stakeholders to recognize those resources—as they become important to the process; and (e) that stakeholders not be actively pursuing other purposes counter to the social change objectives. This approach has the effect not only of fostering Mutuality of Success (see the next pillar), but also of inviting resources, benefits, and innovations from unexpected places. Focused Purpose Sharing is anchored in ideas such as "shared values," and "shared purpose" (Boncheck 2013), but carries them further down the value chain.

Mutuality of Success: Following on the heels of Focused Purpose Sharing, success should be mutual among stakeholders. *Mutuality* of success does not mean *equality* of success. This is not some desire to achieve balanced weights on a scale. Nevertheless, if stakeholders share a social change objective, it is because, by definition, each party has a "stake" in that outcome. To achieve the full benefit of a social innovation, then, those stakes must be met. They may not all be met at the same time, or with the same intensity. They should, however, attempt to reflect the intensity of the stakeholder's commitment and need. That's not the same thing as the share of success reflecting the level of resources a given stakeholder can invest, however. The very disparities social impact initiatives seek to address make resource investment a poor measuring stick for proportionality in success. In the end, success should simply be a mutual experience. When this is the case, goal achievement by some—and in particular, the larger organizations at the table—genuinely benefits or newly empowers all other stakeholders.

Persistent Change Perspective: Achieving true social impact takes time and sustained collaboration. Therefore, we often call for patience. Indeed, "patient capital" has become a watchword of impact investing for that very reason. Persistent Change Perspective, however, is not about patience, but instead about tenacity and perseverance. Rather than being patient for change, it reflects a constant, active striving for it, and the endurance to keep up that striving for as long as its takes. Given the life cycle of everything from grants to elections to attention spans, it can be extremely difficult to achieve the sustained attention and efforts necessary to produce lasting social impact without this kind of perseverance. And while patience is, indeed, essential, the ability simultaneously to be *impatient* with the current pace of change is necessary to maintain inspiration and to invite the kind of risk taking and creative thinking necessary for systems-level change.

Illustrations of the Four Pillars

Part of the reason the Four Common Pillars of Sustainable Social Impact resonate is that they can be applied across types of endeavor, and especially across sectors. For decades now, scholars and practitioners alike have recognized that solving social problems is not the exclusive domain of nonprofits, or of the public sector, or the private sector. Effective, sustainable solutions require deep cross-sector collaboration. The following examples, many drawn from the chapters in *Managing for Social Impact*, demonstrate how the best practices embedded in each pillar provide a framework to be employed by any party or parties organizing a social change endeavor.

Open Circles

Open Circles are characterized by stakeholders who represent formal and informal "players," and who hold formal and informal positional authority. Stakeholders may be corporate, nonprofit, public sector, venture investors, community members, foundations, or social entrepreneurs. Further, Open Circles recognize that expectations and roles change, with active stakeholders often taking on aspects of the others' traditional roles in long-term efforts, or literally coming to represent different stakeholders over time.

Requirements for organizational accountability and transparency are rising, even as models for measuring the return on social investment are hard-pressed to capture all the dimensions of change over the longer periods of time required for addressing embedded problems. Rooted in the perspective of the community itself, stakeholder-led strategies and initiatives may be based on deep local experience, data analytics, or, as recommended in this volume by Ben Hecht in "Co-Creating More Livable Cities," creating a "one-table" framework for planning. Rethinking the role of the organization or the power holder in relation to the community or the individual is a theme that emerges again and again across the landscape of social impact programs and players. Open Circles allow different players to assume power at different times, and allow individuals and organizations dynamically to come in and out of leadership.

Nonprofit organizations tend to be ahead of the curve in using Open Circle strategies, compared to the public and private sectors. Haley House and its Bakery Café offer a nonprofit illustration. In this volume, Bing Broderick describes the launch of the Bakery Café in "Food with Purpose: Dudley Dough and Haley House Bakery Café." Haley House opened the Bakery Café in the Dudley neighborhood of Boston at a time when it was characterized by low incomes, high unemployment, and disinvestment in the physical infrastructure. The Bakery Café was popular, and as it grew in reputation, residents from the neighborhood began offering to add their own skills and flair to its offerings. In response, Haley House demonstrated incredible openness to community ideas and leadership at each stage of the Bakery Café's development. What resulted was a nonprofit business that also became a part of the heartbeat of Dudley, with arts and culture events, new products, and even new lines of business all resulting from being open to the interests of people who self-identified as Haley House stakeholders. Their Open Circle eventually led to one of their program participants, who had spent time in prison, designing and then running a Transitional Employment Program for men and women reentering their communities from incarceration. Opening the circle led not only to a broader community of supporters, but also to shifting roles for stakeholders which ultimately added value to a shared agenda.

The Social Innovation Forum (SIF) offers another nonprofit illustration of Open Circles. In "A Marketplace Approach to Building and Supporting Sustainable Social Purpose Organizations" in this volume, authors Susan Musinsky and Anna Trieschmann present a model of interaction between social innovators and funders they call the "Marketplace." The SIF marketplace pairs social innovators or entrepreneurs with an ecosystem of volunteers and donors who wish to advance the innovators' impact. One idea behind the marketplace is a shift in the traditional power structures between donors and nonprofits. Rather than there being a charity and a giver, there are two parties participating together toward a common goal, each bringing different skills, talents, and resources to the table.

In sociology, this might be known as "reciprocity" (Gouldner 1960). However, reciprocity may not be quite right, as the capacity for equal exchange or benefit is not the threshold for considering a party as a stakeholder in the Open Circle. *Equal* exchange and an *equal* share in defining success are not necessarily the goals. Stakeholders must be interested in and capable of *beneficial* exchange, however. Perhaps the better description is one from marketplace pioneers Bill Traynor and Frankie Blackburn (2015), who write, "Marketplaces … invite people to mix across differences, exchange ideas, advice, and needed items, and to take entrepreneurial action." Open Circles encourage disparate, or even just separate, players to join to take entrepreneurial action on a problem that interests and affects them all. In SIF's marketplace approach, organizations develop new skills and access new sources of funding, while donors and coaches find meaning for their time, talent, and treasure, and engage with social issues at a level that would be difficult to achieve on their own.

Project 20/20 in Battle Creek, MI, also illustrates the importance of opening stakeholder circles to encompass multiple resident perspectives on economic development. Talia Champlin and Amanda Lankerd's contribution to this volume, "A Community-Driven Change Model in Battle Creek: Project 20/20," describes how various official community and business leaders had been collaborating for decades on social change strategies to improve the quality of life in Battle Creek. What Project 20/20 recognized was that successful social change initiatives rely on the buy-in and cooperation of a broader set of constituents than are typically included in economic development and community change planning processes. There were stakeholder perspectives in Battle Creek that had not been fully represented in planning meetings. Residents, leaders of smaller nonprofit organizations, parents, and informal community leaders were all stakeholders, and saw themselves as such. They had the ability to embrace change or slow it down, contribute their resources and ideas, or stand on the outside and be frustrated by strategies they felt missed the mark. Therefore, the city would find itself repeating efforts. Project 20/20 arguably developed a process to facilitate Open Circles, challenging the power holders and the disenfranchised stakeholders alike to change their minds about who should be involved and how.

Project 20/20 also recognized the profound importance of building social capital across stakeholders in order for the change to last. These informal networks of trust, communication, and resources enable the change to penetrate more deeply into the community. They also create a more stable platform on which to build all future social change initiatives.

b.good, a fast-casual restaurant chain headquartered in Boston, offers an example of how smaller local businesses can innovate ahead of large enterprises which often struggle to create open stakeholder relationships. As described by Allison Kroner in "Stakeholder Voices Shaping Community Engagement at b.good" in this volume, b.good considers its customers part of the family and lends its stores, supplies, and brand to social change initiatives created and conducted by those customers. Motivated customers take the lead in selecting social causes and raising donations, knowing that b.good will contribute free food and meeting space. It's a form of crowdsourcing donations, through sharing the use of the b.good brand and resources with customers, who are then empowered to activate their own personal networks on behalf of a social cause.

One manifestation of this approach is the b.good Family Foundation, which makes corporate contributions from funds raised by customer efforts using a customer-driven nomination and selection process. The company understands that today's customer wants a partnership with, and even some sense of ownership of, the brands with which they associate. Therefore, the company puts the customer alongside them in the driver's seat.

This openness to customers playing a different kind of stakeholder role has also allowed b.good to speed up the clock on its CSR efforts. Most small companies don't have the bandwidth for a corporate foundation and a fairly sophisticated CSR operation. Because b.good's bandwidth comes from the customers, the company has created social impact capacity sooner in its life cycle than it might have otherwise.

Focused Purpose Sharing

When a broad range of stakeholders participate in the Open Circle, the various stakeholders' needs, aspirations, and capabilities enter with them. Best practice undertakings will welcome those needs and aspirations, as well as the resources stakeholders can bring to bear. They work to develop a shared vision of success among the stakeholders, and then to think creatively about who brings what to the table, and how to deploy that focus and those resources in the right ways, at the right times, in common cause. The Haley House example demonstrates that relationship. With each new customer who wanted to be part of a vibrant Dudley neighborhood, Haley House gained resources they could deploy toward a focused, shared purpose. The same is true with SIF's marketplace.

The Seattle 2030 District offers an excellent public sector view of Focused Purpose Sharing. As Sandra Wickwire and Matthew Combe explain in this volume in "Transforming the Urban Built Environment: The Seattle 2030 District as a Model for Collaborative Change," the Seattle 2030 District was an aspirational undertaking formed in response to the goals established in the 2030 Challenge—a global effort spearheaded by the architectural community to ensure that all new buildings will be carbon neutral by the year 2030. The organizers and collaborators in the Seattle 2030 District expanded on that goal, adding stringent targets for energy use in new buildings and existing buildings, as well as water use in all buildings and the CO_2 produced from vehicle miles traveled in the city.

The act of responding to the 2030 Challenge and seeking to achieve even more ambitious targets for the city served as an invitation to Focused Purpose Sharing for a variety of stakeholders. Property owners, developers and managers, architects, energy officials, transportation specialists, and conservationists—all could come together to build a set of objectives and a path forward for the Seattle 2030 District. Indeed, the initiative also attracted players from all levels of the public sector—city, state, and federal. Historically, all the stakeholders in the Seattle 2030 District may not have worked together. At times, they even may have perceived other players in the coalition to be at cross-purposes, or at least not in regular, common cause. Here, however, they could deploy their resources toward a focused, shared purpose.

While nonprofits have demonstrated a particular ability to foster Open Circles, many corporations are inclined to align their brands with social causes toward what can become Focused Purpose Sharing. Sometimes companies pursue only the patina of such deep, common cause. Other times, however, they truly connect with stakeholders on focused, shared purpose. In the world of Corporate Social Responsibility (CSR), one could argue that well-developed and well-executed "purpose branding" displays elements of Focused Purpose Sharing. Mark Feldman and Nikki Korn of Cause Consulting offer several examples in "Evolution, Innovation and Best Practices in Corporate Social Impact" in this volume. For example, Chouinard Equipment created the Patagonia brand when the company decided to embrace customer and other stakeholder concerns about the environmental impact of their profitable climbing equipment. IKEA, which normally targets commercial and residential customers, engaged in Focused Purpose Sharing with the UN High Commission on Refugees' Refugee Housing Unit. As Feldman and Korn note,

> It became clear that the company's expertise in design, logistics, and flat packing could help solve some of the emergency shelter challenges. IKEA designed and manufactured safer, bigger, more cost effective refugee housing that was easy to build, could withstand severe weather, and ultimately created a more livable, safe and comfortable home for families.

Liz Delaney's discussion of the Climate Corps program in "Embedding Environmental Advocates: EDF Climate Corps" in this volume offers another look at Focused Purpose Sharing. Created by the nonprofit Environmental Defense Fund (EDF), the Climate Corps provides a robust example of Focused Purpose Sharing between the corporate and nonprofit sectors around the goal of reducing environmental impacts. EDF's Climate Corps embeds graduate students who are trained as climate fellow summer interns into enterprises in order to identify cost-saving, energy-saving initiatives. At the end of the fellowship, these graduate students deliver detailed proposals with the associated business cases to each organization's senior leadership for consideration. Ninety percent of host organizations surveyed by EDF indicate their intention to implement at least one of the recommendations made by their Climate Corps fellow.

This is a model partnership, in which EDF and the more than 400 organizations that have welcomed fellows join in Focused Purpose Sharing. Climate change is not at the heart of the core business for most of the host organizations. Nevertheless, companies such as adidas, Iron Mountain, and Blue Shield of California have implemented extensive energy-saving programs based on the business cases developed by a Climate Corps fellow. Importantly, after their Climate Corps experience, many of the fellows are moving into full-time careers managing sustainability programs in the private sector.

In this volume's "Transformation through Social Impact at Whirlpool Corporation," Bridget Akinc describes the importance of Focused Purpose Sharing to the brand identity and CSR efforts of the Whirlpool Corporation. As part of a long-term CSR strategy, Whirlpool Corporation and its employees have spent years engaging in economic development work in Benton Harbor, MI, home of its corporate headquarters. That work has included economic redevelopment partnerships and collaboration with Habitat for Humanity to build hundreds of units of affordable housing for Benton Harbor residents.

In the process of a company-wide innovation effort, Whirlpool's employees began to recognize the role the company and its products could play in affecting the challenges of peoples' everyday lives. After conducting market research to validate this idea, they transformed their brand strategy, creating an "Every day, care™" campaign, which seeks to develop and sell appliances that meet the real-life needs of today's chaotic families. Each step for Whirlpool Corporation was an attempt at Focused Purpose Sharing, culminating in a stronger brand for the company via a better understanding of what Whirlpool and its customers both wanted for customer families.

Mutuality of Success

Mutuality of Success builds naturally from Focused Purpose Sharing. Such shared success is, or should be, the ultimate end goal of collaborative approaches. Once again, mutual success does not necessarily mean that each stakeholder experiences the *same* success, or the same *amount* of success. Instead, the idea is that all stakeholders in the Open Circle, and who have engaged in Focused Purpose Sharing, should experience outcomes that achieve the purpose, and also benefit their interests in the social change. Once again, note a special emphasis on ensuring that successes are seen as such by the most disenfranchised. It's also worth noting that the emergence of both social ventures and benefit corporations, or "B Corps," is based on making mutuality a priority. That's one reason both organizational forms are such an important trend in the social change landscape today.

For a nonprofit illustration of Mutuality of Success, one can return to the Social Innovation Forum. The entrepreneurial actors in SIF's marketplace include nonprofit leaders, social enterprise founders, donors, executive coaches, and professional service providers (Musinsky and Trieschmann). They all enter the marketplace with Focused Purpose Sharing around scaling effective solutions to specific, complex social problems. They also enter with different metrics of their own success, however. The nonprofit leader wants funding and brand recognition to expand the organization's level of service. The volunteer executive coach wants to help transform the nonprofit leader's skill set. The donor wants an investment that works, and that makes meaning for her with her time and money. When all three are achieved, not only is the focused shared purpose achieved, but each stakeholder also experiences success for himself or herself.

UTEC, a nonprofit in Lowell, MA, embodies Mutuality of Success. Croteau et al. describe the organization and its approach in this volume, in "Social Enterprise for Economic Opportunity at UTEC." UTEC works with youth who have demonstrated risk of becoming "disconnected" or involved in the criminal justice system. UTEC engages the youth in positive life changes, supporting them to achieve their high school equivalency, develop job skills, achieve sustainable long-term employment, and become active in social justice issues. One way UTEC does this is through employing the youth in a number of social enterprises, revenues from which then also help cover UTEC's bottom line.

UTEC pursues a deep commitment to the Cities of Lowell and Lawrence, MA, their families, and their young people. At first blush, one might think that UTEC is a basic "get youth off the streets" program. The organization's vision is more profound than that, however, because it does believe in Mutuality of Success. The vision is one of vibrancy and prosperity for the young people who engage with UTEC, creating young people who believe in themselves and what they can do for their communities.

That vision is pursued with the express belief that transformation for these young people can and ultimately will transform the community as a whole, and vice versa. Steady incomes and lack of recidivism, therefore, are insufficient accomplishments. Those successes might be good for UTEC's funding case, but they don't offer the shared transformation that UTEC, its young people, or its supporters seek. That's why UTEC builds businesses the youth feel a part of, helps them pursue education at the highest level each youth wants, and builds concepts of social activism and community engagement into all aspects of their culture. It's also why, when UTEC needed a bigger headquarters, they added 8000 square feet of space right where they were in downtown Lowell, and turned the existing part of their building into the oldest LEED Platinum-certified building in the USA (UTEC 2016). UTEC youth helped transform the existing space and build the addition, and UTEC expanded its catering business to include Café UTEC on the first floor, offering affordable, healthy, preprepared foods in a part of Lowell known to be a food desert. Each of these investments represented a commitment to Mutuality of Success for UTEC, its young people, the people of Lowell, and the city itself.

These efforts have demonstrated consistently that as the youth become socially and economically stable, the entire community *does* benefit each stakeholder in a different way. UTEC produces more transitional jobs in the community, and gets revenues for its operations. The community has more workers, taxpayers, and informal community leaders while also achieving reductions in crime, incarceration, and recidivism. Businesses have a strengthened labor force, and customers of the social enterprises—which include catering, woodworking, and mattress recycling—get quality providers who meet their needs, but who also allow them to invest in a social purpose with their consumer dollars. Not every stakeholder experiences success proportionately. As noted earlier, that's not the goal. But stakeholders do benefit according to their needs, and as UTEC's success grows, so does theirs.

Public–private sector partnerships enhance the potential for Mutuality of Success by opening stakeholder participation and building purpose sharing into the fundamental design of social impact projects. All three pillars are embedded in the "one-table" model that Living Cities implements in its programs (Hecht). Living Cities is a nonprofit that convenes public and private resources to support cities or municipalities in improving opportunities for their low-income residents. TII, or The Integration Initiative, is a program of Living Cities that offers multiyear financial and planning support to cities prepared to target their specific, and most challenging, social issues. Living Cities has pursued TII through two rounds, investing first in five cities for three years, conducting a robust evaluation, and then seeking to deploy those lessons learned with a second group of cities while continuing to support the first group.

Through that learning, Living Cities has identified four key elements necessary to bring TII efforts to scale in cities. The first of those is "Success must be clearly defined, shared and supported." They found that pursuing such mutual success challenged the players in a city to ask from the beginning, "What can we do together that we could not do alone?" This question underscores the relationship between Focused Purpose Sharing, Mutuality of Success, and achieving sustainable, systems-level change.

The Smart Cities movement also demonstrates Mutuality of Success. It is a global movement focused predominantly on using technology to improve city efficiency, environmental impact, and effectiveness on behalf of residents in response to rapid urbanization. As Ruthbea Clarke demonstrates in this volume, in "Measuring Success in the Development of Smart and Sustainable Cities," a Smart Cities approach focuses on a flexible infrastructure of people and processes prepared to identify and leverage new technologies to meet any of a number of city challenges. The ultimate point is to ensure that cities work for all of their residents while improving overall sustainability. Therefore, technology improvements that make, for example, municipal offices more efficient can, when deployed with Focused Purpose Sharing to improve quality of life for low-income residents, also improve access to resources that low-income residents need. For example, San Francisco has driven down the number of people dropped from Supplemental Nutrition Assistance Program (SNAP) benefits by sending enrollees nudges by text to keep them from missing re-enrollment deadlines (Hecht).

In impact investing, a private sector endeavor, the purpose is to make financial investments that drive success in businesses with either an express or a secondary social purpose while ensuring financial returns for investors. It is an investment practice born specifically of a desire to create Mutuality of Success. Michael Gilligan offers an example from his own investment philosophy as founder of Urban Catalyst impact investing in "Catalyzing Social Impact Investments" in this volume. Gilligan highlights 99Degrees Custom—a custom apparel producer in Lowell, MA, that employs immigrants from the Dominican Republic who bring with them extensive experience in textiles—specifically because the company leveraged the skills that workers from the Dominican diaspora could offer while creating a profitable product. Investors, 99Degrees, and the employees from the Dominican diaspora each achieve success in their own goals while pursuing Focused Purpose Sharing for profitability and viable employment for workers in Lowell.

When thinking about the private sector as a whole, customer expectations have reached a point at which corporations are hard-pressed to achieve business success without some investment in mutual success with and among stakeholders around social impact. Consider the case Jen Anderson and Jessica Abensour make in "Measuring Your Company's Impact: How to Make the Most of Sustainability Reporting Frameworks" in this volume, regarding the ubiquity of environmental, social, and governance (ESG) reporting. They note that the percentage of the Standard and Poor's 500 companies publishing regular sustainability reports grew from 20 in 2010 to 75 in 2015. As they explain, "Reporting is evolving because companies' role in society is evolving … expectations have shifted so that stakeholders including customers, advocacy groups, community members and government entities, are looking to business to help solve societal problems."

Steps toward social impact without ensuring true *mutuality* of success are insufficient, however. Whirlpool Corporation learned this lesson in Benton Harbor, a struggling city with high levels of poverty and unemployment. At a key inflection point for the company, Whirlpool made the commitment to keep its corporate headquarters in Benton Harbor, and then invested hundreds of millions of dollars in local economic development, including environmental cleanup and affordable housing (Akinc). It joined a coalition that created a PGA-rated golf course and a luxury residential complex. While these efforts produced tangible economic development results and drew some praise in Benton Harbor, the company also drew criticism from local residents for prioritizing local investments that were not matched with resident needs and priorities. Whirlpool Corporation continues to engage with the residents of Benton Harbor to create a broader sense of mutual success among community members, reflecting the importance of a Persistent Change Perspective (see next pillar) for creating a deeper sense of purpose sharing and mutual success over time.

Persistent Change Perspective

In the field of education, "grit" has become a topic of discussion. Grit is a personality trait often equated with success, and is defined as "perseverance and passion for long-term goals" (Duckworth et al. 2007). A Persistent Change Perspective takes grit. It takes a decision to maintain "perseverance and passion," and to manage strategies, incentives, and people in support of that perseverance. In the Persistent

Change Perspective, grit is accompanied by an absolute unwillingness to accept the status quo. Not only is that unwillingness an essential source of the passion for social change, but it also ensures that, even while organizations may ask for patience from funders and other stakeholders when change is slow to come, slow change is nevertheless recognized as unacceptable. As such, every stakeholder in an Open Circle must possess the Persistent Change Perspective to achieve sustainable social impact. At the same time, strategies themselves must facilitate persistence and adaptation, in order to be able to address systemic issues both over the appropriate time horizon, and in their changing manifestations.

UTEC's approach demonstrates Persistent Change Perspective at the organization level. As Croteau et al. explain, UTEC's values are core to their approach, and their first value is *Chipping Away*. "UTEC Streetworkers may spend years in conversation with a youth before that young person decides to participate in UTEC programming." Time is of the essence, and Streetworkers hope that a young person will accept their invitation the first time. But they understand that it takes time to build trust and credibility, and so they never give up.

Their social enterprises must facilitate the same. UTEC's mattress recycling business lends itself well to putting the program before the enterprise while meeting the demands of being a competitive business. UTEC figured out how to control for the production interruptions that their as-many-chances-as-it-takes approach to their workforce might produce. Croteau et al. write:

> As outlined earlier, youth attendance is inconsistent, so UTEC's workforce for the enterprise is variable. This makes it difficult to project how many pieces the warehouse can cut at a given time. To solve this problem, UTEC Mattress Recycling hired two reliable, part-time workers from outside the program who come in four days per week to cut mattresses and box springs, ensuring that the operation can keep up with the number of pieces coming into the warehouse. These workers also enable youth programming to proceed without interruptions from truck arrivals or other deliveries.

Living Cities provides an example of Persistent Change Perspective through public–private partnership, and at the systems level. Grit has been at the heart of President and CEO Ben Hecht's focus, and he asks in his chapter about the organization's city innovations, "Can it stick?" Rather than wondering, however, or patiently tracking results over time to see if it does, Hecht and Living Cities worked with their stakeholders to launch a City Accelerator initiative to help ensure that city innovation can and does stick over time. The City Accelerator initiative "bakes in" systems-level perseverance strategies through ideas like "create a staff culture of innovation," and "bake innovation into individual departments."

One can return to Bridget Akinc's chapter on Whirlpool Corporation for another private sector example of Persistent Change Perspective. Whirlpool began with their commitment to reinvest in Benton Harbor and its economic viability, rather than relocating their headquarters. This decision triggered the significant financial investment mentioned earlier, as well as a long-term partnership with Habitat for Humanity. Whirlpool's community commitment helped to inspire company-wide innovation efforts, most recently culminating in a rethinking of corporate purpose and brand strategy.

Whirlpool hit bumps along the way that could have either derailed their commitment or incentivized them to do less. But they showed grit. While the verdict is still out on the long-term social impact of the "Every day, care™" brand strategy, Whirlpool demonstrated with its hiring, investments, collaboration, and perseverance that it could grow and change with a community, and that doing so would help the company itself grow and change in profitable ways.

In "Impact Investing at the Base of The Pyramid: Unitus Seed Fund" in this volume, coeditor Mary Cronin describes the impact investing strategies of the Unitus Seed Fund. This fund demonstrates both Mutuality of Success and a Persistent Change Perspective. Indeed, it's their reason for being. As an impact investor, Unitus wants to alter dramatically the capacity for economic development in India as well as generate positive financial returns for Fund investors. That's an ambition that certainly requires long-term, persistent strategies. To do so, Unitus Fund partners target enterprises that will increase economic well-being for those at the "base of the pyramid," or BOP. Unitus partners recognized that there was a "strong and growing supply of quality entrepreneurs in India," and that investing in those entrepreneurs could prove their belief that "locally initiated entrepreneurial solutions can create a stronger and ultimately more sustainable economic development and improved quality of life" for India's BOP consumers. Ultimately, their investments help enable an ecosystem of BOP mentors, entrepreneurs, and investors in India, with the potential to alter radically economic participation for a massive percentage of India's populace.

Challenges to Achieving Sustainable Social Impact

The Four Common Pillars of Sustainable Social Impact demonstrate a framework of best practices that can help drive lasting, shared social impact. They also require managers to embrace a new level of enterprise responsibility. One can't simply identify Open Circles or Mutuality of Success as aspirational states, or incorporate them into a core values statement, for example, and then hope for the best. To the contrary, they require focused, sustained commitment and active strategic management. Choosing responsible enterprise means choosing to manage for it over the long haul.

In addition to active *management*, sustainable social impact requires active *managers*. It has to be someone's job—or the job of several "someones"—to build and steward the processes necessary for achieving the four pillars. Further, those managers must themselves embody the Persistent Change Perspective. Managing continuous implementation of the four pillars requires tenacity, combined with the kind of neutrality that Living Cities recommends with its "backbone function" (Hecht); in order to sustain all collaborators at "one table," some neutral party must help identify, coordinate, and assign roles, and then be able to support shifts in roles and responsibilities, across multiple players and across time. If neutrality isn't possible, then managing for social impact at least requires an ability—by position and/or by personality—to be ecumenical about aspirations, processes, and outcomes.

Why such a heavy emphasis on active management and the embodiment of Persistent Change Perspective? Because there are some widely shared challenges that have emerged as organizations become more ambitious and more inclusive in their efforts. Enterprises interested in producing lasting social impact must confront and navigate these challenges successfully. The three most fundamental are **scaling, sustainability,** and **measuring the return on social impact innovations across time and multiple stakeholders.** All three elements require active management in any social change initiative, whether on a municipal or global scale, and whether originating from a public, private, or nonprofit-led initiative.

Scaling

This chapter has noted already that social impact innovations must be capable of scaling along with stakeholder needs and aspirations, including those of the operations itself. This means employing adaptive strategies capable of achieving more than one kind of scale. Social impact scale can happen across at least two dimensions: expansion and depth. Achieving either can be challenging.

Expansion

For some, scaling means the obvious—expansion to new customers, markets, or territories. This is the kind of scale one would see with Unitus Seed Fund and their investment in social enterprise in India, for example, or with global adoption of the Global Reporting Index (GRI).

Scaling social innovations via expansion can raise a number of challenges. What if the social problem manifests differently depending on geography or population? Can you work toward enfranchising disconnected youth the same ways in an urban environment as a rural one, for example? What if government structures differ? Given the differences among municipal funding structures and regulations governing public–private partnerships around the world, for example, the Living Cities TII framework may not adapt easily to other countries.

Using strategies that incorporate the Four Common Pillars from the beginning can help anticipate these challenges and prepare for them. For example, embracing Open Circles means that, from the beginning, the change initiative has been capable of responding to multiple stakeholders and their aspirations at different stages in the life cycle. The management practices among collaborating parties that allowed for that flexibility in one place should allow for it in another as well.

Family Independence Initiative (FII) demonstrates several of the pillars in its work, and embodies how they help FII manage for expansion. Founded in Oakland, CA (MacArthur Fellows Program 2012), in 2001, FII is rooted in the aspirations of its members. Indeed, their entire model is based on incentivizing groups of members to form small communities, set their own goals, and then track their success using computers and a data tracking system built by FII. FII unites these aspirations in a common data platform into which participants all over the country put their results each month, allowing FII to find and represent back to them patterns of success, results, and best practices. It also gives FII incredible data to use for public policy advocacy (Stuhldreher and O'Brien 2011).

The model now has demonstration sites in CA, LA, MI, and MA (FII 2016) and shows strong, positive results. In Boston, for example, families in their first two years achieved on average a 181 % increase in savings, while 80 % of their youth improved school attendance and grades ("Success Groups" 2015).

Arguably, FII's strategy embraces all of the pillars. Individual families become core stakeholders and take on a broad array of roles, from organizers to data reporters and trackers and to mentors for other family groups. Focused Purpose Sharing happens among and between families, family groups, and FII itself. Mutuality of Success is baked into the model, with FII's success literally being defined as family success, and family groups identifying those success objectives for themselves. Lastly, the model is built for Persistent Change Perspective at several levels. For example, family groups stay together, adapting their goals and aspirations as life changes (Stuhldreher and O'Brien 2011). Further, FII continues to track family data and advocate with it in perpetuity. As long as there's poverty, FII will use its data to change what affects one's ability to leave it.

FII started in Oakland, CA, and has expanded to an additional site in California as well as into three other states. Within a given location, families do the recruiting and manage the expansion, employing an Open Circle philosophy that outstrips what FII staff could do alone. FII Boston quadrupled its number of families in its first four years (Giving Common 2012).

Perhaps most interesting in terms of expanding impact, however, their data now allows them to make cases for federal public policy changes that would help not only their families achieve success, but also other families who aspire to the same results that FII families do. FII uses its data to paint a clearer picture of how federal policy affects efforts to leave poverty (Lim Miller 2015) and therefore advocates for changes to sweeping policies such as the Earned Income Tax Credit, and practices such as the way HUD (US Department of Housing and Urban Development) does case management (Stuhldreher and O'Brien 2011).

Depth

Scale also can mean deeper engagement with an existing business challenge, population, or social problem. Complex, systems-level problems manifest themselves in a variety of ways. Poverty, for example, can affect health, education, urban infrastructure, and public safety, to name a few. Scale can also mean, then, confronting multiple manifestations of a single, systems-level problem within a given community or population over time. Whirlpool pursued this kind of scaling by going deeper and deeper in its economic development work in Benton Harbor (Akinc).

One might argue that scaling through depth particularly manifests the tenacity and systems-change element of Persistent Change Perspective. It's a strategy that seeks to stick with the problem through all its manifestations, seeking change and more change until the whole system is transformed.

LIFT Communities' approach demonstrates best practices from the Four Common Pillars, and how they allow LIFT to pursue scale through depth. LIFT currently works in four large US cities—Chicago, Los Angeles, New York, and Washington, D.C. Their volunteer advocates support members facing a range of problems resulting from poverty, while those members pursue self-defined goals across personal development, social capital, and financial well-being (LIFT 2016b). Via this approach, LIFT embodies Open Circles by embracing what others might consider a "client" as a "member," Focused Purpose Sharing by prioritizing that member's goals as LIFT's own, and Mutuality of Success because success for members can translate into success for their families and communities. As LIFT (2016b) explains it:

> The Member, not the Advocate, takes the reins. After all, it is the Member's goals that we're tackling and the Member's dreams that we're fulfilling. Advocates are rigorously trained in supporting them to success. By setting their own goals and working to achieve them, Members are better equipped to get a job, a safe home, and an education for themselves and their children. They also build a support network, confidence in what they bring to the table, and the skills to manage tough times in the future.

One way LIFT tracks scale is by tracking the depth of success and change made by its members (LIFT 2016a). Yes, they track growth in their member count (10,200). Their 2014 data report, however, also tracks changes in how frequently members come to LIFT (6 %); increases in progress per person (53 %); and the number of milestones achieved by LIFT members (2500). LIFT's model allows for this scale-by-depth approach because it is rooted in the aspirations of its members. The work can change with the needs and aspirations of this, its most essential stakeholder.

Sustainability

Sustainability is a core issue for social endeavors, as for any other kind. As Persistent Change Perspective suggests, one aspect of sustainability is the sustained commitment and attention span of the stakeholders involved. Two other, more obvious aspects include sustaining results and resources, especially funding.

Increasingly, nonprofit organizations are turning to social enterprises to help improve sustainability. Philanthropic dollars tend to be of shorter term, often close ended—meaning grants cannot be renewed in perpetuity—and often don't cover an organization's general operations. Earned income can help offset these limitations in the nonprofit capital market, as UTEC and Haley House both demonstrate. UTEC, for example, is on track to break even with its mattress recycling business in the next few years despite the fact that it first and foremost achieves a social purpose, with an approach rooted in Mutuality of Success and Focused Purpose Sharing (Croteau et al.). Haley House's Dudley Dough seeks to break even while being able to pay its workers living wages (Broderick).

Arguably, use of the Four Common Pillars helps *create* the conditions for sustainability. A company attractive to impact investors should inherently be one that embodies Mutuality of Success. That embodiment draws in the capital necessary for growth and long-term survival. Focused Purpose Sharing develops communities of people who share common cause and are ready to pool their resources toward its end. That idea is at the heart of crowdfunding on platforms like Kiva and GoFundMe.

SC2 is a public sector initiative that demonstrates how the best practices manifested in the four pillars can help drive sustainability. SC2 stands for Strong Cities, Strong Communities, launched out of the White House in 2011 as part of President Obama's economic mobility agenda. The White House describes it as follows (SC2 2014):

> The SC2 concept was developed through engagement with mayors, members of Congress, foundations, non-profits and other community partners who are committed to addressing the challenges of local governments. SC2 and its partners are working together to coordinate federal programs and investments to spark economic growth in distressed areas and create stronger cooperation between community organizations, local leadership, and the federal government.

Fundamental to SC2's approach is coordination across federal government departments, such as Housing and Urban Development (HUD) and the Environmental Protection Agency (EPA). They remove regulatory barriers to collaborative funding, and place support teams of federal staff on the ground in city government to do capacity building in support of local city agendas around economic development and sustainability. By 2014, SC2 was working with 14 US cities, and had harnessed $368 million in federal money toward shared purposes with these cities (SC2 2014).

Of particular note is the potential of the SC2 approach to sustain local progress in the face of changing resources and leadership. Because federal agencies work with cities to develop and pursue Focused Purpose Sharing, they are able to develop local capacity for success that can outlast any of the current players. Their consultations build not only the strength of city workers, but also improve and help coordinate across city systems themselves. Mutuality of Success ensures that it is in the best interest of the federal agencies to deploy their resources to the cities, and in the best interests of the cities to develop their internal capacity to invest that money toward positive outcomes. While President Obama no longer will be in office in 2017, and no one can say for sure if his successor will continue the SC2 initiative, by then the 14 cities should have built local infrastructure around the problems they wish to address. Career employees of various federal departments already will know how to get around regulatory barriers to cooperation. They will have built work patterns with that adaptation in place. There's no reason to believe that they will arbitrarily stop using these best practices themselves, or that new work processes will necessarily disappear as people naturally shift roles or leave various departments.

Measuring Impact

The field of social impact measurement has produced a robust set of concepts and frameworks for "understanding, measuring, and reporting the social, economic and environmental value created by an intervention program, policy or organization" (Banke-Thomas et al. 2015). Such frameworks are important, delivering not only a way to count outputs and, hopefully, outcomes and impact over time, but also another method for reaching agreement on terms and the definition of success (Clarke).

Any attempt at social impact measurement offers challenges, however. These range from facilitating common definitions of success to creating baseline data across diverse measurement systems, to tying technical results to social change, and to capturing the more difficult to quantify social impact of a given innovation. Measurement frameworks and standards that seek to address these challenges run the risk of being buried under their own weight.

As Ruthbea Clarke notes in her chapter, for example, Smart Cities measurement frameworks facilitate "everyone speaking the same language when discussing complex topics" while allowing cities to "take a baseline of where they are, define where they want to go, and understand the gap between the two." Clarke offers three measurement frameworks that cities can use to determine whether they are being "smart" and having impact. These include The Maturity Model by the British Standards Institute, ISO 37120 Standard Indicators for City Services and Quality of Life, and IDC's Smart City MaturityScape. Together, she argues they focus on the "what" and the "how" of Smart City implementation. Clarke feels that they are best used in tandem. Employing these three frameworks can be quite complex, however. Further, each has its own complexities, built in to ensure each framework accounts for the wide variety of cities that might wish to employ smart strategies and then compare themselves to each other. As Clarke notes, the ISO standards alone include 46 core indicators and 54 supporting indicators across 17 themes.

As this example illustrates, differences in culture, industry, and regional contexts may require any standardized measurement framework—whether for Smart Cities strategies or measuring a company's ESG impact—to be so broad and thorough as to be burdensome. In addition, impact measurement is difficult under any circumstances, especially long-term impact, and especially for nonprofit organizations (Ebrahim and Rangan 2014). Nonprofits aren't alone in this struggle, however.

In their chapter, Anderson and Abensour note that the GRI is one of several global ESG reporting frameworks available to corporations seeking to measure their social impact. Since 1997, the GRI has produced four versions of the framework, the most recent being G4. Anderson and Abensour suggest that, while the GRI is the most attractive ESG reporting option, it currently lacks "the ability to translate the data that a company reports into an overall expression of the company's broad social impact." They note that a 2016 update of the G4 seeks to rectify that problem by requesting new content reporting specifically focused on impact. That the GRI is one of the more recent frameworks in the reporting landscape, however, and still is evolving in trying measure true social impact, is telling.

Similar challenges in measuring social impact in impact investing are leading to a new set of standards there. Recognizing the varied landscape of impact investing measurements being used, and the need to settle on some common definitions and approaches, GIIN created IRIS. IRIS is a "catalog of generally accepted performance metrics used by impact investors to measure and manage their returns on investments" (GIIN 2016b). GIIN created IRIS because "investors need a common language to describe and compare the social, financial and environmental performance of their investments." IRIS, in turn, combined forces with Aeris, the rating service for Community Development Financial Institutions (CDFIs), to cluster the metrics CDFIs use most commonly in determining the impact of their own investment performance (GIIN 2016a).

According to IRIS, CDFIs report across the following five categories (GIIN 2016a):

- **Housing** (home ownership, lending, voluntary metrics)
- **Health and Food Access** (food access, health)
- **Environment** (improvement of physical environment, energy efficiency, fossil fuel reduction)
- **Education**
- **Economic Security** (consumer finance, income generation, voluntary metrics)

IRIS offers 37 measures across these five categories, some with multiple types of data tracked. Of the 37, well over half represent output measures—counts of things, such as number of loans disbursed or total number of client individuals. A handful—in Education and Environment—arguably track outcomes, such as amount of water conserved or percentage of students advancing a grade. Even these, however, fail really to get at long-term social impact. This is not to denigrate CDFI attempts—or GIIN's attempts—to quantify the "impact" in impact investing. Instead, it underscores the challenge, even for a mature industry like CDFI lending, in demonstrating change in social problems that span time and complex systems.

To measure its impact, the Seattle 2030 District first had to establish baseline data that required collecting information across multiple data platforms, and multiple data owners (Wickwire and Combe). They used one tool to track data on building energy performance (ENERGY STAR Portfolio Manager), developed another tool for data on vehicle emissions (Seattle Climate Partnership carbon calculator), and pieced together a third through strategic partnerships between the city and a voluntary organization in order to collect data on water use intensity. While the Seattle 2030 District did it, the complexity is worth noting. Imagine taking that approach to scale across multiple cities, or into other, non-environmental metrics about quality of life within Seattle, as a desire to measure impact for residents ultimately suggests will need to be done. Achieving that kind of data coordination requires creating the myriad conditions for sharing, through thoughtful management of people, partnerships, and processes.

Strategies that employ best practices represented by the Four Common Pillars help create the conditions for sharing data, bridging cultural and practice divides, and capturing changes important to a broader range of stakeholders. In keeping with the adage, "we perform to what we measure," the next iteration of measurement both to help demonstrate and drive sustainable social impact will be not so much in new metrics of outputs or outcomes, but instead in measures of processes and practices that can (a) expand the impact of social innovations; (b) ensure sustainability; and (c) measure that impact at scale. Kate Ruff and Sara Olsen (2016) assert in the *Stanford Social Innovation Review*, "The next frontier in social impact measurement isn't measurement at all." With respect to Ruff and Olsen, it can be argued that one must find a way to measure even that next frontier. Such measurement will be, however, additive, and will get as much at practice and attitude as at any particular investment in, say, a green technology or a specific community public health outcome.

Defining the Long-Term Return on Social Innovation (ROSI)

> *How these changes are translating into improved outcomes for large numbers of low-income residents ... will not be evident for a number of years. This is not a limitation of TII or the evaluation, merely a reflection of the realities of efforts ... that were designed with an understanding of complexity and an ambition around transformative change, not smaller scale programmatic outcomes.* — Mt. Auburn Associates (2014).
>   *There are two levels of change that we are working on; short-term, incremental changes that are more like a sprint and the systemic change that is more like a marathon.* — Angela Taylor, Network for Economic Opportunity, New Orleans, LA (Hecht)

Persistent Change Perspective requires persistent change measurement. When Living Cities set out to launch The Integration Initiative, they developed a logic model with a 10-year timeframe (Hecht). Anything less would have failed to take into account the complexity of the systems change cities needed to tackle. Therein lies the "marathon" Angela Taylor of New Orleans described in that city's work with TII to reduce a 52 % unemployment rate among working-age black men. Baltimore had a marathon to run, too, as it worked on jobs and workforce development for its TII initiative. The director of Baltimore's integration partnership noted, "Making inroads into Baltimore's deep socio-economic challenges is bigger than the individualized efforts of any one organization or government" (Hecht).

Time Frames for Persistent Change Measurement

For measuring Return on Social Innovation, or ROSI, it's about longevity. Across all the various stakeholders, the complexity of the targeted social issue, and the number of systems involved in a particular "systems change," it's about conditioning the endeavor to run a marathon, not a sprint. The best practices represented in the Four Common Pillars of Sustainable Social Impact drive ROSI. They push responsible enterprises beyond programmatic-level focus, where one initiative seeks to make short-term, incremental changes on a single problem. They push for the courage to embrace complexity, which, in turn, requires strategies that integrate the four pillars—the courage to collaborate, to open strategies to partners one doesn't entirely control and whose agendas one doesn't entirely share, to take risks on endeavors whose returns won't be measurable quickly or easily, to define success beyond the threshold of any one organization, and to stay in the thick of it all for time periods well beyond standard reporting cycles.

While it may be difficult to measure long-term impact at the systems level, enterprises can and must improve their ability to measure the processes, attitudes, and practices that sustain complex social change efforts over time, driving them *toward* impact. That's the next horizon. Responsible enterprises will have to be prepared to sign up for this kind of grit—in the time horizons of their investments, in longevity of their staffing, and by ensuring ongoing commitment even during leadership changes and shifts in the marketplace. They also will have to develop blueprints for social change that map the varied path of outputs and outcomes that in total will create that change, but that represent smaller hash marks along the way. What should we be seeing in year one, and in this location? In year two in another? How do those accumulate to a year five change? Year ten? Then, with that blueprint in place, they must have the intestinal fortitude to perform to those hash marks, even when the endgame is not yet visible to investors or stakeholders.

Measurement approaches seeking to track the emerging best practices represented by the Four Common Pillars of Sustainable Social Impact also must allow for other kinds of variability. Over a 10-year time horizon, for example, results will not be steady. More likely, successes will happen in bursts. Returns won't be equally distributed across all stakeholder groups, either—nor necessarily should they be. Setbacks, whether in resources, public policy, or even community acceptance of the changes, will halt or even reverse progress at times. Changes in leadership still may cause disruptions in buy-in or participation. While implementing the four pillars will, hopefully, help mitigate these disruptions, they still will happen. Measurement practices will have to account for them, and help drive the will to persevere.

Granted, short-term gains and clear outcomes remain important. They are the price of entry to engage in longer-term social change. If pursued alone, however, the kind of change that enables what Living Cities calls the "new normal" (Hecht), or the Smart Cities movement calls "maturity" (Clarke), won't take hold. Battle Creek Project 20/20 offered one potent illustration of this point when explaining why the initiative emerged in the first place. After decades of willing local leaders investing resources in the city's most intractable problems, things didn't stick as they should have (Champlin and Lankerd). The solutions didn't align with local people's views of their needs, and the community didn't sustain buy-in in ways that permanently changed the way the city, its people, and its social capital operated.

Progress Toward Persistent Change Measurement

A number of global frameworks already have begun to try to capture some of the emerging best practices represented in the pillars, and that drive ROSI. Of the Smart City measurement frameworks, for example, the British Standards Institute's Maturity Model rates leadership from "Lagging" to "Driven," depending on the level of leadership fragmentation versus integration. IDC's Smart City MaturityScape rates city strategies as more mature if they are "repeatable," versus ad hoc (Clarke). In global ESG reporting, the GRI approach requires that corporations "ask your stakeholders which economic, environmental, social topics are most important to the company" (Anderson and Abensour), through a Materiality Assessment, which then should guide investment priorities.

The patchwork of these indicators across various frameworks is, however, just that—a patchwork, incomplete and not integrated into a set of measures that would allow enterprises to determine whether their strategies were employing the four pillars effectively and consistently. They also beg the question of "vertical integration." What is the set of measures that helps determine effective, sustained implementation of the pillars in one or two TII cities, or Smart Cities, or SC2 cities on the one hand, but also in a multinational corporation or a global sustainability initiative on the other? If the Four Common Pillars represent best practices at any scale, then any frameworks for input and process measurement that help drive their implementation also must function at varying scales.

Further, even with the measurement advances that already have been built into some of the best frameworks currently available, it remains difficult to resist the pressure *not* to go "all in," maintaining instead a sole focus on the enterprise in the shorter term. Anderson and Abensour list five key principles for CSR measurement today in their chapter. Number three is "Focus on what the program can truly impact: Don't spread the program too thin." While that advice is not misplaced, ROSI calls for organizations to reach beyond what they can impact alone, and to stretch themselves to a level that might, in the early years, very much look "thin."

And even as Mark Feldman and Nikki Korn of Cause Consulting declare this to be the Era of Innovation in CSR in their chapter, they caution that pressure to perform to stakeholder expectations "can result in poorly planned and executed activities that are designed to look good rather than to make a measurable difference." Even the most committed stakeholders become impatient for results. Faith in that required blueprint of changes—even one developed using Open Circles and Focused Purpose Sharing—can be shaken as people get tired, problems persist, or funding challenges emerge, and they always do.

One way to tackle this challenge is to capture the kinds of practice inputs that should remain steady over time, even when results do not. That's why, for example, UTEC asks its employees in every performance evaluation to demonstrate how they have shown "respectful curiosity" and an ability to see "beyond the mask" with their young people (Croteau et al.). They know that these cultural values determine in part whether their team can sustain the UTEC approach. It's also why the Seattle 2030 District sets a best practice of recruiting board members that represent the diversity of District members and leaders from "all categories (property, professional, community)" (Wickwire and Combe).

Another is to use the cumulative effect of many, many small changes. At no time in its first, say, five years was FII going to demonstrate that it had built the path out of poverty for the residents of Oakland, CA. Indeed, after more than 15 years, the path ahead undoubtedly still is long and winding for all the communities that have engaged the FII model. Nevertheless, the persistence of individual family and family group successes, measured month after month, and year after year, forms a pattern that is directionally correct, that offers enough inspiration to keep all FII's stakeholders going, and that charts enough of the blueprint to maintain faith in the viability of a systems change outcome.

As noted at the start of this chapter, cross-sector participation and investment in social impact initiatives are gaining global momentum. In the process, public and private sector organizations are building much-needed capacity for tackling the world's most challenging social problems. But we are still very early in the process of creating the necessary metrics for assessing the return on broad-based social innovation. This is true both for society at large and for stakeholders in each sector. The development of a valid, widely adopted measurement framework needs to be on the table, even as the work of strengthening and implementing the pillars for cross-sector collaboration continues apace.

Conclusion

On June 22, 2016, corporate leaders and entrepreneurs gathered for a summit in New York led by the United Nations. The focus was on creating a new era of sustainability. UN Secretary-General, Ban Ki-moon, addressed this 2016 UN Global Compact Leaders Summit. He exhorted participants to pursue an ambitious, truly inclusive agenda.

> We need new ways of living that will end the suffering, discrimination and lack of opportunity that define the lives of billions of people around the world, and that drive instability and conflict. The solutions must involve everyone, from world leaders and chief executives, to educators and philanthropists. We must work together—across sectors and industries—in broader and deeper partnerships.

The UN Global Compact is the world's largest corporate sustainability initiative, focused on implementing the UN's 2030 Sustainable Development Goals. At its heart are ten principles, covering subjects ranging from human rights to the environment and to government corruption. The goal of the summit was, according to the UN, "to jump-start business action everywhere on the [Sustainable Development] Goals" (UN 2016).

There was a time when the ambitiousness of this agenda would have appeared ridiculous. Maybe corporate leaders would have attended—and maybe with NGOs standing outside, protesting the practices of those located within—but such attendance would have been to mark a sort of general, broad support for the ideas of a Global Compact, not a serious attempt to achieve them. Such ambition would have seemed impossible.

Today, it's not. The world has come to recognize that our most complex problems can and must be addressed, and that enterprises of all kinds have a role in doing so. Leaders recognize a responsibility to social impact regardless of the form or sector of the institutions they run, as well as the need to define that impact in terms broader than the individual interests of those institutions. Further, sustained collaboration, while extremely difficult, no longer exists in the world of unicorns and other pipe dreams.

Most promising is the realization that successful examples are not one-offs. They are real, and they can be sustained. Further, they are beginning to demonstrate patterns of practice—a framework for such collaborations—that could apply across endeavors, and allow for standardization of some practices, processes, and cultural norms that improve sustainability and the promise of real impact, beyond outputs and outcomes.

There's a long way to go. Nevertheless, a common path to achieving sustainable returns on social innovation is now visible. 2030 is not as far away as it seemed at the beginning of the millennium.

References

Banke-Thomas A, Madja B, Charles A, Broek N (2015) Social return on investment (SROI) methodology to account for value for money of public health interventions: a systematic review. BMC Public Health 15:582. doi:10.1186/s12889-015-1935-7.

Boncheck M (2013) Purpose is good. Shared purpose is better. Harvard Business Review. https://hbr.org/2013/03/purpose-is-good-shared-purpose

Buchanan P, Glickman J, Buteau E (2015) Investing and social impact: practices of private foundations. Center for Effective Philanthropy. http://www.effectivephilanthropy.org/wp-content/uploads/2015/05/Investing-and-Social-Impact-2015.pdf

Clolery P (2014) Troubling numbers in volunteering rates. The Nonprofit Times. http://www.thenonprofittimes.com/news-articles/troubling-numbers-in-volunteering-rates/

Duckworth AL, Peterson C, Matthews MD, Kelly DR (2007) Grit: perseverance and passion for long-term goals. Journal of Personality and Social Psychology 92(2007):1087–1101

Ebrahim A, Rangan V (2014) What impact? California Management Review 56(3):118–141. Business Source Complete. http://www.hbs.edu/faculty/Pages/item.aspx?num=47515

FII (2016) FII demonstration sites. http://www.fii.org/contact-us/. Accessed 14 July 2016

The Foundation Center (2012, 2013) Foundation stats. http://data.foundationcenter.org/#/fc1000/subject:all/all/total/list/2012. Accessed 28 June 2016; http://data.foundationcenter.org/#/foundations/community/nationwide/total/list/2013. Accessed 28 June 2016

GIIN (2016a) Community investing. Global Impact Investing Network. https://iris.thegiin.org/community-investing-metrics. Accessed 14 July 2016

GIIN (2016b) What is IRIS? https://iris.thegiin.org/. Accessed 14 July 2016

GIIN (2016c) What you need to know about impact investing. https://thegiin.org/impact-investing/need-to-know/#s2. Accessed 14 July 2016

Giving Common (2012) Family Independence Initiative: Boston. The Boston Foundation. https://www.givingcommon.org/profile/1124934/family-independence-initiative---boston/. Accessed 14 July 2016

Gouldner AW (1960) The norm of reciprocity: a preliminary statement*. American Sociological Review 25(2):161–178.

Kania J, Kramer M (2011) Collective impact. Stanford Social Innovation Review. http://ssir.org/articles/entry/collective_impact

LIFT (2016a) Our impact. http://www.liftcommunities.org/why-lift/our-impact/. Accessed 14 July 2016

LIFT (2016b) The LIFT solution. http://www.liftcommunities.org/why-lift/the-solution/. Accessed 14 July 2016

Lim Miller M (2015) The poverty line—a false target. FII Blog. Family Independence Initiative. http://www.fii.org/blog/the-poverty-line-a-false-target/

MacArthur Fellows Program (2012) MacArthur Fellows:meet the class of 2012. MacArthur Foundation. https://www.macfound.org/fellows/871/

Mt. Auburn Associates (2014) The integration initiative: three year evaluation report. Living Cities. https://www.livingcities.org/resources/282-the-integration-initiative-three-year-evaluation-report

Mudaliar A, Schiff H, Bass R (2016) Annual impact investor survey. Global Impact Investing Network. https://thegiin.org/assets/2016%20GIIN%20Annual%20Impact%20Investor%20Survey_Web.pdf. Accessed 18 July 2016

National Center for Charitable Statistics (2012) The nonprofit almanac 2012. http://nccsdataweb.urban.org/NCCS/extracts/nonprofitalmanacflyerpdf.pdf

Porter M, Kramer M (2011) Creating shared value. Harvard Business Review. https://hbr.org/2011/01/the-big-idea-creating-shared-value

Ruff K, Olsen S (2016) The next frontier in social impact measurement isn't measurement at all. Stanford Social Innovation Review. http://ssir.org/articles/entry/the_next_frontier_in_social_impact_measurement_isnt_measurement_at_all

SC2 (2014) National fact sheet. White House Council on Strong Cities, Strong Communities. https://www.huduser.gov/portal/publications/pdf/SC2_National_Fact_Sheet_2014.pdf

Stuhldreher A, O'Brien R (2011) Family Independence Initiative: a new approach to help families exit poverty. http://www.fii.org/wp-content/uploads/2014/01/newamericafiipaper_2011.pdf. Accessed 18 July 2016

Success groups: a partnership project between Family Independence Initiative and New Life CDC (2015) New Life CDC. http://newlifecdc.us/wp-content/uploads/2015/12/FIIFamilyIndependenceInitiativeStrategicDocSuccessGroups-5.pdf

Traynor B, Blackburn F (2015) Circles and marketplaces: spaces for transforming community life. Communities and Banking 26(4). Federal Reserve Bank of Boston

United Nations (2016) UN summit jump-starts global drive for responsible business actions on sustainable development goals. UN News Centre, United Nations. http://www.un.org/apps/news/story.asp?NewsID=54296#.V4gBQ5MrLyh

United Nations Global Compact (2016) What is UN Global Compact? https://www.unglobalcompact.org/what-is-gc. Accessed 18 July 2016

UTEC (2016) World's oldest LEED platinum certified building! https://www.utec-lowell.org/greenbuilding. Accessed 14 July 2016

Social Justice and Sustainable E

A Marketplace Approach to Building and Supporting Sustainable Social Purpose Organizations

Susan Musinsky and Anna Trieschmann

Abstract The Social Innovation Forum (SIF) builds the capacity and funding base of promising social innovations, both nonprofit and for-profit. SIF uses a marketplace approach, connecting social purpose organizations with a community of professionals who can provide financial, technical, and coaching support. The idea behind the marketplace is that all participants give value to, and receive value from, each other.

SIF's marketplace consists of two accelerators: the Social Innovator Accelerator, focused on nonprofit *Social Innovators*, and the Social Business Accelerator, focused on for-profit social business *Impact Entrepreneurs*. Before, during, and after the accelerator experience, SIF pairs participants with philanthropists, coaches, and professional service providers who become deeply engaged in the organization's work. The accelerator participants gain professional development and an opportunity to bring their organizations to the next level, while investors and volunteers have an opportunity to make meaning with their time and money by becoming part of a solution to a critical social problem. This marketplace improves the work of the nonprofits and business enterprises on the ground, strengthens their leadership and long-term capacity, introduces new resources (time, talent, and treasure), and creates the opportunity for lasting relationships between and among marketplace participants.

Keywords Social innovation • Social Business Accelerator • Social Innovator Accelerator

Introduction

Imagine a town square where people come together not only to exchange resources, but also to connect with each other in order to increase the overall wealth and well-being of their communities. Such a "marketplace" may evoke images of people in

S. Musinsky (✉) • A. Trieschmann
Social Innovation Forum, One Congress Street, Boston, MA 02109, USA
e-mail: smusinsky@socialinnovationforum.org

© Springer International Publishing Switzerland 2017
M.J. Cronin, T.C. Dearing (eds.), *Managing for Social Impact*,
Management for Professionals, DOI 10.1007/978-3-319-46021-5_2

medieval clothing bartering over bread, fish, and fruit, but this marketplace is anything but old-fashioned. Instead, it represents an innovative approach to engaging a broad community in the work of social change. In *this* marketplace, market-goers exchange resources (time, money, expertise, and social capital) in order to collaborate on creating social impact. For volunteers, philanthropists, and social impact investors, this marketplace is a structure that affords them opportunities to engage in meaningful ways, to "give back," to have deeper impact than they could on their own, and to become part of innovations beyond their own imaginations. For mission-based organizations, it is a way of connecting with people who are eager to support their work with time, talent, and financial resources that would otherwise be hard to obtain. By facilitating connections, this marketplace for social change goes beyond the transactional relationships often seen among funders, volunteers, and nonprofit organizations. This marketplace has a broader purpose of building community and mutual exchange among people who are committed to positive social impact. Through this community, relationships develop, organizations grow, and social impact emerges at levels that otherwise would be impossible to achieve.

The marketplace described above is at the heart of the Social Innovation Forum (SIF) and its work. SIF combines capacity building and network development to advance promising solutions to the community's most pressing social issues. SIF runs two accelerator programs—one for nonprofit organizations (Social Innovator Accelerator) and one for for-profit social impact businesses (Social Business Accelerator)—which actively connect supporters (funders, investors, and volunteers) and practitioners (nonprofit and social business leaders) to build productive relationships focused on growing social impact. Figure 1 briefly describes the accelerators.

Massachusetts is home to over 34,000 registered nonprofit organizations (Office of the Massachusetts Attorney General n.d.), many of which struggle to gain traction, to scale themselves, and to make substantial, lasting impact on the social issues that they address.[1] This is particularly true of smaller organizations. Meanwhile, philanthropists, foundations, and other funders, who collectively give away $4.9 billion each year in Massachusetts, struggle to find the time, focus, and expertise to assess organizations and find matches that give the most meaning to their resources (The Chronicle of Philanthropy 2012).

Those passionate about creating positive change in their communities are also exploring for-profit solutions to social issues. They are launching social impact businesses that require mentoring and investment in order to scale their product or service. Beyond philanthropy, investors are increasingly seeking opportunities to yield *both* social and financial returns. Yet, in a 2015 report by the Global Impact Investing Network (GIIN) and JP Morgan, impact investors reported a "shortage of high quality investment opportunities with track records" as being a major barrier to making impact investments. By fostering community and facilitating relationships among these groups, SIF addresses the needs of each in a way that allows them to achieve sustainable impact together.

---

[1] Massachusetts public charities increased 45 % from 1999 to 2009, based on the Massachusetts Nonprofit Database.

	Social Innovator Accelerator	Social Business Accelerator
Participants	Nonprofit organizations	For-profit, social impact businesses
Duration	24 months	12 weeks
Applicants*	171 → 8 Innovators	52 → 6 Entrepreneurs
Volunteer roles*	115+	20+
Capacity Building Components	• One-on-one consulting • Executive coaching • Graphic design • Presentation coaching • Relationship building • In-kind partner support • Showcase events • Opportunities to connect with diverse community of funders, philanthropists, and business leaders	• Workshops • Guest speaker sessions • One-on-one advising with mentors from business and startup communities • Showcase event • Opportunities to connect with investors who seek both financial and social impact returns from their investments
Started	2003	2013
Portfolio (to date)	75 organizations	24 businesses

* 2015-2016 program year

Fig. 1 Comparison of the two Social Innovation Forum accelerators

Over its 13-year history, SIF has grown from a volunteer-led initiative to an independent nonprofit organization with an active community of more than 6,000 funders, volunteers, and social purpose organizations. In the process, it has engaged more than 100 funding partners and built a committed network of more than 2300 philanthropists, foundation staff, and business leaders; worked with 75 nonprofit Social Innovators and 24 for-profit social business Impact Entrepreneurs; moved over $24 million in cash and in-kind services to its portfolio organizations; and attracted more than 10 long-term, in-kind partners.

SIF's marketplace approach is helping promising leaders in the social sector to do their work even better, and helping philanthropists and investors to create meaning with their work, wisdom, and wealth. On average, nonprofits in the SIF portfolio more than double their revenue within four years after engaging with SIF, a growth rate significantly higher than state and national averages.[2] Collectively, organizations in the SIF portfolio impacted more than 200,000 lives in 2015 across a range of social issues including early childhood education, healthy aging, environmental sustainability, homelessness, youth development, and the arts.

---

[2] SIF calculated MA and national nonprofit growth rates with the following data on public charities with <$5 million in annual revenue. 2010: MA—3.49 %, USA—3.06 %, SIF—12.29 %; 2011: MA—5.78 %, USA—7.28 %, SIF—18.69 %; 2012: MA—1.62 %, USA—7.95 %, SIF—13.94 %; 2013: MA—2.41 %, USA—.40 %, SIF—13.94 %; 2014: MA—2.19 %, USA—2.55 %, SIF—21.14 %.

The Marketplace in Action: Veterans Legal Services

To illustrate how the marketplace approach works, consider the story of Veterans Legal Services, a nonprofit organization that provides free legal services to homeless and low-income veterans. When SIF chose Veterans Legal Services (VLS) for its 2014 "Social Innovator Accelerator" cohort, VLS was a 23-year-old organization that, while successful in its work, had grown little over the previous two decades. Serving 350 veterans each year at three partner sites, its three staff members worked out of donated, long-outgrown office space on the campus of the Boston College Law School. Anna Richardson and Sarah Roxburgh, attorneys who started with VLS as program staff, had recently become codirectors and wanted to move the organization to the next level.

SIF matched Anna and Sarah with a consultant who worked with them to articulate a growth strategy and to develop a fund raising plan to support it. The consultant helped VLS craft compelling materials to showcase its work to potential investors, particularly those outside the legal field. SIF also introduced VLS to a high-level business professional who volunteered his time to help them refine their message into a compelling pitch. Through this process, Anna and Sarah began to develop an "impact per investment" mindset by looking at VLS's work more strategically, articulating short-term and long-term capital needs, and using business language to frame their communications to resonate more clearly with a funder audience. Presentation coaching helped Anna and Sarah adapt VLS's messaging to authentically connect with a wider range of audiences while conveying their passion and enthusiasm. As with so many leaders of effective organizations, they were adept at reaching the people they served. Now, they needed the tools to be equally adept at reaching those who could fund them.

With a new spotlight on this established organization, Anna and Sarah took advantage of the SIF network of in-kind partners to access additional graphic design services and develop a new logo and branded look for the organization. After six months with SIF, Anna presented to an audience of more than 300 people at SIF's annual Showcase event. Because of their work with SIF, Anna was better able to articulate VLS's mission, value, and opportunities for growth and impact in ways that would best resonate with interested funders.

After the Showcase, SIF matched Anna and Sarah with trained executive coaches—one for each—who committed to work with each of them pro bono for six months. Although Anna and Sarah were initially reluctant to invest scarce time in the unknown outcomes of executive coaching, they found that setting leadership development goals and working both individually and as a team helped them leverage their respective strengths in order to work more effectively, both with each other and the VLS board of directors. SIF's executive coaching engagement complemented the capacity building and consulting support VLS had received, and it enabled Anna and Sarah to steward the organization through challenging times and to begin to build a committed community of supporters beyond their immediate, existing network.

VLS has continued to benefit from the lessons learned and relationships formed through the SIF community. So have the people who worked with them. Inspired by the leadership and mission of the organization, the graphic designer that VLS met through SIF's in-kind partnerships joined the VLS board of directors. Both executive coaches became deeply invested in Anna's and Sarah's personal and professional success; they continue to work with VLS today, including participating on its Governance Committee. Within 12 months of their engagement with SIF, Veterans Legal Services secured $300,000 in commitments from new funders. This funding allowed VLS to move into new office space located closer to its constituents and supporters, add essential staff to increase capacity, and to serve an additional 100 veterans in each of the last two years. Anna Richardson sums up the experience as follows:

> Our organization has changed significantly since our selection as a Social Innovator. Every time we have had a breakthrough, we have seen a connection back to the process with the Social Innovation Forum.

History of the Social Innovation Forum and Evolution of the Marketplace Approach

Founding Vision

The Social Innovation Forum was founded in 2003 by Andrew Wolk, CEO of the national nonprofit professional service organization Root Cause, as an experiment in bringing together Boston-area leaders in nonprofits, business, philanthropy, and government to focus on allocating resources to nonprofits on the basis of their performance. Andrew sought to bring best practices from the business world, and specifically for-profit venture forums like the MIT Enterprise Forum, to promising nonprofit organizations so that they could attract the resources needed to grow and extend their impact. He recognized that effective nonprofits were highly skilled in service delivery, but not necessarily in the art of making their cases to the business world where they would need to communicate effectively to secure sufficient resources to succeed. In its first year, SIF helped six organizations to pitch their missions, impact models, and needs at a showcase event, allowing prospective funders to make more informed resource allocation decisions.

Since then, SIF has refined its model each year, seeking out organizations with effective solutions to the community's long-standing social issues and providing them with a range of supports to help them better articulate their work and impact to the funding community. Attracting people who share an interest in supporting effective organizations, SIF has also built its community of funders and investors through its annual Showcase, educational events, and meaningful volunteer opportunities. These funders and investors learn new models of impact, stay up to date on innovations, and connect their resources with social change at a level that it would be hard for them to do alone.

In 2013, SIF began expanding its work beyond nonprofit organizations to include for-profit businesses that focus on social impact. This part of the SIF portfolio appeals to investors interested in investing capital for a social and financial return. Still in its early stages, this work with for-profits is structured around an accelerator (the Social Business Accelerator) and draws on the same marketplace approach.

Building the Marketplace

As mentioned earlier, SIF focused in its early years on developing its approach to accomplish two things—building the capacity of effective nonprofit organizations and advancing resource allocation based on performance. Under the leadership of Susan Musinsky, who joined in 2005 with a focus on community building and further developing the marketplace approach, the program, known today as SIF's Social Innovator Accelerator, has grown to provide consulting, executive coaching, presentation advising, performance measurement, graphic design, and other supports delivered by a constellation of staff, contract consultants, skilled volunteers, and in-kind partners. Quite intentionally, the SIF model seeks to create space and time for leaders to ask hard questions, to take stock of their assets, and to leverage their SIF experience to build a new community of support. As its core program has matured and spun out of Root Cause, SIF has continued to focus on building community and the marketplace approach.

Figure 2 depicts the Social Innovation Forum's marketplace approach. The "Investors and Supporters" side of the model represents a community of philanthropists, foundations, skilled volunteers, connectors, and collaborators, many of whom come from the corporate world. The "Innovators and Entrepreneurs" are the nonprofit organizations and for-profit social impact businesses that participate in SIF's two accelerators.

SIF is in the middle, representing its position as the *marketplace* for social impact. In creating this marketplace, SIF not only facilitates the exchange of resources, but also works to *connect* people within the marketplace, leveraging every role in the ecosystem for social purpose.

The Marketplace in Action: Stories of Give and Take

In the usual nonprofit narrative, donors and volunteers are the "givers" and nonprofit organizations are the "receivers." SIF fosters a reciprocal give and take in the marketplace. The benefits to the participants might be tangible (such as money) or intangible (such as an opportunity to be a part of social change), but real value is exchanged in a way that provides a "win-win" to all parties and keeps the focus on advancing the larger goal of social impact. Stories from SIF's community illustrate the give and take of the marketplace.

THE SOCIAL INNOVATION FORUM
builds networks that create social change

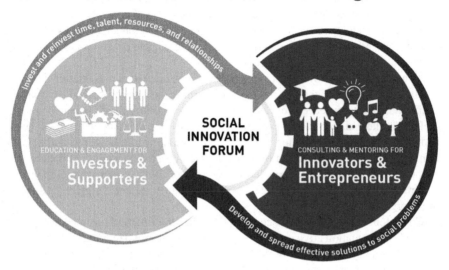

Fig. 2 The Social Innovation Forum marketplace model

Innovators and Entrepreneurs

My Life My Choice (MLMC)

The experience of My Life My Choice (MLMC) offers an example of an Innovator that benefitted immensely from SIF's technical support, network building, and ability to shine a spotlight on a particular issue. My Life My Choice is an initiative designed to stem the tide of commercial sexual exploitation of adolescents. When MLMC was selected for the 2010 Social Innovator cohort, the commercial sexual exploitation of adolescents was a significant issue with little visibility and even less funding in the local community. Between 2005 and 2009, the SEEN (Support to End Exploitation Now) Coalition in Suffolk County, Massachusetts, received over 300 referrals of exploited or high-risk youth, with many more victims likely going uncounted. At the same time, the SEEN Case Coordinator position was reduced and then temporarily eliminated due to lack of funding (Piening and Cross 2012).

Although now a nationally recognized program and model for others across the country, in 2010 MLMC was a 7-year-old organization that effectively served about 125 girls each year while facing significant financial and organizational challenges. My Life My Choice had no board of directors, and cofounder and director Lisa Goldblatt Grace was struggling to pay the staff. In addition, because the organization was focused on short-term financial stability, it had no structured plan in place for the future. Lisa and MLMC cofounder and associate director Audrey Morrissey, a survivor and strong voice on the sexual exploitation of adolescents, were eager to engage in the SIF process. They knew that more girls needed them, and they would have to grow to meet those needs. Lisa and Audrey worked with their SIF consultant to shape a plan for long-term sustainability by looking to diversify revenue streams. Together, they created a clear articulation of the organization's message and vision for impact, and they created materials designed to engage potential financial supporters in the organization's future.

To help refine Lisa's financial pitch, SIF matched her with a presentation advisor, a retired wealth management professional turning his energy to contributing to social change after a successful career. The advisor was unsure of the match at first, feeling that he had no personal experience or expertise in the issues that MLMC was addressing. The SIF team supported him in the relationship, however, and helped him to see how his skills could be valuable. He provided coaching, guidance, and support to MLMC, and after concluding his advisor role, he found the relationship so rewarding and MLMC's impact so profound that he became a significant funder of the organization's work.

Consistent with the marketplace ideal, while he gave time and financial resources, MLMC's presentation advisor also received much in return. He found an extremely rewarding engagement for himself where he, too, gained new skills, broadened his knowledge of social issues affecting his community, felt the impact of his investment of time and capital, and expanded his own network significantly. More than five years later, he continues to support MLMC and is an active member of the SIF community, as a funder, connector, and strategic advisor.

Joining the SIF community gave My Life My Choice access to a new network of funders and potential supporters who were eager to learn about the organization's approach to this critical, yet challenging, issue. Shortly after the Showcase, an individual in SIF's network made a $100,000 commitment to the organization. He later joined MLMC's newly established board of directors. MLMC received help from several of SIF's in-kind partners, including database support from Analysis Group and presentation coaching from the Ariel Group.

After completing the formal SIF accelerator, Lisa and Audrey led the organization through a period of remarkable growth, which has raised their profile nationally and increased their impact in addressing commercial sexual exploitation. Lisa Goldblatt Grace notes,

> Working with SIF made an enormous impact on the growth and sustainability of My Life My Choice. We were named a Social Innovator at a time when our organization was at a real inflection point. Since that time, our budget has grown six fold to more than $1 million and our staff has increased from three to 17.

GRIT

GRIT (Global Research Innovation & Technology) is dedicated to building technology that improves the lives of people with disabilities, primarily through creation and distribution of an affordable, all-terrain wheelchair originally designed for people in developing countries who are often isolated as a result of their disability. When GRIT applied for the Social Innovation Forum's first Social Business Accelerator cohort in 2013, the company had started offering its initial product, the Leveraged Freedom Chair, in developing countries, but had not yet entered the US market or begun raising growth capital. Although GRIT had gone through other start-up accelerators with financial success, CEO and cofounder Tish Scolnik and her team of MIT-trained mechanical engineers were eager to learn from companies specifically focused on social impact. Tish also wanted to connect with the growing community of investors and mentors specifically interested in mission-driven companies.

SIF worked with GRIT to focus on highlighting the social impact part of its work alongside the financial return. Tish had the opportunity to share experiences with and learn from like-minded leaders facing similar challenges. During the program, mentors from the business community asked tough questions that helped GRIT deepen its presentation content and hone its message. Through SIF, the GRIT team gained visibility and exposure to potential investors, particularly those who were looking to back companies that promised both financial and social returns. Through SIF, Tish met Jeff Kushner, former CEO of BlueMountain Capital, Europe, and an active social impact investor. Jeff later became a lead investor and GRIT board member. Drawing on the materials created with SIF, GRIT began actively fundraising, and in July 2015 closed its first funding round, raising $650,000 from 16 impact and angel investors, many of whom came through the SIF network. To date, GRIT has distributed more than 2000 Leveraged Freedom Chairs in the developing world and is now making the Freedom Chairs available in the USA, where the current addressable market includes over three million wheelchair riders in the USA alone[3] (Brault 2012).

Investors and Supporters

Reynders, McVeigh Capital Management (RMCM)

SIF's hands-on, responsive relationship management has led to the success of innovative partnerships, such as a corporate partnership with Reynders, McVeigh Capital Management, LLC (RMCM). RMCM is a Boston-based investment management firm focused on socially responsible investments, creating portfolios comprised of companies that emphasize sound financials plus social impact. Like so many others in the SIF community, RMCM met the Social Innovation Forum through another company in the network. After getting to know SIF's work, an exciting idea for collaboration emerged.

While RMCM has expertise in managing socially responsible investment portfolios, the leaders of the firm, Chat Reynders and Patrick McVeigh, wanted to find a way

---

[3] 3.6 million: Number of people 15 and older who used a wheelchair to assist with mobility. This compares with 11.6 million people who used a cane, crutches, or walker.

for their company and its staff to become more deeply involved in the local, early-stage social impact community in greater Boston. RMCM joined the SIF funding community as a corporate sponsor. The Social Innovation Forum engaged RMCM staff in a range of volunteer roles throughout a full cycle of both of the accelerators. RMCM staff members were invited to participate in every aspect of SIF's work, including evaluating applications, participating in interviews, serving on pitch panels, mentoring social impact start-ups, and attending SIF events. RMCM staff learned about pressing social issues in greater Boston and used their business skills to support SIF's cohort of Social Innovators and Impact Entrepreneurs. RMCM staff, equipped with new experience and learning, then came together and chose one SIF organization to receive the first "Reynders, McVeigh Social Innovation Prize." In turn, prize recipients have used the award to leverage additional public relations attention, credibility with donors, and new funding, including investment from RMCM employees and clients. Since the partnership began, RMCM has awarded three prizes to organizations in both SIF's nonprofit and for-profit cohorts. The RMCM staff has become deeply involved in SIF's work, including a match between one RMCM employee and the board of an organization she supported through the SIF process.

Schrafft Charitable Trust

Partnerships with local philanthropic foundations have been an important part of SIF's marketplace approach. Many of the foundations that support SIF act as "social issue track partners," sponsoring a specific social issue for a given year in the Social Innovator Accelerator. This role gives foundations the opportunity to learn about SIF's approach to selecting and supporting organizations, to be a part of a larger conversation around a specific social issue, and to have more flexibility than they might have within their own portfolios to explore different social issues or work with earlier stage organizations. The Schrafft Charitable Trust, a private foundation established in 1946, had a strong record of supporting inner-city Boston nonprofits focused on educating disadvantaged youth. In partnership with SIF, they engaged in valuable learning while achieving impact in a new social issue area with an organization in the early stages of development.

The Schrafft trustees had attended events and served as evaluators in the Innovator selection process. After 25 years of focusing their grant-making on education, the trustees became interested in urban environmental sustainability. In 2013, the Trust joined the SIF funding community as a track partner for a "Sustainability in Our Communities: Building Greener and Healthier Cities" social issue track.

Partnership with SIF gave the trustees confidence to explore this new social issue area. Working closely with the SIF team, Schrafft trustees learned about urban sustainability, explored organizations working on this issue in greater Boston, and received guidance from experts and other funders. In 2014, after six months of evaluation, the "Sustainability in Our Communities" track selected a Lowell-based organization, Mill City Grows, as its Social Innovator. Mill City Grows was a smaller, younger organization than the Trust had supported historically. SIF's evaluation and due diligence process gave the Trust the opportunity to meet the organization's leadership and more fully understand the potential in, and implications of, investing in an earlier stage organization. Thrilled with its first experience as a track partner, the Schrafft Charitable Trust signed on to support a second sustainability track the following year and chose the Mystic River Watershed Association (MyRWA) as a Social Innovator. According to Lavinia Chase, a Schrafft Trustee:

> For a long time at Schrafft, we focused primarily on education in Boston. A new area arose as a concern for us: the effect of climate change on our cities. Partnership with the Social Innovation Forum educated us in urban sustainability and gave us confidence to involve Schrafft in newer and smaller nonprofits.

The experience of narrowing the field through applications and evaluation, meeting the finalists through interviews and site visits, and learning from SIF's comprehensive selection process has enabled Schrafft trustees better to understand the field of urban environmental sustainability and to direct their resources toward organizations that are best positioned to leverage engagement and financial support. The trustees continue to partner with SIF and remain actively engaged in urban sustainability issues and in the work of Mill City Grows and MyRWA.

In addition to partners like RMCM and Schrafft Charitable Trust, SIF also engages a large community of passionate individuals who bring diverse skills, professional experiences, and interests to the marketplace. These individuals contribute immensely to emerging mission-driven organizations through hands-on mentoring, coaching, advising, and often funding and, in turn, find meaningful opportunities to give back, expand their own networks, and sharpen new skills through their work with Innovators and Entrepreneurs.

A Closer Look: Key Features of the SIF Marketplace Approach

The examples above illustrate the elements that make SIF's marketplace approach so effective in bringing together funders, investors, and practitioners to create positive social impact: a rigorous selection process that engages the community; thoughtful, intentional matching of skilled volunteers with nonprofit and social business leaders; deep connections with institutional partners; an emphasis on performance measurement; and ongoing support. This next section explores each component of the approach in greater detail.

Rigorous Selection Process

As with every aspect of SIF's process, the selection of innovative, diverse, mission-driven nonprofit organizations and social impact businesses for the accelerator programs is intentional, hands-on, and provides an opportunity to bring together stakeholders and build networks.

For the Social Innovator Accelerator, SIF engages the community through its intensive, 6-month selection process, which includes nominating, evaluating, and interviewing committees comprised of issue experts, community leaders, funders, practitioners, business people, and representatives of the populations being served by the organizations. This structure brings more than 90 people into the selection process each year and provides SIF with opportunities to engage and educate people about critical social issues and the range of organizations working in those areas. Also, broad participation makes the selection process more transparent and brings critical expertise and perspectives to the decision making.

The Social Innovator selection process begins with 150+ applications each year, yielding 25–30 finalists and an Innovator cohort of six to eight organizations. Through two rounds of written applications, evaluation committees, in-person interviews, and due diligence, the SIF selection process is intentionally designed not only to benefit the selected SIF Innovators and Entrepreneurs by guiding them through a period of intense self-reflection, but also to add value to other applicants by helping them connect with new organizations every year, providing in-depth written and verbal feedback, and offering guidance and support from SIF's accessible staff.

Applicants report that the process helps them reflect on their organizational goals and impact, and they appreciate the input and feedback they receive. Groups that are selected as finalists or participants in SIF accelerators carry a recognized "imprimatur" of having been thoroughly vetted by SIF. Funders and volunteers benefit from the work done by SIF to identify and assess organizations in a way that they might not be able to do on their own. In this role, SIF often acts as a complement to private, family, and community foundations, as even established funders sometimes will seek information from SIF about promising organizations in their fields of interest.

Leveraging Highly Skilled Volunteers Through Intentional Matching

Effectively leveraging highly skilled volunteers represents an important pillar of the marketplace approach. While SIF staff and contractors provide some technical assistance to portfolio organizations, SIF deliberately spends significant time and energy building up its community of supporters and investors, nurturing relationships with them and between them, and helping them to help the Innovators and Entrepreneurs in the portfolio.

It is not simple to choreograph an effective program made up of highly skilled volunteers, most of whom have been leaders themselves. This approach requires deep engagement with volunteers, Innovators, and Entrepreneurs to make intentional introductions, provide guidelines, and support ongoing work. However, SIF has found that by successfully sourcing, cultivating, and supporting high-level volunteers, not only is the value of volunteer time leveraged to provide more direct support than SIF could afford to fund directly, but it also creates more long-term impact through the level of commitment and enduring relationships that can develop.

The executive coaching component of the Social Innovator Accelerator demonstrates the increased trust, strong relationships, and deep impact that come from a thoughtful process utilizing skilled volunteers. In their first year with SIF, Social Innovators are matched with high-level, volunteer executive coaches to work on individualized leadership goals. SIF begins by sourcing an extensive pool of trained executive coaches and then carefully reviews their applications and conducts interviews to learn more about each. SIF then matches coaches with Innovators based on the coach's experience, personality traits, and skillset alongside the Innovator's particular leadership challenges. With support from SIF staff, two "lead" coaches regularly check in with each coach/Innovator match to ensure that the engagement is going smoothly. In addition to the obvious benefits of executive coaching for Innovators, this approach provides value for the coaches themselves—diversifying their experiences, sharpening their skills, and helping them to feel deeply connected to social purpose organizations while they develop a close-knit peer network.

This level of community engagement and volunteer management takes time and energy to build, but it is critical to the marketplace approach. SIF has found that highly skilled volunteers and other supporters crave opportunities to be a part of this type of network. They want engagement with real meaning. As individuals become less involved in traditional, geographically based communities such as neighborhoods or churches, people are eager to connect with a community that shares their values. Additionally, as people live longer but retire earlier, they retain professional skills that they want to keep using. According to a report by the Corporation for National and Community Service, baby boomers (Americans born between 1946 and 1964) tend to volunteer at higher rates and to have higher levels of education compared with previous generation (Foster-Bey et al. 2007). SIF provides both community and skilled volunteer opportunities, and by investing time in meeting new people, it grows a community through nurturing relationships, and meaningful, structured opportunities for individuals to apply their skills to projects that matter.

Deep Connections with Institutional Partners

In-kind resources are often critical to building a sustainable nonprofit business model. As such, they have been an important component of SIF's marketplace approach. In-kind partners are companies and organizations that offer professional talents and skills, providing meaningful, hands-on support to current and past Innovators and joining the SIF community in long-term relationships. SIF provides in-kind partners with a customized structure that allows the partner's employees to give of their time and talents, expand their own skills by working on unique projects, and become a part of the broader SIF community committed to social change in greater Boston. In 2015 alone, SIF partners contributed more than $325,000 in in-kind services, including graphic design, data analysis, presentation advising, and development consulting.

Drawing on the in-kind support of partners provides much-needed professional services to SIF's Innovators while enabling SIF to extend its per-dollar impact.

The organization continues to expand and refine the suite of services available through in-kind partnerships, engaging companies interested in giving to their communities and broadening the support available to the organizations in the portfolio. The following examples of in-kind partnerships show the range of resources that enter the marketplace in this way.

The Ariel Group, an international training and coaching firm comprised of performing artists and business professionals, provides Social Innovators with group training on presence and storytelling as well as individual presentation coaching. Over a 10-year partnership with the Ariel Group, SIF's Innovators have learned to deliver compelling, authentic pitches, and the Ariel Group's coaches and staff have developed deep bonds and long-lasting relationships with inspiring social sector leaders.

Another in-kind partner, Opus Design, has worked with SIF for the past seven years to provide each cohort of Social Innovators with substantial graphic design support. Each year, Opus designers get to know the Innovators and work with them to design professional PowerPoint templates and customized graphic depictions of their program and impact models. Opus consistently makes an extra effort to ensure that each Innovator has materials that reflect the organization's specific culture and personality. Innovators often engage Opus to do additional graphic design work, capitalizing on the opportunity to work with a designer who already understands and cares deeply about their organization to develop new logos, marketing materials, or annual reports.

Analysis Group (formerly Public Service Economics) regularly works with both current Innovators and past Innovators who may have completed their formal SIF engagements as many as five or 10 years prior. Analysis Group provides pro bono economic consulting services from survey design to data analytics. Teams of Analysis Group consultants work with Social Innovators to assess and develop projects that address their needs, working with Innovators on projects ranging from three months to more than a year, and providing more than $100,000 worth of services to SIF Innovators annually. Past projects include cost-effectiveness studies, statistical analyses, survey design, and database design.

Performance Measurement

Recognizing that performance measurement can be challenging, particularly for smaller, early-stage organizations, SIF helps its portfolio groups to advance their efforts in this area, regardless of their starting points. In the selection process, applicants must present whatever impact data they have. This helps ensure that every group begins with some baseline for measurement. Then, SIF consultants work with Innovators to set measurable performance targets in three key areas: program performance, organizational health/capacity building, and social impact. Following the Showcase, SIF holds quarterly check-in calls with Innovators to track their progress toward these goals and discuss the successes and challenges they have experienced.

Eighteen months after selection, SIF publishes a "Performance Measurement Report" for each Innovator and shares these results with the broader community. In the report, Innovators share their progress in the key areas mentioned above and reflect on successes and lessons learned. They also present 1-year accomplishments, current capital needs, and ways to invest in the organization's growth. The SIF performance measurement process provides frameworks and tools for assessment, but also for learning, at the individual, organizational, and community levels. In addition, SIF regularly conducts its own performance measurement to track the program's overall effectiveness and report out to stakeholders. The performance measurement work allows people entering the SIF community to see how SIF and its portfolio groups are progressing toward shared goals of creating social impact.

Ongoing Support

Given SIF's deep, long-standing commitment to the selected organizations, the staff continues to work with portfolio groups in a range of ways after the formal conclusion of their SIF engagement. The staff stays closely tied to many organizations, celebrating successes while also supporting them through difficult times. All past Innovators and past Entrepreneurs have access to the services of several in-kind partners and are invited to events and skill-building workshops. SIF has helped organizations through staff transitions and rebranding, through intense growth and periods of struggle, and even with seemingly small (but important) details like how to prepare for a funder meeting. Perhaps most important to sustaining the marketplace approach, SIF continues to actively make introductions and connections between the two sides of the marketplace to help its portfolio organizations grow and its supporter community find meaningful engagement.

InnerCity Weightlifting

The relationship between SIF and InnerCity Weightlifting (ICW) shows the mutually beneficial effects of the ongoing commitment and connection that characterize this marketplace approach.

Since becoming a Social Innovator in 2012, Jon Feinman, founder and executive director of ICW, has been an active participant in the SIF marketplace. ICW uses fitness as a tool to reduce youth violence by connecting young people who are gang and/or criminally involved with new networks and opportunities, including a meaningful career track in personal training. Jon has met a number of large funders and supporters through SIF, worked with in-kind partners, built out his first corporate training program with SIF partners at Microsoft, and helped other Innovators along the way. "SIF helped us to think strategically, communicate our story, and measure success for our students," said Jon. "Then SIF introduced us to a network that made our growth possible."

Staying true to ICW's mission, Jon has grown the organization with a sharp focus on strengthening the skills and social capital of his students, making sure to foster meaningful relationships between them and the supporters in ICW's community, often people in networks previously out of the students' reach. This exchange exposes network members to something new, too, and helps change their own beliefs about segregation and social isolation.

Within six months of completing the SIF engagement, InnerCity Weightlifting had nearly doubled its budget to $500,000 and opened its first gym in Boston's Dorchester neighborhood. In 2014, when ICW wanted to expand further, an introduction from SIF helped the organization secure a $400,000 commitment to support a second location in Cambridge's Kendall Square, a hub for innovative companies. Today, InnerCity Weightlifting has a budget of more than $1 million, serves more than 250 students each year, and has attracted a roster of 350 individual and corporate personal training clients whose sessions give student trainers an income. Of ICW's clients, 78 % report a shift in their perceptions about ICW students and 96 % report a positive relationship with ICW students. At the same time, 95 % of students report increased hope for the future—which is, from ICW's perspective, the most essential metric to consider.

Conclusion

From its beginnings, SIF carved out a distinctive place in the greater Boston landscape. As founder Andrew Wolk once noted (2012):

> I have watched [SIF's] market-minded approach change the relationship between nonprofits with innovative ideas and the people who provide resources to them …. The dialogue between these groups has become honest and transparent. In addition, a shared understanding of the targeted social issues and performance data has become a primary basis for decision making.

SIF's work complements that of consultants in strategy, evaluation, and development, technical assistance providers, and other groups that support social purpose organizations.[4] SIF provides a pipeline for larger local and national funders who help proven organizations go to scale. SIF supports individual donors and lightly staffed foundations, which often lack the time and expertise needed to make informed decisions about where to allocate their resources of time and money. In sum, SIF offers a way for individuals and institutions to engage in improving the community, making a difference that none could achieve on their own.

SIF does this through an intentional, relational, rigorous process: selecting nonprofits and social impact businesses for its accelerator programs; leveraging highly skilled volunteers and in-kind partners to provide capacity building support in critical areas; creating meaningful, individualized opportunities for engagement and

---

[4] SIF collaborates with organizations like Social Venture Partners Boston, the Draper Richards Kaplan Foundation, MassChallenge, and others.

impact; tracking performance measures and showing evidence of impact; and building and sustaining a community by making introductions, offering support, and responding to the interests and needs of funders, investors, and practitioners.

With all that SIF has accomplished, much work remains to be done. In the next phase of development, two key questions stand out as being essential to SIF's success. The first is a question of scale. Challenges to scale are inherent in the marketplace model, which thrives due to the high-touch, local, and relationship-based nature of SIF's approach. As more community building moves onto digital platforms, the SIF team has both an opportunity and a challenge to navigate the implications of existing in a digital age with a model based largely on personal interactions. Of course, any question of scale also comes with questions of funding. Given the smaller subset of funders interested in supporting capacity building models versus direct service organizations, SIF has to demonstrate the value of this approach to ensure sufficient support in its next phase.

Another key element to SIF's future success is increasing the diversity of the organization both within SIF's own staff and in the broader community. As the SIF team and its community grow, it will be essential to strengthen relationships and recruit in ways that intentionally build an inclusive network that is representative of the diverse communities, populations, and social issues addressed through SIF's work. Increasing diversity within the SIF community will allow the organization to move its work forward more effectively by having a broader set of perspectives helping to guide it into its next phase.

As it has over the past 13 years, SIF's modern-day marketplace continues to evolve, as the organization works to refine its model, expand diversity, ensure sustainability, and measure results. More than just demonstrating how resources can be effectively and efficiently allocated to social purpose ventures, though, SIF itself models how an organization can create a mission-focused community. The SIF team is encouraged by the national and international interest in its work and excited about opportunities to share this approach with others. The authors hope that an expanding number of organizations will be inspired to develop active marketplaces for social change in their own communities.

References

Brault M (2012) Americans with disabilities: 2010. United States Census Bureau. www.census.gov/prod/2012pubs/p70-131.pdf. Accessed 21 June 2016

The Chronicle of Philanthropy (2012) How America gives. https://philanthropy.com/interactives/how-america-gives#state/25. Accessed 21 June 2016

Foster-Bey J, Grimm R Jr, Deitz N (2007) Keeping baby boomers volunteering. http://www.nationalservice.gov/pdf/07_0307_boomer_report.pdf. Accessed 21 June 2016

GIIN (2015) What is the current state of the impact investing market? https://thegiin.org/impact-investing/need-to-know/#s9. Accessed 21 June 2016

Office of the Massachusetts Attorney General (n.d.) Public Charities Annual Filings. Commonwealth of Massachusetts

Piening S, Cross T (2012) From 'the life' to my life: sexually exploited children reclaiming their futures. http://www.suffolkcac.org/assets/pdf/From_the_Life_to_My_Life_Suffolk_Countys_Response_to_CSEC_June_2012.pdf. Accessed 21 June 2016

Wolk A (2012) Social impact markets. Stanford Social Innovation Review. http://ssir.org/pdf/Winter_2012_Social_Impact_Markets.pdf. Accessed 21 June 2016

Social Enterprise for Economic Opportunity at UTEC

Gregg Croteau, Ed Frechette, and Dawn Grenier

Abstract UTEC is a nonprofit organization in Lowell, MA, that serves proven-risk young people—those who actively have demonstrated risk factors for incarceration and criminal activity. UTEC works in Lowell and Lawrence, MA, two cities with substantial immigrant populations experiencing income inequality and significant gang activity. UTEC helps proven-risk youth transition from gangs and/or incarceration to achieving sustainable employment and completing their educations.

As part of its strategy, UTEC has developed three social enterprises in food, woodworking, and mattress recycling. These enterprises not only allow UTEC to take a patient "mad love" approach to working with their young people, but also provide core operating revenues for the organization. While the earned income is attractive, the young people come first, and the social enterprises are part of a carefully constructed set of values, cultural practices, and approaches designed to walk with the young people from disenfranchisement to education and to stable, long-term employment.

This chapter explores UTEC's overall approach, and then dives deeply into UTEC's Mattress Recycling program, the first point of entry for its youth. As authors Gregg Croteau, Ed Frechette, and Dawn Grenier note, "The business side of each social enterprise must work around the programming side, not the other way around." Mattress Recycling is a competitive enterprise that is structurally suited to the level of engagement, supervision, and multiple chances to which UTEC is committed.

Keywords Proven-risk youth • Social enterprise • UTEC • Mattress recycling

Jeff's Story

Jeff was born in Lawrence, MA. His father, originally from the Dominican Republic, was deported the next year. Jeff lived with his mother and stepfather once his dad was gone, but struggled. He was diagnosed with anxiety and depression at a young age and didn't do well in school. His mother and stepdad tried to protect him and

G. Croteau (✉) • E. Frechette • D. Grenier
UTEC, 15 Warren St, No. 3, Lowell, MA 01852, USA
e-mail: gcroteau@utec-lowell.org

© Springer International Publishing Switzerland 2017   51
M.J. Cronin, T.C. Dearing (eds.), *Managing for Social Impact*,
Management for Professionals, DOI 10.1007/978-3-319-46021-5_3

encouraged him to stay close to home, but Jeff rebelled. By his junior year of high school, Jeff was in trouble with the law. He left school without his diploma. He was arrested and convicted for auto theft at age 18, serving 6 months in jail. When he got out, he returned to the same friends and same situations, got arrested again, and this time served 2 years in the county jail.

UTEC is a community-based nonprofit organization that provides work experience as part of a holistic model for those specific young adults who have the highest potential for negative impact on society based on their proven risk factors. UTEC serves youth from Lowell and Lawrence, MA, who are 17–24, out of school, and who are gang or criminally involved. UTEC Streetworkers visit the correctional facilities that serve Lowell and Lawrence regularly to get to know the young people there before they leave and return to their communities.

During one of these prerelease visits, UTEC's Streetworkers met Jeff. They encouraged him to think about where he was headed when he got out. They knew that the choices a young man makes in his initial days after leaving incarceration have a dramatic effect on whether he goes back to jail (Ball et al. 2008).

Jeff didn't think much of the visit from the UTEC Streetworkers at the time, or when he was released from jail. After his release, he obtained, but quickly lost, a job at a temp agency. Jeff then reconsidered his decision. He had a friend who had joined the UTEC program and encouraged him to try it. "It was a way I could get my GED and have a job at the same time, so why not?" he said.

Like all young people joining UTEC, Jeff started in the organization's mattress recycling enterprise, where youth deconstruct mattresses and recycle the component parts. "I didn't know anyone, and I don't like meeting new people, but it worked out okay," Jeff said. "I liked that I had a job and we had a great crew." Jeff moved through the program's Transformational Beginnings introductory stage in just 3 weeks—faster than usual—and advanced to the Workforce program, where he could pursue his high school equivalency credential while continuing to work in one of UTEC's other social enterprises, which include Food Services and Woodworking.

Jeff left the county jail at age 21. Now 22, he completed his HiSET (High School Equivalency Test), the recognized high school equivalency degree in Massachusetts, in his first month in the program, when he also joined the UTEC Woodworking crew. In Woodworking, Jeff is learning shop and carpentry skills doing hands-on projects, including building display racks for a local Whole Foods Market as part of a contract UTEC has with the company. In a *Lowell Sun* article about the local Whole Foods Market's grand opening, Jeff proudly stated: "I'm not used to the glow. Now we're shining" (Hanson 2016).

Lowell and Lawrence, Massachusetts: Gateway Cities

Lowell and Lawrence are located in Eastern Massachusetts. Each was a planned industrial community. During the nineteenth century, Lowell and Lawrence were thriving centers of wealth and industry, attracting immigrants and migrant workers to their textile mills—an attraction that persists today despite increasing economic hardship for many area residents.

Following the overall arc of America's post-World War II industrial decline, these once-prosperous communities have struggled for decades. Lowell and Lawrence have poverty rates at 19.1 % and 28.5 %, respectively. In Lowell, 21.9 % of residents don't have a high school degree, and 78.4 % didn't graduate college (U.S. Census 2016a). Lawrence's numbers are higher, at 31.5 and 88.1 % (U.S. Census 2016b). Lawrence ranks as the poorest city in Massachusetts and one of the poorest in the USA (Atkinson 2012). The unemployment rate for these two cities is also higher than that of Massachusetts as a whole. In the early 2010s, Lowell's unemployment rate was typically about 2 % higher than the state average, while Lawrence's unemployment was nearly double the state average (Labor Force/Unemployment Rates Database 2016).

Both Lowell and Lawrence are "Gateway Cities," 2 of 26 such cities in the Commonwealth of Massachusetts (Forman et al. 2007). According to the Commonwealth's Department of Housing and Economic Development, a gateway city has a population between 35,000 and 250,000, a median household income below the state average, and a rate of higher educational attainment below the state average (2016). These smaller gateway cities bear the brunt of a geographic concentration of poverty driven by rising income inequality. They lack sufficient resources to help disadvantaged residents reach their potential and participate fully in the state's knowledge economy (Carr and Foreman 2015). The state's economic growth has been fueled by knowledge-intensive industries, which offer few opportunities for low-income workers with lower levels of educational attainment. For example, the minimum educational requirements for the 25 highest-demand occupations in Lowell include a college degree (Kottcamp et al. 2015).

In addition to being hubs for income inequality, gateway cities tend to be home to large concentrations of immigrants—hence the idea of being "gateways" to the USA for aspiring new Americans. According to the 2010 Census, Lowell, MA, located just 35 miles northwest of Boston, is a diverse community of 109,945 residents and the fourth largest city in Massachusetts, with the second-largest Cambodian population in the USA. Lawrence, MA, is fewer than 30 miles northwest of Boston and has a population of 78,197, of which 74 % is Latino.

Challenges for Justice-Involved Young Adults

Young adults are more impulsive and more likely to make poor decisions. This has notable consequences for criminal justice; as a Mass Inc. policy brief summarized, "Young adults ages 18 to 24 are the most likely demographic to find their way into Massachusetts prisons and the quickest to return to them upon release" (Forman and Yee 2015). Disengagement from school, exposure to violence, poverty, race, and being a young parent can all correlate with a young person's likelihood of involvement with the criminal justice system.

Recidivism rates, the rate at which people reoffend, are consistently high for young adults. For example, one analysis covering 30 states found that the 3-year rearrest rate for prisoners released in 2005 was 78 % for 18–24-year-olds, compared to 72 % for all released prisoners (Durose et al. 2014). In Massachusetts, young adults represent the highest rate of incarceration among any age group. Nearly one-quarter of the house of correction (county jail) population are between the ages of 18–24 (Mosehauer et al, 2016, Research Addendum). This age range also has the longest length of stay, and thus the highest costs of incarceration. Most critically, young adults demonstrate the highest rates of recidivism. Within one year of release, more than half of all young adults (ages 18–24) recidivate: 52 % of young adults released from jails and 56 % released from state prisons will be re-arraigned. The rates are similar for three-year recidivism rates, with 55 % from jail and 51 % from prison re-offending (Mosehauer et al, 2016). Conversely, recidivism rates for young people served by UTEC are significantly lower. Among youth who have left UTEC programming, only 17 % had been arrested in the two years since exiting (UTEC, 2016), and less than 5 % had been convicted of a new offense. These rates are significantly lower than the recently-released Council on State Governments Justice Center data for Massachusetts, which shows 37 % of young adults reconvicted within two years of release (2015). In addition to meeting UTEC's internal targets for reducing recidivism, this significant drop in new offenses reflects increased public safety and a public benefit in cost savings associated with law enforcement and incarceration.

Beyond age 24, criminal involvement tends to drop off: it is rare for those who are criminally involved to have committed their first offense beyond this age (Schiraldi et al. 2015). For this reason, UTEC focuses on keeping proven-risk youth productively engaged during that critical highest risk period of 17–24 years. With resources and positive support up to age 24, proven-risk youth are more likely to succeed in their mid-20s and beyond. In addition, research shows that after 6 or 7 years without criminal activity, an ex-offender's risk of future criminal activity is almost the same as for their peers without a criminal record (Kurlychek et al. 2007). This suggests that if UTEC can keep youth with prior criminal records engaged for up to 6–7 years without further criminal involvement, those youth will have a very low likelihood of reoffending.

Based on this research, UTEC's primary hypothesis has two parts:

1. If proven-risk youth are productively engaged in UTEC activities and supports for an extended period of time during the critical ages of 17–24, then by age 25, they will have the skills and resilience they need to maintain stable employment and avoid further criminal activity.
2. If UTEC is able to specifically target and serve those proven-risk youth (through the age of 24) who are most likely to recidivate and cause harm in our communities, success will also translate into a significant return on investment from a public health, public safety, and economic development perspective.

UTEC's model aligns with best practices emerging in young adult justice and reentry fields and was cited by the National Institute of Justice as a model for working with justice-involved young adults. Notably, UTEC's work in direct service, policymaking, and performance measurement support all four recommendations from the Council of State Governments Justice Center in its brief, *Reducing*

Recidivism and Improving Other Outcomes for Young Adults in the Juvenile and Adult Criminal Justice Systems (2015):

1. Tailor supervision and services to address young adults' distinct needs [including career pathways, life skills training, and connection to a supportive adult]
2. Reduce barriers across service systems to meeting the distinct needs of young adults
3. Improve data collection and reporting on young adult recidivism and other outcomes
4. Build the knowledge base of "what works" by testing promising and innovative supervision and service delivery approaches, and direct funding to programs proven to be effective

UTEC's History

UTEC was founded in 1999 in Lowell, MA, as the United Teen Equality Center. It was created by youth, for youth, looking for a safe place to gather in downtown Lowell. A large influx of Cambodian refugees started in the mid-1980s, and the 1990s saw a significant increase in gang conflicts between Asian and Latino gangs. It was in this context that a group of 15 youth leaders, with assistance from a few adult volunteers and street outreach workers from the City of Lowell, approached city officials for help in developing a center where they and their neighbors could come together without fear of violence. UTEC's very first funding source was a Housing and Urban Development (HUD) Enterprise Community grant of $40,000, sub-granted through the city. The Lowell Downtown Neighborhood Association advocated for support from the community and downtown businesses; its president was the founding board chair for UTEC.

Gang violence escalated during UTEC's early years. According to the Robert Wood Johnson Foundation (Croteau 2015), by 2002, "an estimated 1500 to 2000 young people [were] involved in the 25 to 30 active gangs in the city, with the highest incidence of gang violence being between immigrant Latino and Southeast Asian—mostly Cambodian—youth." That year, there were 12 gang-related murders in this relatively small city, and 16 shootings within 5 months. Throughout the growth in homicides, overall gun violence, and shots fired in Lowell in the early 2000s, research shows that "Lowell homicide and serious gun assault incidents were concentrated among young, minority males residing in disadvantaged neighborhoods" (Braga et al. 2006). Gangs drove the violent crime. Between 2000 and 2002, "73.7 % of 19 homicide offenders, 45.5 % of 22 aggravated gun assault offenders, 47.1 % of 17 homicide victims, and 29.4 % of 51 aggravated gun assault victims were active gang members" (Braga et al. 2006).

Selected members of the founding youth leaders served on the board; helped develop the bylaws; participated in the hiring of Gregg Croteau, the first and current executive director; and helped shape the initial programming for the center. A local church offered space for UTEC operations in its first years, and hundreds of young people visited UTEC each week.

For roughly 10 years, UTEC functioned as a drop-in center serving local youth aged 13–23, with an average age of 16. The center provided a safe haven from gang violence and offered a range of programming. UTEC's on-site resources like pool and ping-pong allowed young people to interact informally, and a small team of staff offered planned programs ranging from graphic arts and hip-hop to a culinary program and local community organizing initiatives.

Street outreach workers, originally employed by the City of Lowell, became part of the UTEC Streetworker program, which grew to a staff of four by 2007 and achieved national recognition. Researchers from the Johns Hopkins University Bloomberg School of Public Health conducted an 18-month evaluation of UTEC Streetworkers with funding from the Robert Wood Johnson Foundation. The study resulted in two peer-reviewed journal articles and a congressional briefing hosted by then MA Senator John Kerry's office in Washington, DC, in 2010. Among other data points, the researchers found that 82 % of UTEC youth who participated in mediation/peace activities successfully resolved their conflicts. More than half of all youth, particularly those gang involved and those most disengaged, reported that they could not have connected with the services they received without the help of UTEC.

Refining Programs to Address Youth Needs

The Johns Hopkins study confirmed the Streetworker program's success in engaging hard-to-reach young people and supporting them as they worked toward personal goals. It also highlighted that many of UTEC's young people needed more than a safe place with assorted programming: young people needed help finding work and continuing their education.

In 2010, UTEC's leadership stepped back from day-to-day operations and raised the question of how the organization should evolve over its second decade. Rather than continuing to serve all youth in Lowell, UTEC decided to target its efforts on a more specific subset of young people—youth who were not just "at risk" or even "high risk," as was generally the practice for other organizations, but who were already "proven risk," meaning they had actively demonstrated specific risk factors for incarceration and criminal activity. UTEC intentionally seeks to serve young people who have not succeeded in other, shorter term programming or who may have been deeply involved with the criminal justice system. Interestingly, research has found that even probation officers spend more time and resources on younger youth, pointing to a gap in the attention and investment in older youth who may be perceived as "too far gone" (Schwalbe et al. 2009; Schwalbe and Maschi 2009). UTEC's focus became, and remains, on young men and women aged 17–24 with histories of serious gang or criminal involvement, the majority with past felony arrests. When these youth succeed through UTEC, the community sees the greatest positive impact on public safety, public health, and economic development. UTEC outcomes also represent a cost savings. The Massachusetts Department of Corrections spends approximately $45,500 annually per inmate, while UTEC provides positive outcomes for approximately $25,000 annually per youth served, including a job for 20 or more hours per week (Cannata et al. 2015).

Today, UTEC's mission is to ignite and nurture the ambition of the most disconnected young people so that they will trade violence and poverty for social and economic success. Through its holistic program model, the organization works with youth over 4 or more years—an average of 2 years after enrollment, and with follow-up services for 2 years after program exit—to enable them to find their own paths to success.

Youth Outcomes: Social and Economic Success

UTEC tracks three key outcomes for its youth: reduced recidivism, increased employability, and increased educational attainment. Each of these metrics includes well-defined goals. UTEC invests considerable resources in tracking outcomes for each youth as he or she progresses through the program.

UTEC uses this data to nurture a culture of learning and continuous improvement. All staff have at least some level of involvement in entering or reviewing data: while the Evaluation department coordinates this process, evaluation is a shared responsibility across the organization. Data review is integrated at all levels, with tailored reports built into staff meetings at every level—from direct-service teams to the board of directors.

UTEC is set up to track youth on several levels of their journey through the program. UTEC tracks attendance, performance, and outside issues that could be impacting youth. UTEC tracks youth while they are with the program, actively follows up with youth who disengage from the program, and commits to 2 years of follow-up after youth move on to external employment, postsecondary education, or both.

The results are positive. Of the youth engaged in 2015, for example, 85 % demonstrated an increase in work performance reviews, and 55 % of those without a high school degree obtained the high school equivalency credential. Additionally, 84 % of those who attended workforce programming had no new arrests, and more than 95 % had no new convictions. Of youth who completed UTEC programming 2 years prior, 87 % had not been arrested since leaving UTEC, and 83 % were currently employed (UTEC 2016). These outcomes compare favorably to statistics for the state of Massachusetts, where only 20 % of incarcerated men aged 18–24 have attained a high school diploma or GED, former inmates earn 40 % less than if they had not been incarcerated (Forman and Larivee 2013), and about 78 % of young adults released will be rearrested within 3 years (Schiraldi et al. 2015).

Values and Culture Make the Difference

While UTEC is focused on achieving youth outcomes, it is equally committed to doing the work in a way that is consistent with a set of values that serve and honor its participants. UTEC sees its organizational values as a critical part of the program model's implementation.

UTEC's values do not exist merely on paper. Staff and young people alike discuss the values in action, in day-to-day life. The values are prominently displayed in the main entry hall of the program center. They represent the key ingredients to the organization's culture, which outlines what UTEC asks of each new staff member joining its team.

Moreover, UTEC's training and professional development specifically include values, culture, and community expectations, regularly reinforcing them. Even staff performance reviews are structured around implementation of the values as a key measure of success. For example, UTEC performance reviews ask how well a given staff member demonstrates "respectful curiosity" with young people. They also ask staff members for self-reflection on how well they are advancing the value of "seeing beyond the mask" that a given young adult may wear when first walking through UTEC's doors.

UTEC cultivates continuous self-assessment and self-improvement, at both the individual and organizational levels. Therefore, the organization's theory of change goes through a regular process of examination, and UTEC consciously systematizes its values in order to scale the culture simultaneously with the service model.

The "values wall" pictured in Fig. 1 embodies not only UTEC's beliefs, but also how the organization incorporates the intentional fostering of its culture in every aspect of its work. Three values in particular reveal the essence of UTEC's work:

- **Chipping Away**: UTEC Streetworkers may spend years in conversations with a youth before that young person decides to participate in UTEC programming. The Streetworkers will approach a young person continuously, even when rebuffed, and offer services or resources, reminding them that UTEC is there for them if and when they are ready for a change.

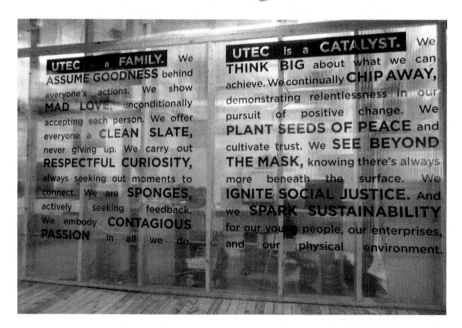

Fig. 1 The UTEC "values wall," prominently positioned at the front of the building

- **Clean Slate**: All youth come into UTEC with a clean slate. UTEC doesn't judge anyone based on their past, and once at UTEC, the organization never gives up on them. If a young person makes a mistake, UTEC will wipe the slate clean again. UTEC does not refer to itself as a "second-chance" organization. Rather, grounded in the belief that working with such proven-risk youth requires a multiple chance framework, its model allows for the ability to be a seventh-, eighth-, or ninth-chance organization depending on the needs of that individual.
- **Mad Love**: UTEC practices unconditional love of its youth. That may be part of the reason many of them consider UTEC a second family.

An Integrated Program Model

The UTEC model has four phases, starting with outreach to young people who are unlikely to seek assistance and extending through each youth's transition beyond the organization.

Phase 1: Outreach

> *Sako [UTEC staff member] helped me with advice on how to tell my friends that I was leaving the gang. He's the father figure I've never had. I can go to him for anything; I've called him at midnight, and he was there with a couple of Streetworkers to help.*
> *Nico R.*

Efforts to connect with youth start with youth engagement out on the streets or in the jails. UTEC Streetworkers meet young people "where they're at." They target those young people who are most disengaged and deeply involved in local youth gang networks or those who are incarcerated. UTEC recognizes that moments of crisis are also windows of opportunity, when young people may be most open to considering change. These windows may open while a youth is on the streets, but Streetworkers also reach out to young people in the aftermath of violence—at the hospital or at a funeral. The widest window of opportunity often comes when a young person is locked up, which is why Streetworker visits to jail and prison facilities are so critical.

The Streetworkers' recruitment and relationship building set the stage for gang peacemaking work and to bring disconnected youth through the doors at UTEC. For those who observe the Streetworkers' daily work, the "chipping away" is obvious. Streetworkers may follow up with a youth for a few weeks or for more than a year before that youth decides to join the program.

As noted earlier, UTEC has been granted prerelease access to juvenile detention facilities, to state prisons by the Massachusetts Department of Corrections and to county jails through the Sheriff's office for a given geographic area. In a weekly visiting rotation, Streetworkers visit correctional facilities to meet young men and women who are in UTEC's age range, plan to return to their home communities of Lowell and Lawrence, and are scheduled for release in the next 3–6 months. Streetworkers make these young people aware of opportunities through UTEC and stay connected until they are released. Streetworkers are often the ones who pick up young people when they are released, to ensure that the critical first hours back in the community support positive choices.

Phase 2: Engagement

Once Streetworkers identify a youth who is interested in joining the program, that youth is invited to participate in an orientation session and to begin work in the Mattress Recycling social enterprise. UTEC refers to this introductory stage as Transformational Beginnings (TB). Young people are paid minimum wage for their work in the mattress recycling warehouse. A new group of youth starts TB each month, and its shorter hours and basic work skills offer a transitional period for youth to get a sense of what UTEC is about, what a regular work commitment is about, and for UTEC to get to know the youth. Consistent with "seeing beyond the mask," staff realize that this early phase is designed to best understand the needs and goals of each young adult—knowing full well that each young person may walk through the doors with their own mask, one that can rightfully be worn due to years of valid mistrust for other adults who may have promised to be there for them and weren't. Once a youth enters into this stage, he or she is paired with a transitional coach who conducts an extended intake assessment and starts to help the young person identify goals. UTEC intentionally uses the term "coach," not "case manager," as young adults do not want to be referred to as "cases." Transitional coaches have life portfolios that average 1 coach per 18 youth. Young people stay in the mattress recycling program for an average of 2–3 months, depending on their level of engagement.

Phase 3: Transformation

Once a youth has demonstrated consistency in the mattress warehouse, earned an OSHA 10-h certification[1], and committed to engaging with UTEC further, he or she will come to the UTEC center in Lowell to participate in a blended learning program (working toward both their employment and educational outcomes). At the same time, youth continue to work with their transitional coaches on major life challenges and obstacles, including housing, finances, family relations, physical and emotional health, and legal matters.

While in the transformation phase, youth can pursue their HiSET credential and work in one of UTEC's social enterprises. Youth are required to enroll in UTEC's

---

[1] The OSHA 10-h certification demonstrates "an entry level construction worker's general awareness on recognizing and preventing hazards on a construction site" (OSHA 2016).

on-site HiSET preparation classes, which focus on blended, project-based learning and integrate the organization's values of civic engagement and social justice. They are encouraged to pursue education beyond HiSET, through either enrollment in secondary education or specific trade programs.

The Workforce Development program provides youth with paid on-the-job experience. UTEC's agency-operated social enterprises are a core component of its model. UTEC developed its social enterprises in order to create its own rules for employment, as detailed in *UTEC Social Enterprises: Supporting the Youthwork Outcomes* section. This includes the ability to offer a "clean slate," starting fresh each day, and offering repeated opportunities to succeed.

Civic engagement themes are connected to all programs, reflecting UTEC's "igniting social justice" value. Staff-led workshops and youth-led organizing initiatives expose emerging leaders to principles of social justice and community organizing, learning skills that will allow them to systemically address the problems and inequalities they see first-hand in their communities.

Phase 4: Pathways

Youth progress at their own pace through the first three phases. Enrollment averages nearly 2 years. Once a young person has advanced through various levels (based on regular work performance reviews and attainment of his or her HiSET), he or she transitions to the pathways coordinator, who begins conversations and preparation for a move to employment or education beyond UTEC. Pathways activities include workshops on financial literacy, successful resume writing and interviewing, and goal setting. Youth decide what type of external employment to pursue, whether to apply to postsecondary education, or whether to opt for a combination of both. The pathways coordinator identifies potential employers for the youth, assists with placement and then maintains contact with the employer to identify issues and supports needed from their perspective, and provides follow-up services for 2 years after the youth leaves UTEC.

Social Enterprises: A Triple Bottom Line

The corporate triple-bottom-line framework typically measures social, environmental, and financial benefits. UTEC defines the triple bottom line slightly differently for its social enterprises.

1. Youth outcomes: individual progress in recidivism, employability, and education
2. Financial value: unrestricted earned revenues to support UTEC's model

3. Community impact: positive economic and environmental benefits through waste reduction, material reuse, and local food distribution, in addition to contributing to the local economy

UTEC's program is structured around industry-specific social enterprises. Each enterprise aligns with an industry area that is "CORI friendly," or accessible to workers with criminal records, and offers the opportunity for real career growth without postsecondary education. Current enterprises include the following.

- **Mattress Recycling**: As detailed below, this high-volume, low-skills warehouse process is an ideal point of entry for young people who need first to focus on positive work habits rather than specific hard skills. This social enterprise collects mattresses from individual and institutional (e.g., colleges, hospitals) customers, deconstructs them into component materials, and recycles up to 85 % of materials to reduce landfill.
- **Food Services: Café, Catering, and Retail Food Production**: Teaches youth the skills necessary for successful employment in culinary and event management positions. One of UTEC's two commercial kitchens prepares catering for onsite and offsite orders and preps meals for the retail Café UTEC, onsite at the UTEC program center. Through Café UTEC, youth learn additional skills such as vendor relations, inventory management, financial management, and marketing while working in a café environment. UTEC's second commercial kitchen focuses on mass food production for high-volume customers, such as Whole Foods Markets, who also partner with this social enterprise.
- **Woodworking**: Teaches youth basic safety and tool skills, modeling and construction skills, and custom woodworking using repurposed materials. Cutting boards made from hardwood scraps are the primary item for ongoing production.

UTEC Social Enterprises: Supporting the Youthwork Outcomes

UTEC social enterprises are designed with two primary objectives: to operate in a way that prioritizes and complements programming needs, and to generate revenues that offset operating costs. While a wide range of businesses might generate sufficient revenues to help offset operating costs, UTEC must select industries that align naturally with the youth programming needs. Each social enterprise must accommodate five key elements of UTEC's social enterprise philosophy.

"Our business. Our rules": Young people with no work experience and proven risk factors are unlikely to succeed in traditional employment right away. Many do not succeed even in more traditional, short-term job training programs. At UTEC, a primary assumption is that proven-risk young people need multiple chances to succeed. Operating its own social enterprises allows UTEC to provide young people with paid work experience, on the agency's own terms—taking into account the possibility of relapse and building in multiple chances and returns. For each social enterprise, UTEC has set up the business so that staff can dictate the operations, as well as the rewards and consequences.

For example, UTEC hopes that all youth will show up every day to work. Unfortunately, that is rarely the case given the various challenges they face. At the early stages of the program (while in Transformational Beginnings), UTEC prepares for this behavior and does not punish youth for missing work. Youth are not paid for days they do not work, but they are welcomed back without further consequence. In fact, if they are out, UTEC staff will try to reach them to encourage them to come back.

Extending the Clock: Given UTEC's commitment to proven-risk youth, job training must be provided through real-world social enterprise experience that extends across *multiple years, multiple chances, and multiple pathways.* UTEC understands the barriers youth face and knows that youth will likely relapse and make poor decisions after years of trauma, criminal involvement, gang involvement, or unhealthy relationships. Traditional short-term job training programs simply don't allow enough time for transformation. UTEC's social enterprise model allows UTEC to extend the clock for training while still empowering young people with paid work experience.

"Presence" as Priority: UTEC recognizes that many of the most significant challenges of its target population are tied directly to life skills, personal presence, and relationship management. On-the-job training in the social enterprises provides youth with opportunities to learn: (a) industry-specific skills in fields that offer appropriate entry-level positions for youth at the point of graduation (e.g., jobs that do not require postsecondary credentials), and (b) job and life skills required to excel in any workplace. UTEC commits significant time and energy toward developing the social and community skills that many target youth lack upon enrolling in programming. Without these so-called soft skills, proven-risk youth struggle to engage peers, providers, and potential employers, and they remain unlikely to establish positive employment histories as stepping stones to success.

Enough Work for a Crew: UTEC seeks out enterprises that enable the work crew to have anywhere from 6 to 8 youth working at a time. The combination of labor-intensive work and a group setting is essential for young people who need to practice teamwork and communication, and who will benefit from opportunities to develop positive peer relationships. Many enterprises are worthwhile ventures and consistent with the organization's value of financial sustainability, but their daily operations do not require a large group to function profitably. For example, UTEC considered but declined to pursue composting based on this requirement. The work must also be consistent, to ensure that youth who commit to UTEC have productive work experiences awaiting them. That rules out, for example, seasonal work such as landscaping.

Line of Sight Supervision: Enterprise operations must also be relatively contained; along with the crew size requirement, this ensures that a single staff member can supervise the entire crew. This ratio also allows for one-on-one conversations with youth to talk about their progress, their plans, and any performance issues that arise. Sometimes, there is a design component to promoting line of sight supervision. The mattress recycling warehouse, for example, is a wide-open space where staff can see all the activity from one vantage point and can interact with youth throughout the day.

Mattress Recycling as First Work Experience

UTEC wants to make it as easy as possible for young people to keep coming back so they will engage with the program and move on to the next phase of programming. Mattress recycling is an ideal point of entry for young people with no or very limited previous work experience. The mattress deconstruction process is labor intensive but not time sensitive. New youth have the opportunity to contribute and learn from the first day they are in the warehouse. Deconstruction leaves a safe margin for error, and progress is visible as mattresses are broken down into their components, and the stockpile of waiting mattresses gets smaller.

From a business standpoint, youth learn basics about warehouse operations and the specifics of mattress deconstruction. Some youth will ride on the truck with staff to pick up and load mattresses from customers, both residential and institutional. All participate in the unloading of the trucks and staging the pieces for deconstruction. Youth learn how to deconstruct the mattresses, sort the various materials, bale the various materials, and stage them for trucking. Perhaps most importantly, they learn the importance of working in a clean and safe environment.

While essential safety and tool skills are part of the instruction, the deconstruction process is largely unskilled labor. This is ideal from a programming standpoint, allowing UTEC staff members in the warehouse to focus on basic skills such as teamwork, responsibility, and problem solving. For most youth entering the program, teamwork is a fairly new experience. For some youth, working in the warehouse also means working together with rival gang members. The Streetworkers and staff are sensitive about who may be working in the program at the same time and conduct meetings in advance with youth to address potential issues before they occur. Weekly "pipeline" meetings review the status for incoming individuals who are returning from incarceration or identified in gang peacemaking efforts; staff identify potential conflicts and work to ensure a balance of participants, so that any given gang set is not overrepresented in UTEC's enrollment.

As part of its engagement phase, UTEC Mattress Recycling structures time for relationship building and developing positive communication skills. Because UTEC makes the rules, it can build in time during the day for this type of activity. Each workday begins with a circle that includes a "mood check" and an activity like a question of the day. This check-in offers staff a heads-up when young people are facing issues outside of UTEC. Group circles are an important part of programming. They get young people to interact and share what they might be thinking or feeling. Young people are encouraged to ask questions and offer suggestions on how to do things better.

Program staff monitor youth attendance and performance as they participate in Transformational Beginnings. Those youth who come regularly and bring a positive attitude and strong work ethic can move up in a matter of weeks. Others who attend irregularly, or don't participate actively, will take longer to move up. Some take several months; the average length of stay in TB was 3 months in 2015. UTEC staff from the main program center visit the warehouse periodically to introduce themselves and begin to build relationships with the young people in advance of their transition into Phase 2 at the program center. Youth will also shadow the range of programs at UTEC once they do transition so they can get a good sense of how things will work for them.

UTEC Social Enterprises: Supporting Financial Outcomes/ Business Operations

The business side of each social enterprise must work around the programming side, not the other way around. UTEC does not want to compromise youth programming in any way. At the same time, the social enterprise needs to generate as much revenue as it can to offset its own costs. To that end, UTEC has built a business model rooted in several factors critical for it to be successful within a programmatic context. These include fulfilling a market need, partnering with an anchor customer, securing a broad customer base, and finding both public and private partners willing to help.

Fulfilling a Market Need

Currently, in Massachusetts, roughly 200,000 mattresses and box springs go to landfills or incinerators each year. By all accounts they are a nuisance. The springs clog up grinders as mattresses are prepared for incineration and mattresses take up an inordinate amount of space in landfills. They don't compress and can "float" through piles of waste, rising to the top surface or creating air pockets that lead to underground fires.

Before UTEC entered into the recycling business, there was just one company in Massachusetts recycling mattresses. Businesses, organizations, and individuals had few options for disposing of their mattresses beyond the waste stream. As socially responsible organizations and individuals started learning about the recycling option, they were open to the idea.

Launched in earnest in early 2014, UTEC Mattress Recycling pursued a range of channels in the search for mattresses. High on the list were universities, hotels, and nearby municipalities. The first task was making potential customers aware that a recycling option existed. Second was getting potential customers to value the recycling option, based on a potential cost increase for some given their current spending on disposal. In its first year of operation, UTEC Mattress Recycling landed the municipal contracts for Lowell and Newburyport, MA, and lined up six schools and two hotels. The operation recycled roughly 6,500 pieces. With experience and growing awareness, UTEC expanded its reach into more towns, more schools, and more hotels, growing the business in its second year to over 12,000 pieces. UTEC Mattress Recycling is now on pace to grow into one of the largest mattress recycling facilities on the East Coast. In 2016, this enterprise was recognized with MassRecycle's 21st Annual Recycling Award.

UTEC picks up used mattresses from municipalities, schools, and hotels for a fee. At a dedicated mattress facility, UTEC then deconstructs the mattresses, salvaging and selling some portions and discarding the rest. A mattress has several layers. Starting from the base, these include springs or solid foam; then a layer known as "grey shoddy" is attached to the springs; the next layer is either cotton or a layer of foam; this is followed by a top, or pillow, layer, sometimes referred to as a "topper." In the case of box springs, there is usually just a wood frame with or without a set of springs.

Materials are separated into basic material groups: steel, wood, foam, grey shoddy pads, cotton, and toppers. Each is placed into 500–800 pound bales using large baling machines. For the box springs, the steel is stripped away from the wood using a table shearing machine that literally rips the metal off the wood using a hydraulic wedge. UTEC uses a forklift to move the large bales around the warehouse and to load materials onto trucks to send to aftermarket customers. Altogether, UTEC recycles, on average, about 85 % of each mattress by weight.

In 2015, UTEC Mattress Recycling diverted from landfills over 100 tons of steel, 37 tons of polyurethane foam, and 63 tons of wood through aftermarket channels. Every piece of a mattress UTEC recycles is a piece of a mattress that doesn't go into the trash. The organization is constantly looking for ways to reuse or repurpose materials ranging from coconut shells (used as a liner in old mattresses) to the felt pads that line most mattresses above the springs. It also looks for buyers and/or potential re-use of the cotton and wood. Currently, UTEC is designing prototype models for a new line of dog beds made from recycled foam. UTEC's goal is to reach 95 % recycled material in the next 2 years.

Partner with an Anchor Customer

Nearly as important as being in an in-demand industry is identifying a reliable and consistent source of volume. UTEC wanted to be sure that it had mattresses coming in regularly. To ensure that flow, UTEC actually has several anchor customers in the form of municipalities across the state. UTEC Mattress Recycling has agreements with nearly 20 cities and towns to pick up their unwanted mattresses. UTEC picks up from some as often as weekly and others every other month, but they provide a steady flow of materials.

These agreements with the municipalities were accelerated because of a grant from the Massachusetts Department of Environmental Protection (MassDEP). Interested in promoting mattress recycling, MassDEP provided funding to pay for the transportation of mattresses and their deconstructions for cities and towns that were willing to collect the pieces. In 2015, UTEC Mattress Recycling was identified by MassDEP as one of the three state-approved vendors to recycle the mattresses and box springs from the municipalities. This had an immediate effect on enterprise growth. As of early 2016, UTEC was contracting with 17 different Massachusetts municipalities and has done work with 12 universities and 7 hotels. Matthew Beaton, MA Secretary of Energy and Environmental Affairs, commented:

We applaud UTEC's efforts to expand the mattress recycling program not only as a way of diverting tons of materials away from the waste stream, but as a way of creating jobs and new products through innovative reuse while providing job training for disconnected youth in the Merrimack Valley.

In addition to direct contract growth, the partnership with the Commonwealth offers other potential benefits. This growing supply of mattresses helps to reduce per unit processing costs, making mattress recycling competitive with the cost of disposal, and thereby driving more demand for services. Engagement in and awareness of mattress recycling by so many municipalities could ultimately provide support for policy changes that would further accelerate mattress recycling in general. It also could lay the groundwork for other nonprofit social enterprises to receive contracts for their services.

Identify a Range of Customers

While UTEC values its municipal contracts, it didn't want to rely exclusively on towns for its volume. UTEC Mattress Recycling has contracted with over a dozen colleges and universities and various hotels to dispose of their unwanted mattresses as well. Ideally, UTEC will work with additional industry groups or consortiums to reach these potential customers efficiently. The organization continues to look for more areas of opportunity. As a state-approved vendor, UTEC can access other state organizations, ranging from state universities to hospitals or veterans centers where customers do not have to bid out their jobs. UTEC is also looking to make inroads with private institutions such as furniture stores, private hospitals, or senior centers, as well as to extend its operations to neighboring states. Michael Orr, former Sustainability Coordinator at Lesley University, notes that recycling through UTEC amplifies the school's positive social impact:

> Being able to recycle our mattresses is important for our commitment to sustainability at Lesley University. We switched our mattress recycling vendor when we learned that UTEC supports at-risk youth. Their professionalism and ease of recycling made the transition very simple.

Find Private and Public Partners Willing to Help

Capital expenses associated with running a mattress recycling enterprise are significant. At a minimum, to launch operations, UTEC Mattress Recycling needed a box truck to pick up mattresses, a forklift to move them around the warehouse, and a baler to compress the materials coming out of the mattresses and box springs. These initial costs totaled approximately $63,300. As the operation grew, the warehouse needed a machine to strip steel away from box springs and a second baler. UTEC was fortunate to have two major partners in MassDEP and the Cascade Alliance, which helps nonprofit organizations take control of their financial futures by transforming them into self-sufficient, job-creating community enterprises, to help with the acquisition of these pieces of equipment. Terry McDonald, Executive Director, St. Vincent de Paul Society in Eugene, OR, commented:

> [Since 2012] the St. Vincent de Paul Society of Lane County has worked closely with UTEC to launch and support the agency's mattress recycling program … UTEC has demonstrated that they can manage large-scale corporate customers as well as individual pickups from highly populated urban areas.

The financial goal for UTEC Mattress Recycling is to generate sufficient revenue to cover all of its operating expenses. The revenue side of the equation is fairly straightforward. UTEC needs to find more organizations willing to pay to dispose of mattresses through recycling rather than incineration. This includes covering the cost of transporting the mattresses from their location to UTEC.

The vast majority of the revenue comes from the pickup fees customers pay UTEC to collect the mattresses. There is some revenue from recycling the steel and foam, but prices are relatively low and fluctuate with the commodity markets. For example, UTEC Mattress Recycling recycled nearly 100 tons of steel in 2015. Three years ago, buyers were paying over $100 a ton for steel. In 2015, the price dipped to below $20 a ton. UTEC sells the foam to a company that makes carpet underlining. The price per pound also fluctuates and doesn't generate significant revenue.

UTEC is looking into other ways to make products out of the materials themselves instead of passing them on as commodities. For example, the organization is exploring the idea of making dog beds out of mattress foam. This would provide UTEC with more revenue than it could get from just the foam itself. As with the overall enterprise, UTEC will need to confirm that there is a market and find an anchor customer.

Not surprisingly, managing expenses is just as important as generating revenue. The UTEC program model for youth employment creates several obstacles that a similar, for-profit enterprise would not face. As outlined earlier, youth attendance is inconsistent, so UTEC's workforce for the enterprise is variable. This makes it difficult to project how many pieces the warehouse can cut at a given time. To solve this problem, UTEC Mattress Recycling hired two reliable, part-time workers from outside the program (prioritizing past UTEC graduates) who come in 4 days per week to cut mattresses and box springs, ensuring that the operation can keep up with the number of pieces coming into the warehouse. These workers also enable youth programming to proceed without interruptions from truck arrivals or other deliveries.

A final major expense is the transportation of the mattresses. Initially, UTEC rented a U-Haul truck when it needed to move mattresses. Once the operation was making two to three trips each week, it recognized the need for its own truck. With the help of MassDEP, UTEC Mattress Recycling purchased a used 24-ft box truck that can take roughly 50 pieces at a time, depending on the size of the mattresses. The organization will purchase its own roll-off truck by end of 2016, thanks to support from MassDEP, so it can move large containers and haul its own trash, further reducing expenses.

The Mattress Recycling business grew significantly over its first 3 years and is expected to continue to grow through 2018 with a goal of reaching 40,000 pieces for the calendar year. While UTEC Mattress Recycling has yet to generate a profit,

Table 1 UTEC's key indicators for the mattress recycling business

	2014	2015	2016	2017 (projected)
Units (mattresses or box springs)	6500	12,500	19,000	30,000
Municipalities served	2	12	24	34

it now expects to break even within 5 years of first beginning its operations. The organization has its costs under control, so the biggest variable will be identifying more mattress customers who are willing to support the environment and the youth work (Table 1).

Next Steps in Integrating Social Enterprises and Youth Supports

UTEC recognizes that the success of its social enterprises also depends in part on its capacity to further integrate key supportive services that can help enhance a youth's consistent participation in its social enterprises. For example, gang conflict, court involvement, and substance abuse are common barriers to attendance and involvement. As such, its core model is designed to help reduce such barriers through the program as outlined above, in addition to onsite mental health counseling and substance abuse counseling through ongoing partnerships.

However, key barriers still remain. For example, nearly half of the young adults enrolled at UTEC are also young parents; the availability of dependable childcare is a never-ending obstacle. UTEC is moving forward with a new two-generation approach that includes an onsite early-childhood education center, scheduled to open in the 2017 program year.

Transportation is another significant barrier, particularly for youth who successfully move into UTEC's Pathways phase and are ready for external employment. In response, UTEC is in the planning stage of a partnership that can provide for transportation back and forth to employers while ultimately hoping to place all graduating young adults into their own reliable vehicles as a means to further expand their employment options. Both of these initiatives fit into UTEC's overall growth plan over the coming years. In short, they aim to continue serving more youth while digging deeper by also adding key supportive services.

Conclusion

UTEC Mattress Recycling is an example of how a social enterprise can achieve programming objectives, sustain the environment, and generate income. While UTEC continues to rely on fund-raising to support its comprehensive program model, the efforts and progress demonstrate how a holistic model that includes social enterprises can succeed on many levels. In addition to sharing findings with other practitioners, UTEC actively seeks ways to connect social enterprise models with policy opportunities, such as establishing preferred procurement for social enterprises. In 2015, UTEC's Executive Director, Gregg Croteau, was appointed to the Massachusetts Governor's task force on Economic Opportunity for Populations Facing Chronically High Rates of Unemployment. The task force issued its final report in January 2016, which recommends that the state "identify meaningful ways to support and engage with social enterprises, which are nonprofit or for-profit entities that create social impact while also generating revenue" (MA Executive Office of Labor and Workforce Development).

UTEC sees opportunities to share its programmatic and business criteria with other nonprofit social enterprises in order to best support triple-bottom-line investments of public and private funds. Rather than seeking to replicate its own model in other service areas, however, UTEC is focused on formalizing and codifying its findings in order to create a national teaching and learning center for other community-based organizations that serve proven-risk young adults.

The triple-bottom-line approach offers positive framing for public policy and value to taxpayers. UTEC's social enterprises offer direct economic and business benefits to customers. UTEC's programmatic success in reducing recidivism and increasing employability is significant, particularly for a population that might otherwise remain reliant on public assistance and are instead able to be active participants in the labor market. Beyond the benefits of actual mattress recycling, UTEC is demonstrating its success with a targeted social enterprise model that decreases recidivism, increases participant earnings, and reinvests public resources from corrections to job training and economic development.

References

Atkinson J (2012) City of the damned. Boston Magazine. http://www.bostonmagazine.com/2012/02/city-of-the-damned-lawrence-massachusetts/. Accessed 22 June 2016

Ball D, Weisberg R, Dansky K (2008) The first 72 hours of re-entry: seizing the moment of release. The Stanford Executive Sessions on Sentencing and Corrections. http://law.stanford.edu/wp-content/uploads/sites/default/files/child-page/266901/doc/slspublic/Seizing_the_Moment_Release_091208.pdf. Accessed 22 June 2016

Bernstein J (2016) Incarceration trends in Massachusetts: long-term increases, recent progress. Massachusetts Budget and Policy Center, Boston

Braga A, McDevitt J, Pierce G (2006) Understanding and preventing gang violence: problem analysis and response development in Lowell, Massachusetts. Police Quarterly. doi:10.1177/1098611104264497

Cannata N, Eaves C, Feagans D, Longton A, Matthews H, McDonald S et al (2015) Prison population trends 2014. Massachusetts Department of Corrections. http://www.mass.gov/eopss/docs/doc/research-reports/pop-trends/prisonpoptrends-2014-05042015-final.pdf. Accessed 22 June 2016

Carr G, Foreman B (2015) Leading together. MassINC. http://massinc.org/research/leading-together-6/. Accessed 22 June 2016

Croteau G (2015) Providing a safe haven from gang violence for immigrant youth in Lowell, MA. Robert Wood Johnson Foundation. http://www.rwjf.org/en/library/articles-and-news/2015/03/providing-a-safe-haven-from-gang-violence-for-immigrant-youth-in.html. Accessed 22 June 2016

Durose MR, Cooper AD, Snyder HN (2014) Recidivism of prisoners released in 30 states in 2005: patterns from 2005 to 2010. U.S. Department of Justice, Bureau of Justice Statistics. www.bjs.gov/content/pub/pdf/rprts05p0510.pdf

Forman B, Larivee J (2013) Crime, cost, and consequences: is it time to get smart on crime? MassINC. http://massinc.org/wp-content/uploads/2013/03/Crime_Cost_Consequences_MassINC_Final1.pdf. Accessed 22 June 2016

Forman B, Warren D, McLean-Shinaman E, Schneider J, Muro M, Sohmer R (2007) Reconnecting Massachusetts gateway cities: lessons learned and an agenda for renewal. Brookings. http://www.brookings.edu/research/reports/2007/02/regionsandstates-muro. Accessed 22 June 2016

Forman B, Yee S (2015) Viewing justice reinvestment through a developmental lens. MassINC. http://massinc.org/wp-content/uploads/2015/12/young.offenders.brief_pdf. Accessed 28 June 2016

Hanson M (2016) Whole foods opens in Westford. Lowell Sun. http://www.lowellsun.com/business/ci_29853913/whole-foods-opens-westford. Accessed 22 June 2016

Housing and Economic Development (2016) Gateway cities and program information. http://www.mass.gov/hed/community/planning/gateway-cities-and-program-information.html. Accessed 22 June 2016

Kottcamp R, Francis D, Kiliroy G, Pierce D, Powell V (2015) Massachusetts labor market and economic review, 2014. Massachusetts Executive Office of Labor and Workforce Development. https://www.doleta.gov/performance/results/AnnualReports/docs/2016_State_Plans/Economic_Reports/Massachusetts/MA%20Economic%20Analysis%20Report.pdf. Accessed 22 June 2016

Kurlychek MC, Brame R, Bushway SD (2007) Scarlet letters and recidivism: does an old crime predict future reoffending? Crime & Delinquency 5(3):483–504

Labor Force/Unemployment Rates Database (2016) Massachusetts Labor and Workforce Development. http://www.mass.gov/lwd/economic-data/labor-force/labor-forceunemployment-rates.html. Accessed 22 June 2016

MA Executive Office of Labor and Workforce Development (2016) Report and recommendations of the EO 561 taskforce. http://www.mass.gov/lwd/docs/executive-office/eo-561-task-force-report508.pdf. Accessed 22 June 2016

Mosehauer, K., Allen, S., Peters, M., & Warney, C. (2016). Working group meeting 3 interim report, July 12, 2016. Washington, DC: The Council of State Governments Justice Center.https://csgjusticecenter.org/wp-content/uploads/2016/07/Justice-Reinvestment-in-Massachusetts_Third-Presentation.pdf

OSHA (2016) OSHA 10-hour construction training course. http://www.osha.com/courses/10-hour-construction.html. Accessed 22 June 2016

Schiraldi V, Western B, Bradner K (2015) Community-based responses to justice-involved young adults. National Institute of Justice. https://www.ncjrs.gov/pdffiles1/nij/248900.pdf. Accessed 22 June 2016

Schwalbe CS, Hatcher S, Maschi T (2009) The effects of treatment needs and prior social services utilization on juvenile court decision making. Soc Work Res 33:31–40

Schwalbe CS, Maschi T (2009) Investigating probation strategies with juvenile offenders: the influence of officer's attitudes and youth characteristics. Law Hum Behav 33(5):357–367

Tansi R, Ponikiewski J (2015) Juvenile recidivism report. Massachusetts Department of Youth Services. http://www.mass.gov/eohhs/docs/dys/dys-recidivism-report-2015.pdf. Accessed 22 June 2016

The Council of State Governments Justice Center (2015) Reducing recidivism and improving other outcomes for young adults in the juvenile and adult criminal justice systems. https://csgjusticecenter.org/wp-content/uploads/2015/11/Transitional-Age-Brief.pdf. Accessed 22 June 2016

U.S. Census (2016a) U.S Census Bureau. http://www.census.gov/quickfacts/table/PST045215/2537000. Accessed 22 June 2016

U.S. Census (2016b) U.S Census Bureau. http://www.census.gov/quickfacts/table/RHI805210/2534550. Accessed 22 June 2016

UTEC (2016) UTEC outcomes & impact report FY2015. https://www.utec-lowell.org/uploads/uploads/utec_outcomes_report_fy15_final.pdf. Accessed 22 June 2016

Food with Purpose: Dudley Dough and Haley House Bakery Café

Bing Broderick

Abstract Haley House has sustained a tradition of community service and community engagement since its founding in 1966. What began as a very personal project by its two founders to engage with homeless men in Boston's South End neighborhood has grown over the years through creating two social enterprises, the Haley House Bakery Café and Dudley Dough.

Building off the work of its South End Soup Kitchen, Haley House opened the Haley House Bakery Café in Boston's Dudley neighborhood in 2005, training and employing workers with barriers to employment in a nearly self-sustaining nonprofit restaurant while offering delicious, healthy food in a vibrant community setting. Haley House welcomed the ideas and inspiration of Dudley residents, becoming a multifaceted hub for community engagement, all rooted in the food. When the City of Boston declared Dudley an Innovation District, Haley House launched Dudley Dough, a social enterprise pizza shop in the District's anchor building, as a way to offer fair wage employment and an economic future for residents who might otherwise be priced out, and forced out, of the community. Throughout it all, Haley House has remained committed to providing "Food with Purpose," and the strong community ties it engenders.

Keywords Social purpose business • Job training • Community engagement • Haley House • Gentrification

Connecting Pizza and Economic Justice

At Dudley Dough, the menu features mocha lattes, kale smoothies, and specialty pizzas like cauliflower béchamel. This bill of fare and the restaurant's sleekly modern décor would be at home in any health-conscious, affluent US suburb. But the sign on the door reads "Pizza with Purpose" and the location is Dudley Square in Roxbury, a long-neglected inner-city neighborhood in Boston.

B. Broderick (✉)
Haley House, 23 Dartmouth Street, Boston, MA 02116, USA
e-mail: bbroderick@haleyhouse.org

© Springer International Publishing Switzerland 2017   73
M.J. Cronin, T.C. Dearing (eds.), *Managing for Social Impact*,
Management for Professionals, DOI 10.1007/978-3-319-46021-5_4

JUSTICE pops out in bright red on the menu's front page and that repeated word underscores the recipe for neighborhood revitalization proclaimed in the 2016 Dudley Dough Manifesto:

> Dudley Dough celebrates the labor of exceptional workers who nourish our community with healthful food—empowering them with just pay, dignity, and a voice in their workplace. We pursue social wealth, not greed, as the driving force of commerce. We believe that individual and societal well-being are bound together.

The focus on justice in the menu and manifesto make it clear that more is happening behind the Dudley Dough counter than preparing delicious pizzas. This welcoming restaurant is structured as a social enterprise, designed to serve its local community and to provide stable employment. Its presence in the Roxbury neighborhood of Boston reflects the social justice mission of Haley House, a Boston nonprofit that "uses food and the power of community to break down barriers between people, transfer new skills, and revitalize neighborhoods" (Haley House 2016).

For 10 years prior to the launch of Dudley Dough, Haley House owned and operated the Haley House Bakery Café, a popular restaurant and neighborhood cultural center that had served and helped to stabilize the Dudley area of Roxbury. As a small nonprofit committed to "Food with Purpose," Haley House staff were very conscious of how under-compensated the workers in typical restaurant kitchens are, often working paycheck to paycheck and struggling to support their families. The group envisioned Dudley Dough as a model for self-sustaining, community-oriented social enterprise restaurants with a primary mission of investing the staff in the success of the business and sharing the rewards with them.

A parallel mission for Dudley Dough was forged in the context of rapid neighborhood transition. Boston City planners had identified Dudley Square, with its long-neglected storefronts and underserved residents, as the promising hub for a Roxbury renaissance, designed to become an innovation district with newly constructed residential and office buildings to attract high-tech businesses and young professional workers. This planned redevelopment raised concerns around displacement and gentrification in a setting where entry-level employment was scarce and long-term residents were at risk. As a social enterprise, Dudley Dough is structured to offer accessible economic opportunities for workers and provide Dudley's residents with an anchor to secure their own place in the future of Boston.

The connection between pizza and economic justice, like the Haley House mission to serve and empower Boston residents, goes back several decades. This chapter tells how the principles behind Haley House have created a powerful force for social justice in Boston and an innovative, scalable social enterprise model for serving food with purpose.

Feeding and Housing Homeless Neighbors in Boston's South End

Haley House's 50-year history is unique for its continual envisioning of creative responses to societal injustice. Its story begins in 1966, when a group of young activists residing in Boston's South End neighborhood identified unmet needs of their neighbors who were struggling on the streets, largely men whose lives had been undone by alcohol. Kathe and John McKenna were at the core of this activist group, and one cold day in February 1966 John McKenna brought home one of their rootless neighbors, Tom Flynn, whom he had discovered freezing in a snow bank.

For the first year, their apartment was an incubator for social action. John taught school to fund their generosity of spirit, while men were unequivocally welcomed to share their home and their food. Kathe and John were inspired by the principles of the Catholic Worker Movement, such as "personalism," honoring the inherent worth of every individual; living in solidarity with the poor; living out the works of mercy; and recognizing that when one of us is vulnerable, we are all vulnerable. Friends of the McKennas were moved by their ideals and brought support in many ways, often volunteering to help directly.

By the end of the first year, the group had identified a building that was slated for demolition and that could be a perfect home for what was already an inspiring movement. With the help and generosity of a few friends, they were able to purchase the building and to convert the storefronts into a soup kitchen — the only soup kitchen in Boston at the time. Above the soup kitchen, there were four floors of rooms where they were able to accommodate volunteers willing to serve without pay. In its earliest years, as homelessness in the South End and other Boston neighborhoods began to reach critical proportions, nonprofit and city services — including shelter for the homeless — lagged behind urgent daily needs.

It soon became clear that food alone was not enough, leading the group to acquire permanent housing for struggling neighbors in order to offer a foundation to prevent further displacement. Over the next 30 years, many social justice initiatives developed at "Haley House," named that first year to honor a fellow activist, Leo Haley, who died after helping some strangers on the street. As Boston's South End neighborhood began to gentrify, pricing out its immigrant and working class members, Haley House acquired a separate rooming house to preserve a place for folks who would otherwise have been pushed out. In the years to come, Haley House expanded its housing portfolio to include over 100 units throughout the South End. Today, the units include a mix of government-subsidized housing for lower income families and single rooms for individuals who have experienced homelessness, as well as one building that includes a unique model of mixed-level rents. This model is possible because Haley House has owned the building outright since the 1980s, allowing for flexible rental rates that are discounted (or not) according to a tenant's ability to pay.

Food and housing are essential human needs, but by the 1990s the Haley House founders and supporters realized that these fundamental services were not enough in themselves to reverse the drastic cycle that drove individuals from disenfranchisement-to-addiction-to-prison-and-back. To help individuals break this cycle, Haley House developed its first economic empowerment initiative, a supportive training program that developed organically through the work taking place in the Soup Kitchen.

In the mid-1990s, Jane Moss, a volunteer in the Soup Kitchen who knew the craft of bread baking, started sharing her baking talents with some of the guests. This marked the beginning of Haley House's first training program, with three Soup Kitchen guests and four formerly homeless men (living above the Soup Kitchen) helping to run the operation. Soon, South End neighbors who were seduced by the smell of the good bread came in wanting to support the initiative as customers. In response, the training program carved out a corner of the Soup Kitchen and opened a bakery shop. Volunteers and trainees took turns in staffing the shop. Trainees were paid minimum wage to support their move to independence.

Thanks to its long history of neighborhood service, Haley House had become a place where socially minded individuals could identify a need and strategize how to address it, using minimal funds and accessing the social capital available through the support of the organization's friends and volunteers. In the collaborative process, community was built, and the individuals in that community led the charge in developing what was to become the Haley House Bakery Café.

For the next 10 years, the South End bakery continued to train and grow, sending its graduates out into the restaurant world. In 2001, local chef Didi Emmons approached the bakery to make pizza dough for her new venture, Veggie Planet, which had limited space for food production. Haley House also began selling fresh-baked scones and muffins (based on Didi's recipes) to 15 shops and cafes around Boston.

Even with its tight margins, this wholesale business was a great support to the training program. Haley House was working with a broad range of trainees, men and women facing a variety of barriers to employment. This program gave them an opportunity to learn skills (both culinary and work readiness) that allowed them to move on to jobs in other bakeries and workplaces. Working in the corner retail shop helped them to hone their social skills and their sales and marketing abilities. By 2004, the Haley House wholesale bakery business had grown to a point where it had reached full capacity in the Soup Kitchen. The trainees were using the Soup Kitchen's only oven, and there was no room for a second oven.

The lack of kitchen space was not the only barrier to expanding the scope of social enterprise at Haley House. To create long-term growth and provide employment for more local workers and trainees, the bakery business needed to shift from relying primarily on volunteers and philanthropy to become more self-supporting. There was also a discussion of where an expanded Haley House bakery should be located. The South End had become one of the most fashionable and high-priced neighborhoods in Boston; its brownstones were selling for millions of dollars to wealthy professionals. Other Boston neighborhoods, however, were still lacking in fundamental services including restaurants serving healthy, reasonably priced food. One such Boston neighborhood was the Dudley area of nearby Roxbury.

Food with Purpose: Social Enterprise in an Underserved Boston Neighborhood

Haley House founder Kathe McKenna was already spending time in the area around Roxbury's Dudley Station, serving a weekly breakfast to men and women on its streets. The Roxbury section of Boston, while adjacent to the South End, had not experienced the same type of gentrification. According to 2000 US census data, 63 % of Roxbury's residents were black, 24 % were Hispanic, and 5 % were white. The median household income was $27,133 compared to a 1999 median income of $41,590 in the South End. The 2000 census recorded that 27 % of Roxbury residents were below the poverty line and over 74 % of households were characterized as on low to moderate income (City of Boston Department of Neighborhood Development 2006).

Dudley had once been a hopping commercial district in the center of Roxbury, with movie theaters, jazz clubs, restaurants, dance halls, and more, but by the early 2000s, due to years of red-lining and disinvestment, most had shut their doors. There were few options for healthy food or eat-in dining available. Even McDonald's Express had closed its doors. As Haley House looked to expand the bakery, along with its training program and the economic opportunities it provided, the Roxbury community beckoned. Some Haley House friends and supporters in the neighborhood urged a move to Dudley to open an expanded "Haley House Bakery Café" in an abandoned warehouse building, once a storage facility for corrugated cardboard, near Dudley Station.

The move out of the Haley House Soup Kitchen in the South End to Dudley was a risk. In its new stand-alone location, Haley House Bakery Café would need to become a more formal, revenue-generating business operation. To meet the cost of monthly rent and salaries, it would have to attract a larger base of customers, or find additional sources of income. The first step was to write a business plan articulating what the organization hoped to create, outlining a clear vision and mission for Haley House Bakery Café. The business plan projected that the Café would be able to achieve break-even status by year three. This goal would allow Haley House to be less dependent on philanthropy to cover the costs of the training program. But to get up and running the organization needed to convince more funders to believe in the Haley House vision and to donate money to prepare the new café space and fund the move and related setup costs. As with most things at Haley House, volunteers were essential to getting the new Bakery Café operation off the ground. Over the summer of 2005, crews of students did whatever work needed doing to transform the Dudley Square warehouse into a comfortable dining spot, by upholstering the seats and painting the walls.

Didi Emmons, whose Veggie Planet restaurant was now running smoothly, offered her gifts as Haley House Bakery Café's founding chef. She developed a menu comprised of healthier spins on classic American and African-American comfort food.

When Haley House Bakery Café opened its doors near Dudley Station in Roxbury in August 2005, the mission was relatively simple: to offer healthy food options in a neighborhood where there were few dining spots, to provide job training to under-employed individuals and to create sustainable, Criminal Offender Record Information (CORI)-friendly jobs. Members of the community who have spent time in prison are frequently blocked from employment due to their past history, even though they have served their sentences. Many employers establish policies to require these CORI checks as a condition of employment, even when the jobs involve no security risk. As a result, few legitimate opportunities are available to citizens returning from incarceration.

The Bakery Café had a clear sense of its social impact goals and mission, but it also faced the daunting challenges of launching a restaurant, a famously risky prop-osition. Close attention needed to be paid to adjusting the menu and to the design and systems of the restaurant. Issues had to be addressed promptly in order to ensure the success of the business. We soon discovered that the vitality and identity of our enterprise depended on our ability to adapt and respond to opportunities and ideas that were presented to us.

I arrived at Haley House Bakery Café a few days after the doors had opened, and received a crash course in restaurant management. What place did I, a middle-class white guy, have in running a nonprofit café in the largely working class hub of Boston's African-American community? I had no training in business, social work, restaurants, or any of the critical areas in which we were working. Before Haley House, my career had been in grassroots marketing, in film and music. Prior to com-ing to Dudley, the skills I had developed were largely in finding unexplored outlets for music and film and in building partnerships to help to raise the profile of these cultural assets. Initially, the connection wasn't clear, but soon it began to reveal itself.

Dudley had long been dismissed by many as a place where nothing good could happen, but that was not what I was seeing or experiencing. In my role as manager, I found myself working with members of our community to help to showcase and celebrate the abundance of talent in our neighborhood. This work energized me. As is evident from our origins, a core value at Haley House has been to welcome those who walk through the door. As people identify needs and offer solutions to address them, we build community together. These threads resonated, too, at Haley House Bakery Café, with hundreds of new people engaging with us every day, traveling across former neighborhood barriers to meet, converse, and engage with each other. I often found myself introducing people who shared common interests, but whose paths might not have otherwise crossed if not for the café. I felt like I ran a "pub with no beer" (that is, until we got a beer and wine license).

After a few weeks, a customer approached me, saying that she had a board meet-ing that evening. Could we possibly put together a platter of wraps and drop it by her office at 5 pm? Even though catering was not a part of our Bakery Café business plan, I ran out and bought a platter, and we delivered a platter of wraps to her that evening. Thus began our catering business, which has continued to grow and sup-port the rest of the café operations. This ad hoc introduction of catering to the Bakery Café business plan is a lesson in the importance of adaptability in the suc-cess of a social enterprise. Catering expanded our customer base significantly and it allowed our fellow nonprofits and like-minded for-profits to support us while addressing their own needs for food at meetings and events. This advent of catering also coincided with the rise of the "Fair Trade" movement, and our friends supported us in that spirit. People who had never heard of Haley House were ordering from us because our food was consistently good and healthy. We wanted the food quality to be as important as the "social good," so that people would continue coming back to us. It is quite possible that without catering we would not have survived our leaner years as a business.

Becoming a Dynamic Community Hub One Neighbor at a Time

This same responsive approach to our neighbors' input would also enrich the Haley House Bakery Café programming and deepen our connection in the community, defining us as a community hub. On one of the first days we were open, Lana Jackson walked in and identified something that was missing: "You need art on these walls." With the curatorial help of her photographer friend, Lolita Parker Jr., we were soon setting up shows for artists from the community, launching six exhibits every year. Another customer, Nina LaNegra, approached us asking if we might consider hosting her performance series embracing food, art, culture, and spirituality, "Art is Life itself!," which had been running in a bar up the street; it has now been a staple of Café programming for over 10 years.

Boston Police Officer Bill Baxter had been developing a curriculum using food as a vehicle to break down stereotypes in order to reduce gang violence. He asked, "Would you be interested in working with me on this?" Within a few days, after the café's 4 pm closing, a dozen students from the nearby Timilty Middle School gathered for a class taught by the charismatic Officer Bill (aka "Officer Donut") and chef Didi. This evolved into our "Take Back the Kitchen" program, with classes in health, nutrition, and culinary arts, offering instruction to over 300 students each year.

Our response to these ideas led other community members to propose programming. Soon we were presenting a Dinner & A Movie series with the Color of Film Collaborative and History Nights in partnership with Discover Roxbury and the Roxbury Historical Society. Two women who were prominent figures in the Cambridge poetry "slam" scene approached us to establish a Boston-based slam. From the beginning it was a hit, and after a year, the "House Slam" took a team to the National Slam Competition, returning with all of the lead prizes.

After the Café had been open for about 8 years, it became evident that while one of our goals as an organization was to break down barriers, our menu prices represented a barrier to an individual or a family who might not be able to afford to go to a restaurant. A member of our residential volunteer community, Albert Ramirez, helped us to launch Community Tables, a Saturday-evening, three-course dinner, offered on a "pay-what-you-can" system. Each week, we reach out to neighborhood churches, mosques, housing complexes, and support agencies to invite our neighbors in to share a meal together, regardless of their ability to pay. With donations from area farms like The Food Project and ReVision Urban Farm, and vendors such as Iggy's Bread, we have been able to expand our reach more widely in the neighborhood.

The dynamic Fulani Haynes serves as Community Tables' host, welcoming in families and friends, and creating an environment where all are truly welcome. A retired nurse, Fulani has been involved at Haley House Bakery Café from the very beginning—performing with the Fulani Haynes Jazz Collaborative, hosting a Jazz Brunch, and teaching classes for Take Back the Kitchen. Fulani embodies the spirit of hospitality that is central at Haley House: welcoming people, encouraging engagement, and building community.

Every summer, we host an *outdoor* Community Tables banquet, with 250–300 guests in attendance. Both the weekly Community Tables dinner and the annual outdoor event have deepened our relationships with our friends and neighbors. It has become one of our eagerly anticipated signature events.

Early on in our existence, we were approached by Sandra Casagrand of the Bay State Banner, the newspaper of record in the local African-American community, offering to help us showcase the cultural events at the Bakery Café. She worked with us to put together a marketing plan that was within our budget, so that people could consult the Banner to find out what events were happening that week at the Bakery Café. Our weekly ad in the Bay State Banner has reinforced our place in the local Roxbury community and certainly has helped boost attendance at our events.

Although it was not our motivation at the outset, in establishing these partnerships, Haley House Bakery Café has become a dynamic community hub—a place where things that mattered to Roxbury residents could happen—one friend describes it as a place of "positivity." Others call it a "third space," a place where people convene and connect outside of work or home.

Through our food and our newfound cultural connections, we had grown strong connections with our friends at Hibernian Hall and Discover Roxbury. We were invited to join the Roxbury Cultural Network, a consortium of a dozen local arts organizations, working to support and promote arts in our community. Soon we were among the founding members of Common Thread Dudley Square, a coalition working to organize monthly outdoor events in our community. We found ourselves very engaged in our community.

Volunteers have also played a central role in our move toward sustainability. One summer, in the early years of the Bakery Café, Matt Hamilton joined us as an intern. Matt loved the Bakery Café's signature chocolate chip cookies, and when he returned to Boston College in the fall, he convened a meeting exploring how BC might help Haley House by purchasing Haley House cookies to sell to students in its dining halls. Ever since then, BC has been buying the cookies to sell in its dining halls, as a support to our programs. Over that time, the cult of the Haley House chocolate chip cookie has grown, and on June 8, 2011, the Boston City Council named the day "Haley House Cookie Day," officially honoring Boston's favorite chocolate chip cookie.

Carol Kong arrived at the Bakery Café as a volunteer in its early days, cooking during our Thursday evening performance series. She soon joined the staff as Bakery Café manager, and before long she was running the entire operation. She holds the bar high for her staff and supports them every step of the way. Carol's ability to identify the work that needs to be done and build a team to do it has enabled the Café to grow and build steadily.

While the Bakery Café expanded its business model to include catering services, our staff training program operated much as it had out of the South End Soup Kitchen. At a certain point, we had a waiting list for the program of 50 people—essentially a 5-year waiting list for a 6-month training program. Questioning our impact in this program given this logjam, we took a few months' hiatus to reflect. During this time, our catering manager, Danny Cordon, expressed his vision for a training program focusing exclusively on men and women coming out of prison, helping them through their transition back into society.

A visionary leader, Danny himself had spent time in federal prison and knew the immense challenges faced by returning citizens. In Danny's vision, the focus of the trainees' work would be on the production of cookies for Boston College, but their training would emphasize the importance of "life skills" and deeper conversations about trust, respect, family, community, and more. Danny led the launch of the Transitional Employment Program (TEP). Today, Jeremy Thompson brings his own experience to leading the program, which has grown to include computer training, mindfulness training, and financial literacy, with "life skills" training provided by friends at the Harvard Graduate School of Education. TEP is now 6 years old, with its graduates offering a valuable network of mentoring support to newer trainees. The transformation of our training program has changed our organization at its core, involving our entire staff in addressing the crisis of mass incarceration and the "School-to-Prison Pipeline." In supporting individual men and women as they transition from incarceration, we have built a deeper relationship with our local community.

Expanding the Impact of Food with Purpose: A Social Justice Restaurant Model

While the original Haley House Bakery Café business plan projected reaching break-even status by 2008, it became clear early on that our goal was too ambitious. In a few more years, we were generating 90 % of our operating budget through sales. One might argue that it is more efficient to hire accomplished culinary professionals than to train inexperienced people to do the same work, but for us, training and job creation took priority over efficiency. And, as we compared our figures with other fledgling social enterprises, we recognized that generating 90 % of our operating budget in a relatively short period of time was quite remarkable. We adapted our expectations, because we did not want to reach a break-even point at the expense of our staff and our social justice mission.

Today, Haley House employs 34 people at the Bakery Café, in addition to paid employment for five returning citizens through TEP. Haley House Bakery Café's sales revenue breaks down as follows: 39 % café sales, 44 % catering, and 17 % wholesale.

Fortunately, Haley House was able to buffer shortfalls in anticipated revenue growth during the early years of the Bakery Café thanks to its organizational history. Through decades of buying property as part of its housing mission, Haley House had maintained minimal debt and set aside funds for future projects and capital needs. Nonetheless, even with this capacity to cover short-term gaps in the Bakery Café's operating budget, we recognized that building a self-sustaining restaurant business was the best path to offering more training and expanding our social impact. The success of a social enterprise restaurant model could also serve as a powerful statement about overcoming the dismal wages and employment conditions typical of the restaurant industry in Massachusetts and across the United States.

Issues of low income, poor health, and high rates of violence and incarceration disproportionately affect the residents of inner-city neighborhoods of color. With limited opportunities available, many inner-city residents seek jobs in the food industry, where minimal education and experience are required. According to the National Restaurant Association (2016), in 2016 Massachusetts restaurants were expected to register $16.5 billion in sales, with 10 % of the population working in this industry. Between now and 2024, they project a job growth rate of 8.1 %. Sadly, however, neither of these patterns of growth has translated into increased worker pay. Federal labor statistics indicate that the "13 million-plus restaurant workers in the U.S. face a poverty rate nearly three times that of the rest of the country's workforce, and the industry hosts seven of the ten worst paying jobs" (Fuchs 2014).

Throughout the history of the Bakery Café, Haley House has been approached regularly by leaders in neighboring districts, asking if we might consider opening an operation in their neighborhood. Some of these Boston neighborhoods were similar to Dudley, commercial districts that would benefit from a catalyst to stimulate local business. As our business grew, and with it we built a bigger staff, we realized that the model of interconnected retail, wholesale, training, and catering divisions that had evolved over time at the Café did not lend itself to replication. We began to consider how we might create a more streamlined, replicable social enterprise model that offered a faster path to financial growth and break-even sustainability while providing stable, fairly compensated employment for staff.

As it happened, the first opportunity to broaden our social impact emerged right around the corner as an offshoot of the efforts by the City of Boston to jump-start economic development in the Dudley neighborhood. By 2014, Boston's economic growth and escalating cost of housing had set off a construction and redevelopment boom all across the city, this time including Roxbury. Dudley was in transition as city planners designated it as a new "innovation district" and approved multiple new construction projects. The City also announced plans to redevelop the Ferdinand building, one of Dudley's original landmark stores which had been vacant for decades.

Situated at the center of Dudley Square, "Ferdinand's Blue Store" was an iconic furniture showroom once flanked by the old elevated Orange Line train that had been dismantled and moved in the 1980s. Ferdinand's was a business that allowed customers to pay on "layaway," and many older members of the community remember it fondly. The business itself closed during the infamous "Blizzard of '78," a storm that paralyzed traffic in Boston for over a week. Following the storm, Ferdinand's never reopened. Its abandonment came to symbolize the overall neglect and disinvestment in Dudley.

Now, the City was soliciting proposals for new retail and restaurant operations to help anchor a modernized Ferdinand building. While we welcomed the idea of neighborhood economic development, we also recognized the risks to long-time residents and small businesses. Because of high rates of poverty, more than 75 % of the housing in the pre-redevelopment Dudley neighborhood is government subsidized. The scarcity of market rate housing has resulted in a greater demand for it, often resulting in artificially inflated rents and sale prices. The city's stated plan was to increase housing density, in order to accommodate more affluent newcomers without displacing the existing residents. In theory, this strategy reduces the percentage of affordable housing without reducing the actual number of affordable units, but longtime merchants and service providers now need to pay higher rents to continue to serve their clientele in this market.

Residential gentrification puts upward pressure on commercial rents, often driving out small storefront businesses that are replaced over time with upscale restaurants and higher priced stores. In many Boston neighborhoods, independent businesses are giving way to higher priced, less community-minded stores. Dudley businesses have always had a distinctively independent character, and it was important that this be true of the new Dudley development.

In the South End, Haley House had witnessed how gentrification drives out long-term residents and local businesses with escalating rents and property values. If Haley House had not purchased the building for our Soup Kitchen in 1967, we could not have afforded the cost of staying open in the South End, and we likely would not exist today. With that hindsight, as investment in the Dudley neighborhood deepened, we felt the strong need to secure our Café's future there, if possible through purchasing our Café building. The owner had indicated early on, however, that he was not interested in selling to us. With redevelopment moving forward in Dudley, the ground was starting to shift beneath our feet. In 2014, we appealed to our landlord. This time, much to our relief, he agreed to sell us the building. Ownership ensured that the Café's role as a dynamic community hub reflecting the needs and priorities of Dudley's residents would continue.

Concurrently, we began to move forward with a plan for a second social enterprise that would provide sustainable and more adequately compensated restaurant employment as well as healthy food. We responded to the City's "Request for Proposals" for a retail space in the newly renovated Ferdinand building with a proposal for a healthy fare pizza restaurant. We had chosen to design our new model as a fair-wage restaurant, co-op or other similar employee-ownership model, with the core value of investing employees in the success and outcome of the business. Uncertain of our prospects for designation, we also applied to a special fund at the Herman and Frieda L. Miller Innovation Fund to research and develop a new, more equitable restaurant model for future execution.

Within a few weeks of our hearing that we could purchase our Café building, the City of Boston approved our proposal for launching Dudley Dough, and we received the grant from the Miller Innovation Fund to design a socially equitable restaurant model. Suddenly, we found ourselves undertaking three major projects at once.

Anchoring a Community in Transition

With the city's Innovation District designation, active construction projects, and the redevelopment of the Ferdinand space into the renamed Bolling Building, a different "Dudley Square" identity was emerging. Even the name was newly formalized, since it was always simply Dudley to longtime neighborhood folks. While there were some new assets to celebrate, the community was quickly losing some longtime pillars of the commercial district, due to rising rents and changing tides. The rebranding as an Innovation District meant that Bostonians who had never before come to Dudley were now comfortable doing so, and they were beginning to price out some of the longtime residents.

Just as Haley House learned the importance of owning our building for the longterm sustainability of our operation in the South End, we know how critical it is to provide economic opportunity and stability for a neighborhood's long-term residents particularly in the face of gentrification. We envision Dudley Dough as a social enterprise model that will benefit local workers, and provide a fair share in the economic benefits associated with development. Without such local, sociallyminded business models, many Roxbury residents will be hard-pressed to support their families and move up the employment ladder.

So again, "Food with Purpose" guides us—to provide Roxbury with more healthy food choices *and* economic empowerment for its residents. We are seeking to bridge a disconnect between local residents and access to the benefits of economic development, in which residents might otherwise be displaced, and to expand our impact to serve an even broader community by creating a self-sustaining and replicable business model.

The model we articulated for our second social enterprise, Dudley Dough, is the one offering higher wages for restaurant staff and greater investment in the success of the business. Staff is being trained in reading profit and loss statements, basic business practices, customer service, food costing, and more. In addition to the main attraction, pizza (which can be quite healthy and has a greater markup than most restaurant items), we have differentiated Dudley Dough from the Bakery Café with other offerings: specialty coffee drinks (the café offers drip coffee only), smoothies, and beer on tap. Dudley Dough is designed to celebrate the dignity of workers and labor, with an eye-catching mural of working people visible from the lobby of the Bolling Building.

With our new model, we seek to address the issue of income inequality in our community and to offer the restaurant industry an alternative to the $9/h standard for restaurant kitchen workers. We hope to liberate our staff from working paycheck to paycheck while holding down multiple jobs. By including some part-time staff in the mix, we are also able to offer higher wages to people with caregiving responsibilities or goals for advancing their education.

Dudley Dough has benefited from the track record of the Bakery Café in numerous ways. When the Bakery Café first opened in 2005, those who knew the name "Haley House" associated it with our Soup Kitchen, making it a challenge to market our café as a restaurant for everyone (where people pay money for food). After 10 years, we have firmly overcome that challenge, and the inclusion of "Haley House" in Dudley Dough's logo has helped the pizza shop through positive association with the Bakery Café. Similarly, as we seek funding to get Dudley Dough off the ground, we have been able to return to several funders who supported the launch of the Bakery Café. The proven success of the Bakery Café makes Dudley Dough an attractive enterprise to fund.

We were fortunate early on to find a great candidate for the role of the Dudley Dough team leader. Luther Pinckney grew up in nearby Highland Park. He had worked as a manager in numerous area restaurants and knew exactly how hard it was for restaurant workers to make due. From his "front-of-house" experience as a host, he was adept at welcoming people and ensuring that their experience is a good one. Through years in this role, he had become a community leader and recognized figure. He has worked closely with our founder, Kathe McKenna, through the build-out of Dudley Dough and its early months as an enterprise.

Conclusion

Reflecting back on the original business plan for the Bakery Café, I found that so many things have changed and grown that we could not possibly have foreseen. Inevitably, in the earliest days of the organization, energy was expended on addressing the immediate issues. Over time, we have been able to build capacity and take a longer term view.

Here are some of the lessons we have learned from our experience in Dudley:

- Invest the community in your work—the resulting vitality and impact will be greater for all.
- Be flexible in order to adapt your model. Our key example of flexibility is adding the catering service. Without it, the Bakery Café might not have survived. As Dudley Dough moves forward, we are mindful of this. If our strategies change, we are guided by our values, which have been the foundation of our community trust.
- You need good stewards to keep things together and moving forward: without Carol at the Bakery Café and Luther at Dudley Dough, neither enterprise would succeed.
- Activate your space—become a crossroad.
- Know your market and grow your market. Are you able to serve a greater part of your community—who is missing from the equation?

- Determine an acceptable and sustainable level of outside funding for your program—but be flexible with it. This should be an ongoing conversation with your various stakeholders.
- Try to create an economic buffer. The organizational history of Haley House and our mix of programs helped to overcome shortfalls in projected revenue as the social enterprise got up and running.

Our near-term goals are to bring Dudley Dough to the point where it generates enough financial success that we can share that success with employees in the form of increased earnings. Further down the road, the goal is to reach a point where we can use that success to make similar investments in other neighborhoods by building on the model and lessons learned at Dudley Dough.

Since the Bakery Café produces dough for Dudley Dough, the Bakery Café will also benefit from this replication. Soon, we also hope to expand the Café facility, building an annex toward the street, to connect it more directly to the community and to significantly expand seating and capacity for the Bakery Café, offering even more jobs in the community and more space for connection and partnerships. If we succeed, we can then apply some of the lessons learned at Dudley Dough back to the original model of Haley House Bakery Café, raising hourly wages and offering more investment there, too.

From its earliest days, Haley House has sought to break down barriers, build bridges, and establish channels to empowerment for people in the margins—Dudley Dough is the latest manifestation of our mission.

References

City of Boston Department of Neighborhood Development (2006) Roxbury data profile. http://www.cityofboston.gov/DND/PDFs/Profiles/Roxbury_PD_Profile.pdf. Accessed 22 July 2016

Fuchs T (2014) For many restaurant workers, fair conditions not on the menu. Boston Globe. https://www.bostonglobe.com/opinion/editorials/2014/02/16/service-not-included-restaurant-industry-serves-injustice-workers/NNnE0dNzQ8dLne00EjbxZJ/story.html. Accessed 23 June 2016

Haley House (2016) Our vision. http://haleyhouse.org/who-we-are/mission/. Accessed 21 July 2016

National Restaurant Association (2016) National Restaurant Association forecast. http://www.restaurant.org/News-Research/Research/Forecast-2016. Accessed 23 June 2016

Part III
Rethinking Corporate Social Responsibility From the Outside In

Evolution, Innovation, and Best Practices in Corporate Social Impact

Mark Feldman and Nikki Korn

Abstract This chapter summarizes the evolution of the corporate social impact field, from corporate philanthropy and volunteerism to the rise of Corporate Social Responsibility (CSR) and to today's Era of Innovation. Tracking this evolution, it presents examples ranging from Patagonia to Unilever's Dove brand. In each case, a company of a different size and industry seeks to apply the power of its assets in new ways to proactively and intentionally deliver positive business and social impact.

The authors characterize the Era of Innovation as defined by exploration, innovation, and risk-taking, providing examples of how these traits will guide the next stage of corporate social impact over the next decade. They track the successful harnessing of corporate assets for social impact including products, business acumen and expertise, brand, and communications. The chapter concludes with advice for managers seeking to implement a corporate social impact strategy.

Keywords Corporate Social Responsibility • CSR • Corporate social impact • Brand purpose • Corporate citizenship • Corporate philanthropy • Employee volunteerism

A Pioneering Direction

In 1957, Yvon Chouinard was an experienced young rock climber who started a business selling rock-climbing hardware to fellow enthusiasts. Demand for the pitons and other climbing products made by Chouinard Equipment grew over time, as rock climbing became a popular amateur sport. As described by the founder, "By 1970, Chouinard Equipment had become the largest supplier of climbing hardware in the U.S. It had also become an environmental villain because its gear was damaging the rock. The same fragile cracks had to endure repeated hammering of pitons, during both placement and removal and the disfiguring was severe" (Patagonia 2016).

M. Feldman (✉) • N. Korn
Cause Consulting, 18 Newbury St, Boston, MA 02116, USA
e-mail: mfeldman@causeconsulting.com

© Springer International Publishing Switzerland 2017
M.J. Cronin, T.C. Dearing (eds.), *Managing for Social Impact*,
Management for Professionals, DOI 10.1007/978-3-319-46021-5_5

89

Facing this dilemma, Chouinard and his business partner, Tom Frost, made a risky business decision. They stopped selling traditional pitons, even though this equipment was at the core of the company's product line. They introduced an alternative product—aluminum chocks—that left no scars on the rocks. This decision to prioritize environmental protection in parallel with commercial growth became the hallmark of the Patagonia brand, which Chouinard and Frost launched in 1973. Patagonia became known globally as a company that sells gear for the most rugged outdoor activities while simultaneously protecting the environment that its customers and employees care so much about. In the process, the company pioneered a model for integrating corporate responsibility with business strategy.

Decades later, Patagonia retains its commitment to the environment and to positive social impact for its multiple stakeholders. The Patagonia brand has become an internationally recognized example of a company that regards corporate responsibility as an embedded element of its business, not an afterthought. Patagonia was also a harbinger of the ever-increasing expectations that consumers, community members, executives, and shareholders have about corporate social responsibility.

Consumers, nonprofit groups, and socially committed investors regularly pressure today's companies to demonstrate a strong commitment to sustainability, employee well-being, and social causes. Visionary founders and seasoned executives understand the powerful relationship between social innovation and commercial success. Patagonia was an early leader and continues to be a trailblazer, but it is now one of many companies with robust social impact strategies.

Over the years, this field and the language used to describe it have grown. Companies now use a variety of terms for their social impact efforts, including Corporate Social Responsibility (CSR), corporate citizenship, sustainability, and environmental, social, and governance (ESG) programs, among others. This chapter uses the term social impact strategy (SIS) to describe corporate social initiatives.

Social implies a commitment to the greater good. A best-in-class social impact strategy is based on broad, long-term goals such as changing lives for the better, transforming communities, addressing climate change, improving public health, or tackling pressing economic problems.

The word *impact* reminds us that the ultimate objective of these programs is to foster positive social and economic change. They seek to deliver measureable internal and external results that benefit society and support their business goals.

Finally, *strategy* refers to thoughtful planning, a long-term view, and use of businesslike methodologies. When companies approach business and social challenges in a coordinated, strategic way, they can strengthen their organizations *and* positively impact society, creating sustainable solutions for a variety of stakeholders.

Today, corporate application of social impact has evolved from just a few smaller pioneering companies like Patagonia, seeking to make a difference through business, into a well-developed business discipline and field of strategy. Almost every US business school offers coursework in sustainability, business ethics, and related social impact topics. Whether or not they use social impact-related terminology, many of the largest companies in the world consider sustainability, community, and the environment to be fundamental components of their business practices.

Fig. 1 The evolution of corporate social impact © Cause Consulting

In fact, the corporate social impact field has become too large, complex, and fast-changing to be easily captured in any one publication. This chapter briefly summarizes how corporate social impact work evolved to become an accepted and standard business practice, and then it highlights examples of how companies continue to experiment and expand the boundaries of the field. It presents examples of how companies harness the power of their assets in new ways to proactively and intentionally deliver positive business and social impact. This new era, defined by exploration, innovation, and risk-taking, will guide the field over the next decade.

The Evolution of Social Impact Strategy

The world of corporate social impact has evolved gradually to the dynamic environment we see now, with a few notable inflection points. Basic ideas like corporate philanthropy and employee volunteerism have become strategic. The introduction of CSR brought important frameworks, measurement tools, and new methods of engagement to the field. And progress continues, with many companies today innovating to meet their dual goals of strengthening business and impacting society (Fig. 1).

In the Beginning: Corporate Philanthropy and Volunteerism

Two of the basic building blocks of social impact strategy are philanthropy and volunteerism; each has long been a fundamental way that companies give back to society. Both continue to play an important role in social impact work and are increasingly becoming more aligned with business strategy and desired social impacts.

Corporate Philanthropy

Corporate philanthropy—defined as financial or in-kind contributions—is a traditional path for companies of all sizes to activate their support for local community activities and address social issues. There are thousands of targeted local ways to give, and no shortage of causes that need support.

Corporate philanthropy and grants are made from two primary sources within a company, *Corporate Giving Programs* and *Corporate Foundations*. Both can accept proposals and channel financial support to select nonprofit organizations and social causes. Corporate giving budgets are captured within a company's financial management and reporting systems and have more flexibility to support various types of giving-related activities, such as sponsorships and cause-related marketing.

Many larger enterprises establish corporate foundations. These entities are legally independent from the companies that create and fund them, and are usually overseen by staff and boards of directors that are affiliated with the company. As charities, corporate foundations are required to follow a stricter set of laws and regulations governing how they operate and make grants. The Council on Foundations (http://www.cof.org/content/leading-corporate-philanthropy) is one trusted source to learn more about these structural and giving requirements.

The amount of aggregate philanthropy made by corporations has been growing over the past decade, with expected ebbs and flows that follow broader economic conditions. Giving USA (2016) reported that corporations donated $18.45 billion to charities in 2015, an inflation-adjusted increase of 3.8 % over 2014.

The related 2016 Giving in Numbers Report, produced by the Committee Encouraging Corporate Philanthropy (CECP) in association with The Conference Board, includes key trends on corporate philanthropy based on input from hundreds of responding companies. The report dives deeper into industry-specific data and summarizes the most popular giving practices and cause areas. Education-focused efforts consistently top the list of corporate grant-making priorities.

Although corporate philanthropy represents a significant amount of money, it is important to note that corporations actually only account for a small portion of the $373.25 billion dollars donated to charity in 2015 from all sources, including individuals, companies, and non-corporately affiliated foundations. Corporate giving represents a relatively small investment compared to the enormity of the social needs it tries to impact.

Facing internal and external pressure to drive more business and social value from corporate philanthropy, practitioners began to take a much more strategic approach to giving during the late 1980s. Many companies began to evolve from *reactive* giving—fulfilling ad hoc requests—toward *proactive* giving—developing more sophisticated programs, collaborations, and processes to focus resources and make decisions. For many companies, this included a move toward making fewer, larger, multiyear grants to nonprofit partners versus trying to spread the same amount of money across a greater number of organizations.

The most effective proactive strategies apply specific criteria and an intentional approach to giving. More and more companies use the 70/30 rule, where 70 % of corporate giving is planned and proactive, but 30 % is budgeted for other types of giving that can't always be foreseen or is a "must do" for the business. Corporate philanthropy has also become much more aligned with the mission, products, culture, and industry of the company and connected to achieving corporate objectives.

Within the planned 70 %, *Signature Cause Programs* are widely used to focus and communicate initiatives under a theme or branded name. Using philanthropy as one foundational element, signature programs become an umbrella for the coordination and activation of a broad range of corporate resources including employees, marketing, and in-kind contributions, among others. Avon's Breast Cancer Awareness Campaign, Adobe Youth Voices, and Samuel Adams Brewing the American Dream are a few examples of signature programs that use philanthropy as a driver for engaging the business and its consumers to drive toward increased social impact.

Employee Volunteerism

Recognizing that their true power to impact social issues lies beyond just activating philanthropy, corporate social impact practitioners sought to utilize other company resources and assets to address change. Employee volunteerism emerged as one way to simultaneously demonstrate the company's concern for community and social issues and also provides opportunities for employees to participate.

GE's Elfun Society, established more than 85 years ago, is an early example of companies encouraging employee and retiree volunteerism. In the early 1980s, the employee volunteer movement gained momentum with the rise of local organizations like New York Cares and Hands On Atlanta that help companies connect employees with local community needs. It continued with initiatives like the launch of President George W. Bush's Points of Light Foundation in 1990. For the subsequent three decades, US companies formalized ways to engage their employees and track their volunteer hours. CECP (2016) reports that corporate volunteer participation rates continue to increase throughout the world.

Similar to trends in corporate philanthropy, employee volunteerism has gradually evolved beyond an early focus on "activity," such as counting volunteer participation by numbers of hours. Many companies now have departments or team members dedicated to creating and managing volunteer activities. Employee volunteering has become significantly more strategic, with issue-focused global volunteer days that simultaneously engage thousands of employees around a theme and with skill-based volunteering. In the latter, employees apply their professional knowledge toward helping nonprofit organizations achieve their missions.

The terminology for the field has also begun to change. *Employee engagement* is replacing "volunteerism" as the language used to link volunteering to increases in employee morale, retention, and productivity—metrics regularly measured by human resource teams and tied to real business costs and investments. Employee engagement programs are used to identify potential corporate leaders, provide training opportunities, and expose employees to new markets, communities, and issues relevant to their work. Current and prospective employees now expect that meaningful volunteer opportunities will be a part of their corporate culture.

The Rise of Corporate Social Responsibility

Around the same time that corporate philanthropy and employee engagement were becoming embedded within corporations, many companies also began to look more deeply at how core business practices influenced economic, social, and environmental issues. This field and overall movement, as referenced earlier, are often referred to as Corporate Social Responsibility (CSR).

For generations, being compliant with relevant laws and regulations was a perfectly acceptable definition of responsibility for most companies. Covering the basics, like operating within existing regulatory boundaries or ensuring employee safety procedures, was the minimum required and expected of business. Economist Milton Friedman described this when he wrote a 1970 *New York Times* article, "The Social Responsibility of Business is to Make a Profit." His declaration fueled a widespread movement to make profitability and increasing shareholder value the primary goal of corporate executives, boards, and shareholders to the detriment of other stakeholders.

CSR brought a new lens to business thinking. At its core, it prioritized the understanding that companies are responsible to a variety of stakeholders beyond their investors—employees, communities, customers, consumers, and even future generations.

CSR moves well beyond the philanthropic and volunteer activities discussed earlier. It requires companies to take a much closer look at their governance, supply chain, energy use and emissions, transparency, diversity, and other business practices. Embedded in CSR is the understanding that compliance with laws and regulations is simply the basic requirement for companies to operate, but that stakeholders expect—and increasingly demand—much more.

In the mid-1990s, business author John Elkington (2004) introduced the Triple Bottom Line (TBL) as a new language and accounting framework to help companies begin to measure the CSR-related, nonfinancial aspects of corporate performance. TBL goes further than the traditional measurements of profits, return on investment, and shareholder value to include environmental and social dimensions. Sometimes the TBL dimensions are called "the three Ps," for people, planet, and profits.

More recently, focus has shifted toward shared social and economic value creation. In 2011, Michael Porter and Mark Kramer (2011) coined the term "creating shared value" as a management strategy focused on companies creating measurable value by identifying and addressing social problems that intersect with their business.

Continuous improvement is a fundamental component of CSR, and practitioners often refer to their work as a "journey." Recognizing that companies had few markers for how to chart the approach, progress, and priorities of their CSR efforts, Philip Mirvis and Brad Googins developed the *Stages of Corporate Citizenship* (Googins et al. 2007). This framework helps companies identify their advancement toward best-in-class corporate citizenship practices and impact. Their model describes five stages of corporate citizenship, from the simply compliant or "elementary," through "engaged," to the most advanced, or "transformative."

As companies adopt CSR approaches, they modify their organizational structures and add new business titles. Just as there is no standard term for social impact management, there is not necessarily one specific department or line of reporting for these activities. In one company, the person leading social programs may be the Vice President of Corporate Citizenship, in another the Chief Corporate Responsibility Officer, Director of Community Relations, or the Head of Communications and Public Affairs.

There is no one best way to name the person responsible for all of the above, but companies are best positioned to make a positive social impact when different business units, functional areas (like marketing or procurement), *and* the foundation or community affairs division all work together to drive social impact. The language and structure used to describe "Who's Who" in CSR are still evolving, but a team effort is usually involved.

By their very definition, CSR and social impact strategies exist to make a difference. What quantitative and qualitative data can companies collect and analyze to calculate a return on investment? This question is one of the hardest in the field to answer, and has been challenging to practitioners since the early days of CSR. There are a few industry tools to measure and report consistent data points, which allow for benchmarking and comparison.

The Global Reporting Initiative (GRI) is an international independent standards organization that helps businesses, governments, and other organizations understand and communicate their impacts on issues such as climate change, human rights, and corruption. The GRI created, and periodically updates, a framework for sustainability reporting that is used by many of the world's largest companies.

Similarly, the Carbon Disclosure Project (CDP) works with companies to report, share, and track key environmental indicators, mainly greenhouse gas emissions. According to Lord Adair Turner, Chairman, UK Financial Services Authority, "… in business what gets measured gets managed. The Carbon Disclosure Project has played a crucial role in encouraging companies to take the first steps in that measurement and management path" (CDP 2016).

Social impact metrics are difficult to quantify, compare, and aggregate across companies. Under pressure to report results, companies have a tendency to measure outputs, rather than impact. To be clear, measuring quantitative input and output isn't wrong—it is important to know and track employees' volunteer hours, philanthropic donations made, and other investments. These measurements, however, do not necessarily indicate whether or not social impact has been achieved—although sometimes they serve as the best available proxy. Advanced companies have moved beyond simply counting outputs in favor of measuring outcomes. They are reporting on lives saved, behaviors changed, and economic impacts.

The acceptance of CSR as a management best practice continues to increase. One indicator is the tracking of companies publicly reporting on their CSR-related issues by the Governance & Accountability (G&I) Institute. They found that in 2015, 81 % of S&P 500 companies published a Sustainability or Corporate Responsibility report, a significant increase from just 5 years prior when only 20 % of those companies published such a report (G&I 2015). This is a clear sign that not only are more companies increasing transparency; they also are developing complex CSR strategies. CSR, including corporate philanthropy and employee engagement, has become a standard, expected, and accepted corporate social impact discipline.

The Era of Innovation

As CSR has become embedded within companies, the frontier of the corporate social impact field has shifted. Today, companies of all sizes and in all industries seek to harness the power of their assets in new ways to proactively and intentionally deliver positive business and social impact. This era, defined by exploration, innovation, and risk-taking, is driving new ways of thinking. There is a perfect storm of influences that make this the ideal time for companies to think bigger, differently, and in disruptive ways.

First, more employees are ready to take action. They are looking for more than a stable environment and a good paycheck. They increasingly demand meaningful work and want to play a role as catalysts for social impact on the job. Net Impact reports that 49 % of Generation Xers and 52 % of Baby Boomers want a job that impacts causes that are important to them (Zukin and Szeltner 2012). A 2016 Deloitte study found that while two-thirds of Millennials express a desire to leave their organizations within 4 years, retention improves if they feel that they are working for more than a paycheck; 88 % of Millennials who say that their organizations have a "sense of purpose" plan to stay more than 5 years. In fact, 6 in 10 young workers say that sense of purpose is the reason they chose their current employers.

Second, consumers are also ready to take action through how they shop and give permission to companies to address social issues. They are increasingly searching for brands that share their sense of purpose and goals. In one of the most watched TED talks of all time, *How Great Leaders Inspire Action*, management consultant Simon Sinek frames how consumers are really looking to buy not what brands are selling, but what brands *believe* (2009). Research from Nielson, Globescan, and others regularly suggests that consumers are willing to pay more for a product if they believe that a company is committed to social impact.

Third, the recent and seemingly overnight success of completely new ways of doing business has inspired hope that new social change models are within reach. The rise of Uber, Airbnb, and Zipcar, and even the Human Genome Project, offers inspiration for companies and entrepreneurs who seek to take a disruptive approach to social impact. A generation armed with new technology tools, shared-economy philosophies, and entrepreneurial passion is unleashing fresh approaches to social impact.

And finally, this storm is global. As the world gets smaller, the realities of social, economic, and environmental challenges arrive directly via everyone's handheld devices every minute. It is not hard to see the interconnectivity of our lives and our dependence on one another's success. We are only one call, one flight, one picture away. The bottom of the pyramid is no longer hidden from view.

The time is right for big ideas and new approaches; however, companies also face new types of obstacles to taking action. As CSR and social impact programming have become formalized and stakeholders' expectations grow, managers feel increased pressure—both internally and externally—to get it right. This pressure is not necessarily bad, but it can result in poorly planned and executed activities that are designed to look good rather than to make a measureable difference. For example, companies claiming to be environmentally friendly, when in fact they are not, have been exposed and accused of "greenwashing."

These negative practices, however, have both educated consumers to be more sophisticated in evaluating initiatives and pushed companies to be more transparent and committed to demonstrating impact. In this environment, companies are exploring new ways to create change. They are looking for solutions at the intersection of business and society. Here are some of the ways that companies are exploring how to harness the power of their assets to impact social change.

Harnessing the Power of Products

From big business to smaller social enterprises, designers, engineers, and scientists seek to solve problems through product innovation. Social impact driven from within established global businesses has become a model for a new generation of ideas and experimentation.

Safe drinking water is a problem for nearly one billion people. Every day, over 1,000 children die due to contaminated water-related illnesses (United Nations 2016). In 2004, Proctor & Gamble launched a new water purification packet developed in collaboration with the US Centers for Disease Control and Prevention. This technology enables people anywhere in the world to purify dirty water in a simple, affordable, and convenient way. One packet is able to quickly turn 10 liters of unsafe water into clean and drinkable water. The packet has been proven to remove waterborne bacteria, viruses, and other microorganisms that cause diseases such as diarrhea. P&G laundry scientists originally invented the technology as they were trying to separate dirt from used laundry water.

Through the Children's Safe Drinking Water philanthropic health and hygiene program, P&G has provided clean water in more than 75 countries and helped to raise awareness of the clean water crisis through a diverse network of 150 partners (P&G 2016a). Global relief nongovernmental organizations such as CARE and Save the Children have been using P&G packets since 2004 to save lives (P&G 2016b).

Some product innovations don't even involve new products, but rather repurpose existing ones. Intermarché, a large supermarket chain in France, decided to address the issue of food waste. Approximately 1.3 billion tons of food globally is wasted—roughly one-third of the total of all food produced (United Nations 2016). Since fruits and vegetables have the highest wastage rates, the company launched the "Inglorious Fruit" campaign in 2014 to sell fruits and vegetables which look abnormal but are as healthy and tasty as their perfectly formed counterparts. Intermarché reported in 2016 that the campaign increased store traffic by 24 %, and the "Inglorious" items routinely sell out. Many large food retailers around the world are now following suit with similar results. Small companies such as California's Imperfect Produce have even formed specifically to deliver "ugly fruits" directly to consumers' front doors.

Inspired by the power of innovation to save and transform lives, an exciting variety of new businesses and products are launching almost every day. Established brands like Kohler are designing waterless toilets for the developing world. Newer social enterprises are introducing products such as Alter Eco's compostable food packaging to reduce plastic in landfills, Because International's adjustable shoes that protect children from soil-transmitted diseases, and Janma, a simple, low-cost clean birth kit, assembled by women in India to ensure safe and sterile conditions during delivery (Kopernik 2015).

Harnessing the Power of Business Acumen and Expertise

Human capital is (literally) the heartbeat and one of the most crucial elements of a company's success. As companies look at how they can make an impact in critical social issues, they are pushing the boundaries around how to apply their unique skills and business acumen to create change. They are becoming more and more strategic around how to align human capital with the specific societal issues and the needs of NGOs.

In 2016, according to the United Nations Refugee Agency (UNHCR), approximately 59.6 million people have been forcibly displaced around the world because of conflict or persecution (2016). This crisis has mobilized companies and their foundations to tackle the immediate and long-term challenges faced by refugees. IKEA and United Parcel Service (UPS) are two businesses that apply their expertise on behalf of those refugees.

In 2008, the Refugee Housing Unit located in Stockholm, Sweden, started working on a new initiative to improve the effectiveness and sustainability of refugee shelters. Extreme weather conditions often posed a threat to refugee housing; Johan Karlsson, Project Manager at the Refugee Housing Unit, recalls that "humanitarian aid should not only contribute to saving lives, but also to creating sustainable communities after disasters" (IKEA Foundation 2013).

IKEA and the IKEA Foundation worked together with the Refugee Housing Unit to identify and deploy the unique resources, skills, and knowledge that IKEA has to offer in building low-cost shelters for refugee camps. It became clear that the company's expertise in design, logistics, and flat packing could help solve some of the emergency shelter challenges. IKEA designed and manufactured safer, bigger, more cost-effective refugee housing that was easy to build, could withstand severe weather, and ultimately created a more livable, safe, and comfortable home for families. In 2013, the Refugee Housing Unit project won a World Design Impact prize (World Design Impact 2013).

In addition to housing challenges, refugee camps struggle with identification, tracking, and record keeping associated with their operations. As UNHCR delivers a range of humanitarian support to refugees, the collection and consolidation of data for each refugee are critical to the organization's ability to manage and provide food and other relief items to millions of people worldwide. This is where UPS and the UPS Foundation applied their logistics expertise and supply chain management to help optimize distribution and tracking of critical supplies. UNHCR and UPS reviewed the current systems and processes and created "UPS Relief Link." This technology represents the combination of a handheld scanning tool and durable identification cards to deliver efficiency by eliminating paper records in refugee camps. According to UNHCR and UPS, the piloting and testing of this technology and leveraging of UPS's proprietary Trackpad™ technology have lowered wait time for refugees to receive critical, life-saving items and helped manage and distribute supplies more efficiently (UPS 2015).

Harnessing the Power of Brand and Communications

Companies recognize that their brand reach, communications channels, and voice can be powerful tools to address social issues. Brands have the ability to influence and engage millions of global consumers. They can inspire them to take action and change their personal behaviors.

To address the negative impact of decades of advertising imagery portraying unrealistic standards of beauty on women and young girls' self-esteem and self-confidence, Dove launched the Campaign for Real Beauty in 2004. This integrated communications, marketing, and philanthropic initiative aimed to change the global conversation about female beauty.

Through an initially unorthodox and attention-grabbing series of advertisements, fashion shows, videos, workshops, books, and other activities, Dove sought to inspire women to have the confidence to be comfortable with themselves and their bodies. By featuring diverse, real women—not models—in their communications, they prompted consumers to think differently and aimed to ignite a global conversation about the perception of beauty.

The campaign was not without its critics. Some raised questions about the initial self-esteem research, and many pointed out that Dove's parent company, Unilever, markets the Axe brand which has been criticized for sexism in its advertising. Despite the controversies that continue to surround this campaign—and perhaps because of them—it provides a solid example of how a brand can lead, share its voice, and engage its consumers around a social issue to raise awareness, inspire dialogue, and drive change.

The business results were encouraging. During the first decade of the campaign, product sales increased from $2.5 billion to $4 billion. Unilever reports that of the more than 400 brands it sells, those with the strongest sustainability credentials—such as Dove, Ben & Jerry's, and Comfort—have seen sales grow at a high single-digit or double-digit rate over the past 3 years (Unilever 2015).

Brands can also put the power of their communications reach to work driving behavior change, not just attitudes. In 2015, CVS announced that its stores would stop selling cigarettes and mobilize consumers to stop smoking, sacrificing an estimated $2 billion in annual revenue. The move was part of a greater effort to position CVS as a health brand.

Under the communications umbrella of "Let's Quit, Together," the company also committed to help consumers stop smoking. In partnership with the American Cancer Society and American Lung Association, among others, CVS launched in-store, online, and community programs where consumers can get advice, peer-to-peer support, and access to a range of smoking cessation-related resources and products.

Just as Dove's social impact efforts met with skepticism from some observers, so have CVS's decisions. They have become vulnerable to legitimate questions about other products on their shelves, like soda and junk food. This example highlights that tensions exist when a company seeks to simultaneously drive business and social objectives.

CVS has set a series of 5-year goals including reducing the national youth smoking rate by 3 %, cutting the number of new youth smokers by 10 %, and doubling the number of college campuses that ban tobacco use (Bomey 2016). Stakeholders will be watching closely as CVS dedicates its leadership voice and resources to drive social impact around this cause (Fig. 2).

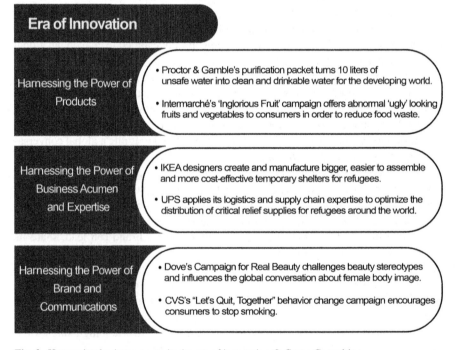

Fig. 2 Harnessing business assets in the era of innovation © Cause Consulting

Implementing a Successful Social Impact Strategy

A world-class social impact strategy doesn't happen overnight; creating one takes time, effort, and investment. It also takes very dedicated people, who are willing to do the challenging but incredibly rewarding work of designing and implementing these strategies. Many companies with effective social impact strategies follow the advice below.

Pick the Right Issue: What issue best matches a company's products, customers, or community? When a company's existing expertise and business acumen can be used to address a social issue, and its stakeholders can help, a natural fit exists. Following this advice helped brands like IKEA and UPS create strategies that make sense for their businesses and make a difference for society.

Design for Easy Wins: Big picture goals are important, but so are short-term successes that happen early on. Companies need these to get traction and inspire long-term support—and to build internal champions for the strategy. An easy win can be defined as taking a foundational step in a social impact initiative, such as convening key players, conducting and reporting preliminary research, or launching an initial web portal. Milestones in a project's early days matter even though greater impact will come with additional time and investment.

Find the Right Partners: Collaboration can produce positive results, but finding the right partners is tricky. Reputations can go south; even marquee nonprofit brands like the Wounded Warrior Project and the American Red Cross have stumbled. Criteria to consider when selecting partners for collaboration include cultural fit, leadership buy-in, and capacity to deliver results. Because the ability to measure impact is increasingly important, partners need to be willing and able to do that. Finally, there must be mutual support and enthusiasm for the mission and the cause. Without that, no partnership can reach its full potential.

Focus the Investments: When companies generously fund programming that aligns with their social impact program's core mission and their partners' needs, the work will make a difference. Spreading smaller donations around is less effective, so those who control the resources need to be comfortable saying, "No." This will be easier and kinder if there is a clear strategy and criteria to share with potential partners or others who request support. "No" is hard to hear, but it goes down better with understandable rationale.

Whenever Possible, Measure Impact Rather than Output: This advice is easy to give, but hard to follow. Nevertheless, the pressure to measure impact is increasing. If the goal of a social impact strategy is to change lives, how will a company know if it's working? As companies plan their strategies, they must spend the time and resources to scope them properly and study the ability to create change. Determining what and how to measure must be part of the planning process. If an organization funds programs that a nonprofit partner delivers, leaders should understand the ways that

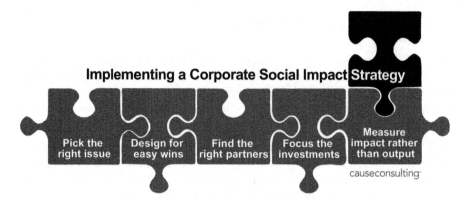

Fig. 3 Five key steps to implementing a corporate social impact strategy © Cause Consulting

nonprofit evaluates impact. It's not necessary or possible to measure everything—selecting a few key metrics that are most important is perfectly acceptable (Fig. 3).

Conclusion

Yvon Chouinard made a bold decision when he stopped selling pitons because they damaged the environment. Patagonia made another in 2011, buying a full-page ad in the New York Times featuring a photo of their product and the headline, "Don't Buy This Jacket." The text described the environmental impact of producing that jacket—the water, the carbon footprint, and the raw materials—and told readers that really, they should repair their clothes and buy less new stuff—even from Patagonia.

How could Patagonia run an ad asking people *not* to buy its products, and expect that to be good for business? It worked because the ad was consistent with Patagonia's brand purpose and values. The brand's customers and employees believe what Patagonia believes. They trust Patagonia and love what the company stands for.

What is the secret to Patagonia's success? Actually, it's no secret. Patagonia is a well-known example of the approaches described in this chapter. Beyond developing powerful marketing campaigns, the company's leaders apply business acumen to an integrated social impact strategy, from continuously improving their supply chain and the lives of the workers who make their garments to ensuring that all its products and initiatives reinforce the brand purpose and are designed to protect the environment.

As the social impact field continues to innovate, we can expect to see more companies harnessing the power of their assets in new ways to proactively and intentionally deliver positive business and social impact. This new era, defined by exploration, innovation, and risk-taking, will guide the corporate social impact field over the next decade.

References

Bomey N (2016) CVS launches $50 million anti-smoking campaign. USA Today. http://www.usatoday.com/story/money/2016/03/10/cvs-smoking-prevention-campaign/81574276/. Accessed 19 June 2016

CDP (2016) Catalyzing business and government action. https://www.cdp.net/en-us/pages/about-us.aspx. Accessed 18 June 2016

CECP (2016) Giving in numbers brief 2016. http://cecp.co/research/benchmarking-reports/giving-in-numbers-index.html. Accessed 19 June 2016

Deloitte (2016) The Deloitte millennial survey 2016. http://www2.deloitte.com/global/en/pages/about-deloitte/articles/millennialsurvey.html. Accessed 19 June 2016

Elkington J (2004) Cannibals with forks. Capstone, Oxford

Friedman M (1970) The social responsibility of business is to make a profit. The New York Times Magazine

Giving USA (2016) 2015 was America's most-generous year ever. http://givingusa.org/giving-usa-2016. Accessed 14 June 2016

Googins B, Mirvis P, Rochlin S (2007) Beyond good company. Palgrave Macmillan, London

G&I (2015) FLASH REPORT: eighty one percent (81%) of the S&P 500 Index companies published corporate sustainability reports in 2015. http://www.ga-institute.com/nc/issue-master-system/news-details/article/flash-report-eighty-one-percent-81-of-the-sp-500-index-companies-published-corporate-sustainabi.html. Accessed 19 June 2016

IKEA Foundation (2013) Designing a better home for refugee children. https://www.ikeafoundation.org/stories/designing-a-better-home-for-refugee-children/. Accessed 19 June 2016

Intermarché (2016) Inglorious fruits. http://itm.marcelww.com/inglorious/. Accessed 19 June 2016

Kopernik (2015) Janme clean birth kit. http://www.kopernik.ngo/technology/janma-clean-birth-kit. Accessed 19 June 2016

Patagonia (2016) Company history. http://www.patagonia.com/us/patagonia.go?assetid=3351. Accessed 24 May 2016

Porter M, Kramer M (2011) Creating shared value. Harvard Business Review

Proctor and Gamble (2016a) The P&G children's safe drinking water program: the power of clean water. https://www.csdw.org/csdw/childrens-safe-drinking-water-impact.shtml. Accessed 19 June 2016

Proctor and Gamble (2016b) A simple way to clean water: the science behind the P&G packet technology. https://www.csdw.org/csdw/pur-packet-technology.shtml. Accessed 19 June 2016

Sinek S (2009) How great leaders inspire action. ted.com. https://www.ted.com/talks/simon_sinek_how_great_leaders_inspire_action?language=en. Accessed 27 June 2016

Unilever (2015) Unilever sees sustainability supporting growth. https://www.unilever.co.uk/news/press-releases/2015/unilever-sees-sustainability-supporting-growth.html. Accessed 19 June 2016

United Nations (2016) Goal 6: ensure access to water and sanitation for all. United Nations Sustainable Development Goals. http://www.un.org/sustainabledevelopment/water-and-sanitation/. Accessed 18 June 2016

UNHCR (2016) Figures at a glance. http://www.unhcr.org/uk/figures-at-a-glance.html. Accessed 19 June 2016

UPS (2015) The UPS Foundation links advanced tracking technology with global humanitarian relief efforts. https://www.pressroom.ups.com/pressroom/ContentDetailsViewer.page?ConceptType=PressReleases&id=1429104592455-974. Accessed 19 June 2016

World Design Impact (2013) Refugee housing unit. http://worlddesignimpact.org/projects/project2013/32/. Accessed 27 June 2016

Zukin C, Szeltner M (2012) Talent report: what workers want in 2012. John J. Heldrich Center for Workforce Development. https://www.netimpact.org/sites/default/files/documents/what-workers-want-2012.pdf. Accessed 27 June 2016

Transformation Through Social Impact at Whirlpool Corporation

Bridget Akinc

Abstract Within the cost-pressured, competitive environment of American manufacturing, Corporate Social Responsibility is often thought of in terms of an additional set of reporting requirements for environmental impact, philanthropy, and volunteering. But corporate social responsibility and a commitment to positive social impact are not just check box items, or add-ons to the work at Whirlpool Corporation, the world's largest major home appliance manufacturer, headquartered in Benton Harbor, Michigan. Since 2000, Whirlpool's work as a catalyst for economic development in its hometown, and as a consumer-focused partner to organizations like Habitat for Humanity, has become core to its business strategy. Whirlpool engaged in a strategic innovation effort to understand genuine customer needs in order to create breakthrough products that would cultivate long-term customer loyalty. Simultaneously, Whirlpool Corporation engaged with community partners, state and local government, and employees to understand and improve the economic conditions of Benton Harbor, Michigan. This chapter analyzes how an intensive focus on helping families has played an integral role in how Whirlpool designs products, models innovation, and recruits new talent. With customers as the focus and innovation as the method, Whirlpool undertook to transform its business for long-term success. In the process, it discovered the power of purpose-driven engagement with employees, customers, and its community.

Keywords Purpose branding • Corporate Social Responsibility • CSR • Corporate philanthropy • Economic development • Benton Harbor

Introduction

In 2000, Whirlpool Corporation, the largest appliance manufacturer in the United States, was facing steep market competition and stalling sales growth. The 90-year-old corporation faced significant costs and increased price pressures, particularly

B. Akinc (✉)
Carroll School of Management, Boston College,
140 Commonwealth Avenue, Chestnut Hill, MA 02467, USA
e-mail: bridget.akinc@bc.edu

© Springer International Publishing Switzerland 2017
M.J. Cronin, T.C. Dearing (eds.), *Managing for Social Impact*,
Management for Professionals, DOI 10.1007/978-3-319-46021-5_6

from manufacturers outside the United States. Although profits were still holding constant, much of this profitability was due to significant cost cutting the company had imposed throughout the 1990s. The industry as a whole appeared stuck in a commoditized environment where differentiation, let alone innovation, seemed impossible. "It's a stalemate industry," Whirlpool Vice President Nancy Snyder admitted. "If you walk into the appliance department at any retailer, everything looks the same. We call it the sea of white" (Parks 2003).

As Whirlpool was experiencing these challenges in the marketplace, the core urban areas of Benton Harbor, Michigan, where Whirlpool had been based for almost 90 years, were also in trouble. Benton Harbor's economic conditions had declined along with other manufacturing hubs across the Great Lakes region, suffering thousands of job losses, and subsequent poverty, unemployment, and education challenges.

CEO David Whitwam, Whirlpool Corporation's chairman and CEO in 2000, conceived of a way to rejuvenate the appliance manufacturer and think about competing on a global scale: by engaging employees on innovation from within. Whirlpool embarked on a prolonged, intensive effort to understand and respond to genuine customer needs in order to create breakthrough products and services that would cultivate long-term customer loyalty. Simultaneously, Whirlpool engaged with community partners, state and local government, and employees to understand and improve the economic conditions facing the urban areas of Benton Harbor, Michigan. With customers as the focus and innovation as the method across a global landscape, Whirlpool embarked on a journey to transform its business for long-term success. Whirlpool shifted from competing primarily on appliance features and price to a strategy of understanding and meeting deeper consumer needs. In the process, it discovered the power of purpose-driven engagement with employees, customers, and its community.

Today, Whirlpool's sense of purpose drives its product innovation as well as its engagement with customers and the local community. Whirlpool differentiates itself through a clear sense of purpose, grounded in the values of community, family ties, and care for one another. On its corporate website, Whirlpool states: "We exist to create purposeful innovation that helps keep homes running smoothly so personal and family lives can flourish" (2016b). While many companies make similar declarations, Whirlpool executives will tell you that the challenging decision to stay and invest in the community of Benton Harbor, after most local manufacturers had moved or closed down, ignited a transformation at the core of its business. Whirlpool's mid-level managers who have joined the company in the last decade point to the company's commitment and reinvestment in Benton Harbor as playing a central role in its values as a business. This chapter analyzes the evolution of Whirlpool's commitment to local corporate responsibility and broader social impact during the period between 2000 and 2016. Starting with the Board's decision to stay in Benton Harbor and double down on economic redevelopment projects locally, it explores how prioritizing social impact helped to trigger a dramatic shift in the trajectory of a company entering its second century of business.

Headquartered in Benton Harbor, Michigan

Whirlpool Corporation, the world's largest major home appliance manufacturer with $21 billion in annual sales in 2015, is headquartered in Benton Harbor, Michigan. On the surface, this location may seem inconsequential. The century-old company started out as a family business in 1911 in the tiny community of Benton Harbor, on the eastern shore of Lake Michigan (Whirlpool 2011a). Whirlpool began as the Upton Machine Company when founder Lou Upton, along with his uncle, Emory, and brother, Fred, joined together to produce a motor-driven wringer clothing washer. By the 1950s, Benton Harbor had become a Midwest manufacturing metropolis, serving as a manufacturing center during WWII, and booming through the postwar period. Well into the 1960s, Benton Harbor was economically vibrant and racially mixed, and its population grew to a high point of 20,000. But, by the final decades of the twentieth century, Benton Harbor had declined along with other manufacturing hubs across the Great Lakes region, suffering a similar fate of job losses, poverty, unemployment, and economic decline. All across the region, previously local manufacturers sought cheaper labor in the South and overseas, shutting down their Michigan operations. Benton Harbor lost the majority of its manufacturing jobs between 1970 and 1990; in just one 18-month period in the mid-1980s, the area sustained a loss of 5500 jobs (Dumke 2008).

By 2000, Benton Harbor had become the poorest city in Michigan and its population had declined to only 11,000. The per capita income of its remaining residents was roughly $10,000 and about 60 % of its population was on some form of public assistance. Approximately 90 % of the residents of Benton Harbor were African-American (Mahler 2011). The negative effects of corporate relocations and massive factory closures were felt by the land, as well as by its people. Over the decades, departing manufacturers left behind hundreds of acres of polluted brownfields and wetlands, including a 17-acre Superfund site contaminated by more than a dozen types of contaminants, including arsenic, PCBs, and asbestos.

For 50 years, Whirlpool had been one of the major economic engines of the Benton Harbor area. But as it faced increased pressure from global appliance competitors, the company was not immune to the pressures that had sparked the exodus of so many manufacturing jobs from Michigan. In 1986, Whirlpool announced the closing of its last large plant in the area, with a loss of 1050 jobs (Elsner 1987). By the early 2000s, the company's executives were confronting the question of whether it still made sense to maintain a corporate headquarters in Benton Harbor. Even though neighboring St. Joseph remained a stable lakefront community of 8000 residents, there was no denying that the local area, and Michigan as a whole, was in serious economic trouble. It was becoming difficult to attract new college graduates, midlevel, and senior management staff to positions at Whirlpool headquarters. The buildings themselves needed renovation and expansion. Staying put was not viable without a significant change in the local situation.

In 2003, Benton Harbor made national headlines when a 2-day riot occurred following the death of a 28-year-old black man who crashed during a chase with police.

As Governor Jennifer Granholm ordered the National Guard troops to Benton Harbor, it was clear that decades of rising unemployment and poverty, inadequate housing and education, social inequality, and class conflict had come to a crisis point. The headlines about the poverty, violence, and racial strife in the area further deterred potential new hires from accepting positions at Whirlpool Corporation headquarters. Whirlpool was faced with the decision of staying in Benton Harbor and reinvesting in its roots, or moving on to another location where the local economy might better serve its growing business.

Innovating Out of the "Sea of Sameness"

During this period, Whirlpool's leadership also recognized that the company was engaged in an unwinnable battle in the marketplace, particularly in North America. The "sea of sameness" across all products left cost and quality as the only two levers. Whirlpool began a major initiative to innovate across its products, its processes, and its brand, with attention to the needs of customers around the world. CEO Dave Whitwam wanted to transform Whirlpool from a margin-driven appliance business to a customer-focused organization capable of outperforming in global markets (Maruca 1994).

Whitwam believed that Whirlpool's long-term competitive advantage in the market would come from an emphasis on customer-focused innovation plus global expansion. Whitwam reflected, "Too many companies implement one improvement program after another but ignore the larger picture, which has to do with establishing enduring relationships between a company and its customers. Many companies would like to think that if they become 'world-class' in cost and quality, they'll win. But it takes more than that" (Maruca 1994).

Whirlpool embarked on creating innovation as a source of competitive advantage, and has stayed the course with this initiative for 20 years. Whitwam engaged innovation expert Gary Hamel to pick cross-functional teams to head up a "new ideas" initiative, and allocated $50 million (20 % of the entire research budget) to get the new ideas launched in 2003 (Parks). Across its many brands and global expansion, Whirlpool emphasized the vision to be one branded company. Whirlpool made innovation integral to its business success, with the objective of its innovation efforts to deliver shareholder value in the top 25 % of publicly held companies in total returns.

Innovations over the next decade encompassed product design changes, entrance into new markets, and processes driving efficiency globally, but they also included innovations in the company's engagement with the community. Reaching beyond traditional corporate philanthropy, community relations, and local community volunteerism by employees, Whirlpool's model looked for innovative, transformative solutions and practical social impact partnerships in the Benton Harbor community. Whirlpool made substantial financial and leadership commitments to the economic redevelopment of Benton Harbor through local and national partnerships. As its work on innovation was sparked in 2003, the field of social innovation was just emerging. Leading universities were launching academic centers for social innovation, and the White House Office for Social Innovation was created to "develop policies and programs to accelerate economic recovery and create stronger communities" (2016). Whirlpool reflected this larger trend, at the same time that it embarked on an effort to integrate social impact at a deeper level across the entire company.

Catalyzing Community Transformation

In tandem with its corporate innovation goals, Whirlpool as an organization evolved a core social impact purpose of improving the lives of individuals, families, and communities around the world. Whirlpool had a tradition of local corporate citizenship, volunteering, and philanthropic contributions, dating all the way back to its founders. Lou and Fred Upton established the Whirlpool Foundation following World War II, making a promise to reinvest in the community through financial and leadership support for nonprofit organizations dedicated to improving the quality of life in communities where Whirlpool operated. The Whirlpool Foundation regularly contributed to Benton Harbor causes and nonprofits, but a decision to stay in Benton Harbor for the long term would require Whirlpool to make a much more significant financial and resource-intensive investment in the local community.

When Whirlpool Corporation decided to recommit to Benton Harbor, it charted a course for substantial investment in the economic development of the community. The call for a transformative structural redevelopment required changes in the way Whirlpool approached community relations. Just as for the business initiatives requiring innovation, incremental improvements in community work were not enough. Whirlpool looked to a strategy and engagement model that extended far beyond volunteer hours and philanthropy. In its plan, Whirlpool Corporation envisioned massive investments of resources, time, and energy, not as an add-on social impact initiative, but as a necessity for doing business in the community where its company had started. Whirlpool took on the role of a corporate catalyst to this economic revitalization, and embraced a vision for collective impact with partners from nonprofit organizations, local community members, state and local government, other companies, and federal contributions to support the environmental cleanup.

Whirlpool invested resources and time into the planning for the Benton Harbor initiative through a nonprofit organization, the Council of World-class Communities, which would mature into an organization known today as the Consortium for Community Development. The mission of this coalition and its initiatives was to (2016):

> ... provide a whole-system approach to dramatically intervene into the issues and causes of chronic generational poverty and to drive a transformation in the quality of life in the greater Benton Harbor area.

Working with community leaders, organizations, and citizens across the area, the Council of World-class Communities adopted a vision to serve as a "catalyst for the transformation of the greater Benton Harbor area, ensuring a responsive, effective and sustainable local government and public school system with a community of engaged and self-sufficient residents" (Whitwam 2010). Members of the consortium included some Benton Harbor residents, businesses, government officials, and community leaders, working toward the Benton Harbor Transformation Strategy. The Consortium was one of several local nonprofit organizations partly financed by Whirlpool Corporation, to encourage redevelopment of the town. Through the experience of working with these coalitions, Whirlpool adopted a Model for Collective Impact for its social impact work, which recognizes that "no one organization alone can achieve communities' wide transformation. It takes everyone working together" (Whitwam 2010).

With a $3 million investment from Whirlpool, the Council of World-class Communities hired the Kaleel Jamison Consulting Group in 2001 as "diversity consultants" to spearhead work with community leaders and local residents of Benton Harbor and St. Joseph to come up with ways to address some of the problems caused by the poverty, unemployment, and contamination in the region (Stevens 2002). The nonprofit organizations worked collaboratively with 23 members of Governor Granholm's Task Force for Benton Harbor, to focus on ways to improve the quality of life in Benton Harbor. The Governor's Task Force noted in October 2003:

> Benton Harbor has historically been the subject of numerous studies and notable community-wide initiatives that have promised wide ranging systemic change, but have yielded limited results … The recommendations in this report are meant to address some of the most persistent challenges facing the Benton Harbor area community.

The Governor's Task Force identified four critical needs in the area of economic development: a job development strategy, the use of the community's natural resources to target tourism, greater access to capital for businesses, and the goal of eradicating substandard housing in Benton Harbor by 2025 through community and government efforts. Out of these discussions, the idea for Harbor Shores was born— a recreational facility, golf course, and resort housing that would allow for the cleanup and repurposing of the contaminated sites to generate economic development and job opportunities in recreation and tourism. Along with its support for Harbor Shores, Whirlpool joined other community groups in a major initiative with Habitat for Humanity to develop high-quality, low-income housing for residents of Benton Harbor.

Objections to Community Investment Priorities

Whirlpool's deepened involvement in the economic development of the region over the past decade has garnered community criticism and negative headlines as well as praise. Much of the criticism has focused on an early decision to combine the much-needed environmental cleanup with the development of a professional golf course and resort community. Consistent with the recommendation of the Governor's Task Force to find a way to bring tourism to town, the golf course and surrounding beachfront were designed to combine "the charm of a small town with the year-round amenities of a world-class destination, ideally located just 90 min from downtown Chicago" (Harbor Shores 2016). From Whirlpool's perspective, this combination attracted more financial partners to the larger community redevelopment effort as well as offered the potential of increased property values and economic stabilization. But the investment in a $500-million golf resort known as Harbor Shores and a $68-million investment in a new Whirlpool North America Region headquarters campus overshadowed the efforts being made to revitalize the depressed downtown of Benton Harbor and to build new housing for its residents. Whirlpool CEO, Jeff Fettig, noted in 2014, "Our confidence in this area is so strong today that we as a company have committed almost $100 million in new facilities and investments, mostly in downtown Benton Harbor" (Echlin 2014). While economic development in Benton Harbor might benefit the city overall, it seemed unlikely to residents that they would benefit proportionately from Whirlpool's investments.

Reporters venturing to the Harbor Shores development in 2011 focused on the headline-worthy contrast between the resort homes being built on a new golf course with the impoverished city beyond it (Mahler 2011). Critics cited a mismatch between the Harbor Shores development and the needs of the Benton Harbor community for jobs, improved education, and affordable housing. The Harbor Shores Community Redevelopment group pointed to the golf course as "the economic engine that will get Harbor Shores to attract hotels, second-home buyers, developers and commercial and retail businesses" (Draeger 2008). Stipulations were put into place to ensure that residents be given discount rates to the golf course, local high school competitions would be hosted there, and at least 40 % of golf course employees be Benton Harbor residents (Benton Harbor 2010). Further, it was established that any profit from the course would go to the city of Benton Harbor, not Harbor Shores, to support community programs "for the improvement of, among other things, literacy, adult education, housing, minority contracting, and transportation to the Park" (Benton Harbor 2010).

Community advocates for Benton Harbor were quick to point out that it would likely be years before the golf course turned a profit, and had anything to reinvest. Cornerstone Alliance, one of the leading nonprofits, highlighted the importance of the immediate environmental investment: "We have budgeted over $8 million for environmental cleanup. The whole purpose is not to better our golf games. It's to provide an opportunity to transform this community" (Draeger 2008).

Practical Partnerships Tied to the Business

While Whirlpool chose to invest in economic revitalization through Harbor Shores, the company also expanded its direct service role in Benton Harbor, through a combination of expanded corporate giving and employee volunteerism. Whirlpool had begun a partnership with Habitat for Humanity for charitable contributions in 1999, but in 2003, it moved that partnership beyond monetary donations to volunteering and product contributions. Whirlpool partnered with Habitat for Humanity and the Jimmy and Rosalind Carter Work Project to address the immediate housing challenges in Benton Harbor. The Carter Work Project and Habitat for Humanity selected Benton Harbor, along with Detroit, as sites for building over 200 homes in a blitz construction week. Former President Jimmy Carter explained the rationale for selecting these two cities: "Both communities suffer from social and economic tension and decaying neighborhoods. Both have areas people would rather drive around than drive through. There are good people in Benton Harbor and Detroit who have lost hope and need our help" (Crowell 2004). Along with thousands of volunteer hours, Whirlpool Corporation contributed products (a range and refrigerator) for every newly constructed house. This was the beginning of a long-term partnership between Whirlpool and Habitat for Humanity, which has continued through 2016. Whirlpool developed active Habitat for Humanity programs in more than 45 countries with a commitment of more than $90 million, and over 8000 employee volunteers, and for 15 years has quietly donated a range and refrigerator to homes for over 85,000 families (Habitat for Humanity 2015; Whirlpool 2016d).

In 2004, Whirlpool Corporation's new CEO, Jeff Fettig, encouraged employees to look for practical solutions and business involvement as drivers for Whirlpool's ongoing community work. Fettig took the generic promise of the founders to "reinvest in the community" to a new level of strategic focus for initiatives contributing to the "social concerns in our home communities ... centered on quality family life, cultural diversity and lifelong learning." Driven by the strategic alignment with the business- and employee-directed programs, Whirlpool launched collaborative programs with schools and Boys and Girls Clubs. Initiatives emerged from individual brands like KitchenAid's partnership with the Susan G. Komen breast cancer organization in a program called Cook for the Cure (J. Noel, VP Communications and Public Relations, personal communication, June 16, 2016). With these new areas of focus, community work tied much more directly back to the business and the people of Whirlpool Corporation. It was clear that both long-term social impact work like Harbor Shores and immediate community partnerships were becoming increasingly important to Whirlpool.

Measuring Outcomes from Social Impact Investment

Once the Harbor Shores golf course was completed, the Jack Nicklaus-designed course was ranked Number 3 on the 2010 Best New Courses You Can Play list compiled by GOLF Magazine. In 2010, the PGA of America announced the selection of Harbor Shores as the site of its annual Senior PGA Championship beginning in 2012. In his announcement, PGA of America CEO Joe Steranka welcomed "a legendary partner of the business community in Whirlpool Corporation, one of the world's most respected and recognizable companies" (PGA 2012). In sponsoring the Senior PGA Championship through the KitchenAid brand, Whirlpool

Corporation found "an opportunity to show how business and golf can help to strengthen and transform lives and communities." In the words of Jeff Noel, corporate vice president, Whirlpool Corporation, it was Whirlpool's hope that hosting the championship would "turn the eyes of the golf world to Benton Harbor Michigan, where the Harbor Shores development is already making a difference and driving positive, lasting change in our community" (PGA 2012).

The arrival of the Senior PGA Championship gave Benton Harbor a needed boost in driving tourism and visibility to the region. During the development of Harbor Shores, more than a dozen types of contaminants had been removed from the site. Benton Harbor's Mayor, James Hightower, highlighted the positive impact on the community, saying: "I remember riding through this site when I was a little kid on a bicycle going to Jean Klock Park and it was all factories. Over the years they shut down. It became a dilapidated just a total eyesore; rusty buildings. And now to see it like it is today … its transformation" (Smith 2012). The physical transformation was just one measure.

The outcomes sought by Whirlpool included further economic investment by other organizations in the region, improved recruitment for top talent, and measureable gains for the community organizations. Following the PGA announcement in 2010 was the announcement in 2013 for Harbor Village, a $114-million project including a hotel, marina, and residences "envisioned as a catalyst for the next phase of Benton Harbor's economic development plan" (Harbor Shores 2013). This development planned for the creation of an estimated 230 direct jobs in the region. At the time of the announcement, Whirlpool employed 4000 individuals in a combined community of St. Joseph and Benton Harbor with 20,000 residents, and was growing.

An important component of that growth was its success in recruiting from a pool of top new talent that the company had set its sights on a decade before. The decision to invest in the economic development of Benton Harbor deeply shaped its approach to recruiting talent who want to share in this effort (Whirlpool 2015b). As Harbor Shores topped headlines with the positive stories of a lakefront with a purpose, Whirlpool Corporation was successful in recruiting a new generation of midlevel managers and executives to the region. Whirlpool was able to recruit top technical talent like MIT-educated Chief Information Officer for North America, Matt Meier, in 2016, who noted the "values and the place are an integral part of the opportunity for myself and my family. From its products to community, innovation is embraced here" (personal communication, June 29, 2016). Whirlpool joined companies like Google, Apple, Nike, and Proctor & Gamble in leading its industry sector in Fortune Magazine's list of Most Admired Companies for five consecutive years, from 2010 to 2015 (Whirlpool 2016f). The corporation found that it was attracting top talent in teams from marketing to engineering who valued the company's heritage and community values, and were eager to be a part of its social innovation efforts.

Perhaps most important to members of the community and these new employees of Whirlpool was the growing evidence of the company's local social impact. As part of its work with organizations like Habitat for Humanity, Whirlpool sought data measuring the efficacy of the community programs it was investing in. At its 100-year anniversary in 2011, Whirlpool produced a video celebrating the partnership with Habitat for Humanity, in which it highlighted important social outcomes for families helped by Habitat for Humanity, including greater stability for children, improved health, safety and security for families, and better educational and job prospects (Whirlpool 2011b). Whirlpool relies on its partners to measure social impact, such as research conducted with Wilder Research across 400 homeowners, where Habitat for Humanity pointed to measureable outcomes for improved quality of life for families in their new homes, including increased feelings of safety, improvements in respiratory-related health challenges, and improvements in children's school attendance and grades. Two-thirds of the homeowners said that they get along better with their families and 70 % spend more time with their families (Mattessich and Hansen 2015). The outcomes for families who were housed by Habitat for Humanity's new homes were intended not as a one-time donation, but as an attempt to break the cycle of poverty by working in partnership with low-income families in their community. This felt like something to build upon.

Reinventing a Company Through Social Impact

Having been personally drawn to the Benton Harbor/St. Joseph community by the company's story of the community transformation, Whirlpool managers, from the Vice President of Brand Marketing in North America, Bill Beck, to the Director of Global Reputation and Community Relations, Deb O'Connor, found that the story of Whirlpool's investment was incredibly powerful in their decisions to relocate their families to Michigan to join the company. However, it seemed that these values of the organization and the social impact work were largely unknown by customers. Whirlpool products were still caught in the "sea of sameness," where customers who viewed a Whirlpool brand advertisement would often confuse Whirlpool appliances with those of competitors, like Samsung and LG. Consumers saw little to distinguish one company's products from another. Appliance marketing had long been about product features and reviews—"cold metal" as Whirlpool Senior Brand Manager Jon Hall described it. In order to innovate in its marketing, products, and customer experience, Whirlpool looked to consumer research to more deeply understand consumers' needs.

Through market research, Whirlpool learned that even though most people recognized the corporate brand name, consumers didn't really know what Whirlpool stood for. Whirlpool brand's new managers and executives began a massive reexamination of the company, its brand, and its products, trying to uncover how to make a deeper connection to consumers. With insights from focus groups and interviews with existing and potential customers, Whirlpool embarked on a major shift of focus from marketing its products to meeting the needs of the customer.

Through its consumer research, Whirlpool came to understand more deeply the pressures on family life and heads of households, who were more time-pressed than ever in caring for their families. They heard from consumers about how much pressure families were under to live up to unreal standards. People talked about how the American Dream seemed to be more focused on status than on family, and consequently how rising expectations for the "perfect home" were actually undermining the role of family. With popular press attention from Annemarie Slaughter's article in *The Atlantic*, "Why Women Still Can't Have It All," to Sheryl Sandberg's *Lean In*, Whirlpool heard women leading households voice a struggle in running the new American family—torn between both career and family demands. In all of these conversations, appliances were not an explicit focus, but the care that is given through them was. Mothers and caretakers said that the pressure for a *perfect* home was coming at the expense of a *loving* home. They wanted to bring the human connection lost behind schedules, screens, and texts back into focus in day-to-day living. Consumers voiced that family care was the glue holding their modern families together.

Whirlpool's team learned that just like the value found in homeownership for families partnered with Habitat for Humanity, measureable value could be seen from families who eat meals together, and do chores together. In shifting its market research focus from the appliances to customers' use of the products, Whirlpool uncovered a number of salient studies about the importance of care:

- Conversation at a family dinner has a bigger impact on vocabulary and GPA than reading (Burns et al. 1999).
- Kids who eat a family dinner are 24 % more likely to eat healthy food and 12 % less likely to be overweight (Hammons and Fiese 2011).
- Lack of clean clothes to wear to school is a top contributor to school truancy (Baltimore Sun 2013).

To learn more about the consumer-focused use of their products for family care, Whirlpool teamed with Richard Rende, an Associate Professor of Psychiatry and Human Behavior at Brown University Medical School, to sponsor research studies that would better understand the value of family time together, and the long-term positive effects of chores (2015). Richard Rende's research looked at the value of household chores, those cleaning and cooking tasks that all families deal with, through a lens of outcomes from family care. Rende's research suggested the need to help caretakers and youth alike reframe their thinking about the role of chores, from the negative aspects of chores as a shared responsibility to an opportunity to express support for each other through care. The research pointed to some important benefits:

- Advanced academic performance in the early school years
- Increased school engagement and decreased truancy rates
- Better social relationships with peers in school
- Higher educational attainment in early adulthood

Reviewing this data drove a transformation within Whirlpool not only for the brand positioning from a product-centric to a customer-centric model, but also in the plans for new products and, indeed, the focus of the corporate strategy. Figure 1,

Fig. 1 Benefits of everyday chores and activities. Source: Whirlpool

which was developed as part of Whirlpool's new brand purpose campaign, illustrates positive outcomes of everyday family activities.

Out of this consumer research, Whirlpool came to realize that they could innovate through a brand purpose that shifted the conversation from cold metal to family care. Whirlpool outlined a strategy for the company, its products, and its marketing for championing the importance of chores as an intrinsic expression of family care in modern families, as diverse as they may be. Bill Beck offered this vision for the campaign: "The campaign is about people, real modern families, and the impact of the care they give and receive every day. It's about proving how often thankless tasks are so important—they are part of the emotional glue holding families together. It's a higher purpose that's driving our brand, and it's a natural space for Whirlpool, because we've been a part of these daily moments of care that have taken place in American homes for over 100 years" (Whirlpool 2014).

Finding a Purpose

With a vision to "become the best branded consumer products company in every home around the world," Whirlpool's marketing team was on the quest to change the way that people think and feel about Whirlpool by using the new insights on the challenges for the modern family. They set a goal for changing the experience its customers had with Whirlpool products—into one more in line with what they wanted for themselves and their families. Whirlpool paid close attention not only to consumer's impressions of its brand within appliances, but also to the increasing importance of a "brand purpose" to consumers overall. Whether reviewing studies from Cone Communications on the importance of purpose to Millennials, or a 2015 study by *Harvard Business Review* and Ernst and Young, data shows that companies with a strong sense of purpose are able to transform and innovate better, as well as improve employee satisfaction (Roderick 2016).

As part of defining its purpose in customer-focused terms, Whirlpool examined its long history of volunteerism and charity partnerships, including the 15-year relationship with Habitat for Humanity, and recognized that these social impact activities were seen as separate and isolated from the company's products and business. Whirlpool employees were logging more than 300,000 h of volunteer time, and the company had made in-kind donations of more than 165,000 appliances for houses built with Habitat for Humanity, but all of these activities were seen as something separate from the core business (Whirlpool 2015a, 2016f). In many ways, the foundation of the company had changed, but the brand hadn't caught up.

As Whirlpool's new branding team examined what made its company and brands unique, the story of the century-old company's reinvestment in its community in Michigan took on new relevance. Whirlpool had cared enough to reinvest in its local Michigan community and make a long-term commitment to the Benton Harbor headquarters. Perhaps the company's appliances could be helping customers meet their own personal and family commitments to care for each other. Whirlpool's marketing team was on the quest to change the way that people think and feel about Whirlpool through the insights on the needs of its customers, with the recognition that consumers were looking for ways to spend less time on chores, and more family time on the things that matter. Whirlpool articulates its brand purpose on its website as follows:

We exist to help families thrive.

Whirlpool has been an authority on family care for more than 100 years. In that time, we have seen the structure of the family change considerably. What hasn't changed is our belief that caring families are the foundation for a better world.

That's why we champion the importance of the care people give to their families day in and day out. We are inspired by this care and we are committed to helping keep things at home working smoothly. This way, people can focus on providing the best care for their families.Defining this brand purpose enabled the entire corporation to coalesce around the needs of consumers in a new way. It motivated Whirlpool to state on its homepage, "We are passionate people who create products and solutions that improve the lives of others" (2016b). With the goal of creating purposeful innovation, Whirlpool's team embraced its purpose in its reinvention of the brand, product innovations, and customer experience.

Reinvention of a Brand

Amidst a sea of sameness, appliances were being marketed through feature wars
between Whirlpool and its competitors, Samsung and LG, where images of the
pristine, perfect home constantly appeared. Despite increased media spending and a
brand built over 100 years, Whirlpool recognized through its languishing brand
metrics that it had no meaningful consumer connection. Understanding and highlighting *why* consumers were using the company's products—what those products
were helping them to achieve—could be a path to reconnecting with customers on
an innovative and deeper level.

Whirlpool created new advertising materials that highlighted realistic scenarios
of families under pressure, with caregivers who were surviving in the midst of various challenges, but not necessarily thriving. For decades, advertisements for appliances and cleaning products featured idyllic homes, pristine kitchens, and mostly
Caucasian families with two kids and a pet. The reality of messy kitchens, flustered
parents, burnt cookies, or family squabbles never appeared. Whirlpool's new ads
offered diverse families and family structures, with single dads packing lunches,
and career moms arriving just in time to pick up kids covered with sweat and dirt
from sports practices. Highlighting how appliances could make things easier was
just a small part of these scenarios—in some ads Whirlpool appliances were not
even mentioned explicitly.

With the backdrop of Johnny Cash singing "You Are My Sunshine," the campaign featured emotional scenes of family life, and spoke about how daily chores
could positively impact family members. They highlighted the care that parents
gave day in and day out, and the love that was shown through their busy schedules
and chores. And, they intimated the benefits of real care from the research that had
been uncovered. Spots that aired were repeated, re-tweeted, and shared more than
any campaign in appliance history. In assessing the outcomes of the campaign,
advertising critics marveled, "It turns out that warming up cold metal can work
wonders" (Neff 2015).

Whirlpool's sales grew by 6.6 % in the first 6 months after the campaign started,
compared to the same period in the prior year, which was four points greater than
the appliance industry as a whole (Neff 2015). Purchase intent scores also climbed
by 10 %, which was reflected in the annual sales growth of 12 %. The campaign
generated more than 120 million video views online in the first 6 months. In the way
a marketing organization measures impact, the brand experienced a jump in its Net-
Promoter-Score, and its social-media sentiment climbed more than six times its
prior level. But, the marketing team's commitment did not just look at purchase
intent and sales, but also to building the relationship of the brand with the consumers and potential customers.

For this long-term relationship building, the brand created a separate Every day,
care™ Project, featuring video diaries, published on the content site Upworthy,
about "sandwich generation families"—a caretaker who is providing both childcare
and elder care in his/her home. One particular video that got more than 2 million

views features the daughter of a Haitian immigrant living in New York with her son, partner, and mother, focused on her feeling that "she never was doing enough." With tears in her eyes, the mother watches the video recording of her mother and her son describing gratefully all that she does for them, in cooking, cleaning, and taking care of them. The diary was capped with the statement, "It's time we acknowledge the value of caring for the ones we love." These moving videos were created not to generate direct sales, but to communicate the values that Whirlpool stands for when it comes to family care.

This project was followed by a customer-generated content campaign, featured in Whirlpool's 60-s ad during the Grammy Awards aired in February 2016. The ad was the culmination of a contest where over 400 participants uploaded videos that featured singing the campaign's theme song, "You Are My Sunshine" and describing a caretaker who had made an impact in their lives. One customer's entry was featured in the Grammy ad, with her own rendition of the song and her own experience receiving care. The winner described her grandmother's care for her while growing up, and her ability now to recognize her granddaughter only when singing this song, as she is suffering from dementia. Not only the winning video, but also hundreds of submissions were shared by thousands of users across the globe.

This campaign reframing the Whirlpool's purpose as Every day, care™ had a strong impact in sales and brand sentiment, as the marketing team had hoped. Interestingly, the campaign and its driving purpose also resonated strongly with Whirlpool's internal product engineering teams and with external retailers as new products were launched in the market.

Purposeful Product Innovations

Inspired by Care as the Whirlpool brand purpose, product design teams started to reshape their conversations in product development away from features and functions to more human dimensions for how to make care easier, less time consuming, and more energy efficient. The design team embraced the tagline "Designed to Simplify," which moved the focus from "bells and whistles" in the design process to making chores simplified and more efficient. Through observational market research on families preparing meals and doing laundry in urban and suburban households at different socioeconomic levels, the Whirlpool product teams focused their innovations on creating "care-driven products" that worked more efficiently for families and were better for the environment.

One such new product was the CookCoach system: a Whirlpool wall oven that contains a digital thermometer, reducing cooking time and measuring food temperatures to alert the home chef to when everything is done. Another innovation came with the HybridCare Dryer that uses a ventless technology to allow families to install their laundry machines virtually anywhere, including tight spaces in smaller apartments and homes, and an Eco-Dry setting that uses 73 % less energy than traditional washer/dryer pairs to help families care for the planet and save on power bills (Whirlpool Brand 2016). Another product, Whirlpool's top load washer, received the top award at the 2016 Consumer Electronics Show as an example of "Tech for a Better World." This new Smart Top Load Washer was one of the first appliance brands to integrate to Amazon Dash Replenishment, so that families would not have to go out to purchase more detergent. Instead, the appliances estimate when detergent is running low and automatically order it from Amazon's replenishment service.

Another innovation that created a new path for shared caring is the Connect to Care feature, for the first time inviting interested consumers to share in and support Whirlpool's work with Habitat for Humanity while doing the laundry. With Connect to Care, families can opt in through a mobile application to make an automatic donation to Habitat for Humanity of 15, 25, or 50 cents with every wash cycle. For each load of wash, the charitable donation is made through Habitat for a family in need. Explained by Ben Artis, the Senior Category Manager for the Connected Home, "We've seen this trend for automated giving and one-for-one donations, but we really haven't seen that take place in the Smart Home. Whirlpool is excited and proud to be the first to recognize that the Smart Home gives us a new platform to extend that donation to those in need." Launched for the 2016 year, the total amount of customer donations during the year depends on the number of participants in the program and frequency and level of their donations, but Whirlpool has committed to a direct donation to Habitat of up to $100,000 in year one as a contribution to the program (Whirlpool 2016c).

These innovations have garnered Whirlpool more recognition than an appliance manufacturer is accustomed to receiving; for example, at the Consumer Electronics Show in 2016, where awards are given to products for outstanding design and engineering across 28 product categories, Whirlpool received an unprecedented nine awards for its appliances, including categories for Eco-Design and Sustainable Technologies. Over the past 2 years, Whirlpool has transformed its company to integrate its purpose in helping families through its product innovations, and tying their products to philanthropy for families in need.

Purpose-Driven Packaging

Mindful that a consumer's experience with a new product begins with the package, Whirlpool's packaging team looked for ways it could also listen to the consumer and create a deeper connection. The packaging team found three ways that it could embrace the brand purpose for families. The first and most obvious example was to ensure that recyclable cardboard was incorporated in the packaging, to minimize the impact on the environment. The two more subtle ways of rethinking appliance packaging materials considered how to reach the families receiving the new packages. First, through observational data, Whirlpool found that a vast number of its customers had children who wanted to take the big appliance box and invent an imaginary toy from it. Embracing the idea of the repurposing of the box for an imaginative toy,

Whirlpool began uploading videos and printing instructions for kids to create different kinds of vehicles, from cars to rockets, out of the huge appliance boxes. This Every day, care™ packaging embraced the whimsical wishes of families to reuse these big boxes for imaginary toys.

Second, Whirlpool created new, Post-Purchase Care Packages. With a note entitled Made with Care "from our family to yours" signed by the Whirlpool employees involved in making and shipping the appliance, the care packages included treats and goodies that can be used with the new appliances, themed to the product category. For example, a new microwave care package for "Family Movie Night" contains microwaveable popcorn, a coupon for free movie rental, a microwave cookbook, and the use and care guide with installation instructions. With this small packet, the ordinary packaging of the appliance manual was transformed into a tangible gesture of support for how customers use appliances in practice.

Purpose-Driven Community Outreach

Through its Every day, care™ initiatives, Whirlpool is emerging as an industry leader in the integration of its care-driven initiatives through every aspect of its business, from product design and packaging to purpose-driven employee volunteerism and to investing in the local community. For every new initiative, whether it is a product innovation, a new packaging, or a new community outreach program, the brand purpose drives the work, by championing the care people give to their families day in and day out. In the early days of the company, the idea of reinvesting in communities guided the company's philanthropy at a high level; now, with social impact as an integral component to its strategy, each new community initiative is evaluated based upon its brand purpose and the business objective.

Whirlpool's commitment to its purpose across the company is evident in its updates to the corporate website, which now includes a headline page entitled "What Matters to Us," alongside "Who We Are" and "Brands We Love." Within this topic of "What Matters to Us," Whirlpool includes topics and pages on purpose, innovation, social responsibility, environmental sustainability and diversity, and inclusion. Whirlpool's description of its purpose includes a video entitled "Moments that Matter" which describes a commitment to helping families not only save time, but also make the most of it. It relates the importance of product design with "people in mind" and illustrates its products serving families by making chores easier, but not by making them perfect.

Whirlpool describes its social responsibility today by saying (2016d):

> We strive to work with other organizations to create a better community, creating a 'collective' impact, first focusing on the social safety net to support the health and wellness needs of area residents, then helping to provide safe and affordable housing to best support youth and education development.

One of Whirlpool's latest social impact investments has grown directly from the Every day, care™ research in a new program called the Care counts™ initiative.

Through their market research, Whirlpool identified in 2014 that a leading cause for absenteeism and truancy for children in poverty is a lack of clean clothes to wear to school (Baltimore Sun 2013) (Banks 2000). In fact, one in five students struggle to maintain access to clean clothes (Whirlpool 2016a). Therefore, the access to clean clothes is a significant barrier to school attendance. A community member voiced an idea for Whirlpool to donate washing machines to schools, just as the company has donated washers and dryers homes in Habitat for Humanity. The goal was for these washers to curb excessive absenteeism by providing access to clean clothes.

In a pilot program during the 2015–2016 school year, Whirlpool worked with two school districts where truancy and poverty were high, one in St. Louis and the other in the central valley of California. Whirlpool's teams worked with the school districts in donating eight pairs of washers/dryers to each district, and allowed the school districts to design outreach to students. Early outcomes of this pilot point to significantly easing the burden on teachers who often pitch in by laundering clothes for their students at home, and improving overall attendance rates (Chelsey Lindstrom, personal communication, June 16, 2016). Upon the first year's completion, the outcomes included reducing the days absent from school by an average of almost 2 weeks per child over the course of the school year (Chelsey Lindstrom, personal communication, June 16, 2016). Students who missed an average of 8.8 days last year, missed only 2.7 days this year on average (Whirlpool 2016a).

As it begins its second year of the program, Whirlpool is partnering with more school districts and the nonprofit Teach for America to expand the program to school districts with similar poverty and truancy challenges across the country. As with any key innovation initiative, Whirlpool teams are engaged with researchers to measure the outcomes for the Care counts™ initiative, including improved attendance and educational outcomes. While the program is clear in the objective to help families by providing clean clothes to students in need, Whirlpool is also deliberate in measuring the role that this campaign has in amplifying the message of Every day, care™ toward elevating consumers' brand preference and purchase intent, in addition to the social outcomes.

Conclusion: Care at the Core of the Business

Whirlpool Corporation product innovations have been recognized with numerous awards, as well as consecutive awards from the Environmental Protection Agency for energy efficiency and the Human Rights Campaign's Corporate Equality index for commitment to diversity and inclusion. Whirlpool brand's marketing campaign for Every day, care™ has propelled it to tremendous success in the marketplace, where sales grew by 6.6 % in the first 6 months of the campaign. Whirlpool Corporation has seen sales grow by 8 % in 2014 and by 18 % in 2015 (Whirlpool 2016g). The community programs with partners like Habitat for Humanity and Care counts™ and the Every day, care™ initiatives in marketing, product innovations, and packaging have been purpose driven, and have fostered customer loyalty, employee enthusiasm, and brand affinity.

As a business, Whirlpool has clearly benefited from its transformation through social innovation to a consumer-focused, purpose-driven brand. From Whirlpool Corporation's five consecutive years at the top of Fortune's Most Admired Companies list for the industry to Whirlpool brand's sales growth and its nine product awards at the Consumer Electronics Show in 2016, Whirlpool is an example of a company that is "doing well by doing good." But adopting a strategy that puts care and innovation at the center of its business creates a higher expectation that Whirlpool will have positive social impact on all of its stakeholders, including its employees and its local community. As a reflection of this commitment to stakeholders, Whirlpool created a new headline on its corporate webpage "Who We Are," which reads: "The Bottom Line isn't our only priority."

In assessing the company's social impact, therefore, it is essential to consider the sustainable benefits Whirlpool Corporation's strategy is creating for employees, customers, nonprofit partners, and the local Benton Harbor community. One such measure for employees is their response to Whirlpool's annual Employee Engagement Survey, where employees have indicated an increased engagement in social impact activities, and the growing belief that the company is "a good company." It's too early to really know what level of social impact will result from brand efforts such as the Connect to care™ and Care counts™ programs, although the data from the first year pilot in two school districts is encouraging. With up to $5 million in product donations and 8000 employee volunteers continuing to contribute to Habitat for Humanity each year, the newest Connect to care™ investment of $100,000 to match customers in daily philanthropy is a small but important step. Whirlpool's long-term commitment to the Habitat for Humanity partnership over a 16-year span demonstrates the alignment of purpose in the two organizations, where the total value of Whirlpool's commitment to Habitat for Humanity is $90 million (Whirlpool 2016e).

When examining the local impact in Benton Harbor, there have been significant changes to the landscape of Benton Harbor since the time Whirlpool Corporation decided to stay. A nationally recognized golf course now encompasses the former Superfund site and areas where three million square feet of old buildings once stood, with lakefront beaches, healthy wetlands fed by Lake Michigan, and a marina and several new commercial and residential properties. Hundreds of new Benton Harbor homes were constructed in partnership with Habitat for Humanity and funding through a federal Hope VI grant and two new facilities have been built for the Boys and Girls Club of Benton Harbor. Jeff Fettig (2016) recently pointed out that "Whirlpool has invested almost $200 million in the last 8 years in our Southwest Michigan facilities, where we employ more than 4200 people." Willie Lark, a restaurant owner in Benton Harbor, noted in 2014, "The change I've seen is that Whirlpool has become a very important instrument in Benton Harbor's growth. They're continuing to build, add on and create high end jobs" (Echlin 2014). When it comes to jobs, the company has been working in partnership with nonprofit organizations like the Cornerstone Alliance to attract new businesses to the area, but the long-term job prospects remain to be seen.

So far, ambitious local employment goals have yet to be achieved. When construction of Harbor Shores began in 2007, Governor Granholm announced that Harbor Shores "will ultimately employ 2000 people, and by expanding the tax base, it will help increase funding for schools and for public safety" (2007). Reports in 2012 noted that only about 100 permanent jobs and hundreds of temporary 4–6-week jobs in service of the PGA event had been created, with an additional 230 jobs expected through Harbor Village (Smith 2012; Harbor Village 2013). Several new education initiatives have been funded, including programs with the Boys & Girls Club and the Benton Harbor Promise, founded in 2011 to allocate private donations to college scholarships for Benton Harbor students. Systemic improvements to the local educational system, however, remain elusive. Benton Harbor's school system as a whole operated at a $15 million deficit in 2015, serving a population of students where 88 % qualify for free or reduced lunch, and 8 % of high school students achieve proficiency in English on state exams and 0 % attain that level in math (Hickey 2015; U.S. News and World Report 2016). Marcus Muhammad, a former liaison for the Michigan Department of Education and now Mayor of Benton Harbor, points out that it may be years before Harbor Shores golf course reaches profitability, in order to provide surplus revenue back to the community. He concludes, "I like to be optimistic. That's good … But you also have to be realistic. They do give money to the Boys and Girls Club, but it has to be more" (Echlin 2014).

In the face of such long-term social needs, it is critical that the company commits to ongoing measurement, evaluation, and transparent reporting on its current and future social impact. Now that the social innovation initiatives have demonstrated real value to the Whirlpool brand, the next crucial stage is to gather data with their partners to ensure that the social innovations are making a significant impact on the long-term challenges they have undertaken. Harbor Shores, for example, was designed to bring "social change to Benton Harbor," according to promotional videos for the project (Walsh 2016). Scholars acknowledge that measuring large societal change like the one targeted for Benton Harbor is challenging, observing that measuring social transformation in a community requires understanding multiple actors and causal mechanisms, over a long time horizon (Hanna 2010). Whirlpool Corporation looks to its partner organizations like Habitat for Humanity and Teach for America for leadership in measuring the social impact of its initiatives, and can help a great deal in emphasizing the need for gathering data to measure long-term, systemic impact.

Whirlpool Corporation had always had a vision and mission regarding its success as a company and its community. Coupled with this vision and mission, the thrust of innovation drove the Whirlpool brand to think differently and innovate to find a "Brand Purpose." Whirlpool tied its new focus on the family and caregivers to its century-old heritage as a company working to improve lives at home. Most importantly, the brand purpose affects how they do business, not just how they advertise. Corporate social responsibility is not a check box, or a wrapper to their work—it is core to the strategy of the business. The focus on helping families has played an integral role in how Whirlpool designs products, models innovation, and recruits new talent. Whirlpool team members will tell you that from engineers to retailers, all appreciate the thought that what they do has deeper meaning. Nowhere is this more evident than among the managers and directors of Whirlpool Corporation who have relocated their families to Benton Harbor to join the company in the last 10 years.

Whirlpool's social impact work in Benton Harbor, from the Harbor Shores initiative and Habitat for Humanity, can be described in many ways: economic development investment, corporate social responsibility, philanthropy, and volunteering. Others have called it corporate self-interest or community gentrification. Whirlpool is acutely aware that the work of revitalizing Benton Harbor to reduce the cycles of poverty and create opportunity is far from done. Jeff Noel, Vice President of Communication and Public Relations at Whirlpool Corporation, emphasizes Whirlpool's role with community partners, businesses, nonprofits, and government: "When we've seen a spotlight on Benton Harbor and the socioeconomic challenges that created tension, they say Whirlpool should just fix it. We can't just fix everything, but we haven't shied away from the tension, and it has actually brought the community together and made it easier to get things accomplished" (Walsh 2016). Social impact innovations and programs by Whirlpool and its partners continue to grow. "Purpose-driven" is the way the new group of Whirlpool managers and directors describe their work.

"Our belief is that caring families are the foundation for a better world," says Bill Beck (personal communication, April 2016). Says Deb O'Connor, who runs Community Relations and is a resident in Harbor Shores: "I don't just agree with what we are doing, I am living it" (personal communication, June 2016).

References

Baltimore Sun (2013) The value of showing up. Baltimore Sun. http://articles.baltimoresun.com/2013-09-29/news/bs-ed-school-attendance-20130929_1_chronic-absenteeism-attendance-rates-middle-school. Accessed 30 June 2016

Banks S (2000) Without clean clothes, tough for kids to rise and shine. LA Times. http://articles.latimes.com/2000/mar/12/news/cl-7891. Accessed 30 June 2016

Benton Harbor (2010) City of Benton Harbor's brief. Documents from the State of Michigan Supreme Court. http://courts.mi.gov/Courts/MichiganSupremeCourt/Clerks/Oral-Arguments/Briefs/01-11/140685/140685-AppelleeBHSupp.pdf. Accessed 11 July 2016

Burns MS, Griffin P, Snow CE (1999) Starting out right: a guide to promoting children's reading success. National Academies Press, Washington, DC

Crowell C (2004) Jimmy Carter hammers at Michigan's affordable housing problem. Michigan Land Use Institute. http://www.mlui.org/mlui/news-views/articles-from-1995-to-2012.html?archive_id=428#.V1K9Eaurics. Accessed 30 June 2016

Draeger C (2008) Harbor Shores fight continues. South Bend Inquirer. http://articles.southbendtribune.com/2008-09-07/news/26903061_1_lawsuits-army-corps-golf. Accessed 30 June 2016

Dumke M (2008) Can Jack Nicklaus save Benton Harbor? Chicago Reader. http://www.chicagoreader.com/chicago/can-jack-nicklaus-save-benton-harbor/Content?oid=1109728. Accessed 30 June 2016

Echlin G (2014) Golf course revitalizes downtown Benton Harbor. WBUR. http://www.wbur.org/onlyagame/2014/05/24/benton-harbor-golf-course. Accessed 11 July 2016

Elsner D (1987) Whirlpool trying not to hang town out to dry. Chicago Tribune. http://articles. chicagotribune.com/1987-01-12/business/8701030963_1_whirlpool-upton-machine-washing. Accessed 15 July 2016

Fettig J (2016) CEO interview: Jeff M. Fettig. Price waterhouse Coopers. http://www.pwc.com/us/ en/ceo-survey/ceo-interviews/jeff-fettig-whirlpool.html. Accessed 11 July 2016

Governor's Benton Harbor Task Force (2003) Benton Harbor: a plan for positive change. https:// www.michigan.gov/documents/BH_final_report_76471_7.pdf. Accessed 30 June 2016

Granholm J (2007) Weekly radio address. http://www.michigan.gov/documents/gov/Radio_ Address_-_Harbor_Google_TEXT_5-18-07_197051_7.pdf. Accessed 11 July 2016

Habitat for Humanity (2015) Whirlpool Corporation and Habitat for Humanity renew 2015 partnership. http://www.habitat.org/newsroom/2015archive/8-24-15-Whirlpool. Accessed 30 June 2016

Hammons A, Fiese B (2011) Is frequency of shared family meals related to the nutritional health of children and adolescents? Pediatrics: AAP Publications, Issue 6

Hanna J (2010) The hard work of measuring social impact. Harvard Business Working Knowledge. http://hbswk.hbs.edu/item/the-hard-work-of-measuring-social-impact. Accessed 15 July 2016

Harbor Shores (2013) Harbor Shores, community partners launch $114 million Harbor Village Development. http://www.harborshoreslife.com/harbor-shores-community-partner.news. Accessed 30 June 2016

Harbor Shores (2016) Harbor Shores home page. http://www.harborshoreslife.com/home2016/. Accessed 11 July 2016

Hickey M (2015) Benton Harbor schools set to reduce deficit in 2015–2016. WNDU. http://www.wndu.com/home/headlines/Benton-Harbor-Schools-set-to-reduce-deficit-in-2015-2016-309966201.html. Accessed 11 July 2016

Mahler J (2011) Now that the factories are closed, it's tee time in Benton Harbor. NY Times Magazine. http://www.nytimes.com/2011/12/18/magazine/benton-harbor.html?_r=1. Accessed 30 June 2016

Maruca R (1994) The right way to go global. Harvard Business Review. https://hbr.org/1994/03/ the-right-way-to-go-global-an-interview-with-whirlpool-ceo-david-whitwam. Accessed 30 June 2016

Mattessich P, Hansen M (2015) Impacts of Habitat for Humanity homeownership. Wilder Research. Wilder Research, Saint Paul

Neff J (2015) Case study: how Whirlpool heated up sales by warming up 'cold metal'. http://adage. com/article/cmo-strategy/whirlpool-heated-sales-reframing-cold-metal/298882/. Accessed 30 June 2016

Parks B (2003) The garage that saved whirlpool's soul. Business 2.0. http://money.cnn.com/magazines/business2/business2_archive/2003/02/01/335987/. Accessed 30 June 2016

PGA (2012) Michigan debut. Senior PGA News. http://www.pga.com/seniorpga/2012/news/harbor_shores_022411.html. Accessed 30 June 2016

Rende R (2015) The developmental significance of chores, then and now. Child Adol Behav 31(1):1–7

Roderick L (2016) Why brand purpose requires more than just a snappy slogan. Marketing Week. https://www.marketingweek.com/2016/02/15/why-brands-must-prove-their-purpose-beyond-profit/. Accessed 30 June 2016

Smith L (2012) Poorest city in Michigan hosts Senior PGA Championship. http://michiganradio. org/post/poorest-city-michigan-hosts-senior-pga-championship#stream/0. Accessed 30 June 2016

Stevens L (2002) Groups focus on much more than race. Herald Palladium. http://www.heraldpalladium.com/localnews/groups-focus-on-much-more-than-race/article_31def7b4-7b86-5ef5-ac3b-5457484ea144.html. Accessed 15 July 2016

The Consortium for Community Development (2016) About us. https://bhcommunity.wordpress. com/about/. Accessed 30 June 2016

U.S. News and World Report (2016) Benton Harbor high school. http://www.usnews.com/education/best-high-schools/michigan/districts/benton-harbor-area-schools/benton-harbor-high-school-9729. Accessed 11 July 2016

Walsh D (2016) Whirlpool seeks socioeconomic balance in its two southwest Michigan homes. Crains Detroit. http://www.crainsdetroit.com/article/20160410/NEWS/160419986/whirlpool-seeks-socioeconomic-balance-in-its-2-southwest-michigan. Accessed 15 July 2016

Whirlpool (2011a) 100 years fact sheet. http://assets.whirlpoolcorp.com/wp-content/uploads/history_100years_factsheet.pdf. Accessed 15 July 2016

Whirlpool (2011b) Whirlpool and Habitat for Humanity: a brief overview. https://www.youtube.com/watch?v=fSZ10fiqOe4. Accessed 15 July 2016

Whirlpool (2014) Whirlpool Brand challenges industry marketing norms; champions the importance of daily tasks. http://investors.whirlpoolcorp.com/releasedetail.cfm?releaseid=875079. Accessed 15 July 2016

Whirlpool (2015a) Social responsibility. http://www.whirlpoolcorp.com/2015Annual/social-responsibility.html. Accessed 15 July 2016

Whirlpool (2015b) Whirlpool Corporation annual report 2015. http://files.shareholder.com/downloads/ABEA-5DXEK8/2333409188x0x879363/40D015BC-1873-46FD-BE50-88113B2751AA/Whirpool_2015AR.pdf. Accessed 30 June 2016

Whirlpool (2016a) Care Counts Research.

Whirlpool (2016b) Our company. http://www.whirlpoolcorp.com/our-company/. Accessed 30 June 2016

Whirlpool (2016c) Smart top-load washer. http://www.whirlpool.com/smart-appliances/smart-top-load-washer-dryer/. Accessed 15 July 2016

Whirlpool (2016d) Social responsibility. http://whirlpoolcorp.com/social-responsibility/. Accessed 15 July 2016

Whirlpool (2016e) Whirlpool Corporation and Habitat for Humanity renew 2016 partnership. http://www.whirlpoolcorp.com/whirlpool-corporation-and-habitat-for-humanity-renew-2016-partnership/. Accessed 11 July 2016

Whirlpool (2016f) Whirlpool Corporation named one of the world's most admired companies for fifth consecutive year. http://www.whirlpoolcorp.com/whirlpool-corporation-named-one-of--worlds-most-admired-companies-for-fifth-consecutive-year/. Accessed 11 July 2016

Whirlpool (2016g) Whirlpool Corporation reports record fourth quarter and full year 2015 results. http://www.prnewswire.com/news-releases/whirlpool-corporation-reports-record-fourth--quarter-and-full-year-2015-results-300211994.html. Accessed 30 June 2016

Whirlpool Brand (2016) Whirlpool Brand earns nine innovation awards at CES 2016. PRNewswire. http://www.prnewswire.com/news-releases/whirlpool-brand-earns-nine-innovation-awards-at-ces-2016-300198323.html. Accessed 30 June 2016

White House Office of Social Innovation and Civic Participation (2016) Our approach. https://www.whitehouse.gov/administration/eop/sicp. Accessed 30 June 2016

Whitwam D (2010) Joining the ongoing journey. The Consortium for Community Development. http://www.harborshoresdevelopment.org/images/stories/pdf/championsforchange.pdf. Accessed 30 June 2016

Embedding Environmental Advocates: EDF Climate Corps

Liz Delaney

Abstract Environmental Defense Fund (EDF), a nonprofit organization founded in 1967, combines policy, economics, and science to design market-based solutions to environmental problems in climate and energy, toxins and human health, oceans and fisheries, and ecosystems. In 2007, EDF had noted that while energy efficiency was widely understood as valuable, both as a business solution and as a climate solution, adoption rates among large corporations were surprisingly low. As a result, it began exploring potential solutions.

To accelerate corporate adoption of energy-efficient solutions, EDF designed Climate Corps, a program that places top-tier graduate students as Climate Corps fellows inside corporations. Over a 10–12-week summer, Climate Corps fellows design customized energy efficiency proposals for their host organizations with the business case for return on investment. Since the program's inception, fellows have identified $1.5 billion in potential energy cost savings, and 90 % of host organizations have implemented at least one recommendation from their Climate Corps fellows. Today, the EDF Climate Corps network consists of over 1000 people who work on a broad array of energy and sustainability issues. This successful partnership between EDF and large organizations produces value for the participants, supports EDF's climate agenda, and has created an effective cadre of engaged climate change professionals from its alumni.

Keywords Climate Corps fellows • Energy efficiency • Environmental Defense Fund • Corporate energy savings

Jump-Starting Large-Scale Energy Efficiency Projects

Energy efficiency has long been touted as a win for both business and the environment. Companies own, operate, or occupy large portfolios of buildings, such as office buildings, data centers, warehouses, and manufacturing spaces, and these

L. Delaney (✉)
Program Director, EDF Climate Corps, Environmental Defense Fund,
18 Tremont Street #850, Boston, MA 02108, USA
e-mail: ldelaney@edf.org

© Springer International Publishing Switzerland 2017
M.J. Cronin, T.C. Dearing (eds.), *Managing for Social Impact*,
Management for Professionals, DOI 10.1007/978-3-319-46021-5_7

buildings consume significant amounts of energy, typically from lighting, heat, and ventilation. It's estimated that US companies spend more than $200 billion dollars annually powering their commercial buildings (U.S. Department of Energy 2012). Buildings serve an important function in our economy, but they often consume energy inefficiently. The energy used to power these buildings comes primarily from burning fossil fuels, whose combustion generates powerful gases that significantly contribute to global climate change. In fact, more than 40 % of US greenhouse gas emissions come from powering commercial and industrial buildings (EPA 2015). The direct environmental benefit associated with improving the efficiency of these buildings is clear, with the additional economic benefit of saving money by using less.

Environmental Defense Fund (EDF), an environmental nonprofit organization founded in 1967, combines policy, economics, and science to design market-based solutions to environmental problems. EDF focuses its efforts on four main areas: climate and energy, toxins and human health, oceans and fisheries, and ecosystems. Across these four areas, a strategic approach to engaging companies in designing and implementing solutions has been a hallmark of the organization's work for the last 25 years. Due to this track record of designing market-based environmental solutions and its history of engaging corporations in environmental initiatives, EDF is uniquely positioned to drive progress in energy efficiency.

In 2007, EDF found itself asking, "If energy efficiency is such a clear business and climate solution, what would it take to get more companies doing it?" For many years the benefits of energy efficiency had been known, and while some organizations had started taking action, little substantial progress had been made. This point was made very clear in a report that consulting group McKinsey & Company published in December of that same year, called *Reducing Greenhouse Gas Emissions: How Much at What Cost?* (2007) The publication underscored the need to take action on climate change and provided an assessment of the cost-effectiveness of many different technological and operational improvements. In the report a (now well-known) cost abatement curve demonstrated that many cost-effective energy efficiency solutions remained unrealized and could dramatically contribute to climate change mitigation efforts, especially if companies acted fast.

The reality was (and continues to be) that despite being cost effective, the practice of implementing energy efficiency is fraught with internal organizational barriers. Primarily, companies find that they lack the time, resources, and expertise to devote their attention to these projects, which are often considered outside of core business interests. And since energy is a commodity that is consumed by everyone across an enterprise, ownership and coordination in managing reductions can be a big challenge. In addition, issues like split incentives (where the financial returns for an investment do not return to the investor), lack of up-front capital for investment, and untested technologies also interfere with the success of these initiatives. Fundamentally, there is a disconnect between the model of investment used for energy efficiency and the mentality of most companies: companies invest money so that they can generate new revenue, through products and services. Energy efficiency does not generate new revenue; instead, it allows companies to save on future operational costs, a distinction which can make it challenging to win financial approval.

Understanding that this was not a policy problem, but rather a people problem, EDF decided to focus on designing a remedy to address the barrier of lack of on-site expertise. It set out to design a program that offered technical expertise to companies that expressed an interest in energy efficiency projects. It soon became clear that providing expert hands-on help that could respond to specific enterprise conditions in an efficient and inexpensive way was a major challenge. EDF knew that companies faced similar barriers to implementing energy efficiency programs. However, they realized that the recommended solutions would need to be based on knowledge of corporate priorities and carefully tailored to each organization. EDF decided to create a model where trained environmental change agents were embedded *inside* organizations, working from the inside out to identify solutions and build the business case for investment in energy efficiency.

This insight became the model for the EDF Climate Corps program. Business students between their first and second years of graduate school generally look for internships to help them demonstrate their newly learned business skills. EDF decided that it would identify business graduate students with an interest in sustainability, train them in the basics of energy efficiency upgrades, and deploy them to leading companies for 10 to 12 weeks over the summer. While the students were working, they would identify equipment upgrades such as lighting, heating, and ventilation, and package them into investment proposals that they would then present to a company's executive team for approval. These students would "speak the language" of investors and effectively bridge the gap between engineers and facility staff and the finance departments of their host companies.

In the summer of 2008, EDF found seven dedicated and capable graduate students who were interested in changing the world. These students were in MBA programs in top universities and were willing to take on the challenge of building the business case for energy efficiency. EDF armed them with training on the latest technologies and cost-cutting efficiency measures, and over that first summer, those seven fellows worked side by side with their managers to uncover almost $35 million in potential cost savings (in net present value) through energy efficiency investments. What's more, when fully implemented, the projects identified would result in reductions of 57,000 metric tons of CO_2e per year, the equivalent of taking 12,000 passenger vehicles off the road.

The Climate Corps Model for Embedded Expertise

It appeared that through its Climate Corps program EDF had hit on a powerful means of overcoming corporate inertia around implementing energy efficiency projects. What's more, using graduate student interns made the model cost effective and reasonably scalable. Participating companies hire the fellows directly onto their payrolls. EDF recruits well-qualified students and provides technical support and training for the program, but it does not charge a fee to the corporations. Initial feedback from corporate participants attributed success to several factors: first, the graduate student fellows themselves. They were ambitious and motivated, but not advanced enough in their careers that they were afraid to ask basic questions, probe simple assumptions, and test out new ideas. The second key attribute of the program was its short length. While there was initial skepticism about what could truly be accomplished in just a summer, it turned out that this compressed time period actually resulted in extreme focus. EDF hypothesized that with a longer time period, fellows might actually become distracted by other opportunities, or scope a project that was too unwieldy. Finally, the third factor that appeared to have a significant impact was the co-location of the fellow with his or her supervisor. Unlike consultants who work externally with companies to design solutions, fellows were embedded *within* the companies, joining staff meetings, getting to know staff, understanding the corporate culture, and ultimately designing solutions that had a higher likelihood of implementation with measurable results.

Embedding students within companies has several advantages. Since energy use is dispersed across every business unit in a corporation, it can be hard for outsiders to identify all of the ways that use can be reduced. By being onsite, fellows can hunt down these opportunities, link them together, and often suggest ways for different departments to collaborate. The fact that fellows are students also gives them the excuse to ask simple questions and brings a fresh perspective to business operations that existing staff may have lost over time. Fellows are armed during their training with a set of recommended interview questions relevant to different departments such as procurement, finance, human resources, maintenance, and real estate. All of these departments play a role in affecting a company's energy spend. Finally, each company has a unique vocabulary and culture. By being onsite, fellows are able to observe that culture and instinctivity tailor their proposals accordingly. For example, at a sports company, a Climate Corps fellow may be able to translate energy savings into equivalent revenue from the number of sneakers sold. Or in a company with a low tolerance for risk, a fellow can focus his or her presentation on justifying how the recommended energy efficiency investments have been tested and will yield predictable results.

Scaling Up the EDF Climate Corps Program

Based on the positive feedback from companies and impressive results of its 2008 pilot, EDF decided to scale the program to keep up with the demand from corporate and organizational participants. Over the last 9 years, the EDF Climate Corps program has grown in size, and matured in its operational practices. From 7 spots in 2008 to 125 spots in 2016, the program engages approximately 100 organizations annually, and in 2014 expanded its operations to China. It found that students with a variety of educational backgrounds besides business were interested in the hands-on, sustainability-focused experience that the program provides, and in 2016 it drew over 900 applicants from business, policy, and engineering programs at almost 200 universities. In addition, EDF found that the energy efficiency challenges and solutions were not unique to just business, and expanded its Climate Corps program to engage large energy consumers in all three sectors, public, private, and nonprofit. Internally, EDF staff managing the program grew from 3 to 15, and EDF was able to streamline and codify its processes for efforts such as company and fellow recruitment, fellow training and technical support, and relationship management of its extensive network. Most importantly, the program broadened its focus to include a wider array of energy-related support and training, including high-level carbon reduction strategy, clean and renewable energy, and more. This allowed the program to continue to meet the needs of its partner companies and provide strong business value for a variety of organizations with varying levels of energy management maturity.

A critical aspect of managing the Climate Corps program is getting the right fellow assigned to each project. Since these fellows are placed inside organizations where they will work across multiple divisions and management levels, it's important that they fit into the culture, bring the right skill sets, and have a strong interest in the work the company does. The EDF Climate Corps project managers take time to get to know all of the host organizations, hear about the work they are doing, and explore what specific skill sets they are looking for from a Climate Corps fellow. Each student is carefully matched to a specific project and organization based on their interests, the requirements of the host organization, their skills and experience, and the judgement of EDF relationship managers who look out for things like personality and corporate culture. This careful process ensures that the fellow not only has the ability to complete the task at hand, but also a strong desire to be at that specific location, and a high probability of "fitting in." Host companies are often amazed at the ability of EDF to match fellows to their organizational needs.

While the specific energy projects that fellows work on have broadened and expanded over the years, most fellows still engage in a fairly predictable set of activities, such as meeting and interviewing relevant stakeholders, researching policies and practices, gathering and analyzing energy data, performing site visits and assessments, and interacting with vendors and technical experts. By working inside an organization, the fellow has access to the wide variety of individuals that will play a role either in moving a project forward or in blocking its implementation. Through face-to-face conversations, potential barriers are identified, and solution designs shift to balance different concerns. At the end of the 10–12-week assignment period, fellows often have the opportunity to present their findings to high-level executives and decision makers, with the goal of gaining approval for the implementation of priority energy efficiency and clean energy recommendations after their departure.

Over the years, Climate Corps has maintained a consistent approach to how it structures its fellowships. For example, it continues to use the short-term internship approach to encourage extreme focus, and has limited its recruitment efforts for fellows only to qualified graduate students. Despite its growing size, the program continues to train its entire annual cohort together, in-person, as the personal connections made during that training prove to be as valuable to the fellows as the technical content covered. EDF also devotes considerable time and resources to maintaining strong relationships with its host organizations, as this ensures that the fellow recommendations will be considered seriously and will have a higher probability of being implemented. EDF insists that each host organization designates a dedicated supervisor for the Climate Corps fellow. This supervisor is expected to be available throughout the summer placement to facilitate internal data gathering, set up meetings with key stakeholders, give the fellow regular guidance and feedback, and provide other key support.

All of these components come together to form what EDF believes is a remarkably effective program. EDF measures the success of its work using a broad array of impact metrics, reliant upon diverse data collection tools. As the program got its start in energy efficiency, the potential energy and cost savings from proposed energy efficiency projects, as well as their associated greenhouse gas reductions, remain core metrics. As more fellows have focused on renewable energy projects (which generate clean energy instead of reducing energy consumption), EDF has started to measure the proposed capacity of these new renewable installations, as well as the proposed investments in clean energy technologies. Through phone calls and surveys, EDF staff work to follow up on the Climate Corps recommendations and track which projects are ultimately implemented by each host organization. EDF additionally collects qualitative data on the impacts of strategic recommendations that fellows make in order to gauge the success of more research or data-focused projects.

An important ancillary goal of the Climate Corps program is to launch the sustainability careers of the young professionals who serve as fellows. Therefore, in addition to tracking the response of the host organizations to fellow proposals, EDF uses surveys and outreach to track how many of its fellows continue to work in energy- and sustainability-related fields once they have graduated. Since the program's launch in 2008, 65 % of the Climate Corps alumni fellows work on sustainability issues upon receiving their graduate degrees. As will be discussed later in the chapter, these alumni now form a powerful and active network of Climate Corps participants made up of over 1000 former Fellows, host supervisors, and technical partners.

Characteristics of the EDF Climate Corps Cohort

It's worth taking some time to understand who these fellows are, in order to understand how they can be so effective. The idea of accelerating progress through the work of graduate students may be met with initial skepticism by some companies, but that skepticism quickly dissipates when they meet their fellows. These students are remarkable in many ways: they are experienced, are highly intelligent, and have demonstrated leadership and accomplishment throughout their careers. They are determined to leverage their experiences in the program to demonstrate immediate business value, and this laser-like focus translates into high-quality energy projects.

Table 1 Core competencies of EDF Climate Corps fellows

Professional experience (minimum 1 year, average 4–5 years)	Passion for environmental sustainability/related career goals
Financial acumen	Energy-related coursework or experience
Demonstrated leadership capabilities	Project-specific skill sets (i.e., electrical engineering)
Current or recent graduate (<1 year) of a masters or PhD program	Positive professional recommendations
Advanced communication skills	Strong academic performance

Host organizations express excitement about the fellows' passion, their business acumen, and their willingness to roll up their sleeves and work.

EDF Climate Corps fellows have a wide range of skill sets and backgrounds, with a vital common interest in engaging in on-the-ground energy and sustainability work. The program screens its pool of over 900 applicants annually for basic core competencies, defined in Table 1. The program currently draws applications from over 200 degree programs, and its top graduate schools are Columbia, Yale, and Duke. Beyond defined core competencies, admission to the Climate Corps program requires several rounds of EDF interviews.

Climate Corps clearly draws a diverse set of fellow applicants, as well as host supervisors. As sustainability and energy management can be housed in many different parts of an organization, the people within companies that host fellows represent a wide variety of positions. Typically, fellows work under energy or sustainability managers, but the department that those managers sit in varies greatly. Fellows have worked within marketing teams, property management and real estate divisions, human resources, procurement, and even regulatory affairs. Which department a supervisor sits within is often irrelevant, as efficiency and renewables projects are inherently multi-stakeholder and involve facets of an entire organization.

EDF has seen over time that potential fellows are looking for this type of intensive hands-on experience when they apply to the program. Applicants are eager for the chance to dig into a sustainability challenge, manage a high-profile project relatively independently, and design a solution that works for a large, prominent organization. Fellows typically have a history of accomplishment prior to joining the program, and want to apply their skills and their newfound content knowledge from their graduate coursework and the EDF training sessions to energy and sustainability issues. Fellows who are career changers find this opportunity particularly attractive, as they haven't had a chance to engage "on the ground" in energy work, while fellows who have a background in energy may want to use their Climate Corps experience as a way to step up and demonstrate advanced, or broadened, management skills and capabilities. Regardless of the specific motivation, over 95 % of Climate Corps fellows to date have rated their experiences positively, and the same percentage credit the program with providing them valuable skills and experience applicable to their current careers.

While some fellowship placements lead directly into employment at the host organization, EDF Climate Corps does not guarantee its fellows employment after they graduate. In fact, organizational sustainability and energy management programs typically do not employ the large numbers of employees that other departments do, so fellows need to rely on a strong network of connections to identify career opportunities and interesting positions. Access to the EDF Climate Corps network of more than 1000 past fellows and hosts serves as a career resource for many applicants, who realize that the common experience they share with other fellows provides them with a strong jumping-off point for networking. EDF facilitates these longer term Climate Corps fellow connections through in-person events, meet-ups, and an online LinkedIn community, with EDF staff who focus on network development and support. Many fellows go on to have successful careers in large corporations, government agencies, utilities, clean tech start-ups, and renewable energy developers, and almost all report that they stay in touch with other members of the network.

Energy Savings and Strategies: Impact on the EDF Climate Corps Host Organizations

Since the launch of EDF Climate Corps in 2008, 400 organizations have taken on the challenge of improving their internal energy management practices by hiring a Climate Corps fellow, many hiring fellows year after year. As priorities change, each year's sustainability project may be different, even within the same organization. EDF works with each host organization to help define the Climate Corps fellow's summer project scope and to shape their onsite work plan. At the end of the summer project, the fellows make recommendations for energy efficiency and renewable energy solutions and describe the financial returns each project will deliver for their host.

Successful energy management inside of a large organization is a complex challenge, and relies upon a diverse set of resources, stakeholders, and tactics. In general, corporate program leaders are responsible for both energy efficiency and renewable energy components, both of which rely on heavy amounts of data collection and analysis. All parts of a business consume energy, making management of that consumption inherently multi-stakeholder, and by nature highly technical. Energy management begins with machinery, devices, and controls and spans all the way to legal permitting, accounting, and capital planning. To carry out their projects effectively, the Climate Corps fellows gain access to existing internal host data and gather even more data during the summer to come up with relevant energy efficiency recommendations and determine the likely cost and payback from implementation.

Table 2 Cumulative impact of the Climate Corps program on host organizations, 2008–2015

Cost savings identified ($)	$1,500,000,000
Potential CO_2e reductions (metric tons/year)	2,000,000
Generating capacity of renewable energy projects (MW)	30
Individual projects implemented (% of total projects recommended)	45 %
Percent of host organizations that implement at least one recommendation	90 %

To respect the confidentiality of internal resources and strategies that host organizations share as part of the program, EDF tracks and reports on the aggregated impact of fellows' recommendations rather than the outcomes and energy efficiency impact at an individual host organization. Table 2 summarizes the cumulative energy impact metrics of the recommendations made by Climate Corps Fellows between 2008 and 2015.

EDF staff members follow up with host companies a year after each fellowship to collect data about project implementation. They estimate that approximately half of all fellow projects are immediately implemented by host organizations, and the other half are either postponed or change enough that they can no longer be considered the direct result of a fellow's analysis. These are impressive outcomes, especially considering that the cost savings from energy projects and the scope of clean energy investment recommendations reflect only the specific recommendations made by Climate Corps fellows during their internships, and do not include more general organization-wide energy cost-reduction and sustainability programs. The implementation rate of projects proposed by Climate Corps fellows is on par or higher than most energy consultancies, and is a strong indicator of the high-quality work that fellows do. At the same time, EDF recognizes that organizations do not always follow up by implementing the recommended projects. There are a number of reasons that specific Climate Corps recommendations may not be implemented, and EDF carefully tracks these reasons. Most projects that do not move forward are hindered by three major factors: lack of capital for upfront investments, organizational discord (mergers, changing CEOs, etc.), and loss of the project champion (i.e., the primary staff person with whom a fellow worked leaves the organization). When surveyed immediately after a fellowship, 90 % of hosts indicate that they intend to implement fellowship recommendations, but it is clear that barriers to implementation still persist.

Two projects from 2015—Blue Shield and Iron Mountain—provide a sense of the sustainability goals of host organizations, how the Climate Corps fellows engage with these goals during their internship period, and the scope of total potential impact that host organizations would derive from implementing all of the Climate Corps recommendations.

Blue Shield of California

Blue Shield of California (Blue Shield), one of the leading health plans in California, hosted its first Climate Corps project in 2015 to support its overall sustainability and renewable energy strategy. EDF matched Blue Shield with Climate Corps fellow Radhika Kapoor, a master's student in International Policy Studies at Stanford University with a concentration in energy, environment, and natural resources and a professional background in corporate sustainability consulting in India. At Blue Shield, Kapoor was tasked with advising Blue Shield on internal and external sustainability targets while also assessing the business model for a solar power purchase agreement for Blue Shield's owned facilities in Lodi, Redding, and El Dorado Hills in California. In her role, Kapoor was also asked to assist with determining the business case and emission reduction potential for specific energy efficiency retrofits and behavior change interventions.

After baselining and benchmarking monthly energy consumption at 13 Blue Shield facilities and documenting all energy and water use in ENERGY STAR Portfolio Manager, Kapoor recommended a broad range of sustainability solutions, including the following:

1. Execute a solar Power Purchase Agreement (3.01 MW DC) at Blue Shield-owned facilities at El Dorado Hills, Lodi, and Redding.
2. Replace MR16 halogen lights with more efficient LEDs in Blue Shield's San Francisco headquarters.
3. Implement behavior change interventions in the form of a "Power Down" campaign encouraging employees to reduce their energy consumption.
4. Set a goal to achieve 30 % renewable energy and 30 % emission reductions by 2020, which would be achievable for Blue Shield if it implements the solar PPA.

Total Potential Impact for Blue Shield
Implementing all of the projects recommended by Kapoor would have a very significant sustainability impact, helping Blue Shield to reduce its carbon footprint and also lower its administrative expenses by reducing energy costs. Collectively, these interventions could help Blue Shield save close to $500,000 every year while reducing its electricity consumption by 4.8 million kWh and carbon footprint by more than 3000 metric tons of carbon dioxide in the first year alone. Overall, this would help Blue Shield reduce its emissions footprint by over 43 % from 2012 levels and increase its use of renewable energy by around 27 %. Over the lifetime of the proposed projects, Blue Shield could reap benefits of over $7 million in savings by implementing all of these sustainability interventions.

Iron Mountain

Iron Mountain, a leading storage and information management service company, had a different project in mind for its Climate Corps fellow—to help identify potential electricity-related opportunities at more than 600 facilities in North America. Iron Mountain had not yet quantified its overall electricity consumption patterns and had not fully evaluated which energy efficiency projects might provide the best return on investment.

EDF matched Jong Tae Park, a recent graduate of the Master of Environmental Management (MEM) program at the Yale School of Forestry and Environmental Studies. Park's summer priority was to gather and analyze energy data from the Iron Mountain facilities in Connecticut and to use this data to estimate the electricity consumption pattern of Iron Mountain's North American facilities by end uses. In addition, Park was charged with formulating possible energy efficiency solutions.

After analyzing the energy data gathered from Connecticut facilities, Park developed a model to quantify Iron Mountain consumption by end use. Then, he calibrated the results to estimate nationwide consumption patterns. Park determined that lighting upgrades, HVAC system control management, and office equipment power management presented the greatest cost-saving and energy efficiency opportunities. For lighting, he discovered that adjusting schedules and operational behaviors as well as reducing the number of light fixtures could help. Upgrading to LEDs in selected areas was expected to reduce energy consumption as well. Park found that the HVAC system could be optimized because the system did not respond to factors other than seasonality. Also, Park identified that a power management program for office equipment including PCs, monitors, and printers could increase efficiency.

Total Potential Impact for Iron Mountain
If implemented, all the projects Park identified could save Iron Mountain nearly $6.5 million annually, cut more than 58 million kWh of electricity per year, and avoid approximately 3500 metric tons of carbon dioxide emissions. At the end of his fellowship, Park presented his findings to senior facility program management. Iron Mountain incorporated Park's research into its energy planning for 2016.

Like Blue Shield and Iron Mountain, each host organization enters the Climate Corps program with general sustainability goals as well as specific projects that are tailored to the intensive but short-term summer internship program. And like Rapoor and Park, typical Climate Corps fellows will deliver a wide range of high-impact energy recommendations to their hosts, along with clear projections of implementation payback periods, lifetime energy savings, and sustainability impact. What varies is the readiness of the host organizations to implement all of the recommendations in any given year. Even if specific recommendations are not followed to the letter, the long-term sustainability benefits are likely to be significant. In some cases, the Climate Corps fellow becomes a catalyst for long-term changes in a host organization's approach to sustainability planning and implementation. The award-winning GreenENERGY Fund at the adidas Group is an outstanding example of the deep strategic impact that the Climate Corps program and its fellows can have.

The adidas GreenENERGY Fund was established in 2012 with a three-part goal of accelerating carbon reduction programs across the adidas Group brands, capturing and verifying energy and financial savings, and sharing best practices across all adidas global facilities. What stands out is that the internal fund is based on a venture capital investment model, the first of its kind for the footwear and apparel sector (adidas 2013).

According to a 2016 case study by RILA (Retail Industry Leaders Association), the GreenENERGY Fund was designed to overcome typical organizational barriers to making significant investments in energy efficiency and renewable energy projects including constraints on budgets and lack of sustainability expertise at specific company locations that would benefit from efficiency projects. Not coincidently, these are the same constraints that EDF Climate Corps was designed to address.

Elizabeth Turnbull Henry, now the adidas Group Senior Manager for Energy and the Environment, was a 2010 Climate Corps Fellow at adidas Group while earning a joint MBA and Masters of Environmental Management at Yale University. According to a recent Bloomberg article on the adidas venture model, during that summer as a Climate Corps fellow, Henry observed that adidas Group would benefit financially by increasing the funds available to energy efficiency projects. When she joined adidas full time after graduation, the pace picked up quickly. Henry was responsible for reducing energy consumption across the adidas Group's global facilities and 2700 stores worldwide. The GreenENERGY Fund became a fundamental tool for accomplishing that ambitious sustainability goal (Martin 2015).

As of 2016, the GreenENERGY Fund has invested $5.5 million in 49 adidas sustainability projects. In keeping with the venture framework, adidas tracks the rate of return on these investments as measured by its projected energy cost savings, with the benchmark being an average 20 % internal rate of return (IRR). A key advantage of the portfolio model is that adidas allows flexibility in achieving that IRR, so that higher cost savings from some energy efficiency projects can help to subsidize other efforts that have a significant carbon reduction impact but may have a lower rate of return. The current return rate is a robust 33 % across the project portfolio (RILA 2016).

In energy efficiency terms, over the lifetime of projects funded to date, adidas will avoid using 118 million kWh of energy. In summing up the multiple benefits of the venture portfolio model in the RILA case study, Doug Noonan, adidas Group Vice President of Corporate Real Estate, notes, "The GreenENERGY Fund has nicely accelerated the pace of investments in energy efficiency in our owned operations. It has also helped to normalize this idea that energy efficiency investments can be great business investments" (RILA 2016).

The Impact of a Growing EDF Climate Corps Network

While the results of the Climate Corps program have been measured for individuals and organizations the broader systemic impact has been apparent qualitatively. Perhaps the biggest demonstration of this is the formation of the powerful Climate Corps network. Now comprised of over 1000 past fellows, host supervisors, and technical partners, the network has evolved into a vibrant community of energy and sustainability practitioners who regularly engage with each other to share jobs, technical resources, advice, and connections. Network members find each other across the country, and across the world, as a large percentage of fellows are international students who then return to their home countries to embed sustainability within their economies. And each person carries with them their enduring connection to EDF, to the Climate Corps program, and to their fellow network members.

While EDF works to engage its entire network, of particular focus are the 700 alumni fellows who have completed the program. Since commitment to sustainability is a criterion for selection in the program, it is not surprising that many fellows dedicate themselves professionally to energy and environmental issues. Approximately 65 % have sustainability-related roles, and more than 80 % are active on energy and climate issues outside of work. Since the inception of the program in 2008, many of these "leaders of tomorrow" have effectively become the leaders of today, with nearly half of them holding managerial positions or higher in their organizations. They are employed in many of the places that are critical for energy transformation, such as clean tech companies, large corporations, utilities, and local and federal government.

Knowledge dissemination is one of the primary goals of the Climate Corps network. Each year, EDF brings together its current class of fellows, fellow alumni, host organization representatives, and other partners in a large event called the "Energy Solutions Exchange." This event focuses on sharing learnings and solutions generated through fellowships and from other like-minded organizations. Participants get to hear about cutting-edge technologies, management solutions, and policy updates, and, most importantly, they make face-to-face connections with other leaders who have a similar commitment to solving climate change. This is the flagship event of the year for the program, but it is accompanied by many regional events in key cities with large populations of network members, such as San Francisco, New York, and Boston. By promoting the sharing of best practices, in person and through documented case studies, this network can catalyze action in other organizations and inspire others to advance their energy management programs.

Fellow alumni are increasingly interested in collaborating with each other and with EDF. An alumni advisory board meets twice annually and is charged with activating alumni in specific regions, pulling together network members for political action, and creating topic-specific working groups. In addition, network members consistently look to each other for job connections and career advice. As EDF continues to grow and cultivate this network, it hopes to offer additional resources such as professional development courses and additional career support. Each network member shares the unique experience of having collaborated with EDF Climate Corps, and knows that they share an interest in and commitment towards environmental issues. Even those who go on to more mainstream business positions consider themselves agents of change and can drive progress and impact. By connecting, empowering, and inspiring this network, EDF hopes to drive even more action towards energy transition.

EDF is now dedicating additional time and resources to supporting the EDF Climate Corps network. From utilities to government to corporations, fellows graduate from their degree programs and go on to work in important and influential places in the energy value chain, and host organization contacts continue to work in sustainability to drive change. EDF sees the cultivation of this network of current and future leaders as an opportunity to support allies for climate change in their careers, and hopes to continue to support them as they drive change from the inside out of their own respective organizations.

What Next?

Over the past several years, a large, global energy transition has started, which has opened doors for companies to go far beyond standard energy efficiency. This has allowed the Climate Corps program to change and evolve significantly, and has both deepened and broadened the work that fellows do. EDF Climate Corps began as a summer fellowship program focused on catalyzing investment in energy efficiency. Today, it has evolved into a large and vibrant network that inspires, connects, and empowers energy leaders as it supports a transition to a low-carbon economy.

While it may be hard to see, the global electricity system is undergoing a massive transition from centralized, fossil fuel-based generation to an increasingly mixed set of generation sources, both centralized and distributed, which include renewable sources such as wind, solar, and hydropower. What is driving this change? There are a variety of societal, technological, and economic factors, from governmental commitments to mitigate climate change, to public support of renewable energy, and to the proliferation of cloud computing. In addition, over the last few years, the costs of renewable energy have decreased precipitously, making clean energy not only socially desirable, but, in many places, also economically feasible. This means that the USA's century-old electric grid will be able to, and will need to, modernize.

The modernization of the electricity grid will fundamentally change the way that it operates. For example, large amounts of distributed energy resources, like solar panels and batteries, make a one-way directional flow of energy, from generator to user, a thing of the past. The grid, constructed to support centralized, fossil fuel-based generators, now has the potential to be outfitted with sensors, monitors, and controls, and balances large amounts of renewable electricity supply and demand in completely new ways. What this means for large organizations, like those who participate in EDF Climate Corps, is that their buildings, once straightforward "takers" in a one-way grid, could have a new and unanticipated role to play. For example, rooftop space can be used to host solar panels, building equipment can store energy, and onsite batteries can be used to control grid electricity frequency.

Companies are now faced with an unprecedented opportunity to engage, influence, and adapt to this evolving electric grid, and go far beyond basic energy efficiency measures. To meet demand, EDF Climate Corps has broadened the work that it does to help support companies in all stages of energy management, from those who are starting out doing basic energy efficiency projects to advanced companies who are developing long-term renewable energy procurement strategies or constructing campus microgrids. Fellows bring to the table the same fresh perspective they have in the past, but are applying their focus to a much wider range of projects. There are many levels of barriers to the implementation of this transformation, and having change agents embedded and doing work at all levels will be critical to sustain this longer term transformation. EDF sees a future where fellows continue to evolve, grow, and expand their project work to continue to support companies as they seek to meet the challenge of deeply decarbonizing their operations. What's clear is that businesses and other large enterprises need to go further, faster, if the catastrophic effects of climate change are to be avoided.

What's also clear is that no one individual is going to solve the challenges presented by climate change. The task is too great, and the solutions are too complex. However, groups of committed, smart, and driven individuals all around the world can make a difference, especially when they are empowered to work together. The EDF Climate Corps network is one of many powerful associations that brings together talented, ambitious, and dedicated professionals and unleashes their impact. As the EDF Climate Corps program gets closer to its tenth year, it looks forward to accelerating the pace of change in the energy sector through the development, deployment, and dissemination of advanced energy solutions.

References

adidas (2013) Green energy fund: key facts. http://blog.adidas-group.com/wp-content/uploads/2013/04/adidas-Group-Green-energy-Fund-Fact-sheet.pdf. Accessed 28 June 2016

Environmental Protection Agency (2015) Inventory of U.S. greenhouse gas and sinks: 1990-2013. https://www3.epa.gov/climatechange/pdfs/usinventoryreport/US-GHG-Inventory-2015-Main--Text.pdf. Accessed 28 June 2016

Martin C (2015) The greening of adidas. Bloomberg. http://www.bloomberg.com/news/articles/2016-05-05/adidas-saving-money-by-treating-energy-costs-like-vc-investments. Accessed 28 June 2016

McKinsey (2007) Reducing US greenhouse gas emissions: how much at what cost? http://www.mckinsey.com/business-functions/sustainability-and-resource-productivity/our-insights/reducing-us-greenhouse-gas-emissions. Accessed 28 June 2016

RILA (2016) adidas Group—venture capital energy fund. http://www.rila.org/sustainability/RetailEnergyManagementProgram/Documents/adidas%20IM%20-%20greenENERGY%20fund.pdf. Accessed 28 June 2016

U.S. Department of Energy (2012) Commercial building energy alliance. http://apps1.eere.energy.gov/buildings/publications/pdfs/alliances/cbea_annual_report_2012.pdf. Accessed 28 June 2016

Stakeholder Voices Shaping Community Engagement at b.good

Allison Kroner

Abstract What happens when a restaurant decides to share its brand with its customers in the quest for social impact? b.good, a "fast-casual" restaurant head-quartered in Boston, MA, decided to find out. Using four methods of customer-led engagement—the Burger Brigade, the b.good Family Foundation, Community Partners, and in-store fund-raisers—b.good has fostered deep community engagement through a wide variety of activities all identified and led by customers.

b.good offers its brand, its restaurants, food, and some resources, including burger suits, to a hearty band who run the Boston Marathon every year and to its customers as they identify social causes and nonprofit organizations they would like to support. The customers do the rest. Over the years, this has led to a customer-centered corporate foundation, a partnership with the Boston Athletic Association, which organizes the Boston Marathon, systematic food donations to local nonprofit organizations, and a host of other initiatives. As b.good expands its footprint, however, its approach to customer-led social impact priorities presents challenges. This chapter concludes with questions about the implications of b.good's innovative community engagement strategy for future demands on staff time and capacity, business focus, and creating deep, sustainable social impact.

Keywords Burgerman • Customer-driven impact • Community partnerships • Brand purpose

Inviting Our Customers In

Since its founding in 2004, b.good has always wanted the communities we're in to be better for us being there. To us, this means giving to the communities around our restaurants in a way that's meaningful and impactful for those

A. Kroner (✉)
b.good, 131 Dartmouth St, Boston, MA 02116, USA
e-mail: allie@bgood.com

© Springer International Publishing Switzerland 2017
M.J. Cronin, T.C. Dearing (eds.), *Managing for Social Impact*,
Management for Professionals, DOI 10.1007/978-3-319-46021-5_8

particular communities. But, how does a business, especially one that's grown big enough to expand beyond the geographical roots of its founders, stay connected to each of the communities in which we establish ourselves? The b.good solution has been to invite our customers into our restaurants, and, indeed, into our brand itself. b.good customers can take over the brand and define for themselves what matters. That becomes what matters to b.good, too. We do this as often as possible, not only to ensure that we're including a wide variety of customers, but also to keep a constant connection with the communities that host our restaurants. We have found that this approach brings both unexpected innovations and challenges.

b.good

b.good is a Boston-based, fast-casual restaurant focused on healthy, farm-to-table fare with stores in the USA, Canada, and Switzerland. Founded by two best friends, Jon and Anthony, who loved fast food but hated the way it made them feel, b.good is dedicated to making and serving "real food." To b.good this means food made by people, not factories. It also means showing customers how the food is made, what's in it, and where it comes from by sharing the stories of the real people who produce, raise, and then cook the food served in the restaurants.

Since the beginning, b.good founders wanted the business to be something that made communities better because it was there. As part of this work, the b.good Family Foundation was founded in 2013, with the mission of using micro-grants to help inspired individuals improve their communities. As of June 2016, the b.good family foundation has given out over $105,000 to 25 community projects through its grant program.

While b.good's corporate philanthropy mission is to give to communities in ways that the community members define as meaningful and impactful, as a for-profit company, ultimately these initiatives must be good for the bottom line. This happens either when the community outreach efforts are in some way revenue generating or self-sustaining, or when they take the place of traditional marketing efforts and generate similar levels of brand awareness. By inviting customers in to help b.good define what matters, the company believes that it can not only give back in a way that is meaningful to communities, but also differentiate itself from competitors in an increasingly crowded "healthy fast food" market. It can drive home the message that b.good is an extension of family and community.

Engaging in Sustainable Impact by "Taking Over the Brand"

Different customers always order different things off the menu. Engaging them in sustainable impact then means giving them a menu of choices. Over the years, customers have reached out to b.good for help in reaching community-minded goals. They helped b.good to identify and establish four recurring opportunities for customers to "take over the brand": the Burger Brigade, the b.good Family Foundation, Community Partners, and in-store fund-raisers. Customers choose the way that is most meaningful to them, and b.good remains open to creating new methods of engagement as opportunities arise.

The Burger Brigade

In the spring of 2009, a b.good customer responded to a marketing e-mail to ask if the company would help him reach a fund-raising goal. He was running the Boston Marathon to raise money for a local charity, and he vowed to run the marathon wearing a burger suit with b.good's logo on it if the company would help him raise money. b.good said yes immediately—who would turn down the chance for your name to be seen by millions of runners and spectators in the world's most beloved marathon? A local sewing shop made the burger suit, but as the marathon drew nearer, the customer backed out.

Not wanting to let the suit go to waste, b.good reached back out to customers in the next regular marketing e-mail and asked if anyone else would be interested in wearing the suit. Someone was, and a customer wore the suit from Hopkinton to Boston as part of his work fund-raising for the American Liver Foundation. A Harvard student also running the marathon saw the runner in the burger suit and reached out to the company to ask if he could wear it the next year. He had been fund-raising on his own but felt that, to date, he had only middling results. He wanted to use the suit and the partnership with b.good to raise more money than he had been able to do on his own.

The customer, Sam Novey, raised $15,000 for Citizen Schools—a Boston-based extended learning program—that next year, $14,000 more than the year before. Sam talked about the burger suit giving him "permission to ask," its silliness making it easier for him to approach strangers to talk about the cause he was fund-raising for than if he were dressed normally. In the suit, Sam adopted a new persona, calling himself "Burgerman." Already a savvy campaign organizer and user of social media, Sam made goofy Burgerman YouTube videos to promote his cause and drive donations. He garnered attention, support, and press mentions.

Burgerman Sam wore his burger suit proudly, the red "b.good" label clearly visible on the front as he introduced himself to the 30 people who assembled for his 2-mile training run. It was part of a weekly series he hosted to promote his quest to raise $100,000 for Citizens Schools, a Boston-based, nationwide program for extended learning time. Donning the persona of "Burgerman," Sam told the group that he was passionate about three things—burgers, running, and education—but that he needed their help to be able to reach his goal of bringing the Citizens Schools program to 20 new classrooms. For their participation in the run, and ideally a donation or two, the runners would receive a free burger from b.good afterwards, a perk that came along with Sam's partnership with the local restaurant.

A junior at Harvard, Sam had fund-raised for local organizations in his previous 2 years of marathon running, but found that his efforts didn't get him very far, raising on average about $1000 each year. He needed access to more people, and more resources to inspire others to participate in his cause. This year, with the resources of a local restaurant behind him and the Burgerman persona attracting press interest, Sam was confident that he could do big things for his favorite cause. He set a bold target of $100,000 for year one, the amount needed to bring those 20 classrooms on line.

In that first year, Sam raised $15,000 for Citizens Schools. While 15 times higher than his previous annual fund-raising total, this fell far short of his ambitious goal. The press he received led the Game Show Network to ask to buy the name "Burgerman," which Sam readily agreed to in exchange for a $5000 donation to Citizens Schools. This was a lucky break, but not a replicable strategy, and activating supporters proved more difficult than anticipated. His weekly training runs, while enjoyable community building experiences, required a lot of work. To encourage attendance, each run had a musical guest and a guest of honor, like a local city councilor, a Harvard professor, or the school's field hockey team, but the bulk of the average 20–40 attendees at each run were people already in Sam's network. What's more, the runs didn't activate a significant number of donations.

Throughout the course of year one as Burgerman, Sam had enlisted his friends to join him on runs and at other events, and throughout the winter and spring three of his friends decided to run the marathon with him the next year as "fries," all of which included b.good's name and logo. Inspired by the somewhat natural formation of a burger-themed marathon team, Sam made a deliberate effort to recruit a larger group in year two. Calling them *The Burger Brigade*, Sam believed that the increase in team members would lead to an increase in connections and eventually donations for the cause they chose. While he had fallen short of the $100,000 target in year one, Sam hoped to make a much bigger impact as part of a team in year two.

Sam's efforts either drew upon b.good's existing networks or brought new people to the store, as with the short "training runs" he held, starting at the b.good store near his campus, and ending there with free food for the runners. b.good provided Sam with resources he simply could not obtain on his own—from restaurant space to free food, to connections, and to customers. In turn, Sam was able to amplify his efforts to raise money for a cause about which he cared deeply. Without needing to hire anyone, or make a direct donation, b.good helped spur positive change in a community, garnered positive press mentions, and interacted with both existing and new customers in the context of supporting a local nonprofit organization. Opening up the brand and allowing Sam to harness it for his own cause did something good for b.good and for the community.

In 2011, Sam expanded the Burgerman concept to encompass an entire group of students excited about combining fitness, raising money for a good cause, and being a part of something unusual. b.good embraced these additional participants. Several new suits later, the Burger Brigade was formed. From 2011 to 2013, the Burger Brigade passed the leadership mantle from one student to the next, from one year to the next—always a student at one of the Boston-area colleges—first Harvard University, then Berklee College of Music, and then Northeastern University. Each year, the leader would identify a participant who wanted to step up, and would hand leadership over after the marathon. The group was largely self-organized and required very little oversight from b.good employees. As with Burgerman's first year, b.good provided suits, t-shirts, free food for fund-raising events, and the use of restaurants and the company's smoothie truck whenever possible. Beyond that, the Burger Brigade did all its own legwork. They held fun runs starting and ending at b.good restaurants and hosted "truck battles" where b.good's smoothie truck would compete against a Ben & Jerry's ice cream truck to garner the most donations in return for free desserts. They created public spectacles by running through the streets of downtown Boston in burger suits, stopping for spontaneous exercise circuits, and then asking friends and strangers alike for donations for their chosen cause.

As with Sam's first year as Burgerman, b.good's resources and platform empowered the students to reach a wider audience and raise more money than they likely would have been able to on their own, resulting in a bigger impact for the community overall and a source of pride for the company. For b.good, this was a marketing "no-brainer." Volunteers did the hard work, organizing organically, and events didn't require much extra staff time or resources beyond occasional free food and costumes. Furthermore, every interaction a customer or potential customer had with the Burger Brigade linked b.good to community outreach and a healthy lifestyle—two values the company cares about deeply.

In 2013, the cause shifted once more as Burger Brigade members decided that they wanted to form a foundation to give the money they raised in increments throughout the year. The team was beginning to raise enough in annual donations that they felt they could reasonably support more than one organization. In addition, because most of the money was being crowd funded through their networks and b.good's customer networks, they wanted a mechanism through which they could engage the public in deciding where the donations should go. As a result, customers drove the founding of the b.good Family Foundation. For b.good, the formation of a charitable foundation bearing its name came much sooner than the business would likely have chosen without customer involvement, and served to differentiate the company from other similarly sized competitors as an organization that took its charitable giving seriously.

That same year, the Boston Marathon bombing happened, forever altering the way the city prepared for and responded to the marathon. While previous Burger Brigade participants had snuck on to the course at the start without official bibs (a frowned-upon, but common occurrence at the time) and run the race in burger suits, the 2014 Burger Brigade couldn't do either. Instead, b.good partnered with the marathon's organizer, the Boston Athletic Association (BAA), to provide free food for the BAA's suite of other races—a 5K run, a 10K run, and a half marathon—in exchange for six official Boston Marathon bibs for the Burger Brigade.

The formation of the 501(c)(3) foundation and the switch to official bibs represented a professionalization of the Burger Brigade. What was once a spontaneous, customer-organized celebration of community and fitness transformed into something requiring more oversight and organization from b.good. This new approach also increased costs for b.good significantly. In addition, with only six bibs, the Brigade had fewer runners raising money, and it became more difficult to justify selecting Burger Brigade members based on cherished qualities such as enthusiasm and leadership ability. While runners were still allowed to set their own fund-raising targets, the emphasis on fund-raising changed the nature of the events the Burger Brigade prioritized. Spontaneous, fluid events such as the training runs in burger suits and exercise circuits downtown were replaced with more structured counterparts that required tickets and b.good staff time. In addition, Brigade members relied more heavily on their own networks of family and friends to provide support the way many other traditional charity runners often do. The Burger Brigade continued in this modified form through 2016, raising between $19,000 and $32,000 each year for the b.good Family Foundation. b.good continued to support the Brigade with in-kind donations of burger suits, food, gift cards, restaurant space, and event supplies, but also ramped up its own commitment, dedicating more staff time to fundraising events.

The Burger Brigade continues to be a differentiator for b.good. They raise the majority of the funds given away by the b.good Family Foundation each year; to date, b.good has not made its own monetary contribution. They also continue to be effective ambassadors for the spirit of the b.good brand. They generate unique marketing content and connection points with customers. As the foundation expands and fund-raising needs grow, however, the Brigade and their events will require increasing oversight, and the marathon will create increasing pressure to select runners based on fund-raising ability. Though it started out as a low-cost, customer-driven community effort, expansion of the business may require that b.good rethink the purpose of the Burger Brigade and how to fund the b.good Family Foundation going forward.

b.good Family Foundation Grantmaking

The Burger Brigade is not the only opportunity b.good has to turn the brand over to customers. Events held by the b.good Family Foundation and the grant program itself provide new opportunities to connect with customers, some of which truly hand the brand over, and some of which provide a new avenue for customers to interact with the restaurant on b.good's terms.

The foundation uses micro-grants to fund local leaders with ideas for improving their communities. These grants are meant to spur civic engagement, allow b.good to serve as a generous neighbor, and keep the entrepreneurial spirit of the early Burger Brigade alive. As noted earlier, without the Burger Brigade, b.good might have been years away from corporate philanthropy. There are risks to starting a foundation, however. With that 501(c)(3), b.good took on more responsibility, setting an expectation with customers and community members alike that the company would bring the same level of community investment everywhere it goes. This means that as b.good grows, so must the reach of the foundation.

Currently, the foundation's funding and grantmaking strategies center on co-creation with customers. That means, while the foundation is largely funded by the efforts of the Burger Brigade, b.good holds additional fund-raising events to which customers can contribute. These include a spring gala—a tongue-in-cheek, "high-end" dinner put on by b.good's chef in one of the local stores—a summer-time outdoor BBQ in downtown Boston, and a holiday calendar sale. Customers are invited to purchase event tickets or calendars, thus engaging with b.good and its food in a new way. Nevertheless, the customers don't take over the brand with these events.

With that money raised, however, the customer takes the lead again. Customers have true leadership during the grant application and winner selection processes. In principle, the b.good Family Foundation micro-grant applicants are customers. b.good advertises grants through e-mails, on Facebook, and through other nonprofit listserves in Boston. The board of the foundation reviews grant submissions, and selects three finalists, and then those three finalists are put out for a vote. Anyone can vote, but the foundation targets members of its listserves and those of the finalists.

b.good empowers customers by offering them a chance to win a grant and by voting for who gets the money. While great for our communities, b.good also gets marketing content focused on positive, community-minded projects, and the non-profits up for a vote promote b.good to their networks. While the model offers a win-win, it also offers two levels of potential challenge. First, there is no way to ensure that grant applicants are actual customers. Second, b.good can't guarantee that the voting process really engages b.good's customers. Are people thinking hard about grant submissions, experiencing their votes as a joint investment in the community? When people do vote, is it because being a b.good customer means something special to them, or, instead, because the finalists mean something to them and asked them to do it? If it's the latter, the selection of a winner is less an expression of the interests of b.good's customers than it is a contest to see which nonprofit can do a better job getting out the vote. How can b.good design this voting process to truly engage customers so that the causes b.good supports are truly reflective of the will of our customers?

The biggest challenge of all, however, is maintaining these various customer touch points—donating, applying, and funding—as the business and thus the foundation scale. As of publication, b.good is in nine states and in Canada, but grants are concentrated in Greater Boston. Without expanding staff to host events in other markets, requiring Burger Brigade members to reach lofty fund-raising goals, or funding the foundation from b.good as a direct corporate gift, the foundation's ability to give grants will be outpaced by business growth. Furthermore, if this issue is addressed and somehow b.good does have funding, the current voting system will be hard to scale, simply because customers would likely start to tune out b.good's requests to vote if they came more than five or six times per year.

Community Partners

b.good regularly invites customers to seize the brand through two other devices: the Community Partners program and customer-hosted, in-store fund-raisers.

The Community Partners program was another innovation born of an inspired customer, a teacher. When she won free food for a year through a corporate promotion, she asked to donate it to a school. b.good did just that. It was an incredible experience for the school and b.good employees, while giving b.good a great story to tell. The teacher kept in touch, and reached back out when she moved to a new school, asking if b.good would come to visit. This request came at the same time that b.good was launching its mobile application and rewards program, designed to give customers gifts of free food in response to reaching certain visit numbers. Customers could redeem the food themselves, or share their credits with a friend. Inspired by the teacher, and wanting to find a sustainable way for b.good to give to the school, the company added a third "donate" option that enabled Boston-area customers to donate their credits to this local school. When the donations reached a certain threshold, b.good would return to the school to take over the cafeteria for the day. This model expanded as b.good expanded, and now whenever b.good enters a new market the company picks a new community partner.

The goal of the Community Partners program has evolved to allow b.good to connect with local organizations in various markets and tie visits to b.good with a chance to support a well-loved community organization. With customers driving donations that would have otherwise been redeemed in store, b.good not only gets to strengthen its reputation as a company that cares about local communities, but also gets to do so in a way that requires limited additional spending.

The tension that arises with this program is that donating food sporadically isn't necessarily impactful for the partner organization. While b.good lets customers drive the donations and the choice community partners can even be inspired by customers, taking over a school cafeteria for a day doesn't have a significant impact on the ability of its kids to access fresh food regularly, for example. Finding a way to make these community partnerships more impactful would likely require investment above and beyond the food donated by customers, which could make a currently sustainable program less so.

In-Store Fund-Raisers

One of the reasons the Burger Brigade model works so well is b.good's ability to offer stores and food as resources for customers to "do good" themselves. In addition to turning over the restaurant for Burger Brigade and Foundation events, b.good offers the restaurant to customers to fund-raise for their own causes. Customers pick a 2-h time slot on Sunday, Monday, or Tuesday nights, and promote the dinner to their network, and then b.good donates 15 % of sales from those 2 h.

While these fund-raising nights are not a unique concept in the fast-casual space, b.good donates 15 % of all sales during a given fund-raising window to the chosen nonprofit, not just the sales of people who identify themselves with the fund-raiser. This ensures that b.good can support the nonprofit by pulling from a bigger pool of transactions, and also gives b.good staff a chance to connect with all customers in the store during the fund-raising window to thank them for helping give to the community. In addition, these fund-raisers are a chance to invite b.good customers to become brand evangelists as they try to drive traffic to the store on the night of their fund-raiser. Finally, these fund-raisers on average increase transaction counts by 70 % and sales by 88 % on typically slow nights, covering the amount of the donation to the nonprofit with increased revenue. With regard to impact on the community however, this program is also limited. Even during an incredibly busy night, with a ceiling of 15 % of sales, the maximum donation is still fairly limited, with the average donation coming in at $173.

Open Questions

While b.good has been thrilled with the impact of its customer-in-control approach, it comes with its own challenges. In particular, the experience has raised four significant strategic questions. First, how does b.good ensure that its giving is also good for its bottom line? Second, these community initiatives market easily and virally. How does that balance against the need to market the company's main product, its food? Third, not all customers are Sam Novey. As the company grows, how can b.good reliably identify the right customers to whom to turn over the brand? Fourth, simply put, how does b.good measure the impact?

Finding the answer to each of these questions is complicated by the operating challenges corporate growth poses. With the Burger Brigade, what would be lost and gained if b.good stopped relying on this model as the main source of funding for the foundation? If the Brigade can't scale with the business, where should the foundation's funding come from?

With the b.good Family Foundation grants, if the goal is to give micro-grants in every community that has a store, how does the voting model scale without exhausting the voters? With fund-raising nights, how can b.good give customer hosts a mega-phone that reaches beyond the doors of the store? And in all these cases, even if b.good solves the problems, are hundreds of small donations in communities really worthwhile beyond the benefit to the brand? What's the aspiration for impact, and how does the company get there?

Conclusion

This is a story in progress. b.good can't answer all these questions yet. Two things are certain, however. First, customers will have to help provide the answers, just as they have led the way at every stage so far. Second, b.good cares about its brand, but a strong brand that doesn't serve communities doesn't meet b.good's corporate values. The foundation, customer passions, and community engagement must scale with the business. The food is the point, but the company is dedicated to nourishing not only its customers, but also the places they live.

Part IV
Public–Private Partnerships to Make Cities More Livable for All

Co-Creating More Livable Cities

Ben Hecht

Abstract Cities are the hubs of twenty-first-century humanity, with fast-growing populations and a disproportionate impact on the environment. The challenge for city leaders, urban community groups, residents, and other stakeholders is figuring out how to house, employ, transport, educate, and ensure access to opportunities for these growing populations. Innovations in city management, service provision, and use of technology are part of the solution. Even innovative cities, however, can still end up working better for some of their residents than others.

Living Cities brings together the world's leading financial institutions and foundations to provide loans, grants, and technical support for more than 100 cities across the USA with a focus on creating opportunities for low-income people, especially people of color. The Integration Initiative (TII), launched by Living Cities in 2010, offers cities financial and strategic planning support to tackle their most pressing social issues. This chapter looks at how Living Cities pursues its work, particularly through TII, and the experiences of two cities engaged in the initiative—Baltimore, MD, and New Orleans, LA. Key lessons include a shared definition of success, distributed leadership among collaborators, harnessing all types of capital, and practicing collaboration until it is the "new normal." The chapter concludes with a brief description of Living Cities' latest initiative, the City Accelerator, which is designed to determine if municipal innovation can be sustained effectively over time.

Keywords Living Cities • The Integration Initiative (TII) • One table • City Accelerator • Urban innovation • New Urban Mechanics

Why Cities Matter

Cities are the hubs of twenty-first-century humanity. They are where the majority of the world's people live, where aspiring US families go to get their piece of the American Dream, and where a rising generation looks for community, work, and prosperity. How well cities work for all of their residents is vitally important.

B. Hecht (✉)
Living Cities, 1040 Avenue of the Americas, New York, NY 10018, USA
e-mail: bhecht@livingcities.org

© Springer International Publishing Switzerland 2017   157
M.J. Cronin, T.C. Dearing (eds.), *Managing for Social Impact*,
Management for Professionals, DOI 10.1007/978-3-319-46021-5_9

Today, nearly two-thirds of America's population lives in cities (Cohen et al. 2015)—ahead of a global trend that, according to the United Nations, will put 66 % of the planet's population in cities by 2050 (United Nations 2014). Indeed, the population density in urban areas in the USA is 46 times higher than outside of them (Cohen 2015). After the economic crisis of 2007, migration to US cities grew at a rapid pace, reversing a long-established trend of people moving to suburbs and exurbs (Frey 2015a). While that new pattern has leveled off generally, more than half of the country's largest cities continue to see population growth (Frey 2015b).

The challenge for city leaders, urban community groups, residents, and other stakeholders is figuring out how to house, employ, transport, educate, and ensure access to opportunities for these growing populations. This task has grown more complex and urgent as the rates of poverty and inequality in cities have increased along with their populations. Around the world, large cities are more unequal than their host countries on average (Royal Economic Society 2014). That is true in the USA as well. From 2000 to 2014, the middle class shrank in more than 200 American metropolitan areas (Kochhar et al. 2016). In turn, metropolitan area inequality is up overall since 2007 (Berube and Holmes 2016).

Ironically, inequality itself is unequally distributed. The growth in urbanization has been accompanied by a growth in what's now known as "income segregation." That means that people increasingly live in neighborhoods or communities with others in similar income brackets—sharing the same access to resources, tax bases, schools and parks, and other amenities. Income segregation has grown rapidly in the urban USA, but "particularly in the last decade and particularly among black and Hispanic families" (Bischoff and Reardon 2013). Indeed, urban segregation can have significant impact on residents' futures. For example, the upward mobility of both white and African-American families is lower in predominantly African-American areas of the country than in predominantly white areas (Chetty et al. 2014).

The problems preventing cities from being sources of prosperity for all their residents are increasingly complex and interconnected. Leaders and organizations in cities across the globe are acknowledging that even their best individual efforts can't stack up against that complexity. Despite good intentions, the myriad of intellectual, financial, and technological resources that cities can bring to bear for their residents still miss entire neighborhoods and income brackets. Diverse groups of local leaders—private, public, philanthropic, and nonprofit—express increasing frustration with the dysfunction around them, and seek new ways to collaborate, learn from each other and their citizens, target the latest technological and social innovations most effectively to resident needs, and create integrated, sustainable communities.

This chapter describes the work of Living Cities, a New York, NY, based nonprofit with a 25-year history of bringing together the world's leading financial institutions and foundations to provide loans, grants, and technical support for more than 100 cities across the USA with a focus on creating opportunities for low-income people, especially people of color.[1] In 2010, Living Cities began deploying a long-term, multicity initiative, called The Integration Initiative (TII), designed to

---

[1]This chapter includes authorized reuse of materials originally written by the author for the Living Cities blog and other Living Cities publications.

accelerate both the pace and the scale of social change in urban America. The early results of that effort speak to both the urgent need and the complex challenges intrinsic in bringing together stakeholders across sectors to improve economic equality and livability for all US urban residents.

The Integration Initiative (TII): Vision, Implementation, and Evaluation

To kick off TII in 2010, Living Cities selected five cities—Baltimore, Cleveland, Detroit, Minneapolis-St Paul, and Newark—and offered them 3 years of financial and planning support to address some of their most pressing social issues. In exchange for this support, the participating cities agreed to adopt a collaborative framework that would incorporate innovative high-impact strategies into their work. TII established the following five goals:

1. **Improve the lives of low-income people in significant, measurable ways.**
2. **Create new "whole system" models of national significance.** Build the new relationships, models, and networks needed to ensure that civic, public, private, philanthropic, and nonprofit leaders and organizations can come together and solve problems from a whole system perspective.
3. **Alter regional dynamics.** Alter regional dynamics that are environmentally unsustainable and that have limited opportunities for low-income people and communities by isolating them from the larger city and region.
4. **Scale change by attracting and blending capital.** Demonstrate how multiple types of funding (grants, loans, PRIs, guarantees, equity) from multiple sources (federal, state, local, private, and philanthropic) can be structured and deployed to maximize impact.
5. **Sustain change by establishing "new normals" that will drive ongoing integration and accountability.** Create a "new normal" by permanently redirecting public and private sector funding streams away from obsolete approaches and applying them to these new solutions; setting new policy priorities and using data to track, ensure, and communicate accountability for results.

As noted in TII's 3-year evaluation, published in 2014 (Hecht):

The problems that these cities were targeting addressed many of the most seemingly intractable urban challenges, such as workforce readiness and jobs (Baltimore), economic development (Cleveland), urban revitalization (Detroit), equitable transit-oriented development (Minneapolis/St. Paul), and health (Newark).... Inherent in the design of TII was the belief that the current methods being used in cities to solve our most complex problems aren't working. Public, private, and philanthropic leadership and capital are not being fully harnessed, deployed, and aligned for maximum impact. TII was going to help us understand what the key elements of a new model of urban practice should be and the challenges and barriers to building it successfully.

The vision for catalyzing change, or "Building a New Urban Practice," in the five city partners was based on implementing the Living Cities' TII framework so that it could be tested, improved, and then replicated in other urban centers. An underlying tenet of TII was the importance of building a resilient, cross-sector civic infrastructure that could tackle the complex challenges facing cities and achieve large-scale results. An important principle of TII's cross-sector framework is referred to as cities creating "one table," where different levels of decision makers and stakeholders come together throughout the implementation process. Implementing this cross-sector civic infrastructure is a critical component of the TII model.

The formation of these "collaborative tables" alone was not enough to bring about the needed changes, however. As noted in TII's objectives, the framework also envisioned its participating cities as moving from consultative collaboration to a "new normal," which is, in essence, a multi-organizational change management process. These cross-sector partnerships, combined with targeted funding from Living Cities, were seen as a way to create openness to change among all TII participants—both in how they work as individual institutions and in how they work with each other to implement far-reaching social improvements.

The TII framework included a process for deploying significant private capital that could be dedicated to specific priorities identified by the cross-sector stakeholders in each city. Living Cities is unique as a philanthropic collaborative, comprised of both financial institutions and foundations and committed to innovating in ways that bring private capital to public purpose efforts. This structure allows Living Cities to leverage precious public and philanthropic dollars and to aggregate a meaningful amount of money for its urban partners. In keeping with that model, the TII program design called for between $10 and $15 million in commercial debt and $3 and $4 million in philanthropic capital to be made available to an approved local lender at each site. That element, of course, meant that there had to be a capable local borrower (such as a certified CDFI—Community Development Financial Institution) to which Living Cities could lend, that they would have experience in distributing loans to activities that promoted the site's programmatic priorities, and that they would be integrated as full partners in the site's collective impact table.

Finally, when launching TII, Living Cities was well aware that working across sectors and institutions towards a shared vision is not a natural act among decision makers in US cities. Once the stakeholders in each city came together through TII, the desired cross-sector collaboration needed to be managed. Hiring a dedicated staff member emerged as a critical component for keeping all the parties and activities moving forward effectively. In summary, "All of these factors aligned to support a TII culture of continuous improvement that encouraged participants to formulate hypotheses around what it would take to achieve the desired results and to experiment, measure and iterate toward what works" (Hecht 2014).

In keeping with Living Cities' commitment to sharing the lessons learned from TII as a foundation for continuous improvement, the organization worked with a third-party consultant, Mt. Auburn Associates, Inc., to conduct a formal evaluation of the outcomes of TII's first 3 years and to articulate insights for broadening the framework to additional cities in stage two. Mt. Auburn's "Three Year Evaluation

Report" (2014) acknowledges that, in keeping with the 10-year theory of change model adopted by Living Cities, the full impact of TII would not be clear for at least a decade after the launch of the framework (Siegel and Winey 2014).

But even though the long-term results of the initiative were not yet visible, some important lessons were already evident by the end of year three (Mt. Auburn Associates 2014):

> When Living Cities launched TII, it had very high expectations that the work would have a transformative effect not only on the five sites that were chosen, but also more broadly in the field. Many of the concepts that were the foundation of TII were relatively untested at that time. These included the importance of cross-sector collaboratives, reaching scale through going beyond projects and programs to changing systems, driving private capital to work on behalf of low-income people, and, finally, the importance of engaging the public sector and the private sector in a new way. That Living Cities wrapped all of these elements together through TII is an indication of the ambition and complexity of the work....
>
> How these changes are translating into improved outcomes for large numbers of low-income residents in each of the five sites will not be evident for a number of years. This is not a limitation of TII or the evaluation, merely a reflection of the realities of efforts such as TII that were designed with an understanding of complexity and an ambition around transformative change, not smaller scale programmatic outcomes.

Among other findings in its report, Mt. Auburn Associates highlighted slower than expected deployment of the commercial debt and philanthropic capital provided to the five participating cities through TII, in part because the form of the financing provided by Living Cities did not meet specific city needs and in part because of lack of collaborative cross-sector capacity in some cities to manage the capital. At the same time, the report noted that the blend of grants and financing capital did serve as an important lever to bring multiple stakeholders into the process. Among the challenges to progress, the report noted that competing local priorities, capacity deficiencies, changes in political leadership, and other factors contributed to "The struggle to identify large-scale results, understand the system challenges, and develop a strategic approach to addressing these challenges [that] was a gap in almost all of the sites" (Mt. Auburn Associates 2014). Such findings could be discouraging, but these and other issues that emerged during the evaluation were not stored up until the end of the project. Through real-time feedback from all the collaborative groups, the lessons learned were quickly integrated into a revised process and updates in the TII framework that were shared with the five original sites and used to inform TII stage two planning.

TII in Baltimore: Progress, Challenges, and Lessons Learned

Baltimore has been much in the news since the death of a resident of its Sandtown-Winchester neighborhood, Freddie Gray, while in police custody in April of 2015. A port city on the East Coast, it has a long history of industry, but also a reputation for segregation, crime, and poverty, as popularly depicted, for example, in the well-known HBO crime series "The Wire."

With a city population of 621,849 in 2014, Baltimore is part of one of the USA's bigger metro areas. In 2014, residents of Baltimore were 32 % white, 63 % African-American, and approximately 5 % Latino. The median household income was $41,819 and 62 % of the population was "in the labor force." 23 % of its residents were living in poverty (U.S. Census Bureau 2015a).

While the country may perceive deep inequality and racial segregation in Baltimore, the actual picture is more complicated. Baltimore does, indeed, demonstrate high levels of racial segregation in its urban neighborhoods. Further, African-American neighborhoods are disproportionately of low income. At the same time, according to the Brookings Institute, Baltimore "boasts a significant black middle class," and ranks second among 35 US metro areas in black median household income (Berube and McDearman 2015). Relative to some American cities, Baltimore is thriving, with the economic, social, and cultural building blocks for prosperity. It is, "by many measures—income levels, educational attainment and concentration of high wage industries … doing quite well" (Vey 2016).

Kurt Sommer, the Director of the Baltimore Integration Partnership (BIP), acknowledges both the city's relative advantages and its daunting economic challenges in a summary of the first 5 years of Baltimore's participation in TII, published on the Living Cities' website in January 2016:

> Baltimore is fortunate to have billions of dollars in active investment underway in water/sewer improvements, schools and redevelopment projects, as well as a very strong set of higher education and medical institutions (a.k.a. anchor institutions) that are the city's largest employers. Yet, we also have systemic economic challenges, poverty and hopelessness that came to a head last April in the uprising following the death of Freddie Gray. In order for Baltimore to make strong inroads into addressing the economic challenges, we need to do a better job of leveraging our assets and investments in new ways.

Baltimore elected to focus on workforce development and jobs as its cross-sector priorities within the TII framework. In describing BIP's positive accomplishments since its formation in 2011, Sommer notes (2016):

> We started new workforce activities and expanded existing efforts in central and east Baltimore. In addition, the BIP made investments in industry based training programs like deconstruction, pre-apprenticeship construction, biotechnology, culinary arts, healthcare and other fields. Through our partner The Reinvestment Fund (TRF), which expanded its lending operations into Baltimore as part of the Integration Initiative, debt financing has supported fifteen projects, leveraging $150 million in investment. Projects include Centre Theater, North Calvert Green and the Chesapeake Building as well as the Hebrew Orphan's Asylum and the Food Hub which are still pending. We set explicit expectations for borrowers, so that the funds were used to further racial equity and inclusion in our work. Borrowers of these funds worked towards local hiring and minority business contracting goals with workforce partners who provided job ready candidates. Over these first three years of work, partners and grantees provided workforce services for more than 1200 individuals, job training for over 500 and placed 800 into job opportunities in the development projects and beyond. Partners also helped move forward a range of new public policies and programs to sustain the goals of the initiative.

At the same time, the lessons from Baltimore underscore barriers to economic inclusion that extend beyond urban boundaries, including structural racism and educational shortcomings, poor transportation options for inner-city residents to reach potential jobs in the suburbs, and lack of coordination among state and regional development programs. Some of BIP's anchor partners, such as public universities, are not legally allowed to prioritize contracting with local Baltimore businesses or hiring inner-city residents, while state and local minority business certification programs turned out to be duplicative and nonreciprocal, adding to the difficulty of building economic inclusion into hiring practices. Such findings underscore the need for cross-sector partnerships, as well as explaining the sometimes frustratingly slow progress on TII initiatives. As Sommer concludes, "making inroads into Baltimore's deep socio-economic challenges is bigger than the individualized efforts of any one organization or government ... we must do things differently, build partnerships, and take risks ... If we don't open up new pathways for Baltimore residents and business, who will?" (2016).

TII Stage Two: Expanding to New Orleans and Other Urban Centers

TII set out to expand its reach in 2014. Living Cities considered 36 possible places, looking to identify local leaders who were committed to building a new type of urban practice focused on addressing inequality and disparate access to opportunity at a systems level. In September 2014, Albuquerque, New Orleans, San Antonio, San Francisco, and Seattle/King County were announced as participants in the second round of TII. Putting one of the insights from stage one to work (that cross-sector groups needed to spend time in planning how to implement the TII framework and deploy debt funding), this round kicked off with a $100,000 grant for a 1-year planning process, with the possibility of being invited to become fully participating sites and receive additional grants and loans. In addition, existing efforts in Baltimore, Minneapolis-St. Paul, and Newark were awarded additional funding for the next 3 years. Detroit opted out of second-stage participation.

One of the new TII participants, New Orleans, had developed a strong public image in the face of tragedy—in this case the disaster of Hurricane Katrina in 2005. More than a decade on, the city has recovered from the hurricane with mixed results. Just over half the size of Baltimore, in 2015 New Orleans had a population of 390,000. Its racial demography is similar to Baltimore's: 33 % white, 60 % African-American, and 5 % Latino. Twenty-seven percent of New Orleans' population lives in poverty, and 34 % has a bachelor's degree or higher—a little higher than in Baltimore. The median household income in the city was $36,964 in 2015 (U.S. Census Bureau 2015b).

In late summer 2015, the nation turned its attention again to New Orleans on the 10th anniversary of Hurricane Katrina. Countless news organizations and think tanks produced stories and reports on the state of the economy, income inequality, racial segregation, and the overall hurricane recovery. Several key themes emerged.

First, tourism has recovered in the wake of the disaster. According to data in *The Washington Post*, tourists brought nearly $7 billion into the city in 2014, ensuring 77,000 jobs (Ross 2015). Second, for parts of the community, the economy is booming. For example, housing prices have increased approximately 50 % since 2005 (Ragas 2015). Third, disparities by race have increased. According to the National Urban League, the black-white gap in median household income grew from about $26,000 in 2005 to about $35,000 in 2013 (Peters et al. 2015). Fourth, New Orleans is experiencing staggering income inequality. In 2014, it ranked fourth in income inequality among metro US areas according to American Community Survey Data (Berube and Holmes 2016). As with Baltimore, New Orleans is a growing city with a strengthening economy, but the city still works better for some of its residents than for others.

For its TII cross-sector collaboration, New Orleans chose the large-scale goal of increasing employment for African-American men. A 2014 study by Loyola University's Lindy Boggs Center for Community Literacy reported that 52 % of African-American working-age men in New Orleans did not have jobs (Sams-Abiodun 2013). Even though a number of the unemployed face seemingly few structural barriers to joining the workforce (e.g., they are not drug users, have adequate education and no criminal record) there's a need to connect them to additional workforce training or to provide a pathway to specific job opportunities. The city's Network for Economic Opportunity aims to bridge this gap through cross-sector collaboration, brining local training providers, social service agencies, the mayor's office, and prospective employers to "one table" to create career paths specifically into the health care and infrastructure fields for residents in New Orleans Claiborne Corridor.

In speaking about the early lessons learned through implementing the TII framework in New Orleans, Angela Taylor, program manager at the Network for Economic Opportunity, highlighted the need for balance between making progress on long-term systems changes in New Orleans with implementing more short-term programs (2015):

> There are two levels of change that we are working on; short-term, incremental changes that are more like a sprint and the systemic change that is more like a marathon. We need to interweave that ... so there's a skill required to manage both paths. The other big lesson is that this work is really hard and demands so much of you on a daily basis. But it's absolutely essential to take the time to assess our progress, the remaining challenges, and what we need to change. Another lesson that we constantly keep close is that we have to constantly revisit important data. We already knew what our large scale focus was, based on the incredible statistic that 52 % of the city's African-American men were not working—that's the big challenge we need to meet. But data is key to helping frame the reasons why all stakeholders, whether they are job seekers or providers need to be at the table. Establishing cross-sector tables is really hard work but it is absolutely necessary. If we don't get the right folks around the table, then we won't have long-term sustainable success. We're learning that incremental, programmatic changes are actually still very helpful strategies for us as we carve the path for the longer systems changes that we need. To keep all the stakeholders at the table, we need those shorter-term incremental wins at the programmatic level to keep the pulse alive, but always on the same path, not ever diverging from the longer-term goals which require systemic change.

Living Cities' Strategies for Scaling Collaborative Urban Change

The recurring themes of process evaluation and lessons learned are fundamental to TII and the philosophy of Living Cities. As summarized in the Living Cities' reflections on TII's first 3 years (Hecht 2014):

> Perhaps the most important lesson we learned as a national funder was that the more ambitious and disruptive you want your initiative to be, the more prominent the role of learning must be in it. We designed TII because we didn't believe that any one institution or sector knew the best ways to increase the pace and scale of change. If no one had the answers, then there had to be a premium put on real time mining and sharing of what was being learned.
>
> We instinctively knew that, but both our understanding of this work's importance and the level of activities required to support it increased over time. By creating a robust information sharing capability among the cities and a forum for teams from each city to come together with each other throughout the year, ideas quickly spread from place to place.

TII demonstrates every day that civic leaders in cities across the country are not waiting for Congress or their state houses to solve their problems for them. They are inventing new ways of working together, realigning resources to achieve better results and setting their cities on a fundamentally different course. Living Cities is committed not only to helping these cities to share their learning with each other, virtually and through biannual learning communities, but also to accelerating change in cities nationwide by disseminating real-world lessons learned in real time on the Living Cities' blog and other social media outlets.

While collaboration is certainly not a foreign concept, Living Cities has observed around the country the coming together of nontraditional partners, and a willingness to embrace new ways of working together. Here are four key elements that stand out from the ongoing assessment of Living Cities' efforts that are essential for achieving scale:

1. Success Must Be Clearly Defined, Shared, and Supported

As Dana O'Donovan of the Monitor Institute has noted (2012), many organizations find collaboration to be messy and time consuming. From the very beginning, one must develop clarity of purpose and articulate, "What can we do together that we could not do alone?" This often means thinking beyond individual projects to whole solutions and big, bold ideas. For example, Corridors of Opportunity, an initiative in the Minneapolis-St. Paul region, and part of the ongoing seven-city Integration Initiative (TII), has brought together a diverse group of policymakers, corporations, foundations, and community organizations to integrate efforts around transit planning and engineering, land use, affordable housing, workforce development, and economic development—all of which had been disconnected. Focusing on the region's growing transit system, the effort aims to accomplish what none of the groups could achieve on their own—expanding access to jobs and transit service for the region as a whole, with particular focus on unlocking employment opportunities for low-income people.

Through TII, Living Cities has also learned that success is unlikely to be achieved unless some type of "backbone function" keeps the group's work moving forward. This idea of a backbone "function" riffs off of Kania and Kramer's controversial *Collective Impact* article in the *Stanford Social Innovation Review* (2011). TII has demonstrated that it can be harmful to ask, expect, or invite one single organization to serve as the backbone. Staffing is essential to ensuring that work is completed between meetings, tracking data, enabling adaptation, disseminating knowledge, and building buy-in and ownership from all participants. Those staff need not be from one single organization. As Living Cities' partner, Strive Together, explains (Edmondson 2013):

> ... what is likely needed is a "backbone function" not a "backbone organization." This may simply sound like semantics, but it leads to a completely different way to approaching the staffing of collective impact work. This shift helps us to see that this work is not about a central power center that gets created in a traditional hierarchical paradigm, but instead is about a set of shared roles that need to be played as we look to connect the dots instead of recreate the wheel.

In facilitating creation of this backbone function, it is essential that some organization act as a neutral convener to help identify and organize the staffing roles to be played.

2. Strong and Distributed Leadership Is Paramount

Multi-sector partnerships require unique leadership traits and skills. One is the ability for individual leaders to transcend parochialism. Too often, individual organizations earmark their participation and resources for activities that perfectly align with their own work or they use the collaboration platform as a way to get other participants to fund their own priorities. While not foolproof, TII has demonstrated that senior-level participation can be an effective antidote to this problem. Senior leaders often have a "balcony view" of the core issue, understanding the needs of the field and the inherent limitations of their own organization's approach. For example, in the SF Hope initiative, a collaboration to battle poverty for the city's most vulnerable citizens, the Mayor of San Francisco, the CEO of the San Francisco Foundation, the Superintendent of the San Francisco public schools, the president of the Chamber of Commerce, and the publisher of the *San Francisco Business Times* are all active participants. They don't send lower level staff who may be unable to transcend politics and self-interest.

They also need adaptive leadership skills. Cross-sector leaders working towards shared outcomes quickly realize that not only is there no formula or roadmap to follow, but also that a comfort with complexity, ambiguity, and "fast failure" is essential to their success. This *adaptive leadership framework* acknowledges the realities of complex social problems by suspending the presumption that leaders already have the right answers while working instead towards solutions by being open to learning and rethinking prior assumptions. Although Living Cities introduced these concepts at the first learning community of TII, it soon became clear that 1 hour sessions on it every 6 months were not enough. TII now uses more training along with positive evaluations and reviews.

Finally, Living Cities found that it is essential to make the work a high priority of the local mayor or another appropriate public official. Public sector resources disproportionately fund many of the problems that these partnerships are working to solve and public officials have to be part of the solution. The higher level the official, the more resources and policy changes were committed. This was most evident in Minneapolis-St. Paul where the Chair of the Metropolitan Council (a regional government body appointed by the governor), two county supervisors, and four mayors served on the governance group. Newark also had strong public sector leadership with the Deputy Mayor cochairing the steering committee and another department head playing a significant role.

3. All Types of "Capital" Must Be Harnessed and Applied to the Effort

Engagement of private markets and capital is critical to sustainability and scale. This means supporting solutions that combine grants with debt to attract private sector money and bring mainstream market goods and services, such as grocery stores and financial services, to underserved people. Integrating capital strategies into larger systems change is not without its challenges, however.

One is the challenge of absorbing, or using, the capital. Even when Living Cities made loans available in TII, some cities had no institutions that could borrow and deploy the funds. Baltimore and Detroit brought in expertise and capacity; Newark created a new financial intermediary. TII spent a lot of time working to understand the problem better and to find ways to help cities innovate to overcome it.

Another challenge has to do with language. The different lexicons of grant makers and lenders at the table must be acknowledged and overcome. Generally, grant makers speak a language of the possible that is not constrained by rigorous underwriting criteria or the need to be paid back. Lenders speak a very different language that is focused on risk mitigation, loan-to-value ratios, and likelihood of payback at the end of the loan term—sometimes 10 years later. Often, that friction is exacerbated by two other factors: (1) neither has much experience working with the other, and (2) the lead time to deploy grants is much faster than the lead time required to identify lending opportunities and to underwrite and deploy loans. Virtually every site Living Cities worked with in the first stage of TII acknowledged the value of intentionally including both perspectives at the table but the pressure to simultaneously deploy capital was not always constructive. Ultimately, based on this learning, Living Cities created a "blended catalyst fund." The fund uses terms that allowed it to blend philanthropic and private capital in advance, so that when an investment opportunity arises, the terms already have been set, and the investment can just go forward.

Leveraging multi-sector partnerships presents unique challenges. However, the possibilities of transformational change that can be accomplished with a shared result, distributed leadership, and a blended capital approach are enormous.

4. Collaboration Must Become a "New Normal"

The formation of these collaborative tables alone is not going to bring about the desired result. Ultimately, behavior change is required. Essentially, TII has witnessed parties coming together and agreeing to what amounts to a multi-organizational change management process. These cross-sector partnerships define an ambitious set of expectations and commit to regular reflection, and create an openness to change in both how they work as individual institutions and how they work with each other. Living Cities often referred to this as creating a "new normal," where cross-sector leaders would agree on where they wanted to go and then align their priorities, activities, and existing resources towards those ends, and stay aligned for as long as it took to achieve them. Here are some lessons learned about the new normal.

The "tables" facilitated important qualitative changes among institutions and the direction of resources. Living Cities used the term "systems change" to capture the vision for the new normal outlined above. One powerful example of what that looks like came out of the work in Minneapolis-St. Paul. Their local effort, "Corridors of Opportunity" (COO), is an ambitious regional partnership cochaired by leaders from the McKnight Foundation and the Metropolitan Council and comprised of top leadership from state and local government, philanthropy, business interests, and key nonprofit organizations. COO was opportunistic, setting out to take advantage of the imminent build out of the regional transit system to improve access to opportunity and, in particular, to ensure that those with the greatest need benefited from that investment and its attendant housing and economic development.

Member organizations used the table to hold each other accountable to the vision—asking each other to present publically how they were making changes internally to support bigger picture, systems changes. In 2012, the Metropolitan Council directed $32 million to support multiple TOD projects in the region and created a $5 million annual TOD grant program, as well as a new five-person Transit-Oriented Development Office. MN Housing and the Cities of Minneapolis and Saint Paul all updated their Low-Income Housing Tax Credit application process to award more points for transit-accessible projects. The Saint Paul Foundation's involvement with COO and its focus on capital led it to create two new programs towards filling system gaps, using program-related investments (PRIs) and loan guarantees. One program, the Accelerator, is financing development projects on the eastern end of the Central Corridor and a new Job Creation Loan Fund is building the capacity of two financial intermediaries (NDC and MEDA) to lend to more midsize companies with greater potential for job creation.

These successes have led to a larger shift in local philanthropy's behavior as well. There is now greater utilization of geographic or issue-area-based funder collaboratives, which are pooling resources to drive towards a shared vision and outcomes (e.g., Central Corridor Funders Collaborative, Northside Funders Group, MSP Workforce Innovation Network).

What's happening here is a prerequisite to long-term change: building of trust, peer pressure, norm making, and changing of the status quo of critical institutions needed to make the shared vision a reality that is reflected in their decision making in areas from programmatic investments to staffing. While, in retrospect, every site had substantial realignment among participating parties, the use of the term "system change" from the outset likely did more harm than good. Since no site was working in one single "system," as they are commonly perceived, such as K-12 education, use of the term was confusing. When people talk about "systems," they are really referring to a set of actors and institutions whose collective practices, policies, and interactions produce a particular result. When defined this way, it is clear that change will not happen in a linear way, and that the change required might actually encompass multiple systems as they are commonly defined. Moreover, Living Cities underestimated how much more it could, and perhaps should have done to help the sites understand and define what "systems change" would mean in their individual contexts.

Urban Innovation, Data, and Citizen Engagement

Cities don't just house the vast majority of low-income people; they also spend billions of dollars annually on education, transportation, and social service supports to improve their quality of life ... with disappointing results. But that is changing. New, ambitious local leaders understand that cities and their resources can play an outsized role in improving the lives of low-income people—and are acting on it. They are focusing on creating a culture of innovation and using data and technology to measure results and reimagine the relationship with their citizens. In large part, municipal innovation is driven by the idea that better-run cities will not only be more effective in tackling poverty, inequality, education gap, and job creation, but also have more money to do so than many other actors. Cities, large and small, are creating innovation offices, like the Offices of New Urban Mechanics in Boston and Philadelphia; forming Innovation Teams, often spurred by support from Bloomberg Philanthropies; applying in large numbers for innovation prizes; and making municipal data available in ways that allow city residents to participate more creatively and actively in solving top-of-mind problems. Municipal innovation is undertaken with the assumption that if it is successful, it will go straight into effect, "intravenously." No annual fund-raising or advocacy is necessary. The innovation and related funding are displacing the old way that city governments did business.

Use of Technology

Innovative use of technology is a common thread through these programs, for example, the crowdsourcing of solutions and participatory budgeting. Technology presents perhaps one of the best tools for city innovators to help low-income citizens become more visible, empowered, and prosperous. By facilitating improved delivery of government services and increased access to opportunity, technology can offer tangible hope for the most disadvantaged. To date, most cities have not taken advantage of technology to reach low-income people. With their increased focus on innovation and civic tech, however, city governments are beginning to recognize the power of technology to improve broken systems and change lives.

Once a city commits to building the innovation infrastructure described above, it needs to explore how to use technology, plus the enormous amounts of civic data on hand, to address pressing problems affecting low-income people in their city. Living Cities' Civic Tech and Data Collaborative, which recently launched in St. Louis, MO, and Boston, MA, bring together civic "hackers," data practitioners, community groups, and government officials to those ends.

In St. Louis, the collaborative is working to make the local criminal justice system easier to navigate. The area's court system uses ticketing to fund municipal operations, a practice that disproportionately affects lower income black residents (U.S. Dept. of Justice Civil Rights Division 2015). The project aims to reduce the inconvenience for citizens to resolve tickets in order to prevent the failure to pay tickets from turning into more serious charges.

The initiative acknowledges the fact that low-income populations must commute and work longer hours in order to make ends meet, making appearing in court and visiting multiple offices to resolve tickets nearly impossible. Unlike most technology projects, it includes citizens in its redesign process. This seemingly simple online innovation could mean the difference between efficient ticket resolution and future incarceration.

Boston's team will streamline their process for placing young people in summer jobs. As the program is currently processed manually, using updated technology will connect thousands of more teens with employment opportunities. These teens will earn a paycheck and start on a meaningful career path, a key step for addressing the city's persistent economic inequalities. Data captured from the updated process will help the team better understand the program's clients and how to enhance the initiative over time.

In addition to these civic innovation programs, city governments are finding simple ways of incorporating technology into service delivery. San Francisco's Human Services Agency keeps people from getting thrown off of SNAP (formerly food stamps) enrollment rolls simply by reminding them to reapply via text message. In New Orleans, they're using social media to help those who signed up for health insurance to use it most effectively.

Technology's virtual nature can free it from socioeconomic and racial biases. Its lack of geographical boundaries and its color blindness can free the human imagination from the laws of physics, or the oftentimes more pervasive laws of society. It can transcend the modern urban theory about how people, places, and things have to interact.

Still, with all this optimism comes caution. The power of technology to do good is not inevitable. For example, robots have fundamentally changed the nature of work and not necessarily for the better. Maximum social benefit will only be realized if city governments champion technology's potential for low-income people. And without political will and capital to ensure that cities stay affordable and livable for all rungs of society, the positive benefits of technology will be limited.

Technological progress paired with making the process of innovation course of business has the power to turn smart cities into equitable cities—if we harness it effectively and responsibly. That is up to us. This century of cities may well be defined by how well we fuel the technology-led, innovation engine of cities for good.

Can the Innovation Stick?

Mayors, like Greg Fischer of Louisville, KY, are building a local government culture akin to that of a high-performing business, but also rooted in the value of compassion. In Nashville, TN, the city's innovation team partners with the Nashville Entrepreneur Center to train human service staff in leading innovation techniques. The participants in turn become ambassadors and skill builders within their departments. In Philadelphia, the city is experimenting with behavioral economics and human-centered design to boost the enrollment of senior citizens in taxpayer benefits with promising results. As these practices reach the core of government operations, the potential for impact is profound. With the burst of experimentation and activity in municipal innovation, Living Cities has asked, "Can it stick?" Can the energy and novelty of these new approaches survive a change in mayoral administration? If so, what can we learn about how these approaches were able to shift a culture in government that can often seem to have its own center of gravity?

City Accelerators

In 2015, Living Cities launched a City Accelerator initiative in partnership with the Citi Foundation and Cohort Lead, Nigel Jacob, from Boston' Mayor's Office of New Urban Mechanics, to answer the question about whether city innovation is sustainable over time. The City Accelerator began working with three cities— Louisville, Nashville, and Philadelphia—that had adopted robust innovation agendas, including two that would change mayoral terms in mid-cohort, to understand what it takes to make innovation "course of business." While the City Accelerator will be evaluated in depth over time, three principles have already emerged:

1. **Build a System**

In many ways, Louisville proved the adage, "from many, one." They had a number of different approaches to innovation which sat in different places, related but largely disconnected. Through the City Accelerator, they've built a sophisticated infrastructure for soliciting and vetting innovative ideas, with a pipeline of more than 50 projects from across multiple agencies, and a staff of 14 that is not only working inside government but now beginning to look outward into the community, and invite external stakeholders to propose innovative ideas and projects that align with the city's strategic plan. They helped people see innovation as more than a series of isolated transactions and brought a discipline and rigor to how change happens, so it can happen over and over again.

2. Create a Staff Culture of Innovation

Much of Nashville's work focused on the individual government employee's role in innovation. Their work revealed that many government employees hold great, potentially innovative ideas in their heads, but rarely have the space and time to think and process these ideas. Nashville has made significant strides in changing the culture of city government, fostering an environment where every employee is given the agency and cover to bring new ideas to the table, and is allowed to fail if that's where the innovation leads. It's a very different and powerful concept. Five months into a new mayor—a former council member—there are promising signs that this culture, and the mechanisms in place to make it stick, will be critical elements of the future.

3. Bake Innovation into Individual Departments

The City of Brotherly Love is focusing on improving how one department better serves low-income residents. Already, the Philadelphia Department of Revenue has shown the value of employing various outside-the-box approaches, like "nudges," to drive a specific outcome—in this case, to increase benefits enrollment by any innovative means is necessary. Successful experiments are rapidly prototyped across all of their work. A dedicated, cross-functional team inside the city department is instituting the principles of lean or agile development by engaging staff at all levels in the department. Encouragingly, the new mayor has selected an advocate for this approach from the former administration to be his new Managing Director.

In many ways, the Living Cities' City Accelerator sites have collectively sketched a blueprint for making innovation the regular course of a local government's business: systematize, empower staff, and intentionally embed it in critical departments. Clearly, the work of municipal innovation is easier said than done. Yet, with so many local leaders committed to working differently, cities really may be on the cusp of something revolutionary across the nation.

Conclusion

Leaders and organizations are acknowledging that even their best individual efforts can't stack up against today's complex and interconnected problems. Diverse groups of local leaders—private, public, philanthropic, and nonprofit—are fed up with the dysfunction around them, coming together to challenge conventional wisdom and fix problems long written off as unsolvable, such as poverty, unemployment, and a failing education system.

Population size, rates of income inequality, age composition, and rates of educational attainment affect levels of income segregation in US cities. In turn, that segregation can exacerbate the relative advantages and disadvantages income already affords. In other words, if you're lower income, it can make it even harder for you to access resources and opportunities as a low-income person than it would have been otherwise (Bischoff and Reardon 2013). The opposite is true, too. If you are upper income, and live with other upper income families in an income-segregated city, access to opportunities and resources could be even easier for you. This, in turn, can have particular impact on children—their future educational performance, job prospects, and income potential.

US cities are a critical resource, and increasingly the gathering places of the nation's people. They don't work equally for all of their residents, however. Making them do so should be an urgent priority. As the Brookings Institution so aptly summarizes, "The American Dream will live—or die—in America's cities" (Rothwell and Reeves 2015).

References

Berube A, Holmes N (2016) City and metropolitan inequality on the rise, driven by declining incomes. Brookings Institution. http://www.brookings.edu/research/papers/2016/01/14-income-inequality-cities-update-berube-holmes. Accessed 29 June 2016

Berube A, McDearman B (2015) Good fortune, dire poverty, and inequality in Baltimore: an American story. The Brookings Institute. http://www.brookings.edu/blogs/the-avenue/posts/2015/05/11-poverty-inequality-baltimore-berube-mcdearman. Accessed 29 June 2016

Bischoff K, Reardon S (2013) Residential segregation by income, 1970–2009. American Communities Project, Brown University. http://www.s4.brown.edu/us2010/Data/Report/report10162013.pdf. Accessed 29 June 2016

Chetty R, Hendron N, Kline P, Saez E (2014) Where is the land of opportunity? NBER Working Paper No.19843. Q J Econ 129(4):1553–1623

Cohen D (2015, March 4) Understanding population density. US Census Bureau. http://blogs.census.gov/2015/03/04/understanding-population-density/. Accessed 29 June 2016

Cohen D, Hatchard G, Wilson G (2015) Population trends in incorporated places 2000 to 2013. US Census Bureau. https://www.census.gov/content/dam/Census/library/publications/2015/demo/p25-1142.pdf. Accessed 29 June 2016

Edmondson J (2013) Backbone organization or backbone function? Striving for Change: Lessons from the Front Line. http://www.strivetogether.org/blog/2013/12/backbone-organization-or-backbone-function/. Accessed 29 June 2016

Frey W (2015a) Migration to the suburbs and Sun Belt picks up. Brookings Institution. http://www.brookings.edu/research/opinions/2015/04/08-migration-suburbs-sun-belt-frey. Accessed 29 June 2016

Frey W (2015b) New census data: selective city slowdowns and the city-suburb growth gap. Brookings Institute. http://www.brookings.edu/blogs/the-avenue/posts/2015/05/21-new-census-data-city-slowdowns-city-suburb-growth-gap-frey. Accessed 29 June 2016

Hecht B (2014) Reflections on living cities' integration initiative. Living Cities https://www.livingcities.org/resources/267-reflections-on-living-cities-integration-initiative

Kania J, Kramer M (2011) Collective impact. Stanford Social Innovation Review. http://ssir.org/articles/entry/collective_impact. Accessed 29 June 2016

Kochhar R, Fry R, Rohal M (2016) America's shrinking middle class: a close look at changes within metropolitan areas. Pew Research Center. http://www.pewsocialtrends.org/2016/05/11/americas-shrinking-middle-class-a-close-look-at-changes-within-metropolitan-areas/. Accessed 29 June 2016

Mt. Auburn Associates (2014) The integration initiative: three year evaluation report. Executive Summary

O'Donovan D (2012) Why bother with next-generation collaboration? Two words: differential impact. Living Cities Blog. https://www.livingcities.org/blog/116-why-bother-with-next--generation-collaboration-two-words-differential-impact. Accessed 29 June 2016

Peters R, Lee S, Simpson L, Govan R (2015) Economic and workforce development. In: McConduit-Diggs E (ed) The State of Black New Orleans: 10 years post Katrina. Urban League of Greater New Orleans, New Orleans. http://www.urbanleagueneworleans.org/ul/wp-content/uploads/2015/08/StateofBlackNewOrleans_TenYearsPostKatrina.pdf. Accessed 29 June 2016

Ragas W (2015) 2015 year end semiannual housing market analysis. New Orleans Metropolitan Association of Realtors. http://www.nomar.org/images/PDF/2015_Year_End_Market_Analysis/Metro_text_December_2015.pdf. Accessed 29 June 2016

Ross J (2015) Katrina may be a metaphor to some, but it's still a reality to New Orleans. The Washington Post. https://www.washingtonpost.com/national/katrina-may-be-a-metaphor-to-some-but-its-still-a-reality-to-new-orleans/2015/08/27/f53bfaa6-4b69-11e5-902f-39e9219e574b_story.html. Accessed 29 June 2016

Rothwell J, Reeves R (2015) The American Dream in American cities: exploring a 'metro genome model' approach. Brookings Institution. http://www.brookings.edu/blogs/social-mobility-memos/posts/2015/10/09-american-dream-cities-metro-model-rothwell-reeves. Accessed 29 June 2016

Royal Economic Society (2014) Inequality in big cities: why urbanisation makes the world more unequal. http://www.res.org.uk/details/mediabrief/7135901/INEQUALITY-IN-BIG-CITIES-Why-urbanisation-makes-the-world-more-unequal.html]. Accessed 29 June 2016

Sams-Abiodun R (2013) Recognizing the underutilized economic potential of black men in New Orleans. Lindy Boggs National Center for Community Literacy. http://www.gnof.org/wp-content/uploads/2015/10/Recognizing-the-Underutilized-Economic-Potential-of-Black-Men-in-New-Orleans.pdf. Accessed 29 June 2016

Siegel B, Winey D (2014) TII stakeholders reflect on the progress and power of the one table approach to achieve system change. Living Cities Blog. https://www.livingcities.org/blog/502-tii-stakeholders-reflect-on-the-progress-and-power-of-the-one-table-approach-to-achieve-system-change. Accessed 29 June 2016

Sommer K (2016) Lessons from five years of economic inclusion and partnership in Baltimore. Living Cities Blog. https://www.livingcities.org/blog/1018-lessons-from-five-years-of-economic-inclusion-and-partnership-in-baltimore. Accessed 29 June 2016

Taylor A (2015) How to achieve large-scale change: thoughts from New Orleans—interview by Raderstrong, J. Living Cities Blog. https://www.livingcities.org/blog/762-how-to-achieve-large-scale-change-thoughts-from-new-orleans. Accessed 29 June 2016

U.S. Census Bureau (2015a) QuickFacts: Baltimore City, Maryland. http://www.census.gov/quickfacts/table/PST045215/2404000,00. Accessed 29 June 2016

U.S. Census Bureau (2015b) QuickFacts: New Orleans, Louisiana. http://www.census.gov/quickfacts/table/SEX255214/2255000,24510. Accessed 29 June 2016

United Nations (2014) World's population increasingly urban with more than half living in urban areas. http://www.un.org/en/development/desa/news/population/world-urbanization-prospects-2014.html. Accessed 29 June 2016

United States Department of Justice Civil Rights Division (2015) Investigation of the Ferguson Police Department. https://www.justice.gov/sites/default/files/opa/press-releases/attachments/2015/03/04/ferguson_police_department_report.pdf. Accessed 29 June 2016

Vey JS (2016) The challenges of Baltimore (and the nation) in context. The Brookings Institute. http://www.brookings.edu/blogs/the-avenue/posts/2015/05/07-challenges-of-baltimore-vey. Accessed 29 June 2016

Transforming the Urban Built Environment: The Seattle 2030 District as a Model for Collaborative Change

Susan Wickwire and Matthew Combe

Abstract The Seattle 2030 District is a public-private partnership focused on meeting, and beating, the aggressive water usage, energy usage, and carbon neutrality goals set by the 2030 Challenge. Founded by Brian Geller, a Seattle architect, Seattle 2030 District was the first of fifteen 2030 Districts in the USA and Canada. In fact, Seattle's initiative set the example for all later 2030 District cities.

Geller's vision was a city whose building owners and managers collaborated to achieve reductions in usage and emissions across water, energy, and transportation. From the germ of the idea in 2009 to now, Seattle 2030 District has become a vibrant community of 120 members—property owners, building managers and professionals, and community stakeholders—who have set the standard for collaboration around reductions in building energy use and transportation emissions, public and regional funding collaborations for the greening of city buildings, and sharing of best practices across building owners and managers. Challenges to tackle next include incorporating more issues of equitable and affordable housing, sustaining member engagement after the initial commitment to take action, and fund-raising to support the infrastructure of the collaboration.

Keywords 2030 District • 2030 Challenge • Built environment • Green development

Introduction

The Seattle 2030 District (the "District") is a groundbreaking, high-performance building district in downtown Seattle and surrounding neighborhoods that aims to reduce dramatically the environmental impacts of building construction and operations through education and collaboration across every sector of the built environment. The District works with its more than 120 members—property owners, building managers and professionals, and community stakeholders—to improve energy efficiency, encourage better management of potable water and stormwater, and promote more sustainable transportation options (Fig. 1).

S. Wickwire (✉) • M. Combe
Seattle 2030 District, 1402 3rd Ave, Suite 301, Seattle, WA 98101, USA
e-mail: susanwickwire@2030districts.org; matthewcombe@2030districts.org

© Springer International Publishing Switzerland 2017   175
M.J. Cronin, T.C. Dearing (eds.), *Managing for Social Impact*,
Management for Professionals, DOI 10.1007/978-3-319-46021-5_10

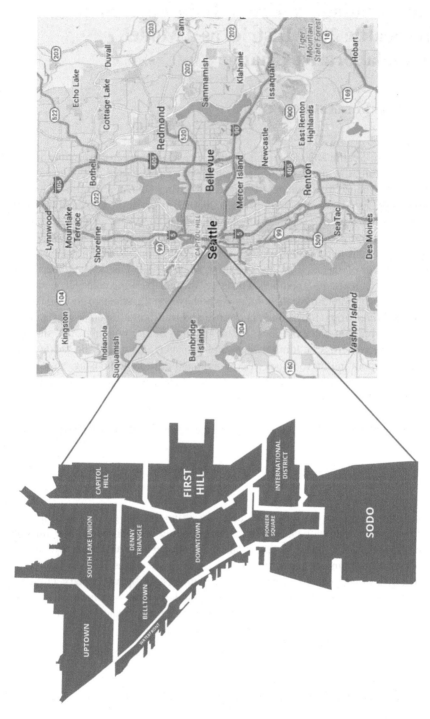

Fig. 1 Seattle 2030 District map of neighborhoods within its boundaries (© Seattle 2030 District, 2016)

In 2011, a group of forward-looking businesses concerned about climate change officially launched the District in partnership with the City of Seattle and adopted the ambitious goals of the 2030 Challenge. These goals call for 50 % reductions in energy and water usage and transportation emissions, with carbon neutrality the aim for new construction and major renovations in 2030 (Architecture 2030 2015b).

The intent of the Seattle 2030 District is to move beyond national benchmarks, targets, and fuel mixes for individual buildings and to define reduction targets and goals for building energy use, water consumption, and related emissions from fossil-fueled transportation for the District as a whole and for each major building type. Individual buildings will have different opportunities for energy reduction. For example, historic buildings may have limitations based on maintaining the exterior shell intact, while some existing older, non-historic buildings may have dramatic opportunities for improvement.

Today, the District seeks to develop realistic, measurable, and innovative strategies to assist its members in meeting their aggressive goals. These strategies include an emphasis on smart building technologies, small buildings that lack resources, green stormwater measures, water-efficient plumbing and irrigation, carbon-free electric vehicles, and commuter amenities to encourage no-carbon trips to work. The District also targets market-based solutions to advance important changes on a broader scale such as private financing, bulk purchasing, and public sector funding in the form of utility incentives and other programs.

The story of the Seattle 2030 District reflects the realization of a vision to achieve measurable impacts at scale. In telling that story, it is critical to focus on the depth and breadth of the commitment made by the founding members, the support of the federal and local governments in getting it off the ground, the conscious engagement with member buildings and the community to keep it going, and addressing challenges along the way. This chapter touches upon all of these facets.

What started in Seattle has now been adopted by 14 other cities in North America—including Albuquerque, Austin, Cleveland, Dallas, Denver, Grand Rapids, Ithaca, Los Angeles, Pittsburgh, Portland (ME), San Antonio, San Francisco, Stamford, and Toronto—and is currently being explored by 5 others, including New York City (2030 Districts 2016c). While the basic blueprint is the same—2030 Challenge goals and substantial private sector involvement—the execution has varied. It speaks volumes for the 2030 model that it can be adapted for local circumstances. Seattle 2030 District's founding Executive Director, Brian Geller, advised those getting a 2030 District launched in Stamford, Connecticut, "Don't ever take the focus off property owners and what they need and what they want," he said. "Don't try to do too much out of the gate" (Spiegel 2014).

Elements of Transformation

Getting Started

The catalyst for creating the Seattle 2030 District was an idea that Brian Geller, an architect, had while working as a Sustainability Specialist at ZGF Architects. He heard about a project in Chicago being undertaken by Adrian Smith + Gordon Gill Architects called "The Decarbonization Plan for Downtown Chicago," which involved studying 550 buildings downtown, and making recommendations for "district-wide" changes focusing on opportunities for buildings to share energy and water resources. Brian was inspired, and contacted some key people he knew at the City of Seattle and others at engineering and architecture firms to discuss the idea of creating a district-scale effort in Seattle.

In December 2009, Brian pitched the idea to this group at ZGF, suggesting the following parameters to make it different than other programs:

- **Physically distinct boundary**: This is a community effort, and we work with everyone inside of that boundary.
- **Property owners and managers are involved from the very beginning**: They take ownership of the Seattle 2030 District and help shape our direction and decisions.
- **Clear metrics and baselines**: We work in three areas: energy, water, and transportation. Each area has very clearly defined and measurable goals and metrics.

More than 40 civic leaders from the public and private sectors joined together to create the Seattle 2030 District Planning Committee, dedicated to achieving the goals of the 2030 Challenge, which had been developed by Ed Mazria and his Architecture 2030 organization (Architecture 2030 2015a).

Formed as an all-volunteer effort, the Committee needed stronger organizational support to broaden its impact, spur action, and advance the goals of the nascent Seattle 2030 District. Start-up funds were essential to developing energy-efficiency services for existing and new buildings, defining membership expectations, and providing stable administrative support.

In the summer of 2010, with the Committee's endorsement, the City of Seattle— an active participant—sought financial support from the U.S. Environmental Protection Agency (EPA) through the Climate Showcase Communities Grant program. The nearly half-million dollars over 3 years would go a long way toward realizing the District and developing the tools needed to achieve its bold reduction goals, while ensuring that the city met EPA's livability principles. The grant was one of 25 chosen for funding out of more than 300 applicants in the fall of 2010, and in spring of 2011 the funding began flowing, allowing Brian Geller to leave ZGF to run the Seattle 2030 District full-time that May.

The Committee met every 2 weeks for over a year to talk through what commitments, resources, and organizational governance would look like. The Committee formally adopted the *2030 Challenge for Planners*, adding reduction goals for water use and vehicle miles traveled to the energy and fossil fuel reduction goals in the original *2030 Challenge*. The Challenge called for the following reductions, as measured against a national baseline:

- **Energy use in new buildings**: 60 % reduction by 2015 and reaching carbon neutral by 2030
- **Energy use in existing buildings**: 50 % reduction by 2030
- **Water use in all buildings**: 10 % reduction by 2015 and 50 % reduction by 2030
- **Carbon dioxide equivalent from vehicle miles traveled**: 10 % reduction by 2015 and 50 % reduction by 2030

As Architecture 2030 founder and CEO Ed Mazria wrote in his letter of support, the Seattle 2030 District would "create the first high-performance building district in the country" and "help Seattle meet its goal of a carbon neutral city by 2030" (City of Seattle 2010).

The City of Seattle's interest in having a public-private partnership promoting sustainability in the commercial core of the city and helping it achieve its own ambitious environmental goals translated into a robust commitment to the Seattle 2030 District's success. Under the leadership of the Office of Sustainability and Environment, which had secured and oversaw the EPA funding, officials from other key City offices such as the Office of Economic Development, Department of Planning and Development, the Department of Transportation, Department of Neighborhoods, Seattle Public Utilities (water and waste), and the municipal utility Seattle City Light participated in a working group. It was charged with:

- Coordinating with the Seattle 2030 District Committee to collect and assemble Portfolio Manager performance data for District project types
- Training property management personnel to complete Seattle Climate Partnership carbon footprints, preparing Portfolio Manager account performance data, and submit results for analysis and development of baselines
- Coordinating with the District Committee to analyze data to establish district-wide average baselines for the major building sectors: office, multifamily, retail sales, restaurants, manufacturing, and hotels
- Helping define project type reduction targets for across the District for each major building type in compliance with the 2030 Challenge

The Challenge of Getting Data and Setting Baselines

Data were needed to establish current baselines, confirm future goals, and define the path (with interim reduction targets) to reach the District goals. The project team involving Committee members and members of the City team used two major tools to collect, analyze, and track the required data on energy, water, and vehicle miles traveled in the District: ENERGY STAR Portfolio Manager and the Seattle Climate Partnership carbon calculator. The project team strongly encouraged submission of performance data from many buildings through these two tools.

ENERGY STAR Portfolio Manager focuses on energy performance of buildings, and in April 2011 the City of Seattle started requiring mandatory annual energy benchmarking reports, using Portfolio Manager, for all non-residential buildings larger than 20,000 square feet. Portfolio Manager is a nationally recognized tool for benchmarking performance against similar projects regionally and nationally. District Committee members willingly submitted energy performance data into the District Portfolio Manager account resulting in performance data for more than 20 buildings as measured by energy use intensity (EUI), energy consumed per square foot. Their cooperation allowed the Committee to conduct some initial analysis comparing performance to national and regional averages of ENERGY STAR performance for the different building types. The project team assembled sufficient performance data to determine locally defined 2030 District-wide average baselines by building sector type as the basis for defining reduction targets for the District as a whole and for each sector type.

To expand beyond energy performance and address the other elements of the 2030 District goals, including vehicle miles traveled (VMT) and water usage, the project team first looked at using the Seattle Climate Partnership carbon calculator. The Seattle Climate Partnership was a voluntary pact among area businesses to take action to reduce their own climate-changing emissions and work together to meet the community-wide goal of meeting or beating the Kyoto Protocol's reduction targets. The Seattle Climate Partnership developed a user-friendly carbon footprint calculator (Excel-based and online versions) to provide users with a planning-level greenhouse gas (GHG) emission inventory to assist in prioritizing and implementing reduction strategies in transportation, energy use, material purchasing (including water), and waste management.

This work led to the creation of the baseline for the transportation performance metric, which is based on the District average in 2010. Through the help of Commute Seattle, a District member, and the City of Seattle's Seattle Climate Partnership, the Seattle 2030 District was able to establish an average mode split and associated CO_2 emissions for commuter transportation within the District boundaries. Commute Seattle had recently completed its *2010 Center City Commuter Mode Split Survey*, which established the average commuter mode split for the area in which the Seattle 2030 District resides. Using the existing methodology from the Seattle Climate Partnership's Carbon Calculator, CO_2 emissions per passenger mile were associated with the given mode resulting in an average of roughly 900 kg CO_2 per commuter per year.

The baseline for the water performance metric was based on the current District average. At that time—and presently—there was no national or local building water use database, so the District had to develop the water baseline through the help of members and partners. Through a Memorandum of Agreement with Seattle Public Utilities (SPU) and the help of District member Partnership for Water Conservation (PWC), the District was able to generate water use intensity baselines for the major building types within its boundaries. SPU was able to aggregate water consumption data for selected building parcels based on the predominant building type and provide annual total consumption for the years 2002 through 2010. PWC members reviewed parcel data and water consumption patterns and provided a recommended assimilation of building types based on similar patterns of water use (e.g., fast food category was combined with restaurants, dormitories combined with multifamily residential).

It was understood that the current baselines were approximations based on the best currently available data and that as more information would be collected on actual building-level water consumption, the baselines would be refined and normalized. This was the first attempt at identifying water use intensity baselines on a square footage basis for 15 unique building types in the Pacific Northwest region, and potentially the entire USA.

Strong Foundations for Success

The passionate engagement of the private sector fueled the Committee to get organized quickly and effectively. Though property owners and managers compete with each other for available tenants and businesses, they understood that by working collaboratively to establish the Seattle 2030 District goals and work toward achieving those goals they could better satisfy customer demands. They could also successfully compete in the national and global marketplace by jointly showing why Seattle is a healthy, environmentally responsible, and financially attractive place to live, work, and do business. These real estate companies included Unico, Hines, Vulcan, CB Richard Ellis, and Kidder Mathews.

They were joined by others from the green building community and those working to support them, including professional service firms, utilities, and nonprofits. A number of leading architecture firms such as ZGF, GGLO, and Mithun participated actively in the Planning Committee as they were already working to advance Architecture 2030's *Challenge for Planning*. MacDonald-Miller contributed its mechanical contractor expertise. Virginia Mason, a prominent healthcare organization focused on sustainability, added its perspective to the Committee as a major energy and water consumer and employer with a large commuting workforce. In addition to Seattle City Light, another utility, Seattle Steam (now Enwave)—a private energy system serving portions of the District—was represented. A number of nonprofits also shared their passion for this work on the Committee: Architecture 2030, Cascadia Green Building Council, New Buildings Institute, and the Northwest Energy Efficiency Alliance (NEEA).

The public sector's support has been equally robust. As described earlier, the City of Seattle committed substantial personnel resources to facilitating the EPA Climate Showcase Community Grant and to supporting the technical foundations of the District. The City of Seattle is a Founding Member in both Property Owner and Community Stakeholder categories with representation on Seattle District 2030's board. As a Property Owner, the City of Seattle has agreed to all of the performance targets for energy, water/stormwater, and CO_2 reductions. As a Community Stakeholder, the City of Seattle has promised support through numerous avenues to help the member property owners and managers meet the District goals. These include but are not limited to a Memorandum of Agreement between the District and Seattle City Light, signed early on and pledging auditing and benchmarking support for six pilot projects; co-development of a Streamlined Permitting Service plan for property developers willing to target the District goals for new construction, which is intended to shorten permit times by up to 12 weeks; and coordination of multiple City department technical assistance and financial incentive supports for projects committing to meet the 2030 District goals.

In 2012, the City of Seattle further cemented its support for the work of the Seattle 2030 District through a contract to help administer the Community Power Works (CPW) program. In April 2010, the City was awarded a $20 million Better Buildings grant from the U.S. Department of Energy (DOE). This award was based on achieving deep energy efficiencies, at least 15 % reduction in energy usage, in multiple building sectors (DOE 2015). CPW was a 3-year initiative that provided innovative incentives to spur building retrofits. The District worked with its members to identify program participants, implement the carbon-incentive component, and track its outreach and performance. Ten member buildings benefited from their participation. The City also asked the 2030 District to sign onto DOE's Better Building Challenge on its behalf due to staff and resource constraints.

King County, in which Seattle and the 2030 District are located, is also a Founding Member as both a Property Owner and Community Stakeholder, and is represented on the board. King County provided funding that helped jumpstart the Green Stormwater Initiative in 2015 and is an active partner in working with members to improve stormwater management in the downtown area. King County is also expanding upon the lessons learned from the Seattle 2030 District High Performance Buildings Pilot by further testing out smart building solutions in five of its own facilities.

The Seattle 2030 District has been fortunate in gaining financial support from national and local sources in addition to what King County has contributed. As a follow-on and supplement to the EPA seed money, the 2030 District received considerable help from Architecture 2030 as its fiscal sponsor and nurturing parent organization in securing funding. Through their engagement, the Kresge Foundation committed $200,000 over 2 years in vital general support, which allowed for flexibility in pursuing several priority areas. A second major source was a grant from the U.S. Department of Energy that was secured by Architecture 2030 and overseen by Lawrence Berkeley National Lab. This funding has made possible initiatives in several 2030 Districts to improve energy efficiency in small commercial buildings under 50,000 square feet. Local funding over multiple grant cycles has come from the Bullitt Foundation, whose mission is to safeguard the natural environment by promoting responsible human activities and sustainable communities in the Pacific Northwest, and the Boeing Company, which was founded in Seattle and has been a generous supporter through its corporate philanthropy program.

Sustaining the Transformation

In 2011 and subsequently, Seattle has had the leaders, innovators, environmental initiative, and critical mass of related efforts to establish and nurture a 2030 District. Enacting the 2030 Challenge on a district scale, rather than building by building, was intended to foster the dramatic changes needed to produce sweeping reduc-tions. The District has showcased solutions in action and has provided a working model and tools that other cities can use to reduce their own impacts of the built environment. However, there are a number of challenges facing the Seattle 2030 District in terms of sustaining the effort over time: transition from a start-up to a mature organization; continuous engagement of members; and alignment of results with the ambitious goals. Fortunately, counterbalances to these challenges exist and are being implemented so that they don't turn into insurmountable barriers.

Responding to Change

There was a considerable amount of passion and excitement around the founding of the Seattle 2030 District. The original catalyst, Brian Geller, with the support of the Planning Committee and the City, guided the organization from its birth in 2011 through a growth phase in membership and recognition. Putting a new environmen-tal nonprofit on the map in Seattle where there are already many established groups took a great deal of networking and relationship building. Several initiatives were launched to provide more focus to achieve the mission. "Assess Target Deliver" engaged members in assessing their energy and water performance and advising on reduction strategies. The High Performance Buildings Pilot allowed a small number of members to test out new analytics that detected faults before they occurred. The Green Stormwater Initiative created a new component for the water goal and identified stormwater management strategies that members could pursue.

The Seattle 2030 District was poised to build off its growing successes when Brian Geller announced his departure in December 2014 to take a high-level sus-tainability position with Citigroup in New York. To his credit, he had laid the groundwork for succession by hiring Charlie Cunniff to serve as the deputy director 6 months prior. Charlie helped create the 2030 District as a City employee and had a great deal of experience in the field.

The Board of Directors contributed substantially to ensuring a relatively smooth transition, which was consistent with its overall enthusiastic engagement in guiding the organization. Many of its members had actively participated on the Planning Committee and remained involved through the board. Led by Chair Brett Phillips from Unico, the board undertook a hiring process to identify a new Executive Director and every member wanted to be on the interview panels. At the same time, the board undertook a strategic planning process to more clearly define the organi-zation's priorities going forward.

Recruiting and Retaining Members

Having board members from all categories (property, professional, community) and from organizations that are District members has helped considerably with the critical task of recruiting and retaining firms to take on membership. In the case of property owners, they have agreed to pursue the Seattle 2030 District goals for new construction and existing buildings (2030 Districts 2016e). In return for their signing a commitment letter, the Seattle 2030 District offers:

- Analysis of current building performance data to set specific targets for the three Seattle 2030 District performance criteria
- Support in benchmarking buildings when this data does not exist
- Facilitation of team meetings to discuss the District goals and means of achieving them
- Outreach to and engagement of additional professionals for project input as appropriate
- Facilitation in engaging service providers to execute and finance improvements and verify performance over time
- Team guidance to ensure that District targets are integrated into any audits and work proposals
- Support for measuring success and making results public

When the District was first forming, property owners were concerned about the new City of Seattle Building Disclosure Ordinance and the impact that it might have on their buildings. Some owners saw it as an opportunity for the District to play a role. If owners were required to disclose their performance then the District could help measure, verify, and compare that data. The District collected the data through Portfolio Manager and provided members with a comparison report, which looked at their individual building and how it was performing compared to the 2030 goals. The report also compared how their building was performing to other anonymous member buildings of a similar size and use type.

This allowed members to see how they were doing compared to the rest of the market; they could choose to publicly disclose that through the District to showcase their buildings efficiencies. The District was able to provide these reports from the beginning, once a member had 12 months of data in their Portfolio Manager account, which was incredibly valuable to owners as the City would not release their own report for another 2 years. That report would give EUI numbers for each building sector as an average, so a one million square foot office building with an average EUI of 32 would be blended with others that might have only 20,000 square feet, making an apples-to-apples comparison impossible.

Another big value proposition for building owners was working toward a common set of goals, the 2030 Challenge. When members signed the commitment letter, they were committing to Seattle achieving a 50 % reduction in energy, water, and transportation emissions as a whole, so they could work to achieve the maximum efficiency possible. Some building owners would be able to achieve 70–80 % reductions and some would only be able to get to a 30 % reduction, but collectively they would contribute to Seattle reaching the 50 % reduction by the year 2030 and put the city on a path to carbon neutrality by 2050.

Networking and education have also played a big part in the value proposition. The building owners would continue to distinguish their properties based on price, square footage, and amenity spaces. Through the District, they realized that they did not have to compete on their environmental impact. For the first time, there was an organization that provided a forum to share ideas and strategies for improved efficiencies and reduced operating costs that they had implemented. If there was an occasion when owners did not know about certain technologies or practices, the District would offer an education session on that topic to deepen owners' understanding of their options and their impacts.

Other Benefits to Members

This sustained effort of the owners toward achieving the goals of the District is critical to the credibility and viability of the 2030 District approach. For that reason, most of the benefits are tailored for them, targeting the barriers that they face to making progress. However, in order for the owners to do the work, they need professional stakeholders, engineers, architects to provide high-performance designs, construct the buildings to meet those designs, and install high-efficiency equipment. In addition to helping sign up at least one building (or have an existing track record of working with member properties), these members commit to:

- Sharing their professional expertise and experience with the Seattle 2030 District on:
  - Opportunities and strategies in building energy use, water use, and Transportation Mitigation Plan (TMP) data
  - Best practices and lessons learned for case studies
  - Challenges in further improvements

- Providing support to Property Owners and Managers in the following programs:
  - ENERGY STAR Portfolio Manager
  - U.S. Green Building Council's Building Performance Partnership (LEED Certified buildings only)
  - Use of the Seattle 2030 District/BOMA CCI Assessment tools when evaluating building renovations

- Supporting the Seattle 2030 District Committee (and later board) through:
  - Participation in District decision making
  - Evaluation of membership criteria for property owners and stakeholders
  - Mentorship for small/sole proprietor property owner and managers
  - Education and training providers in our area of expertise

Essentially, implementing these actions shows building owners and managers the professional stakeholders' commitment to the goals and builds experience in helping others achieve the goals, thereby putting them in a stronger position when bidding for jobs.

The third major category of membership—community stakeholders—has commitments similar to those of the professionals. Those commitments include sharing organizational experience and expertise in areas of the District's core mission, serving as mentors for small property owners and managers, and providing education and training in areas of expertise. They benefit from the alignment of interests as District's efforts assist them in achieving their mission and programmatic objectives, which are primarily focused on greening the built environment, making Seattle a better place to live and work, and protecting the environment more generally. These members include the local chapters of the U.S. Green Building Council and the American Institute of Architects, Preservation Green Lab (an initiative of the National Historic Trust for Historic Preservation), the Downtown Seattle Association, and Commute Seattle. With the involvement of the City of Seattle, King County, and groups such as Emerald Cities Seattle and the Environmental Coalition of South Seattle (ECOSS), there is a growing emphasis on social equity in the midst of an economic boom in the region.

Building performance data is at the heart of what the District does, whether in providing reports to members or using aggregated data to see how the District as a whole is doing. With this in mind, the District recently started a partnership with the Urban Land Institute (ULI) Greenprint Center for Building Performance facilitated by Architecture 2030 (ULI 2016). The District feels strongly that this new relationship will provide great value to its members. While Portfolio Manager will continue to be an important tool, the reporting and data management provided by Greenprint far surpass what is available through that software platform and will allow buildings to better measure and reduce the use of resources. All data contained within Portfolio Manager can be pulled directly into Greenprint, so current data collection methods will not need to change. Furthermore, Greenprint comes from the Urban Land Institute, a trusted, nonprofit, real estate-centric organization. The partnership will allow the District to continue to provide ongoing benefits. Available to all 2030 Districts, these include receiving a discounted access rate, using dashboards and analytical tools to track and report energy, water, waste, emissions, and other information, and verifying and validating building data across a portfolio (2030 Districts).

With its growth over the last 5 years, both in Seattle and nationally, the 2030 Districts organization can provide more tangible benefits to its long-standing members. This not only helps with membership retention, but it also incentivizes deeper engagement and new member recruiting. One of the biggest benefits introduced in 2016 is the 2030 Districts Marketplace, which was developed by Architecture 2030 with the help of the Districts. The Districts-wide Marketplace was created to streamline the procurement process and offer innovative, reliable products at below market prices (2030 Districts 2016d). Available technologies currently include:

- HVAC controls
- Advanced metering
- LED lighting
- High-performance windows
- Electric vehicle charging stations

One last benefit has been the Seattle 2030 District's own annual recognition program to highlight outstanding member accomplishments. The Vision Awards are presented in the categories of energy, water, and transportation to align with the 2030 Challenge goal areas. A fourth Award for Leadership signifies exemplary achievements across all of the goals. A gala dinner is held to raise the profile of the Awards program, and the District issues a press release to further amplify the winners' stories. These Award-winning profiles are added to the existing library of member building case studies on the District website, which serve the important purpose of sharing the ways in which members are working toward meeting their goals (2030 Districts 2016a). Other members and buildings outside the District can learn about which technologies were installed and measures implemented to position the buildings for success in terms of the goals.

Building Alliances

From its public-private partnership roots, the Seattle 2030 District has focused on building collaborative relationships with other active groups in the community in order to leverage their strengths to achieve the mission. In the earlier discussion of establishing the goals and baselines for the water and transportation performance tracking, the contributions of the Partnership for Water Conservation and Commute Seattle were mentioned as critical to ensuring their credibility and viability. The Planning Committee realized that it did not have to create in-house expertise when long-standing organizations could do their own work and benefit from having their missions supported by District members' efforts.

Another early contributor to the emergence and growth of the District was the local chapter of the Building Owners and Managers Association International (BOMA). As there was a relatively small set of owners and managers involved in forming the District, they looked to BOMA to help recruit other owners and managers. BOMA facilitated access to their members and later joined formally as a community stakeholder. They are currently represented on the District Board.

More recently, the District has benefitted from its association with the Smart Buildings Center (SBC), a project of the industry's Northwest Energy Efficiency Council (NEEC). The SBC played a major coordinating role in the Seattle 2030 District's High Performance Building Project designed to test out new building management control and fault detection systems and to demonstrate their benefits for potential wider adoption. The District reached out to member building owners and connected them with software/hardware providers and assisted in the collection and analysis of data and with promoting information exchanges on progress achieved among the buildings and with other community stakeholders. The SBC assists with analyzing the District-wide performance data on an ongoing basis and in formulating quarterly reports. They also offer meeting and training facilities, a tool-lending library that includes diagnostic equipment and measurement devices, and demonstrations of the analytical and visualization applications that can turn building performance data into actionable information for energy savings. The head of the SBC is also a District Board member.

With a focus on energy, water, and transportation, it is challenging for the District staff of five to make significant inroads in each of these areas. There are also numerous opportunities to engage our members and it is critical to be strategic. Working with active and dependable partners translates into far greater progress toward achieving the 2030 goals.

Replicating the Model

From its inception, Seattle 2030 District's vision was that the approach should be implemented elsewhere. When interviewed for an article on 2030 Districts (Lee 2015), Brian Geller said:

> When we created the first 2030 District in Seattle, it was always intended to be a replicable model. We saw room in the green building movement for a private sector focus on uniting downtown property owners and building professionals around a common set of performance goals. The pace of the 2030 District's growth has astounded a number of us, and we are thrilled to see it continue.

The U.S. EPA Climate Showcase Communities program also envisioned that its grantees would focus on sharing their mitigation approaches with other cities in order to amplify the overall impact of the program.

The Seattle 2030 District Planning Committee overcame a range of challenges in getting the District going. One significant challenge, and one shared by subsequent 2030 Districts, was to identity competition. In Seattle, there were a number of other organizations doing similar work, such as the NEEA, the Cascadia Green Building Council, Emerald Cities, the Better Buildings Challenge, and BOMA Seattle-King County's Environment Committee. The District had to define what was unique about the Seattle 2030 District model. It took 6 months before the Committee hit upon what that was—building owners felt like they had a sense of ownership in the organization and its mission.

In particular, at the time the Better Buildings Challenge (BBC) was launching, the City's Office of Sustainability and Environment advocated for the 2030 District to start Seattle under the BBC. Emerald Cities had recently started and was concentrating on energy use in existing buildings. There was a push for them to manage the BBC, and for the District to be the signatory. The City of Seattle didn't want to make the commitment to be the signatory at the time as they didn't have the resources to manage the program and weren't sure how they would benefit from participation.

This conscious and intensive effort in Seattle to assess the existing regional landscape and find the right niche for the District was repeated by several of the other early adopters. For example, the founding group in Cleveland—the second city to have a 2030 District—conducted a thorough assessment of other organizations, although they did so more as a way to identify allies rather than out of a concern about occupying the same space on the environmental/sustainability board. Similar to Seattle, their goal was to create a stand-alone nonprofit. In addition, the City of

Cleveland played an important role in supporting the founding building owners and architects. Architecture 2030 and Brian Geller also engaged fairly closely in getting the Cleveland 2030 District off the ground, but Seattle's capacity-building role diminished somewhat as Pittsburgh launched the third 2030 District.

A number of the subsequent Districts, including Pittsburgh, Stamford, and the Texas cities of Dallas and San Antonio, were launched as initiatives of existing organizations. In Pittsburgh, the Green Building Alliance learned of the idea and made a decision to fit the District into its organization and provide resources and funding to get the program going. One advantage of starting a District this way is that there isn't as great a need to differentiate the 2030 District approach from other organizations, or to have to explain why the mission is meaningful. In Seattle, the founders tried to find a home under other organizations but were unable to find the right fit or an organization that was willing to bring in the District, provide resources, and allow it to be a separate program.

After the four initial Districts were established and a movement was clearly under way, Architecture 2030 and the Districts worked to create a charter so that there would be a more formal, legal basis for all future Districts. The name was also trademarked in the face of enthusiasm from other cities that wanted to use the name but didn't have the necessary critical mass of committed buildings. Processes were set in place to define a 2030 District so that this critical mass could be quantified and an "Emerging" status could become a steppingstone to full-fledged "Districthood." At this point, the 2030 Districts Network started to form (2030 Districts 2016b).

In Seattle, conversations first started in December 2009, and the public launch of the Seattle 2030 District came nearly 2 years later, in September 2011. There was a long gestation period during which the Planning Committee was effectively creating the District model, developing the baselines for the goals, and working out how to measure them and to calculate progress. Most other Districts have followed that timeline of 18 months to 2 years, going from a Prospective 2030 District to Emerging and to an Established. That timeline is necessary to get everything organized and be in compliance with the 2030 District Charter.

Ongoing Challenges

The 2030 District model found fertile ground in Seattle with its long-standing commitment to environmental protection, a City government that had made acting on climate change a priority for many years prior to 2009, and a history of good corporate citizenship, especially in the area of sustainability. But there are ever-present obstacles to success that are shared by other 2030 Districts. Extremely low electricity rates in Seattle and elsewhere (except in California or the Northeast, which have higher rates) make it difficult to justify funding substantial energy efficiency enhancements. The return on that investment for property owners and managers may not compare well to others such as spending funds on a lobby renovation or other more tangible amenities.

In addition, in Seattle, San Francisco, and Los Angeles in particular, commercial energy codes among the strongest in the country make it that much harder to go beyond code to meet the 2030 goals. Developers often feel that they are required to spend substantial amounts just to meet code; they don't want to make additional investments in deeper green technologies for their projects. The problem is even more evident in existing buildings where energy retrofits are minimized so that they don't trigger the "substantial alteration" category of the Seattle energy code, which has similar stringent elements as those for new construction.

Perhaps the biggest challenge, which is not unique to the 2030 Districts, is fundraising. Architecture 2030 and the 2030 Districts Network have financially supported most of the Districts, at least to some extent, to help seed them. There is also flexibility at the District level in pursuing foundation and government grants, contracts from local governments, sponsorship, and even membership dues. In Seattle, the sense early on was that the value of participation had to be demonstrated to members before any fees could be charged. More recently, there has been a realization that it may be difficult to attract outside financial support if the members themselves are not showing their own support with contributions. However, none of the Districts has yet to hit upon a long-term sustainable funding model.

There is also a tension between being opportunistic and being strategic, given the wide playing field of the 2030 Districts. When the Seattle 2030 District first launched in 2011, it had limited offerings, given its very small staff and reliance on volunteer time from members. As the District membership grew in size and recognition, more opportunities arose to work on different projects. These included smart building technologies, financing programs, member engagement programs, and electric vehicles. Throughout the first 5 years, the staff worked on everything that came to them, evaluating how members utilized different services. If it was valuable and if it was something no one else was already providing, the staff increased their efforts. The flip side was, in some instances, giving the appearance of being active but not being able to show tangible accomplishments. "A Vision for 2030: Our Strategic Plan, "created in 2015, documented the priority areas over the next 5 years and helped to defuse that tension significantly (2030 Districts).

This ongoing calibration of the Seattle 2030 District's priority areas has also had to take into account important citywide discussion over social equity and housing affordability amidst the economic boom. Until recently, the District had not focused on these issues, with the exception of working with several affordable housing provider members, including Bellwether Housing, Capitol Hill Housing, and Plymouth Housing. Additionally, because a number of nonprofits have been advancing equity and affordability for some time, there had not been overt pressure on the District to do more in this space. However, as the Mayor's Housing Affordability and Livability Agenda (HALA) has taken center stage in policy considerations regarding zoning and property development, it has become increasingly clear that the District needs to devote more effort to playing a constructive role. Realizing that sustainability can contribute to lower building operating costs and utility bills for lower income residents, there is substantially more work to be done to integrate these regional priorities and translate them into specific policies and actions; the District can be an advocate to promote them among its members and more broadly.

As alluded to earlier in the chapter, it is essential that the members' commitment to achieving the 2030 goals be sustained over time. Otherwise, there is a serious risk of "greenwashing." The Seattle 2030 District recently celebrated hitting two out of the three 2015 interim milestones on the road to the year 2030. The next check-in point in 2020 represents a doubling of effort. Having clear performance goals is extremely helpful for motivating action; they also can underscore glaring failure if they are not met. The Seattle 2030 District has recognized this tremendous challenge and is focusing even more closely on the technologies and practices that will keep moving members along the trajectory of greater and greater reductions.

Conclusion

As explored throughout this chapter, there are several critical elements of the 2030 District model and its development path in Seattle that have made it a vehicle for market transformation. First and foremost is the power of a common set of goals at the District scale. Putting the 2030 Challenge for Planners into action beyond the individual building level was a new and innovative way to harness interest in building sustainability and channeling it. This was not something that could only thrive in a place with a long tradition of passion for protecting the environment. Cities such as Cleveland and Pittsburgh embraced the approach as they sought to make over their aging cities and attract new investment and residents.

A second important factor was the commitment of the private sector, primarily the building owners, managers, and developers but also importantly the architects who acted as catalysts and the engineering and energy service firms ready to help the property members take steps to meet the goals. And it was not simply about climate change and protecting the environment but promoting economic growth and urban livability. There is increasing focus on the value of deep green buildings in the real estate marketplace in terms of higher rents, higher rates of worker productivity in buildings with more daylight and fresh air, greater sale and resale prices, and better constructed buildings that are designed to last longer. More research is needed to quantify and aggregate these economic benefits but they are being more widely recognized around the country.

An additional, and foundational, contributor was strong backing from the local governments. In the case of the City of Seattle, their securing the EPA grant and considerable in-kind support provided the launching pad for the 2030 District concept to become realized. The strong policy imperative to address climate change also provides a context in which to advance 2030 District objectives in terms of incentives for energy efficiency, better access to data, and favorable land-use conditions. Other 2030 Districts have enjoyed similar support which bolsters their credibility in the community and helps attract allies to help achieve the mission.

Although there is a legal structure to the 2030 Districts through the Charter and specified stages of 2030 District evolution from Prospective to Established status, there is also flexibility in how the Districts are formed and what local priorities may be incorporated into the local mission. While the Seattle and Cleveland 2030 Districts are stand-alone nonprofits, Pittsburgh, Stamford, and others are housed in parent organizations, although Stamford is moving toward independence from the Business Council of Fairfield County. In addition, Seattle added a stormwater component to its water goal, while Pittsburgh is looking at adding an indoor air quality goal and Stamford is pursuing how to integrate resilience into its mission. This ability to customize the approach allows for more creative and locally appropriate applications of the 2030 District model.

The 2030 District model arises from a shared vision of what those involved want the future of our cities to look like. It is about intentionally shaping our futures by leveraging the collaborative strength of our communities, businesses, and governments to achieve common environmental, economic, and efficiency goals. It is about being more than a sum of parts; these synergistic opportunities are being led by the private sector and are made up of individual members pursuing shared goals of the community as a whole. This community approach provides a new model for collaborative competition as property owners, managers, local governments, and community stakeholders leverage shared resources for both individual and collective gain.

References

2030 Districts (2016a) Case studies. http://www.2030districts.org/seattle/case-studies. Accessed 24 June 2016

2030 Districts (2016b) Districts. http://www.2030districts.org/districts. Accessed 24 June 2016

2030 Districts (2016c) http://www.2030districts.org/. Accessed 24 June 2016

2030 Districts (2016d) Marketplace. http://www.2030districts.org/marketplace. Accessed 24 June 2016

2030 Districts (2016e) Seattle. http://www.2030districts.org/seattle. Accessed on 24 June 2016

2030 Districts (n.d.-a) Greenprint. http://www.2030districts.org/sites/default/files/atoms/files/Greenprint.pdf. Accessed 24 June 2016

2030 Districts (n.d.-b) Our strategic plan. http://www.2030districts.org/sites/default/files/atoms/files/Seattle_2030_District_Strategic_Plan_Updated.pdf. Accessed 24 June 2016

Architecture 2030 (2015a) Architecture 2030 home page. www.architecture2030.org. Accessed 24 June 2016

Architecture 2030 (2015b) The 2030 Challenge. http://architecture2030.org/2030_challenges/2030-challenge/. Accessed 24 June 2016

City of Seattle (2010) Activating the Seattle 2030 District: a public-private alliance to achieve carbon reduction. http://www.2030districts.org/sites/default/files/atoms/files/Activating%20the%20Seattle%202030%20District%20Proposal_0.pdf. Accessed 24 June 2016

Department of Energy (2015) Seattle helps communities power buildings efficiently. http://energy.gov/eere/better-buildings-neighborhood-program/seattle-helps-communities-power-buildings--efficiently. Accessed 7 July 2016

Lee J (2015) 2030 Districts Piercing boundaries. Green Building Information Gateway. http://insight.gbig.org/2030-districts-piercing-boundaries/. Accessed 24 June 2016

Spiegel J (2014) Stamford joins pioneering energy-saving program. The Connecticut Mirror. http://ctmirror.org/2014/10/14/stamford-pioneering-a-voluntarily-energy-saving-district-for-downtown/. Accessed 24 June 2016

Urban Land Institute (2016) ULI Greenprint Center for building performance. http://uli.org/research/centers-initiatives/greenprint-center/. Accessed 24 June 2016

A Community-Driven Change Model in Battle Creek: Project 20/20

Talia Champlin and Amanda Lankerd

Abstract Battle Creek, Michigan, is a city of people and organizations with great intentions, and persistent challenges. At 52,000 residents, it has a large corporate headquarters, several prominent foundations, a hospital network, and a vibrant non-profit community. Nevertheless, at the opening of this case study, education outcomes were low, dropout rates were high, and health outcomes were poor. Despite the constant presence of community improvement initiatives, it seemed that the dollars and efforts had failed to produce lasting results.

From these conditions emerged Project 20/20, an evolving network of concerned citizens, community leaders, and organizational leaders who set out to build a "public capital" infrastructure that would create the conditions for community change and a shared vision for Battle Creek. Over a period of 9 years, formal and informal leaders carefully built trust among disparate neighborhoods and organizations, a community input process that could undergird multiple community initiatives, and a bulwark of residents used to listening to each other, giving and receiving feedback, and working collaboratively on change initiatives. While Project 20/20 succeeded in building public capital, they also learned about its fragility, and the constant commitment required to make sustained collaboration work.

Keywords Battle Creek • Project 20/20 • Community redevelopment • Public capital

Introduction

In a packed room, another angry resident took the microphone to criticize Battle Creek's Downtown Transformation Initiative. Two disgruntled community members had spoken already, and a significant line of critics stood behind the current speaker, waiting for a turn to add their displeasure.

T. Champlin (✉) • A. Lankerd
317 E. Columbia Ave, Battle Creek, MI 49015, USA
e-mail: tchamplin@battlecreek-homes.com

© Springer International Publishing Switzerland 2017
M.J. Cronin, T.C. Dearing (eds.), *Managing for Social Impact*,
Management for Professionals, DOI 10.1007/978-3-319-46021-5_11

193

What was going wrong? The Downtown Transformation Initiative represented an investment of millions of public and private dollars, all the best in planning and design, and state-of-the-art execution. The "pillars" of the project were carefully conceived by some of the best minds in Battle Creek, and included expansion of downtown employment by the city's major employer—the Kellogg Company— along with new emphasis on food science partners and food science education.

Battle Creek's paper of record had said, "The fact that business, government, philanthropic and education leaders are working together to strengthen downtown Battle Creek offers exciting prospects for this community's future. The benefits of a thriving downtown will reach across this community, enhancing neighborhoods and encouraging business development" (Warner 2008).

None of that effort seemed to matter. As part of its funding contract, Battle Creek Unlimited, the economic development organization for the City of Battle Creek, was holding a community forum on the project's progress. Community residents and downtown business owners turned out and were angry. They criticized traffic disruption, diminished access to local businesses, inappropriate use of public funds, and an over-accommodation for one big employer. They criticized the choices of brick on the sidewalks, the choices of lighting on the paths, and even the choices of benches people would sit on. They expressed skepticism toward development of the project in general, and toward its success.

Staff for Battle Creek Unlimited had done their best to craft a message on the benefits of the project. A media consultant had managed press releases along with many other communications to the community. None of it seemed to matter that night.

FSG, a consultant for the city's largest philanthropic funder, the W.K. Kellogg Foundation, had warned that the Downtown Transformation Initiative could be successful only if the community supported it. No matter what changes were made, residents and downtown employees would need to shop in the resulting retail outlets, eat in the resulting restaurants, vote for the Transformation's success with their approval, and support it with their discretionary dollars. Apparently, the community didn't support it. The planners were baffled, since leaders from across several sectors had been thoroughly briefed. The forum was discouraging. Nevertheless, the Transformation needed to forge ahead.

Battle Creek in Transition

For those who worked to make Battle Creek a better place, community resistance and strong undermining influences were no strangers. Indeed, they seemed like familiar bedfellows. Behind the scenes, as the Downtown Transformation Initiative unfolded, active Battle Creek champions were comparing notes, recognizing that they were working hard, investing time and money in many areas, and not having the impact they wanted.

What happens when well-intentioned plans for community transformation fail to win enthusiastic support from the most highly-impacted residents? What happens when community leaders respond by choosing a different way? In 2006, the City of Battle Creek did choose a different way. Project 20/20 formed as a network of Battle Creek stakeholders who worked with multiple organizations and institutions between 2006 and 2015 to reinvigorate and focus community participation in civic change processes by creating public capital.

In April 2006, a loose coalition of community members who had been reflecting on resistance to various community improvement efforts articulated a common concern. Dedicated citizens were working on the same pressing issues year after year, but didn't seem to be making a sustainable difference. A lot of good projects were completed. Strong leaders set objectives and achieved them, and the community had several generous foundations helping. Still, while wanting to make things better, they were honest enough to admit that they were active, but they were not transformational.

As with so many Midwest cities, Battle Creek had changed over the previous two decades. New corporate leaders weren't engaged in the community the way the Old Guard had been. Increasingly, people worked in Battle Creek but didn't live there. Leaders in recognized positions of authority around the city didn't have a shared vision for Battle Creek. The community was fragmented into municipal configurations that weren't conducive to collaboration, resulting in duplication and territorial behaviors, while creating a climate in which already limited resources were either misallocated or used inefficiently.

Battle Creek could be called an average Midwest City. According to the census, at 52,000 people in 2015 (U.S. Census 2016), it's not too small, but not very big. Residents are about 72 % white and 18 % black, and only about 21 % have a bachelor's degree or higher. The average household income is $38,000 per year. Battle Creek has a successful industrial park comprised of more than 90 companies employing more than 9400 people. A Fortune 500 company—Kellogg—and the seventh largest foundation in the United States—the W.K. Kellogg Foundation— call Battle Creek "home."

Despite these assets, the city had its struggles. In addition to the low college graduation rate, 20 % of students dropped out of the public schools (CEPI 2011). Health indicators were extremely low; the county ranked 78th in the state for health outcomes (livability.com 2016). Overall, the city was not considered "world-class" in quality of life, or any other area of significance.

The informal coalition did not want to create yet another organization, and so began by gathering as many individuals from as many organizations as possible. As the group was trying to understand why the community seemed to be stuck, Sterling Speirn, then the head of the W.K. Kellogg Foundation, brought in Rich Harwood of the Harwood Institute for Public Innovation. The group was eager to gain insight. What was the capacity for our community to make real change? What were the right levers for community change, and how could we put them into play? With Harwood's help, the group discovered its focus: *Battle Creek lacked public capital.*

Harwood defines "public capital" as the connective tissue that shapes the ability and capacity to work together. Two defining characteristics of strong public capital are trust and reciprocity, and it was easy to see that trusting, reciprocal relationships in Battle Creek were rare (The Harwood Institute 1999).

Launching Project 20/20

After several meetings, the group decided that it would pull together a unified network, a group of creative problem solvers, people who could look at the community holistically to accomplish results. Project 20/20 was formed. The first goal was to build public capital, which the coalition had come to believe was the most critical component in achieving collective results.

To build community, the group first needed to establish several things: a shared understanding of the city's challenges and concerns; a format for interaction; a network of connected individuals and organizations; the right formal and informal city leaders in that network; and a way to share ideas and strategies for success. Project 20/20's mission became "Working together, we champion ideas and initiatives that move this community toward excellence." A coalition of groups and individuals came together to be more connected, coordinated, and mutually supportive of work directed toward the greater good.

Despite the many past meetings and projects addressing Battle Creek's community issues, none had been a focused effort to create public capital in support of broad-based transformation. According to Harwood, change efforts are most successful when they are based on community priorities and supported by community passion (The Harwood Institute 1999). Public capital is strong when residents perceive that organizations are acting on their greatest concerns. Residents are therefore engaged, whether by asking questions and making suggestions, by supporting the efforts in conversation with others, or by volunteering to help. Ultimately, that public capital had to be accompanied by a common vision and a network among formal city leaders. But early on, the Project 20/20 coalition didn't feel that it had the authority or efficacy to accomplish those additional tasks—yet.

Now, it was time for some structure. In 2008, Carla Dearing,[1] the CEO of Community Foundations of America, Inc., visited Battle Creek, her former hometown, and met with the group. Experienced in leading community initiatives, she helped formulate the next steps, pull together an Advisory Committee to provide structure and some governance, and identify where to invest in professional guidance. The Advisory Committee secured $10,000 from the Miller Foundation of Battle Creek, added more local supporters, and eventually secured a grant from the W.K. Kellogg Foundation to carry the work forward. At that time, Project 20/20 also developed a guiding statement for the work that held the following aspirations.

---

[1] N.B., Carla Dearing, author Talia Champlin, and editor Tiziana Dearing are sisters.

When we successfully complete Project 20/20, a core network of people will know each other and the community so well that we can mobilize to accomplish any worthwhile task. A larger group will find our mission and norms true and motivating, and could be counted on to help. We will champion ideas and initiatives that create a vibrant community.

We will respect each other, tell each other the truth, insist on looking at things from many perspectives, and continue to work together until quality decisions are made. We will then mobilize to make sure those decisions were implemented, and if possible, are successful. If they are not successful, we will learn from our mistakes, then decide again.

Once the coalition's structure, norms, membership, and research is completed, we think it is likely that an existing organization, such as the Chamber, the Community Foundation, or some other entity, will "absorb" the group. By then, we will have identified the "levers" this community has the energy, influence, and resources to move. We will have learned to support existing pockets of effectiveness, and will be ready to take on some bigger, deeper issues.

To accomplish this vision, Project 20/20 provided structures that allowed residents to:

1. Build community and get on the same page with each other
2. Expand their knowledge and understanding of what was happening in the Battle Creek area
3. Give their input on important topics

This kind of community strength couldn't be built by reading another report or watching another video. To accomplish these things successfully, people representing a diverse range of perspectives had to commit to attendance.

The group quickly learned the difference between "bonding" organizations and "bridging" organizations (Putnam 2000). A bonding organization brings like-minded people together around a common concern. A bridging organization, on the other hand, should partner with many separate initiatives for change, to ensure active community involvement and reduce overlapping silos that are not coordinated across groups.

Finding a format that built community, expanded knowledge, and invited input took time. The coalition experimented with several formats, including one from Juanita Brown and David Isaacs in their 2005 book, *The World Café: Shaping Our Futures Through Conversations that Matter*, and one developed for Project 20/20 by a local consultant, Humanergy. Gradually, the group settled on its final format of 2–3 brief, idea-starting presentations of about 5 min each. The focus rotated across the most pressing topics in the community—economic development, education, healthcare, positive youth development, and leadership. Table conversations consisted of 2–3 open-ended questions designed to accelerate initiatives showing promise. Each table would share a summary of its conversation with the larger group, while someone captured the main ideas in themes. The ideas and materials from every forum went on the Project 20/20 website, www.bcproject2020.com.

Team members coordinated to establish communication among the organizations doing the work and the broader community, ensuring that feedback flowed in all directions. The organizations benefited through clear understanding of the greater community's desires and concerns about their efforts. Community members became knowledgeable enough to actively support organizational efforts, and depending on interest level, some were motivated to get involved.

Project 20/20 topics resonated with the broad Battle Creek community. Attendance at meetings ranged from 50 to more than 100 people, depending upon the subject matter. One forum explored the experiences of successful business owners, asking participants to share ways to make Battle Creek an open and inviting place to do business. Another asked young people to share their thoughts about what youth and young professionals really want in a community. Any "positional" leaders in attendance were required to listen only, so that they could understand better how to make Battle Creek a magnet for young people. One forum brainstormed ways to build support for early childhood education and opportunities to engage businesses in early education so that Battle Creek's youngest citizens would have a great start. Other forums included sharing data on health disparities and gathering community input on how to address them, and local efforts by businesses and post-secondary institutions to expose and connect students to career opportunities in Battle Creek.

Building Public Capital for Battle Creek Community Change Goals

Throughout the process, people would ask, "What does Project 20/20 *do*?" Doing wasn't the main point, though. It was coordinating, leveraging, and connecting. No one organization could spend the time and resources necessary to develop broad trust and reciprocity across the larger community. Networks among leaders and community members, however, could accelerate worthy change efforts—which they called "pockets of effectiveness," drawing again from Rich Harwood's work— by spreading the news, gathering advocates, providing feedback, sharing best practices and lessons learned, and laying the foundation for broader community support. Yet, the city still worked in silos.

It was easy to assume that the silos were intentional, but it became clear that wasn't necessarily true. Yes, some leaders sought to protect their funding sources from perceived "infiltration," but even the well-intentioned organizations could only stretch so far. Collaboration and sharing information were ideal, but every leader faces pressures to avoid "mission creep" and keep scarce resources focused on accomplishing their unique work. Networking with other leaders across the boundaries of sector and priority can be cost- and time-prohibitive, even for organizations that have active board members whose tasks include representing the organization in the community. Project 20/20's job was to grease the wheels of collaboration, helping create a whole Battle Creek that was, indeed, better than the sum of its parts.

Based on numerous discussions with different constituencies, the most pressing topics were economic development, education, healthcare, and vulnerable youth. Therefore, Project 20/20 felt that it could build the most public capital and make the most significant differences if it helped champion worthwhile efforts in these areas. It set out to form strategic alliances with the bridging organizations within each sector, the coalitions who were currently addressing these issues, and with organizations that were most concerned about these issues. For economic development topics, Project 20/20 partnered with Battle Creek Unlimited, the city's official economic development organization. For educational topics, it was the Educators' Task Force, a formal group of local superintendents and college administrators. For healthcare, the Regional Health Alliance stepped up, a group coordinated by the Battle Creek Community Foundation. And for issues involving vulnerable youth there were several partners, including TCC, The Coordinating Council for many local nonprofit organizations. The Strategic Alliances allowed each of these organizations to partner with Project 20/20 to develop forums on the work they were doing that most needed the community's understanding and support.

As the word about Project 20/20 forums got out, new leaders saw value in building public capital and wanted to join the process. In 2014, one of Battle Creek's local school districts, with a student population of 4562, wanted to understand its stakeholders' vision for education and identify opportunities and potential roadblocks to reaching the community's educational goals. The school district reached out to Project 20/20 to facilitate and manage a community engagement process to guide the Board of Education in determining district priorities.

As a result, over 500 people engaged: students in 3rd to 11th grades, parents, representatives of the city's growing Burmese diaspora, business leaders, community members, teachers, principals, support staff, counselors, secretaries, ELL students, and more participated in 51 conversations. The superintendent said to one of the authors about the process, "Project 20/20 was instrumental in our most recent community outreach efforts as they facilitated an engagement process that helped the district transform public input into action while promoting mutual accountability for outcomes in support of sustainable change." The district is currently implementing a "rapid transformation" model to increase student achievement and improve the district.

Public Capital at Work for Economic Development

Battle Creek Unlimited, the city's economic development organization, was an early supporter of Project 20/20. Its previous CEO was one of the founding members; staff members of Battle Creek Unlimited regularly attended Project 20/20 Leadership meetings and Community forums.

A year had gone by since that ugly community meeting described above. Another required community forum was looming in November 2011, and Battle Creek Unlimited's CEO, Karl Dehn, was concerned. During that year, the Downtown Transformation Initiative had made significant progress. Private companies had invested over $87 million during the preceding 3-year period. More than 200 jobs had been created and another 800 jobs had been transferred to the downtown area. The math/science magnet high school for gifted students from across the area had committed to moving downtown. But community members were still upset.

During this same year, Battle Creek Unlimited and Project 20/20 had formed an alliance, and Project 20/20 offered to host the next community forum. BCU learned that, in order to get different results than in past forums, the format, content, and motives all needed to be different. They would need to identify areas where they were genuinely willing to use community input. They would need to cut their presentation down significantly, for the purpose of leaving much more time for listening rather than telling. They would need to include community members as important partners rather than as adversaries, and they would need to be willing to be influenced by what they heard.

Karl and his staff were apprehensive, but willing. They trimmed their stock presentation down to 20 min. They identified topics where they truly wanted help, and topics where they were willing to accept input. They were also transparent about areas where decisions were already made and would not be changed. Project 20/20 members crafted questions with the purpose of gathering necessary input, and BCU promised to listen and respond to that input.

On November 10, 2011, the room was packed again. Attendees included a mixture of community members who had attended the previous forum, and community members who had attended several Project 20/20 sessions. The latter were familiar with the philosophy of finding common aspirations and building on success. Karl kept his comments short and positive. Then the audience broke into small discussion groups and assigned questions for recommendations. BCU made sure that they had enough staff members at the meeting so they could have a representative at every table—not to facilitate, but to listen.

The attendees generated a broad range of ideas and opinions. Organizers validated negative opinions, and then encouraged participants to suggest solutions. Attendees expressed amazement at the results the Transformation was creating. They brainstormed ways to get the word out and accelerate its successes. The meeting ended with positive responses and commitments to champion progress going forward.

BCU did not let the community down. They implemented a range of suggestions and made an effort to report back. They learned that simply bringing "leaders" together to keep them informed was not the same as bringing the community together to influence and be influenced. They understood that one simple meeting was not what made the difference. Project 20/20 had created a subculture of trust and transparency. BCU demonstrated a willingness to be trustworthy and open in a community setting and then acted on what they learned. This turned detractors, along with those who were simply uninformed, into advocates who could help move the Transformation forward.

Lessons Learned

Project 20/20 never incorporated or became a 501(C)3 nonprofit organization. Through its 9-year tenure, it remained what one leader affectionately called a "state of mind." The project had one, half-time consultant. Everyone else volunteered, running on a budget of less than $45,000 per year, along with in-kind contributions from strategic partners. In 2015, the W.K. Kellogg Foundation began its own community-wide engagement process meant to create a common vision for the city. It did not choose to build off of the Project 20/20 infrastructure. Continuing to run a separate program would have been the very duplication of effort that the Project 20/20 founders so passionately wanted to avoid. Project 20/20 disbanded when the current use funding ended.

At its close, Project 20/20 was a trusted "brand" with more than 500 subscribers—residents who had attended meetings, provided input, given time, and donated money. The group's organizers wrapped up respectfully, summarizing accomplishments and archiving the database with a local organization in case its contents could have future community benefit. The project had clearly established the importance of public capital. Indeed, many Project 20/20 volunteers engaged in the W.K. Kellogg Foundation's BC Vision effort.

When Project 20/20 began its exploration of effectiveness, it uncovered some important deficits. Battle Creek did not have a cohesive network of grassroots and positional support for the hard work being done. There did not appear to be a group of champions for ideas and initiatives that could move the community toward excellence. The city lacked a common vision.

Further, there was a profound disconnect between the people doing the work of city improvement and those affected by the work. This wasted time and energy. Workers were frustrated by the lack of appreciation and responsiveness from residents. Residents encountered policies and practices that didn't make sense for their lives. Putting them together was hard, but it made the city work better.

The work of building public capital was much slower and much harder than anyone imagined at the start. The time was worth it, though. Carefully constructed trust and frameworks for participation fostered a growing belief that community input is key to the success and sustainability of projects instituted for the common good. Even so, trust and engagement are fragile; leaders unwilling to be influenced by public voice undermine them. Distrust can return surprisingly quickly.

Project 20/20 participants learned how to ask for input. Even more important, they learned how critical it is to make sure that people feel heard. Alongside that lesson, participants learned from their mistakes the dangers of asking for and then ignoring the perspectives shared. That was worse than not asking at all.

As time went by, people moved in and out of formal leadership roles in the city. Project 20/20 learned the hard way about the importance of careful on-boarding across the community and in its own ranks. Taking time to explore and confirm shared aspirations unleashes great collaborative power. A lack of shared values and beliefs destroys it.

At its end, Project 20/20's progress was incomplete. More trust between the community and organizational leaders still needs to be developed. Managing resident expectations about the pace and scope of action remains difficult. People want to see concrete action, but sometimes the process itself *is* action. For example, having a conversation is action, learning is action, and participating in site visits is action. People are eager to see things happen, but it takes time to bring everyone along in the process—time well spent. Still, and understandably, residents often find the delays of good process frustrating.

Further, staff members at municipalities, school districts, or nonprofit organizations are not always in the habit of engaging the community in their processes. They need support to understand that just because you engage the public doesn't mean that you have to do everything that the public may request. You have to start with small, meaningful steps that make sense. Because leaders are not accustomed to gathering and considering feedback, they rarely have methods in place to communicate back to constituents, either. For continued growth of public capital, leaders need to let the public know that they listened and that changes were made.

Conclusion

Public capital—the careful nurturing of trust and reciprocity among community residents—can be built intentionally. The process takes long-term focus and commitment, but the results can be powerful. Organizations will come and go, as will their leaders. A successful community, however, can steward public capital through these transitions. That stewardship requires shared vision, shared commitment, and a fundamental belief that genuine collaboration—the kind that includes the grassroots, the powerful, the interested, and the disenfranchised—is a public good worth pursuing.

References

Center for Educational Performance and Information (2011) State of Michigan 2010 cohort 4-year & 2009 cohort 5-year graduation and dropout rate reports. https://www.michigan.gov/documents/cepi/2010-2009_MI_Grad-Drop_Rate_345879_7.pdf. Accessed 23 June 2016

(2016) Health and health care in Battle Creek, MI. http://www.livability.com/mi/battle-creek/health. Accessed 23 June 2016

Putnam R (2000) Bowling alone: the collapse and revival of American community. Simon and Schuster, New York, NY

The Harwood Institute (1999) Community rhythms: five stages of community life. http://ncdd.org/rc/wp-content/uploads/Harwood-CommunityRhythmsReport.pdf. Accessed 23 June 2016

U.S. Census (2016) Battle Creek city. Michigan. U.S. Census Bureau. http://www.census.gov/quickfacts/table/PST045215/2605920. Accessed 22 July 2016

Warner R (2008) Downtown poised for revitalization. *Battle Creek Enquirer*, p. A1

Part V
Investing for Scalable Social Change

Catalyzing Social Impact Investments

Michael Gilligan

Abstract Over the last two decades, a growing focus on for-profit investment for social impact has highlighted the opportunity for private capital to play a meaningful role in addressing social change in new, substantive ways. Heightened activity in the public policy arena, growing support from many prominent private foundations, and mounting political will around community-based economic development programs are all contributing to an environment now conducive to attracting private capital with a social mission. Importantly, as more categories of investors seek to make an impact, socially minded investment is beginning to demonstrate its potential to provide market rate returns.

After briefly tracing the evolution and appeal of impact investing in the environmental, health, and education sectors, this chapter discusses how patient capital invested under the right conditions can also achieve significant levels of social impact in the form of economic empowerment for underserved populations through providing quality employment opportunities. When such investments can also deliver financial returns on a par with money invested in "socially neutral" markets, this can translate into major increases in capitalization of socially positive companies especially during their growth stage.

In this context, the author also identifies an emerging opportunity for impact investing in later stage businesses, with the full potential to generate returns that would typically be attractive to private equity investors. The chapter concludes that with well-managed, smaller sized funds, late-stage impact investors can play an important role in enabling social change while also realizing attractive financial returns.

Keywords Socially responsible investing (SRI) • Strategic impact investing • ESG

M. Gilligan (✉)
Urban Catalyst, 51 Melcher Street, Boston, MA 02210, USA
e-mail: michael@urbancatalystpartners.com

© Springer International Publishing Switzerland 2017   205
M.J. Cronin, T.C. Dearing (eds.), *Managing for Social Impact*,
Management for Professionals, DOI 10.1007/978-3-319-46021-5_12

A Need for Greater Impact

The social challenges our nation faces are complex and the pace of change resulting from efforts to confront these challenges has been slow. To date, the innovation initiatives designed to create effective solutions from within the nonprofit and public sectors have been insufficient. More robust, timely responses in the areas of climate change, affordable health care, education reform, income equality, and poverty alleviation, just to name a few, are urgently needed in the USA and around the world. Over time, some profit-seeking businesses and private capital have sought to augment the search for social solutions but these efforts have also met with limited success. That being said, the recent emergence of a corps of private sector businesses and associated investor groups who share a commitment to tackle one or more of these challenges at scale holds great promise. This chapter focuses on the potential for private sector impact investing to become a major force in jump-starting and scaling innovative social solutions developed by businesses.

The notion that investors have a social purpose that accompanies their desire for financial returns is not a modern one. It dates back at least to the seventeenth-century Quakers in England and to US Shaker congregations in the 1800s who aligned their investment and purchase decisions with their social values. As Antony Bugg-Levine and Jed Emerson describe in their book, *Impact Investing,* investment influenced by a social mission then continues to trace "its arc through the environmental movement of the 1970s, the anti-apartheid divestment campaigns of the 1980s, and the modern fair trade consumer and socially responsible investment movements" (2011).

Over the last two decades, a growing focus on for-profit investment for social impact has highlighted the opportunity for private capital to play a meaningful role in addressing social change in new, substantive ways. Socially responsible investing (SRI) in the USA has grown tenfold from $639 billion in 1995 to $6.57 trillion in 2014, now representing nearly 18 % of $36.8 trillion in total assets under management (USSIF 2014).

In its early stages, socially responsible investment activity focused primarily on an ethically driven strategy designed to avoid certain industry sectors (e.g., coal plants or gun manufacturers) or other business practices perceived as morally deficient. Social screening of investments has become available to mainstream consumer investors, with many large mutual funds offering social fund options.

Growth has come as the sector moves beyond a negative screen, now also capturing businesses deemed to deliver positive social benefit, such as environmental sustainability. Investment activity has mostly centered on funds invested in public debt or equity, which are still largely passive in nature, often with broad, general social mandates. For many investors, simple adherence to responsible environmental, social, and governance (ESG) principles and/or defined shareholder advocacy agendas is enough to broadly qualify a business for inclusion as an SRI investment.

More recently, however, strategic impact investing ventures have emerged with more intentionally directed strategies, involving more targeted social mandates and located most often in the private markets. Heightened activity in the public policy arena, growing support from many prominent private foundations, and mounting political will around community-based economic development programs are all contributing to an environment now conducive to attracting private capital with a social mission. While developing rapidly, this activity continues to represent a relatively modest segment of overall SRI, with recent estimates hovering around $300 billion (Sirull 2015).

As impact investors sharpen their focus on increasingly intentional, directed social missions, private capital has the potential to play a more prominent role in identifying solutions and making headway against our nation's social challenges. Greater clarity around the definition of a "social mandate," alongside recent progress identifying effective impact goals and measurement techniques, is also helping to improve the prospect for tangible social impact results.

Adoption of Responsible ESG Practices Is Growing

The ubiquity of social media has enabled social causes to get traction across broad swaths of the population in rapid time frames, heightening social awareness. Naturally, then, good corporate citizens and businesses that are finding ways to "give back" are garnering strong support and loyalty from stakeholders who value those traits. As companies like Patagonia and Ben and Jerry's model exemplary behavior on social responsibility, customers and employees in particular are increasingly making socially responsible behavior a requirement and raising the standards for all businesses with whom they affiliate.

In light of these conditions, leadership teams of virtually all consumer-facing businesses are looking to formalize best practices around ESG principles to ensure that they are managing their businesses responsibly and meeting the expectations of their stakeholders. Leaders with a bolder vision are integrating more intentional social missions to their overall strategy.

Patagonia, for example, directly states its intent to "use business to inspire and implement solutions to the environmental crisis" in its mission statement. It also publically champions six environmental and social responsibility programs as part of imbuing its corporate culture, helping drive the popularity of its brand (Patagonia 2016). Under Armour's Code of Conduct lays out an extensive slate of best practices with employees and suppliers that feature prominently in the articulation of its core values. This carefully developed set of values also contributes meaningfully to UA's positive brand image (Under Armour 2012).

Recognizing these trends among employees and customers, the investor community is lending its support—and starting to see greater alignment with investment performance. While well-known private equity groups like Kohlberg, Kravis and Roberts (KKR) and Bain Capital do not have distinct social mandates that guide their overall investment strategies, each has taken steps to adopt certain socially responsible activities. KKR publishes an annual "ESG and Citizenship Report: Creating Sustainable Value" that demonstrates how they monitor performance against ESG principles across all their investment portfolios. In a more targeted fashion, Bain Capital has established a new, dedicated social impact fund within the Bain family of funds and hired former Massachusetts Governor Deval Patrick to lead that effort (Banerjee and Collins 2015).

Even in the absence of a distinct social mission for the business or investment strategy, these conditions clearly reflect an environment that reinforces and actively supports socially responsible behavior. Impact investing opportunities will continue to build as investors and managers identify and develop distinct, more intentional social missions.

Where's the Impact Now?

A substantial amount of US impact investing is still taking place within defined industry sectors that are commonly regarded as delivering broad social benefits. Three sectors continue to attract significant private capital investments, with examples of groups that are focused on these specific sectors, including:

- **The Environment**: companies that are focused on energy efficiency, waste and water treatment, carbon reduction (e.g., **City Light Capital** at www.citylight-cap.com)
- **Health Care**: general health and wellness, disease prevention, treatment and cure, health care affordability (e.g., **New World Capital** at www.newworldcapi-tal.net)
- **Education**: quality, accessibility at all levels, student retention (e.g., **SJF Ventures** at www.sjfventures.com)

In large part, the businesses operating in these sectors have natural access to various types of capital by virtue of the economic fundamentals of their business models, regardless of any interest from investors seeking social impact. That said, heightened focus on achieving measurable impact in these sectors is helping drive innovation and accelerate the pace of change. This happens in part through the expertise and greater risk appetite that comes from concentrated knowledge, and in part through concessions investors are willing to make on targeted rates of return.

Beyond this market-focused activity, investing for social impact includes investment in for-profit businesses operating in a range of industries that may not deliver social benefit directly through their product or service offerings, but may still do so through other dimensions, such as:

- Support of targeted **economic development** efforts including workforce development, skill training, and employment services as well as certain real estate projects with a community benefit (e.g., **Pacific Community Ventures** at www.pacificcommunityventures.org/)
- Pursuit of **place-based investment** strategies that foster local production capabilities in support of regional economic development (e.g., **Invest Detroit** at investdetroit.com)

- Creation of new **jobs**, especially those that provide living wage compensation for members of low-income communities (e.g., **Urban Catalyst Partners**, described later in this chapter)

Here, again, many of these businesses can attract capital by virtue of their commercial viability and future prospects, independent of their social impact. Nevertheless, they are also attractive to investors with intentions to focus on social objectives such as the creation of quality jobs, and with a commitment to quantify and hold the business and themselves as investors accountable to the social impact.

By way of example, Huntington Capital Management, a highly successful impact investment firm in San Diego, has an investment in Reischling Press (RPI), a leading manufacturer of print-on-demand personalized publishing materials. RPI's social mission is tied to the belief that its business will perform well if it provides a working environment where its employees can thrive. A Gallup Survey finds that enhanced productivity, profitability, and customer ratings among operating entities that have substantially less employee turnover, absenteeism, and safety incidents underscore RPI's objective (Huntington Capital 2014).

Expectations of Financial Returns from Impact Investing

In a 2013 *Stanford Social Innovation Review* article, "Unpacking the Impact in Impact Investing," Paul Brest and Kelly Born analyzed the distinction between investors willing to make a financial sacrifice ("concessionary" investors) and those seeking market returns. They make the case that an investment only has impact if the investor seeks to produce beneficial social outcomes that would not occur but for his or her investment, a concept referred to as "additionality."

Social change agent Jonathan C. Lewis (2015) poses a related question: "I wonder if impact investing in pushing so-called market rate returns is missing an even deeper motivator for attracting private capital?" Lewis adds fuel to a lively debate about the appropriate financial return objectives for social impact investing, lining up with Brest and Born on the notion that concessionary investors are often responsible for driving the freshest and, often, the deepest impact.

Just as angel and other venture capital investors seed the most innovative new business models and spawn new markets independent of social mission, concessionary investors drive many of the most aggressive, cutting-edge innovations in social change emanating from the for-profit sector. Concessionary investors often do have enormous impact as they help get social enterprise ventures that might not yet be commercially viable off the ground, accepting a risk profile for projects that would not be able to attract capital otherwise. Based on the deep wells of generosity and passion for social change in our country, there will always be an active, hopefully deep, community of concessionary investors to drive social impact through their investment efforts.

However, many investors continue to have concern that an investment strategy influenced by a social mission is at risk of generating below-market returns—especially when they thought they were signing up to shoot for market rate returns at the outset. And even some of the most generous philanthropists—also sophisticated financial investors—who believe strongly in social innovation prefer to keep their financial investments and charitable activities separate, reticent to support impact investing until the potential for financial returns becomes more clear.

In fact, while concessionary investors represent a subset willing to accept below-market rates of return in the quest for outsized and/or accelerated impact, mainstream impact investment activity is largely perceived as supporting businesses with value creation potential comparable to other investment opportunities. In a 2015 survey conducted by the Global Impact Investing Network (GIIN) and JP Morgan, 55 % of impact investors professed to be seeking a market rate of return, with 27 % looking to achieve close to market returns and only18 % of respondents expressing a willingness to accept something closer to return of capital, or capital preservation. In a further note, GIIN shares that "respondents also report that portfolio performance overwhelmingly meets or exceeds investor expectations for both social and environmental impact and financial return" (Saltuk et al. 2015).

The market is clamoring for proof that impact investing can consistently deliver returns in line with the socially neutral market. Impact investment strategies that pursue and achieve market returns, therefore, play a vital role in driving broader investor interest in the sector. Moreover, commitment to social impact investment strategies will be underscored, of course, when they demonstrate, as many believe, that business models driven by a social mission can yield exceptional, top-tier returns.

SJF Ventures, a leading impact investment firm in Durham, NC, offers one example of an investment made in a business delivering a social benefit while generating excellent financial returns. SJF led a Series B funding round (a second round of investing) in December 2014 for NEXTracker, a designer of photovoltaic systems for global solar power plants. While SJF was clearly motivated by the role NEXTracker was playing in making solar energy more cost effective and accessible, it was also interested in the financial upside associated with their investment. Furthermore, the company raised funds from other venture capital firms that did not have social mandates, underscoring the fact that NEXTracker's commercial prospects enabled access to capital from socially neutral investors. Flex International acquired NEXTracker less than 1 year later at a valuation that delivered a significant gain for SJF on its investment (SJF 2015).

Over time, more such exits will take place, and successful impact investors will develop the expertise and the track record necessary to broaden the field of investors pursuing more innovative strategies and justifying more patient time horizons for achieving impact while still generating competitive returns. Markets may open more broadly for capital willing to accept discounted returns in light of the impact potential, leading to a stratified investment market. For the most part, though, while the impact investment sector develops, this will need to be applied on a highly selective basis, typically with individual investors. At the current time, investing for social impact will have the broadest reach when a core group commonly achieves returns comparable to investment activity not committed to a social mission.

Needed: Social Capital for Later Stages of Business Growth

In the private investment realm today, impact investment activity is most vibrant with early-stage businesses where an abundance of new ideas and approaches offer great promise of social impact. Innovation is prevalent in the technology space, across many industry sectors (energy, education, and health care, as mentioned earlier), and in the drive to spur local economies—all natural places to find business models providing new solutions to social challenges. To a large degree, innovation and growth in these areas are driving our national economy, so it follows that they would also dominate impact investment activity in the private markets.

In Boston, for example, where technology, life sciences, and financial services are among primary drivers of the regional economy, the community of early-stage investors—angel and venture—actively engaged in impact investing far exceeds those representing the later stage private equity space.

Today's later stage businesses offer real potential to deliver meaningful social benefit. Growing businesses with established value propositions in energy, health care, education, and beyond represent excellent platforms to deliver direct and indirect social benefits, from environmental sustainability to providing greater degrees of quality employment. Private equity capital can fuel the growth and overall health of many such businesses, with multiple dimensions of economic development available as potential social mandate objectives. Currently, however, the potential for later stage private equity investing with a social mandate remains relatively untapped.

Impact Investing Gap

Current market conditions offer impact investing opportunities in both the early- and later stage business segments. On the early-stage side, most incubators and angel investor groups look to invest less than $2 million (with a sweet spot between $500k and $1 million) in seed capital in businesses that are being launched. Increasingly, the venture capital community is favoring later, larger rounds (greater than $2 million) and favors businesses with disruptive strategies and outsized valuation potential. A gap has emerged where postlaunch businesses, often with $1 million or more in revenue and compelling prospects, face insufficient capital flow. For example, Lifecycle Renewables, Inc., a renewable energy business based in Marblehead, MA, and Fresh Ideation Foods, a fresh food purveyor in Baltimore, MD, each have established business concepts and strong prospects for growth and are delivering social impact. Their clean energy and healthy food products, respectively, along with the quality jobs they are creating, represent excellent opportunities for impact investors. In today's market, however, both are finding it challenging to identify viable funding partners.

Classic private equity fund economics are based at least in part on ambitious wealth creation expectations for the principals, driving minimum fund sizes of around $100 million, translating in turn into a minimum investment size in the $10 million range. As a result, businesses seeking less than $10 million in equity-like capital often do not have ready access to formalized funding streams and are forced to opportunistically rely on more creative and flexible, regional sources. Commercial lenders in this space also typically lack the sophistication to lend other than in classic, highly conventional formats which don't work well for businesses in this range.

For investors willing to consider an opportunity to deliver social impact at comfortable compensation levels, however, a smaller fund size ($25 million–$50 million) enabling lower minimum investment thresholds and the ability to focus on smaller businesses can be very feasible. The financial upside and potential for social impact in this sector also provide a natural opportunity for later stage social investor groups to form partnerships with later stage businesses in the lower middle market— comparable to angel investor groups in the early-stage space.

Finally, as today's early-stage investors for social impact seek to realize return on their investments over the next several years they will help generate strong demand for experienced later stage investors to fund the ongoing growth and value creation of these businesses with a sustained commitment to the social mission. The investment portfolios of today's venture capital investors for social impact represent attractive pipelines for tomorrow's later stage impact investors.

Need for Patient Exit Strategies

Investing for social impact does require patient capital. Especially in the lower middle market, business plans take time to develop as talent, capital, and other resources required to fuel profitable growth coalesce. Social impact objectives add another layer of resource requirements. It takes time to shape strategies, attain results, and create real value. None of these factors are deterrents from investment performance when managed well. In fact, the synergies among them enhance the potential for value creation. Focus on a social mission can enhance performance in optimizing the business' commercial value proposition. It can also foster a culture of excellence, enabling the business to attract high-quality employees, customers, and vendors.

Furthermore, longer investment time horizons need not be viewed as a drag on investment performance. While lofty compounded rates of return are challenging to sustain over investment horizons of 5 years or longer, most investors welcome the opportunity to more than double their investment on a business they have come to know, even if it takes an extra year or two. While investors always need to be vigilant about exit timing—and be opportunistic when appropriate—investors for social impact should also be prepared to be patient.

In this context, investors for social impact need to consider the sustainability of the social missions of their portfolio companies as they look to realize return on their investments. Successive investor groups, or potential buyers of the businesses, need to be selected thoughtfully. The growing interest among all stakeholders in socially responsible behavior, and in commercial strategies complemented by social missions, bodes well for an ever-expanding universe of potential investors at the end of an investment horizon. Many observers were concerned when Ben & Jerry's was sold to Unilever, for example, and yet now Unilever is using many of Ben & Jerry's socially responsible management principles as models for how their other businesses might be managed.

Investors for social impact should plan on longer investment horizons—5 to 7 years as compared to the more conventional 3- to 5-year time frame for private equity and venture capital—and attract capital willing to accommodate this reality. Exit strategies should be thoughtfully developed at the outset of the investment and regularly reevaluated over the life of the investment. Furthermore, recapitalizations can also serve as a viable strategy to provide interim liquidity for interested stakeholders and help extend investment horizons.

Private Equity Driving Social Impact

Given the landscape and the potential, then, later stage private equity capital clearly has the opportunity to play a more prominent role in driving social impact. Private equity investors generally deliver meaningful value to their investors and the businesses they invest in through an orientation toward strong results, sophisticated management, discipline, and rigor. These same qualities lend themselves naturally to investment strategies that incorporate a social mission, and seek to drive success toward achieving the social mandate in the context of overall operating performance.

Increasingly, businesses are being called upon to conduct themselves in a socially responsible manner and encouraged to actively incorporate a social mission in their overall strategy. Private equity investors are ideally suited to partner with management teams to ensure responsible practices among the ESG principles businesses touch. In fact, many believe operational excellence in socially responsible practices, as well as adoption of an intentional social mission, enhances a business' commercial value proposition, serving as important drivers of financial success and value creation.

Huntington Capital Management and the Colorado Impact Fund are two models of investors for social impact in the private equity space. "Established with a vision to stimulate the economic well-being of communities while seeking to generate above-market rate returns," Huntington Capital Management has been recognized as a leader in later stage impact investing since 2000. Currently investing its $92 million third fund raised in 2013, Huntington Capital provides growth capital in the form of mezzanine debt and equity to underserved lower middle market companies in the Western USA (HCAP Partners 2016).

The Colorado Impact Fund was formed in 2014 in collaboration with Vestar Capital to make early- and later stage investments in Colorado-based businesses "providing quality jobs, economic development and … contribut(ing) market solutions to social and environmental challenges" (Colorado Impact Fund n.d.).

As investor interest continues to broaden, the universe of later stage private equity models will continue to expand.

A Social Mandate for Urban Catalyst

Driven by a desire to propel social impact, the author recently launched Urban Catalyst, a collaborative investment venture comprised of like-minded investors. Urban Catalyst was created to provide growth and transition capital to underserved businesses in the lower middle market—revenues between $5 million and $50 million—with a focus on creating quality jobs for low-income communities. This new venture seeks to invest in businesses with strong, established value propositions whose model and location, urban or rural, position them to provide a healthy portion of the jobs they create to community members with low-income backgrounds. Urban Catalyst aims to achieve this social objective while generating rates of return in line with socially neutral private equity firms. Once Urban Catalyst establishes a pipeline of investment opportunities and makes a few early investments, the venture may take the step of raising a small, $25 million structured fund.

Urban Catalyst looks to invest in a range of niche market sectors operating in the lower middle market such as precision part manufacturers or food businesses with a regional brand. It will also hold itself accountable to strong creation of quality jobs for members of low-income communities and actively make that outcome a critical piece of measuring success. This social mandate is a key component of both the investment screening criteria and subsequent performance tracking.

99Degrees Custom: Global Growth with Local Economic Impact

As a precursor to Urban Catalyst with the same social mandate in mind, the author recently invested in an early round offered by 99Degrees Custom, a build-to-order apparel manufacturer in Lawrence, MA. 99Degrees Custom was launched in 2013 by Brenna Schneider to capitalize on growing demand among branded active wear companies for customized production capacity in the USA. In an effort to be distinctive and build consumer loyalty, companies like Nike and Under Armour are increasingly interested in offering fresh design changes within a given season along with the ability to order customized apparel product for individual consumers. Both require sophisticated production capabilities and the ability to meet short turnaround times. 99Degrees has established a strong value proposition in order to meet these needs for a number of industry participants and has built an extremely strong pipeline of business (99 Degrees Custom n.d.).

In developing her value proposition, Schneider immediately tapped in to the textile production expertise resident in Lawrence through the local diaspora from the Dominican Republic, until recently the home of a robust garment industry. She also moved swiftly to bring on operating talent well versed in automation and lined up partnerships with companies steeped in the most recent technological advancement in the use of fiber and related materials.

Along with her quest for a commercial leadership position among US apparel manufacturers, Schneider is equally motivated to provide a growing stable of quality jobs for the community of Lawrence. With keen awareness of the competitive realities, Schneider is actively working with key customers to establish operating margin targets that will enable moving the vast majority of 99Degrees' workforce to a living wage over the course of several years along with a program to provide a core set of basic benefits and a fair and engaging workplace. While at an earlier stage of development than Urban Catalyst's core investment model, the author sees the investment in 99Degrees Custom as a prime example of an opportunity to generate an attractive financial return with a business that's committed to providing quality employment for low-income community members and behaving in a socially responsible fashion across all dimensions of the business.

As it grows over the next few years, Urban Catalyst seeks to invest in leading commercial enterprises with a similar social mission.

A World Shaped by Impact Investing

Our country and our world can benefit from new sources of investment in solutions to deter the effects of poverty and climate change and to increase affordable access to quality education and health care. It's heartening to see the burgeoning energy around innovation and a role for private capital and for-profit businesses in the quest for social benefit. While investing for social impact in the private markets is still in its formative stages of development, demand for action among investors is building. Accelerating momentum over the next few years should lead to a more clearly defined market leading to more standardized approaches.

As those approaches standardize, opportunities to invest for strong social and financial returns will develop further at all stages of a business' life cycle. While the availability of capital at different life cycle stages varies by region, there will be a particular opportunity for later stage investors to drive social mission while realizing attractive returns, even as compared to investments without a social mission dimension. This will be true across businesses in which the social mission is part of the core value proposition, as well as those without a direct social purpose but whose operations can, nevertheless, produce positive social outcomes. The opportunity for impact is significant.

References

99 Degrees Custom (n.d.) 99 Degrees custom home page. http://www.99degreescustom.com/. Accessed 29 June 2016

Banerjee D, Collins M (2015) Bain capital hires former Massachusetts Governor Deval Patrick. Bloomberg.   http://www.bloomberg.com/politics/articles/2015-04-14/bain-capital-hires-former-governor-deval-patrick-for-social-fund. Accessed 29 June 2016

Brest P, Born K (2013) Unpacking the impact in impact investing. Stanford Social Innovation Review

Bugg-Levine A, Emerson J (2011) Impact investing. Jossey-Bass, San Francisco

Colorado Impact Fund (n.d.) Colorado impact fund home page. https://coloradoimpactfund.com. Accessed 29 June 2016

HCAP Partners (2016) HCAP home page. http://www.hcapllc.com/. Accessed 29 June 2016

Huntington Capital (2014) Impact case study, quality of workforce. RPI (Reischling Press). Huntington Capital LLC. https://static1.squarespace.com/static/51888c07e4b091a1ff87ef57/t/54be9acae4b0b6737e0993a2/1421777610788/RPI+-+Building+an+Inspired+Culture+-+Nov+2014.pdf. Accessed 29 June 2016

Lewis J (2015) Impact investor motive: money or mission? http://us4.campaign-archive1.com/?u=a7a9993189c38ec285f765cc2&id=41df7c7763&e=b9c773474c. Accessed 29 June 2016

Patagonia (2016) Environmental and social responsibility. http://www.patagonia.com/us/environmentalism. Accessed 29 June 2016

Saltuk Y, Idrissi AE, Bouri A, Mudaliar A, Schiff H (2015) Eyes on the horizon: the impact investor survey. Global Impact Investing Network. https://www.jpmorganchase.com/corporate/Corporate-Responsibility/document/impact-investor-survey-2015.pdf. Accessed 29 June 2016

Sirull B (2015) 2014 Was the year of impact investing: what's next for 2015? Triple Pundit. http://www.triplepundit.com/2015/01/2014-year-impact-investing-whats-next-2015/. Accessed 29 June 2016

SJF Ventures (2015) SJF home page. http://www.sjfventures.com. Accessed 29 June 2016

Under Armour (2012) Code of ethics and business conduct. http://www.uabiz.com/company/ethics.cfm. Accessed 29 June 2016

USSIF Foundation (2014) Report on US sustainable, responsible and impact investing trends. The Forum for Sustainable and Responsible Investment

Impact Investing at the Base of the Pyramid: Unitus Seed Fund

Mary J. Cronin

Abstract The Unitus Seed Fund is an early-stage venture fund focused on investing in companies with innovative, scalable business plans to serve the population at the base of the economic pyramid (BOP). Operating out of Seattle in the USA, and Bangalore in India, the Unitus Fund partners and Fund investors believe that local entrepreneurial activity will provide a strong and sustainable foundation for economic development and improved quality of life at the base of the pyramid in India and other countries. This chapter describes the Unitus Seed Fund investment strategy, profiles the social mission and impact of some of the Fund's portfolio companies in India, and analyzes the challenges of achieving the Fund's dual goals of providing venture investors with superior, long-term capital appreciation by investing in companies that will provide critical services and economic opportunities to millions of BOP individuals in India.

In spring 2016, Unitus Seed Fund launched a second, even larger BOP investment fund that will total $50 million in capital to be used as seed funding for about 30 new social enterprise startups, plus follow on investment in the original portfolio companies. The new fund is raising its capital from many of the original US investors such as Bill Gates and the Dell Foundation, along with more investors from India. As the Unitus Seed Fund looks toward its next 5 years of impact investing in India, the managing partners will apply the lessons and insights gleaned from the current portfolio companies to their future investments.

Keywords Social impact investing • Base of the pyramid investing • BOP • Social impact in India

M.J. Cronin (✉)
Carroll School of Management, Boston College,
140 Commonwealth Avenue, Chestnut Hill, MA 02467, USA
e-mail: cronin@bc.edu

© Springer International Publishing Switzerland 2017
M.J. Cronin, T.C. Dearing (eds.), *Managing for Social Impact*,
Management for Professionals, DOI 10.1007/978-3-319-46021-5_13

The Mathematics of Economic Opportunity

The small group of elementary school students gathered around a table in New Delhi, India, are studying math in a private after-school tutoring program. It's a familiar scene in India's urban landscape, where after-school tutoring represented a US$11 billion market segment in 2013, with projected annual growth rates of 15 % or more (Malani 2016). Many parents rely on private tutoring to make up for widespread failings in the education provided by India's 1.5 million publicly funded K-12 schools. In a 2015 overview of BOP social enterprise models in India, Meghna Rao notes the following telling measures of the public education system. 80 % of India's 250 million public school students drop out before the 8th grade; in fact, almost 50 % of students drop out by the time they reach 5th grade. Even students who stay in government-funded schools through 12th grade may never learn enough to advance economically. Twenty-one percent of grade 4 students in Mumbai can't read first grade texts; 14 % of rural students in grade 8 can't read second grade texts, while 28 % don't know how to divide numbers (Rao 2015).

India's boom in private after-school training is far from a panacea for the shortcomings of public education, however. The highly localized, fragmented, and unregulated tutoring market varies widely in cost and the quality of student learning. That's a source of frustration for parents who pay private tuition, many of whom report being unhappy with the after-school education their children receive. For millions more, the relatively high hourly cost of tutoring puts it out of reach for their families. The eight students learning math around the table in a New Delhi home are studying math exercises from Cuemath, an innovative startup that is tackling the failures in public education by expanding affordable access to high quality after-school education in communities across India.

Jagjit Khurma, a professor with over 30 years of experience in teaching mathematics and his entrepreneurial, math-loving son, Manan Khurma, saw a huge social enterprise opportunity in India's fast-growing but fractured private tutoring market. In 2013, they co-founded CueLearn (the original company name) to deliver afterschool tutoring services, with an initial focus on mathematics training through Cuemath. But the co-founders' passion for mathematics education was not enough to differentiate Cuemath from better-established competition in the crowded math tutoring sector. To create a profitable, high-growth business with a positive social impact, the founders developed a modular, customizable math curriculum for K-8 students with clear, measurable learning outcomes at each stage of the program. Parents can follow along with the weekly lessons, if they wish, and access their children's test grades online. Realizing that many students would not have regular online access, the founders designed Cuemath so that the learning modules could be delivered through paper worksheets as well as mobile devices.

Perhaps the most disruptive aspect of the Cuemath model is the recruitment and training of tutors. Instead of relying on the college grads and traditional teachers who staff many private tutoring programs, Cuemath recruits unemployed, entrepreneurial women and provides special training to prepare them as tutors. Once they are fully trained and certified in the program, the tutors set up micro franchises for Cuemath tutoring services, recruiting students from their local neighborhood. As Manan Khurma, Cuemath's CEO explains, "We empower local women to be teachers. They hold classes out of their homes. This allows us to spend less on infrastructure and, even more importantly, creates a level of trust between the community and our business" (Rao 2015). Training tutors who might otherwise be unemployed, and then supporting their efforts to build micro franchises for local Cuemath programs as independent business people, lowers the costs of customer acquisition and accelerates geographic expansion. It also magnifies the company's social impact by providing a new path to economic opportunity for Cuemath tutors in addition to the educational benefits for students and the affordable tuition costs for parents.

By the end of 2014, just 1 year after its launch, the New Delhi-headquartered Cuemath was overseeing more than 25 local tutoring centers. The co-founders were ready to add new tutors, enhance the curriculum, and expand their operations into more states across India. They needed outside funding to make that growth leap. But early stage, seed investment capital (typically US$100,000 to US$300,000 that is used to validate a business model and demonstrate its ability to scale) is relatively rare in India. Cuemath found the investment that it needed in an unexpected place— the Unitus Seed Fund, co-located in Seattle and Bangalore.

This chapter focuses on Unitus Seed Fund's vision for "activating markets for the masses," particularly at the base of the pyramid (BOP) in India where the majority of the population lack access to quality education, basic healthcare, and opportunities for economic advancement. It analyzes how the Unitus Seed Fund balances the joint goals of delivering strong financial returns to fund investors with catalyzing significant social and economic progress. The business models and social impact of selected Unitus portfolio companies that are aiming to improve the lives of Indians at the base of the pyramid serve as case studies in the potential and challenges of BOP entrepreneurship.

Entrepreneurship at the Base of the Pyramid

"The Fortune at the Bottom of the Pyramid," a 2002 article by C.K. Prahalad and Stuart Hart, highlights the untapped market opportunities embodied in the world's poorest residents. As of 2002, the article defined this bottom tier of the global population as the four billion people worldwide with annual per capita income of less than US$1500. Inside this pyramid base, over a billion people were struggling to live on less than US$1 per day. But even at the lowest income level, the authors argued that goods were being sold and purchased—and that these billions of underserved consumers represented a massive source for commercial growth and profitability (Prahalad & Hart 2002).

A 2007 McKinsey white paper (Ablett et al. 2007) on India's market potential characterized 1.05 billion low-income Indians as living at the base of the economic pyramid, but predicted that a steady rise in business investment and income could reduce these BOP numbers to create a larger, more prosperous Indian middle class by 2015. Business success at the base of the pyramid is far from inevitable, however. Over the past decade, many economists and analysts have challenged the potential for building profitable business models serving BOP populations, in India and elsewhere, noting that, "Stories of well-meaning commercial ventures that couldn't make sustainable profits are all too common in low-income markets" (Simanis 2012).

Independent of the debate about whether the world's poorest consumers have potential to support profitable, high-growth business models, the phrase BOP has come to represent the economic and social struggles of billions of people living in dire poverty, and the multifaceted challenges of improving the lives of such large numbers. How well can social enterprise startups and the funds investing in such companies hope to address these fundamental social issues in a country as large as India, when decades of effort by the public sector and philanthropic giving has not been able to solve them?

Unitus Seed Fund founding partners David Richards and Will Poole were familiar with the debates about BOP challenges and opportunities. Both partners had extensive prior experience working with entrepreneurs and venture funding in India, as well as with social impact investing in the Seattle area. Both had successful careers as entrepreneurial founders and global corporate managers. Based on their experience, Poole and Richards were convinced that a venture capital model providing seed funding would fill a gap in India's startup economy and that the entrepreneurs funded by Unitus could generate significant social and economic advances for India's BOP consumers. Even though India's huge BOP population is facing enormous challenges on multiple fronts, from accessing healthcare and education to finding adequate food, shelter, and employment for themselves and their families, Richards and Poole expressed optimism about an entrepreneurial strategy in a 2012 description of their planned seed fund:

> One impetus for the Unitus Fund founding partners is a conviction that locally initiated entrepreneurial solutions can create a stronger and ultimately more sustainable foundation for economic development and improved quality of life at the base of the pyramid than any amount of external philanthropy or foreign investment … the Fund believes that aid (whether from government or private philanthropy) is a necessary but insufficient approach for bringing economic development to developing countries. Strategic investment is required to sustainably and scalably bring higher living standards in these countries. The Fund intends to pioneer and prove market-based approaches that will help fill this gap.[1]

The managing partners go on to cite this perspective from the International Monetary Fund (2012) on the importance of social entrepreneurship for India:

> India needs to create 10–15 million jobs per year for the next decade to provide gainful employment to its young population. Accelerating entrepreneurship and business creation is crucial for such large-scale employment generation. Moreover, entrepreneurship tends to be innovation-driven and will also help generate solutions to India's myriad social problems including demands for higher-quality education, affordable health care, clean energy and waste management, and financial inclusion. Entrepreneurship-led economic growth is also more inclusive and typically does not involve exploitation of natural resources.

To validate their core strategy of activating and supporting local entrepreneurs who are creating market-based social impact solutions, Unitus Seed Fund founders

---

[1] Unless otherwise noted, quotes from the Unitus Seed Fund founding partners and Fund descriptions are based on private communication between Unitus Seed Fund and the author.

needed more data about the current state of startup activity in India. It was essential to determine if there was an unmet demand for external seed funding and even more fundamentally, if there were in fact enough seasoned entrepreneurs in India committed to generate social change with scalable BOP business models. Prior to the 2012 fund launch, Unitus Labs, an affiliate of the Fund, carried out research in India to more clearly define the venture investment landscape along with the opportunity and challenges for startup businesses seeking to serve BOP populations. In the course of its research study, Unitus Labs staff interviewed over 100 entrepreneurs with experience in sectors relevant for BOP investing, together with leaders of Indian venture capital firms and social impact ecosystem stakeholders.

Based on this research, the Unitus Seed Fund founders concluded the following:

- There is a strong and growing supply of quality entrepreneurs in India with operating experience starting new businesses targeting BOP populations.
- There is a modest amount of "bootstrap" friends and family investment capital available in India for startup businesses to set up and run their initial pilot activities.
- There is a very limited supply of "validation" seed-stage capital (typically US$100,000 to US$300,000) available for businesses in India to validate their business model and prepare the company for the growth phase.
- While there is a reasonable supply of "scale-up" early-stage venture capital (US$500,000 to US$2 million) available from more than a dozen investment funds in India, these fund managers are struggling to find enough companies ready to scale.
- Excluding microfinance, over the 4 year period of 2008–2011, Unitus Labs was only able to identify 21 seed-stage investment transactions (defined as less than US$500,000) in startups serving BOP populations in India—an average of about five seed-stage investments per year in all of India.
- Total investment by "impact venture investors" in 2011 in India was about US$80 million.
- Indian angel investors invested about US$20 million in 2011–2013 in all sectors with the majority of this in the information technology sector.

In summary, the due diligence research conducted in 2011 confirmed that "there is a substantial opportunity to invest at the seed-stage for attractive terms in high-potential businesses which serve rapidly-growing BOP populations in India...India is a frontier, developing economy with substantial natural and human resources, with many hundreds of millions of people striving to attain prosperity" (Unitus Seed Fund 2012).

Strategies for BOP Seed Investing

The research findings, combined with expressions of support from potential fund investors in the USA and partners in India, provided a solid foundation for Richards and Poole, joined by Srikrishna Ramamoorthy, an experienced investor and entrepreneur based in Bangalore, to establish the Unitus Seed Fund in 2012. In keeping with a level of initial seed funding under $500,000 per company, the Fund set a goal of raising enough capital to fund between 20 and 40 startups, with the flexibility to provide larger, follow on investments in portfolio companies that were experiencing rapid growth and meeting revenue goals.

From the beginning, the managing partners sought a balance between providing venture scale returns to Fund investors and generating positive social impact for BOP populations. According to the 2012 Executive Summary of the Unitus Seed Fund private placement memorandum, among the Fund's stated investment goals, the primary goal was "To provide investors with superior, long-term capital appreciation." Providing opportunities to millions of BOP individuals was the next priority, with a third priority being, "To demonstrate the viability of institutional volume investing at the seed-stage for the aforementioned emerging sectors in order to attract additional private capital and generate increased entrepreneurial activity and job creation" (Unitus Seed Fund 2012).

In keeping with the primary goal of achieving a return on investor capital, the Unitus Seed Fund managing partners adhere to the familiar venture capital axiom of seeking seasoned, self-reliant founders with a strong entrepreneurial track record and demonstrated leadership skills. The other desired enterprise characteristics that the Fund's managing partners look for in startups will be familiar to anyone who has been in a position of awarding funds, or pitching a plan for obtaining venture funding in the USA. The partners want to fund companies with a clearly differentiated value proposition combined with a disruptive business model. The startup should have moved beyond concept stage to demonstrate broad market demand and promising unit economics. Founders should have clear strategies in place to build effective distribution and marketing programs and ideally an identified potential future acquirer as well as a realistic chance of attracting a larger round of venture funding within 9–15 months of the seed investment. That $250,000 (or less) to $500,000 of seed funding should have a catalytic impact on the company's implementation cycle, improving their potential for raising additional capital and for successful long-term growth. In general, the business models should be capital efficient—able to scale without incurring high fixed capital expenses for dedicated buildings or infrastructure.

Investing for Impact

Based on this profile of desirable investment targets, the Unitus Seed Fund strategy sounds the same as many other venture funds that make seed-level investments in the United States and globally. What distinguishes the Unitus Fund is the additional screen it uses to assess the potential for its funded entrepreneurs and their business models to generate scalable social impact at the base of the economic pyramid. Unitus defines this quantitatively in its 2012 Executive Summary as "The potential to serve large, underserved BOP populations, including a credible plan to serve

100,000 families (meaning on average over 500,000 people) within 5 years." It looks to invest in companies that will reach those numbers in one or more of the following sectors:

- Livelihoods

    - These businesses seek to provide jobs or increase income generation for BOP populations.

- Education/education technology

    - This is primarily focused on K-12 sectors with an emphasis on supplementary education services, content, and tools which improve learning outcomes for BOP children.

- Basic necessities

    - This includes sectors such as water, energy, housing, healthcare, and food with the goal of providing BOP populations with access to affordable, quality products and services.

Focusing on these sectors helps to ensure that the funded companies—if they do succeed—will meet the goal of impacting half a million people in their first five years. The Unitus Seed Fund is also different from venture investors who consider only models with high profit margins (such as software and technology licensing). The Fund will invest in business models that have relatively low gross margins (because of operating costs) as long as they have the potential for serving large BOP populations and generating proportionately large streams of revenue over time.

Mentoring and advising such startups requires lots of time and attention. The Fund's local presence in India includes a team of nine professionals working for Srikrishna Ramamoorthy in the Bangalore office. This is a fundamental part of the Fund's thesis that strong, indigenous fund management teams are critical to success for early stage investing. Even with such support, the Unitus Fund managing partners recognize that the odds are against seed-level companies surviving long enough to achieve their ambitious goals. So they planned from the outset to make a large number of seed investments to increase the odds of backing successful companies. By investing in multiple sectors (health, education, financial technology, retail, etc.), the Fund also works to mitigate risks that might occur within a single sector. And it uses a cluster strategy (investing in multiple companies in a similar sector which have different revenue models or geographical targets) to leverage expertise and ecosystem partnerships.

Operating out of Seattle as well as Bangalore, the Unitus Seed Fund managing partners and staff were already well connected to a network of global business partners, investors, and well-qualified entrepreneurs in India, thanks to their long-standing association with Unitus Capital and Unitus Labs, which have focused on finance and innovation in India and other developing economies for over a decade. In a 2013 interview about the Fund's launch, Will Poole pointed to this network as an essential factor in identifying promising investments and establishing a robust pipeline of proposals from Indian social entrepreneurs, saying, "There are definitely deals to be done." In prioritizing the returns to Fund investors and the social impact of its portfolio companies, the managing partners acknowledge that at least one component of the traditional venture fund model has fallen by the wayside—they have opted to work for just a fraction of the typical VC fee structure. In Poole's words, "Managing a small fund is not profitable for venture partners. But it can be very profitable for the limited partners [investors]" (Bank 2013).

With a well-defined investing strategy, an experienced team of managing partners, and a successful effort to raise $23 million in capital for seed funding of BOP companies in India, the Unitus Seed Fund was ready to invest in its pipeline of promising entrepreneurs and business models. The next section profiles three of the Fund's early investments.

Three BOP Startup Stories: Education, Health, and Livelihoods

From CueLearn to Cuemath

By 2018, Manan Khurma and Jagjit Khurma, the founders of CueLearn, hope that the eight elementary school students studying Cuemath materials at an after-school tutorial session in New Delhi will be joined by over 500,000 K-8 students and 25,000 home-based tutors operating micro-franchises across India. Each micro-franchise will use the Cuemath platform to create a fast-growing network of after-school education providers. That's an ambitious goal for a company that just launched its services under the name of CueLearn in 2013, but the ability to grow rapidly and scale service delivery with a cost-effective business model are key components of business plans designed to reach India's diverse population. The flexibility to pivot as needed is another essential ingredient. CueLearn founders rebranded their company to do business as Cuemath, leveraging the success of their flagship tutorial program and building on the widespread demand for enhanced mathematics education in India, where math instruction accounts for the majority of the private tutoring market. With a potential market of more than 250 million K-8 students in India, reaching millions of them through widely distributed, low cost math study programs are a focused and potentially very profitable market opportunity. Cuemath's goal of transforming after-school education through a scalable, affordable delivery model that could eventually expand to reach millions of BOP families and K-8 students around India matches up with two of the focus areas for Unitus Seed Fund: enhancing access to quality education and expanding economic opportunity.

By training and empowering previously unemployed homemakers and seniors who conduct the tutorial sessions in their own homes, Cuemath reduces its infrastructure and salary expenses and leverages the built-in incentive for the tutors to actively recruit new students to optimize its marketing and customer acquisition strategies. This model, in combination with a centralized, modular curriculum based on blended learning materials including printed worksheets, removes many of the traditional barriers to rapid expansion into new locations. At the same time, holding regular tutoring sessions and becoming a Cuemath micro-franchise owner provide significant new economic opportunities for entrepreneurial women and senior citizens. While many of the early Cuemath franchises are located in urban centers and serve a diverse economic population, the micro-franchise model can scale over the next few years to expand into smaller cities and even in rural areas.

Cuemath's CEO Manan Khurma and Unitus Seed Fund partner Srikrishna Ramamoorthy summed up these dual benefits in a December 2014 news release announcing the Unitus Seed Fund investment (Unitus Seed Fund 2014):

> Cuemath is disrupting the status quo by providing after-school learning programs for Math and English with a unique distribution model: tapping the incremental efforts of women and senior citizens with basic academic backgrounds, and backing them with by custom-designed learning materials, both paper-based and technology-driven. Cuemath centers are small, home-based setups, with no more than 8 students in each session, ensuring personalized attention to the needs of each learner.
>
> "Our students get a branded and high-quality experience that's fun and produces better results," said Manan Khurma, co-founder and CEO of Cuemath. "Additionally, teachers earn income on a flexible schedule, and parents can be confident their children have what they need to learn, at a price their family can afford."
>
> "Unlike traditional classroom-based tuitions providers, Cuemath is capital efficient and highly scalable, enabling rapid growth everywhere from tier-1 metros to the smallest rural village," said Srikrishna Ramamoorthy, partner at Unitus Seed Fund. "We're excited to provide seed capital and mentoring to help co-founders Manan and Jagjit grow Cuemath rapidly, bringing their superior learning outcomes to the masses in India."

With the Unitus Fund seed investment in hand, Khurma was able to accelerate recruitment of tutors and establish more micro-franchises to deliver Cuemath after-school programs in more Indian cities. This fast early growth and ambitious long-term model for nation-wide franchise development in turn convinced a well-known Indian fund manager and angel investor, Alok Mittal, to invest in the startup in 2015. In a statement at the time of his investment, Mittal (Arora 2015) emphasized the size of the private tutoring opportunity and CueLearn's potential for becoming a leader in the sector:

> "I'm excited about the after-school learning space in India as the opportunity is immense, with no real market leaders at present," said Mittal. "CueLearn's approach to this problem is a business model that is asset-light and extremely scalable, while ensuring high-quality academic delivery. I think the CueLearn team has the strength to execute and I am keen to support them in this endeavor," he added, noting that math learning dominates the after-school private tutoring market in India.

By 2016, Cuemath had expanded its cadre of trained, certified tutors to 1200, with operations in Bengaluru, Delhi, Mumbai, Pune, Hyderabad, and Chennai. The company was ready for another growth spurt, and its business model had been validated to the point of attracting a significant round of new funding. In June 2016, the company received a $4 million investment led by Sequoia India with participation from Unitus Seed Fund. With plans to certify another 5000 micro-franchise tutors by March 2017, Cuemath was on the way to meeting its startup goal of impacting half a million students at the base of the pyramid, providing them with the math skills needed for better paid positions upon completing their education.

Hippocampus Learning Centres

Hippocampus Learning Centres (HLC), India's largest rural preschool chain, is another BOP education provider that benefited from an early United Seed Fund investment.

Headquartered in Bangalore, HLC was founded in 2010 by Umesh Malhotra, who started his tech management career at Infosys then went on to found a successful IT company which he sold in 2002. Prior to starting HLC, Malhotra worked in Europe and the USA, including a stint in Silicon Valley with his family. Watching his young son benefit from the neighborhood library and other Silicon Valley learning experiences inspired an interest in bringing similar resources to the children in Indian villages. In discussing his vision for HLC, Malhotra emphasizes the learning gap that he wanted to fill (Rao 2015):

> The concept of pre-kindergarten schooling is foreign for most children in India. The real issue here is that the void begins even before elementary education. There are no resources to ease children into India's school system. We decided to establish pre-kindergarten and kindergarten schools across rural India. I want these children to have the same excellent education that my son did. The most important thing that I wanted to prove was that you don't need to spend a lot of money to provide quality education.

But the combination of high quality education, an unfamiliar type of service for preschool children, and the conservative culture of India's rural villages posed a daunting challenge even to a seasoned and intrinsically optimistic entrepreneur like Malhotra. In contrast to CueLearn, which developed and quickly scaled a disruptive, low-cost model for expanding within the existing multi-billion dollar market for private after-school tutoring in India, Hippocampus needed time, and venture seed funding, to win parental support and customers for an educational category that was familiar in the USA but unknown to the BOP population in rural India— pre-kindergarten education.

Malhotra launched the HLC model in 2010 with just seven small pilot centers, looking to validate the interest of parents in this type of learning and, importantly, their ability to pay at least 100–250 rupees (about US$2–$5 dollars) a month in tuition. By 2011, it was clear that enough families valued the educational head start that HLC could provide to make a tuition-based revenue model viable as long as overall operating costs could be kept low. HLC launched 18 stand-alone preschool centers and expanded to include after-school learning programs, reaching about 700 children by year's end.

By 2012, it was clear that there was widespread demand from rural parents in many parts of India for the HLC program. HLC was investing in recruiting and training rural teachers to run each center at a relatively low cost, and a program to attract HLC franchise operators was underway. But Malhotra's early funding from friends and family was running low and venture investors were not ready to commit to the level of funding he needed for further growth. The Unitus Seed Fund saw a match with Malhotra's experience and his BOP service vision and the Fund decided to step in with a US$100,000 investment—enough to keep up the growth momentum and to convince other impact funds to make similar commitments to HLC.

"The money from USF came in at the right moment," Umesh Malhotra, Hippocampus's chief executive, said, "We were running out of angel money, and the Series A investors were on the fence. USF coming in was the confidence shot we all needed" (Bank 2013). Even with this essential round of funding, it was clear that HLC would eventually need a much higher level of growth financing to reach its 8-year goal of setting up 100,000 centers to provide three million children with low-cost education. Malhotra acknowledges the challenge. "It's a low-margin business, the impact of good education takes years to demonstrate, and the distributed nature of our business makes it difficult to manage operations," he says. "What attracts funders is potential scale, our ability to reach under-served markets, and making a long-term impact" (Bank 2013).

An early challenge that Umesh and his team faced was finding a way for Hippocampus Learning Centres to integrate their novel approach to learning by experience instead of memorization within the traditional framework of a rural village. One strategy, which also expanded economic opportunities for aspiring teachers living in low employment areas, was to hire HCL teachers locally. As reported by Rao in 2015, Malhotra remembers the importance of establishing personal relationships through these local hires:

> It's a well-known fact that trust dictates the customer flow in rural areas. We had to penetrate the community in order to establish that. After entering a village, the Hippocampus team interviews local young women to hire as teachers. After several rounds of interviews, only 15 % of job applicants are chosen to work at the schools. Each teacher is then connected with an individual from the management team. This helps establish a system of credentials and increases the sense of intimacy we have in our team. When I'd walk into a center, people would see me and say "hey, you're the one who interviewed me, right?"

Now that HLC has expanded to over 200 learning centers and established multiple franchises and school partnerships, its ability to work successfully within the village culture has become a competitive advantage and a barrier to entry for other pre-kindergarten learning providers. According to Nirmala Thyagarajan (Rao 2015), Director of Programs at HLC:

> While Hippocampus' low-cost setup costs and teacher acquisition model are strong enough to scale quickly, the most important factor is aligning with local norms. India is extremely diverse. There are a million different factors that change in rural areas. If you want to successfully scale across all of them, your curriculum needs to be sensitive enough to emanate from each rural area. North India is completely different from Karnataka. Some places are closer to cities than others. Because of this, the Hippocampus team believes that its approach to human led learning is something that won't become outdated. It's hard to even establish a basic understanding of what a rural area needs. You need to hire intelligent teachers that can deliver that.

The boost provided by Unitus seed funding in 2012, and a follow on investment in 2014 by Unitus, the Khosla Impact Fund, and the Asian Development bank allowed HLC to sustain its growth trajectory and to demonstrate the long-term viability of its business model. As of June 2016, Malhotra announced plans to raise an additional US$6 million investment—a big step on the way to achieving his vision of providing three million Indian children with a low-cost quality education by 2018 (Hippocampus Learning Centres 2016).

AddressHealth

At the top of India's $100 billion healthcare sector are many of the world's most highly skilled doctors and care providers, working in state of the art facilities. Access to this top level of care, however, is typically limited to the wealthy. The majority of India's healthcare resources are channeled into large cities and the benefits are concentrated among the top 10–15 % of the population. At the other end of the pyramid, the urban and rural poor suffer from poor quality healthcare even when they seek treatment from high-priced private clinics. The health problems of India's BOP children are often undiagnosed or untreated. According to a 2011 UNICEF profile of children's health and well-being in India, despite some progress in key health indicators India's youngest and poorest residents still suffer disproportionately from chronic, often life-threatening health issues—many of them preventable. As the UNICEF study concludes:

> But with nearly half a billion children in this country, a lot more remains to be done to ensure the survival, growth and development of India's greatest asset: its children. Stubbornly high malnutrition rates, poor sanitation and persistent disparities between states, social groups and the rich and the poor are just some of the obstacles we face in ensuring that every child is reached (UNICEF 2011).

The increasing demand for better healthcare services at the base of the pyramid, like the failures in India's public education system, creates a huge opportunity for impact-minded healthcare entrepreneurs. Two such doctor-entrepreneurs are the co-founders of AddressHealth, which was created in March 2010 with the vision of providing children at the bottom of the pyramid in India with basic health screening and preventative services like vaccination as well as diagnosing and treating prevalent childhood illnesses.

Dr. Anand Lakshman, AddressHealth Co-Founder and CEO, is an experienced public health manager who has developed healthcare policy at regional, national, and international levels, including work with the World Health Organization and the Micronutrient Initiative, an international technical agency, on programs which have reached more than 114 million children. Dr. Anoop Radhakrishnan, Co-Founder, is a doctor entrepreneur with a passion for setting up new generation healthcare ventures. Both were well aware of the gap in health services provided to children at the bottom of the pyramid in India, and determined to create a business model that could reach a significant number of those most in need of healthcare.

AddressHealth's core model was to create "one-stop" Child Health Clinics that serve as a base to reach out to schools, preschools, and residential groups in selected communities. The first clinic was set up in 2010 in Bangalore. Each clinic offers affordable preventive and primary health services to children through an integrated approach, serving as a medical home for children living in a defined geography, providing services for pediatric illnesses, common dental procedures and dental hygiene promotion, vision checks, children's eye wear, and vaccinations. Clinics include a pharmacy that stocks pediatric drugs and vaccines to address the most frequent needs of their patients. While the government is required to provide health services to India's public schools, there is no such support for the growing number of private schools in urban and rural areas. AddressHealth works to fill that vacuum by charging private schools a small fee to participate in their School Health programs. To reduce their own infrastructure costs, they leverage space in private schools to serve as combination school clinics during the day and one-stop Child Health Clinics for all local families during non-school hours.

AddressHealth established a goal of delivering comprehensive primary healthcare services to one million children by the year 2018 with more than 300,000 of them belonging to low-income families. In 2014, after 4 years of operation, AddressHealth was serving more than 28,000 children through its Child Health Clinics and affiliated School Health programs. At that point, it received a seed investment from Unitus. During 2015, the company expanded dramatically to reach almost 100,000 children with some form of health service. This was an impressive growth spurt, but clearly AdddressHealth needed a more scalable strategy and the resources to grow even more quickly for the company to meet its long-term impact goals.

In May 2016, AddressHealth received $1.5 million in funding from a Series A investment led by Gray Matters Capital, with participation from Unitus Seed Fund. The founders celebrated this infusion of capital as an avenue to expanding the impact of their clinics and school-based health services model, with CEO Lakshman stating that, "The funding allows us to expand the reach of our unique model of healthcare, which leverages schools." Co-founder Anoop Radhakrishnan promised, "We will use technology to further expand our reach, reduce costs, and promote proactive preventive health action by parents and schools" (Pitchiah 2016).

These three Unitus portfolio companies, like all the startups funded to date, combine the characteristics that the founding partners outlined for the Fund: venture investment fundamentals such as experienced founders and disruptive, scalable business models together with the potential for impacting millions of BOP users to improve education, health, and economic opportunity. In addition to clustering some of its seed investment in education and healthcare companies, the managing partners have also funded a number of startups in diverse business sectors that offer employment or revenue enhancement opportunities to BOP workers. One such startup, DriveU, illustrates the intersection of savvy investment strategy, an emphasis on competitive business models, and long-term potential for improving livelihoods that characterizes the Unitus Fund approach.

Bangalore-based Humble Mobile Solutions Pvt. Ltd. launched DriveU in July 2015 with a plan to flip the car-on-demand model dominated by Uber (and in India by Ola, a similar service) by providing drivers-on-demand through a mobile app for Indians who owned cars but didn't want to drive and park in congested urban areas, or who just preferred their own vehicle over a taxi service. The DriveU management team met the Unitus Fund criteria for seasoned entrepreneurs—CEO Rahm Shastry had experience with an Uber-like startup that was acquired by Ola for $200 million in 2015; and co-founders Ashok Shastry and Amulmeet Singh had also worked with successful startups. DriveU had also validated the demand for drivers-on-demand by growing 50 % month over month during the second half of 2015, providing over 20,000 paid trips, and expanding operations into Bengaluru, Chennai, Mumbai, and Delhi. Its mobile interface, quality service level, and the thorough vetting of its drivers had all been well received by consumers. The basic model of charging a 20 % commission on the hourly driver fee could generate significant long-term revenue growth as long as DriveU succeeded in capturing a large part of the driver-on-demand market.

DriveU also met the Fund's social impact screen. It was aiming to hire a network of over 100,000 regular drivers in major Indian cities by 2018, paying them between 50 % and 100 % more than typical private driver wages, while providing service training and even health benefits for full-time drivers—a very unusual benefit for BOP employment. Despite these attractive features, the Fund's managing partners saw a risk in DriveU's early success—what would prevent Uber or Ola from simply copying their model by offering drivers-on-demand in tandem with their proven taxi-on-demand model? If those market leaders started competing directly, DriveU could be in trouble. An article in the New York Times (Raghavan 2016) describes how Unitus Seed Fund managing partners spent time probing this issue with the DriveU founders before committing to an investment:

> On a hot afternoon in a two-story house here, as dogs barked and auto-rickshaws sputtered outside, a venture capitalist grilled three entrepreneurs. Their startup, DriveU, provides on-demand drivers for people with cars, differing from Uber or Olacabs, an Indian variant, which offer on-demand taxi services. …"What will it take for someone to come in and replicate this?" asked Srikrishna Ramamoorthy, a partner for Unitus Seed, a venture capital fund started out of Seattle that invests in Indian companies. "Couldn't the Ola guys come in and do this?" … "Essentially they could," said Ashok Shastry, 25, a co-founder of DriveU. "But it would be taking away from their focus." The models for Uber and Ola, he said, are built on the premise that customers do not use their own cars. The venture capitalist persisted. If Uber and Ola were to enter the market, "What would your response be?" he asked.

The DriveU founders received a Unitus Seed Fund investment only after surviving a typically tough venture capital grilling and convincing the Fund's managing partners that their company could compete and survive.

Such careful investment screening helps to explain why so many of the Fund's startups are meeting their business growth and funding milestones. AddressHealth, Cuemath, and HLC have already received a significant round of venture investment by other funds to supplement the capital provided by Unitus. This early success bodes well for the Fund providing a return to Unitus Seed Fund investors. But a solid financial performance is just one of three Unitus Seed Fund goals. The next section will describe how Unitus is measuring the social impact of its portfolio companies on India's BOP population and provide data from the Fund's 2015 Impact Report.

Impact Assessment: Unitus Seed Fund Framework and Outcomes

Since the launch of Unitus Seed Fund in 2012, the managing partners have evaluated over 2000 business plans to select their first 23 portfolio companies. AddressHealth, Cuemath, and Hippocampus Learning Centres are just three of a group of healthcare and education startups; the portfolio also includes companies in the agriculture, financial, mobile, and retail commerce sectors. Each year, the Fund conducts a review of the level of impact generated by the entire portfolio. It divides impact into three categories as follows:

- Social: Portfolio companies have the potential to reach at least 100,000 BOP families, and/or directly employ up to 1000 BOP individuals across geographies in 5 years.
- Financial: Investees are on a path to financial sustainability through increased revenues and additional capital.
- Ecosystem: Every company benefits from, influences, and improves the functioning of the overall market ecosystem.

Figure 1 illustrates the Unitus Seed Fund impact measurement framework, which is based on a logic model that considers inputs, activities, outputs, and the outcomes of the Fund's portfolio companies to assess broad-based impact.

As of December 2015, the Fund reports that its portfolio companies collectively have touched 655,877 BOP lives, including the patients and students served by companies like Cuemath, HLC, and AddressHealth, as well as over 1000 teachers, artisans, store owners, drivers, and others employed by the 23 funded startups. One measure of the business value of its investments—and the very early stage of most of the funded companies—is that the collective cumulative revenue of Unitus Seed funded startups has increased dramatically from just $379,863 as of December 2013 to $5,944,626 as of December 2015.

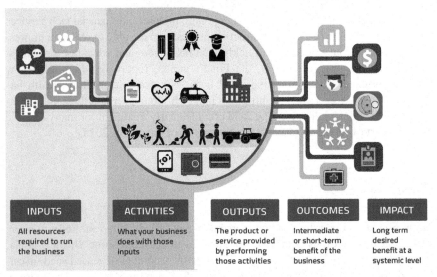

Fig. 1 Unitus Seed Fund impact measurement framework (Unitus Seed Fund 2015)

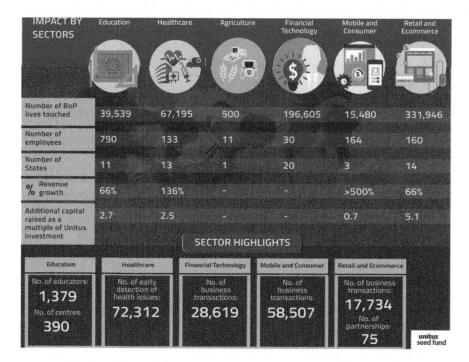

Fig. 2 Cumulative social impact of Unitus Seed Fund portfolio companies by sector (Unitus Seed Fund 2015)

Figure 2 breaks down selected impact measures by industry sector, giving a sense of the pace of growth and the number of lives touched by different types of startup business models at an early stage of development.

It's no surprise that companies providing retail, mobile, and financial tech services (such as shopping and payment transaction processing) are able to reach an impressive number of consumers more quickly than healthcare and education providers. To calibrate the level of impact, the Fund's annual report also highlights how selected companies are improving BOP lives. For example, AddressHealth has already detected over 53,000 health issues in the children it screens through its clinics and 130 school health programs, and provided early treatment for many of these issues as part of seeing 2986 pediatric patients as of the end of 2015.

Conclusion

Unitus Seed Fund investors and partners know that, as with any venture firm, many of the startups that they fund will not succeed in accomplishing all their goals, or even survive in the long run. The failure rate of general US-focused seed investments is estimated to be around 90 % within a 5-year period. In its 2014 report on

"Startup Death Trends," CB Insights notes that, "Companies at the earliest stages are the most vulnerable due to limited financial runway, immature products and businesses and general uncertainty about whether the market needs what they've built." Early momentum is critical—if a startup hasn't raised more capital or identified a potential acquirer within its first 15 months, "things are not looking good" (CB Insights 2014).

For social impact investors focusing on the base of the pyramid there is no comparable data on overall survival rates of portfolio companies, but given the challenges of BOP business formation in general and the infrastructure and operational issues commonly faced by startups in India, it's reasonable to expect that a large proportion of the companies funded early in this decade may not be around in their current form by 2020.

Nonetheless, the Unitus Seed Fund managing partners and investors are convinced that their investment screening and active mentoring strategies will enable enough of their portfolio companies to overcome the daunting odds to yield a superior return on investor capital. There is a growing body of research to back up their conviction. A benchmarking study by Cambridge Associates and the Global Impact Investing Network (GIIN) in 2015 concluded that, "Private impact investment funds—specifically private equity and venture capital funds—that pursue social impact objectives have recorded financial returns in line with a comparative universe of funds that only pursue financial returns." What's more, smaller impact investing funds (defined as under $100 million) often outperformed comparable non-impact investing funds, returning a pooled 9.5 % net IRR (Cambridge Associates 2015).

If the Unitus Seed Fund can meet or do better than this rate of return, the benefits will extend far beyond the financial payoff for Fund investors. The third, and possibly the most impactful goal of the Fund's managing partners is to demonstrate the viability of seed-stage investing at the base of the pyramid in order to attract additional private capital and generate increased entrepreneurial activity and job creation. Delivering market-rate (or better) returns based on a replicable investment strategy is a key element in attracting more social capital and encouraging more investment managers to create BOP seed funds that will support thousands more social entrepreneurs in India and in other countries.

So far, the Unitus Seed Fund track record is impressive. By the first half of 2016, eight of the Unitus startup companies had already raised Series A venture funding, and eight more were in the process of receiving investments. Two had raised a Series B round to support even faster expansion. In total, more than half of their portfolio companies had received additional funding, or were poised to announce an investment soon. There have been just two portfolio company shut downs and two more that were sold at a loss. And there was already one home run, with a portfolio company that generated a 10× return on the Fund's investment through a partial exit. Of course, it's still early in the life cycle of this group of companies; the long-term success rate may more closely map the US averages. But even if just a handful of portfolio companies achieve their impact goals, the Fund will have created significant value for India's BOP population through expanded access to quality healthcare, education, and economic opportunity that will ripple out to the family members and social networks of those who are benefiting directly from the services provided by portfolio companies.

In a broader economic context, every successful Unitus Seed Fund investment provides an incentive to other BOP investors, attracting more resources for innovative Indian entrepreneurs. This creates a virtuous spiral of economic development where it is needed the most. Even that group of startups that don't survive in their current form can provide valuable lessons for both founders and investors. The opportunity to learn from failure and rethink business models can also strengthen local BOP entrepreneurial culture and build capacity for future ventures.

In spring 2016, Unitus Seed Fund launched a second, even larger BOP investment fund that will total $50 million in capital to be used as seed funding for about 30 new social enterprise startups, plus follow on investment in the original portfolio companies. The new fund is raising its capital from many of the original US investors such as Bill Gates and the Dell Foundation, along with more investors from India. As the Fund looks toward its next 5 years of impact investing in India, the managing partners will apply the lessons and insights gleaned from the current portfolio companies to their future investments.

The long-term goals of the Unitus Seed Fund that will continue to guide the decision-making in Seattle and in India are highlighted on the Fund's web site (Unitus Seed Fund 2016):

> We fund and support entrepreneurs who build scalable, sustainable impact businesses and that remains our investing specialty. It is as much about building an economically inclusive India as it is about financial returns. Our philosophy is that impact is maximized when is one is focused on building a scalable and sustainable business. As these businesses serving India's mass/low-income segments scale up and head towards profitability, the impact will also grow in scale.

References

Ablett J, Baijal A, Beinhocker E, Bose A, Farrell D, Gersch U et al. (2007) The bird of gold: the rise of India's consumer market. McKinsey. http://www.mckinsey.com/global-themes/asia-pacific/the-bird-of-gold. Accessed 21 July 2016
Arora V (2015) Tuition startup CueLearn raises angel funding from ex-Canaan Partners MD Alok Mittal. *Techcircle*. http://techcircle.vccircle.com/2015/08/03/tuition-startup-cuelearn-raises-angel-funding-from-ex-canaan-partners-md-alok-mittal/. Accessed 21 July 2016
Bank D (2013) Seeding startups at the base of India's pyramid. *Huffington Post*. http://www.huffingtonpost.com/david-bank/seeding-startups-at-the-b_b_2403144.html. Accessed 21 July 2016
Cambridge Associates (2015) http://www.cambridgeassociates.com/news/articles/private-impact-investing-funds-yielded-financial-performance-in-line-with-similar-private-investment-funds-with-no-social-objective/. Accessed 21 July 2016
CB Insights (2014) The RIP report—startup death trends. CB Insights. https://www.cbinsights.com/blog/startup-death-data/. Accessed 21 July 2016
Hippocampus Learning Centres (2016) Hippocampus Learning Centres home page. http://hlc.hippocampus.in/#1st/1. Accessed 21 July 2016

International Monetary Fund (2012) cited by Unitus Seed Fund executive summary. http://bit.ly/OAVLCK. Accessed 21 July 2016

Malani S (2016) Impact investing in K-12 education in India. Working paper for the Shell Centenary Scholarship Fund, p. 10.

Pitchiah V (2016) Pediatric healthcare chain AddressHealth gets $1.5 mn from Gray Matters, Unitus. vccircle. http://www.vccircle.com/news/healthcare-services/2016/05/25/pediatric-healthcare-chain-addresshealth-gets-15-mn-gray-matters. Accessed 21 July 2016

Prahalad CK, Hart S (2002) The fortune at the bottom of the pyramid. *Strategy+Business*. http://www.strategy-business.com/article/11518?gko=9a4ba. Accessed 21 July 2016

Raghavan A (2016) For Indian startups, tenacity beats high tech. New York Times. http://tech.economictimes.indiatimes.com/news/startups/for-indian-startups-tenacity-beats-high-tech/51789624. Accessed 21 July 2016

Rao M (2015) It's not business as usual: startups in healthcare, education, livelihoods. Capria Ventures LLC, Seattle

Simanis E (2012) Reality check at the bottom of the pyramid. Harvard Business Review. https://hbr.org/2012/06/reality-check-at-the-bottom-of-the-pyramid. Accessed 21 July 2016

UNICEF (2011) The situation of children in India: a profile. UNICEF, p.7

Unitus Seed Fund (2012) Unitus Seed Fund executive summary

Unitus Seed Fund (2014) http://usf.vc/unitus-seed-fund-invests-in-cuemath-bringing-affordable-quality-after-school-learning-programs-to-a-home-near-you/. Accessed 21 July 2016

Unitus Seed Fund (2015) Impact report 2015

Unitus Seed Fund (2016) Impact by numbers: here's the math. Unitus Seed Fund. http://usf.vc/impact-by-numbers-heres-the-math/. Accessed 21 July 2016

Part VI
Measuring and Reporting on Social Impact

Measuring Success in the Development of Smart and Sustainable Cities

Ruthbea Yesner Clarke

Abstract As cities increasingly become hubs for the world's population, their built environments and existing infrastructure are often inadequate to respond to population growth and changing resident needs. In addition, cities contribute disproportionately to climate change. It has become imperative, therefore, to develop methods for creating "Smart Cities," that use technology, design, and metrics to improve efficiency, reduce emissions, and improve lives for their citizens.

The Smart City movement has become global. The movement has, in turn, produced a range of measurement systems available to help cities set and then work toward both smart city and sustainability goals. Three of the most widely adopted are the British Standards Institute (BSI) Maturity Model, the International Standards Organization (ISO) standard indicators for city services and quality of life, and the IDC Smart Cities MaturityScape. Rather than choosing between them, managers tasked with developing smart city approaches would do well to combine the three for the most complete picture. Together, they offer not only quantitative measures, but also aspirational models and a path toward smart city "maturity."

Keywords Smart City • Sustainable cities • BSI Maturity Model • ISO 37120 • IDC MaturityScape

Introduction

According to the United Nations, 2007 was the first year in which the global urban population was larger than the global rural population. Since that announcement, there has been an increasing focus on the importance of cities and, with the advent of technological advances, the creation and growth of the Smart Cities movement.

In 2014, the urban population made up 54 % of the total worldwide population. According to the UN Department of Economic and Social Affairs, this number will increase by an additional 2.5 billion people by 2050 with 66 % of the global

R.Y. Clarke (✉)
IDC, 5 Speen Street, Framingham, MA 01701, USA
e-mail: rclarke@idc.com

© Springer International Publishing Switzerland 2017   239
M.J. Cronin, T.C. Dearing (eds.), *Managing for Social Impact*,
Management for Professionals, DOI 10.1007/978-3-319-46021-5_14

population living in urban environments (2014). This growth in urban population has significant ramifications in regard to climate change, urban resilience, and economic development. Globally, cities generate more than 80 % of the global GDP and are the economic engines of their host countries (World Bank 2016). However, cities are also big contributors to climate change as they consume two-thirds of the world's energy and produce over 70 % of global CO_2 emissions (Sims 2009). Cities are at risk for natural disasters, such as storm surges, given that 500 million urban residents live near coastal areas. And we see evidence today of urban challenges that could worsen if cities and their host nations do not invest in solutions supported by effective policies—increased traffic, lack of affordable housing, lack of access to clean water and other basic services, growth in slums or informal settlements, and increases in crime—all resulting from rapidly growing and concentrated populations. In short, the growth of cities must be managed effectively in order to capture the opportunities they provide (World Bank 2016).

The goal of Smart Cities is to leverage emerging technologies and innovation to attempt to manage this urban growth sustainably and with a view to the future. Smart Cities use technologies (for example, mobile computing, the Internet of Things and connected devices, social networks, and Big Data analytics) to generate information and help:

- **Plan development and land use better**: This can include building roads, hospitals, schools, and libraries where there is the most need and in locations convenient for the most users.
- **Coordinate complex systems more effectively**: Examples here include coordinating traffic signaling for reducing congestion, predicting electricity needs and load distribution, and understanding the flow and movement of people throughout neighborhoods.
- **Optimize the efficient use of resources**: Examples here include using technology to detect water leaks or pressure changes in pipes for faster fixes, scheduling optimal bus routes to reduce traffic and fuel consumption while serving the most people, and providing information to citizens so they can manage their own consumption of water, electricity, and fuel.

The potential impact of a Smart City transformation should not be understated. With current and projected urban populations, these solutions can touch the majority of people in the world, impact the environment in significant ways, and support global economic growth. With the inflexibility of urban-built environments to adapt at the pace of digital transformation, it is up to the cities themselves to leverage data, technology, and people to affect change and to design with sustainability top of mind.

What Is a Smart and Sustainable City?

There is no universal definition of a "city" or urban settlement based on population size or other numeric factors (UN Department of Economic and Social Affairs 2014). Cities can have 200,000 or 15 million residents, and there can be variation in population density, concentration of jobs and/or the availability of infrastructure and services like roads, schools, water, and other public services. The International Organization for Standardization, in its ISO 37101 Sustainable Development of Communities standard, defines a city as an "urban community falling under a specific administrative boundary, commonly referred to as a city, municipality or local government" (ISO 2014). IDC defines a city as a financial, commercial, social, and cultural hub of built infrastructure and resident services where the resident workforce is not involved in agriculture and where there is a high density of available jobs. Within the definition of a Smart City, most of the world takes a broad view of what a city is—it can be a district, town, city, county, and/or metropolitan area—as long as it is a finite entity with its own governing authority that is more on the local than the national level.

The idea of the *smart* city is relatively new and evolving. Every city is unique, with its own historical development path, current characteristics, and future dynamic, but every city also shares many commonalities with other cities, as described above. There are many definitions of Smart Cities, stemming from cities themselves, academics, and technology suppliers, all of which center around similar themes of technology use, sustainability, and quality of life, but which may emphasize different aspects based on varying research focus areas, branding and/or attempts at differentiation. Some cities may focus on being transparent, some on tourism; some vendors focus on connectivity, like Cisco's Smart+Connected Communities, or cognitive computing, like IBM, depending on their offerings. Here are some definitions of smart city solutions developed by thought leaders in the public and private sector:

Singapore: Singapore was one of the first city-states to have a smart city strategy, which it has expanded to "Smart Nation." Singapore states that, "Singapore is pushing towards becoming the world's first Smart Nation, one that will improve the quality of life for individuals and business opportunities for enterprises. In a Smart Nation, we also seek to create an anticipatory Government that can better serve our citizens and better able to use technology to enhance public services, empowering citizens to able to be more participatory in engaging government, as well as businesses, to make more informed decisions and meaningful choices in their daily living" (IDA Singapore 2014).

European Commission: In Smart Cities, digital technologies translate into better public services for citizens, better use of resources, and less impact on the environment (European Commission 2015). In the EIP_SCC strategy, the European Commission offered this definition, "Smart cities should be regarded as systems of people interacting with and using flows of energy, materials, services and financing to catalyze sustainable economic development, resilience, and high quality of life; these flows and interactions become smart through making strategic use of information and communication infrastructure and services in a process of transparent urban planning and management that is responsive to the social and economic needs of society" (European Commission 2013).

Barcelona: "The *Smart City* is a new concept defining a city that works to improve the quality of its citizens' lives by guaranteeing sustainable social, economic and urban development. A *smart city* is based on the use and modernization of new information and communication technologies (ICT) to provide more efficient management of the city's services and resources" (BCN Smart City n.d.).

Smart Cities Council: "A smart city uses information and communications technology (ICT) to enhance its livability, workability and sustainability. In simplest terms, there are three parts to that job: collecting, communicating and 'crunching.' First, a smart city *collects* information about itself through sensors, other devices and existing systems. Next, it *communicates* that data using wired or wireless networks. Third, it *'crunches'* (analyzes) that data to understand what's happening now and what's likely to happen next" (Smart Cities Council 2015).

IDC: A smart city embodies digital transformation in the state and local context. Smart city initiatives are an approach by which organizations use digital technologies to change/innovate operating models, provide improvements on current products and services, and deliver new products and services to residents, visitors, and businesses that are financially, socially, and environmentally sustainable (Wang et al. 2016).

The British Standards Institute (BSI): The BSI defines a smart city as one where there is "effective integration of physical, digital and human systems in the built environment to deliver a sustainable, prosperous and inclusive future for its citizens" (Juvara 2015).

World Bank: "At its most basic level, a city is comprised of a government (in some form), people, industry, infrastructure, education and social services. A smart city thoughtfully and sustainably pursues development with all of these components in mind with the additional foresight of the future needs of the city. This approach allows cities to provide for its citizens through services and infrastructure that address both the current needs of the population as well as for projected growth" (Comstock 2012).As one can observe, regardless of the specifics, all the definitions and descriptions tend to include similar themes, such as:

- Sustainable economic growth, both financially and environmentally (use of resources, ability to sustain and maintain systems)
- Urban livability and quality of life (safety, community engagement, open data, an innovative culture, education, health, less traffic congestion, etc.)
- Economic development (attracting talent, businesses, tourists, etc.)

These themes continue to evolve over time, as shown in Fig. 1. For example, prior to 2014, the Smart City movement was widely viewed as a technology solution to reduce operational costs. In 2015, this shifted to a discussion around smart cities supporting economic development and attracting new business investment or start-ups to an area. In 2016 there has been discussion around the role of smart cities in setting a roadmap for the future investment plans of a city, which are highly important to city residents, investors, and business.

These themes express some fundamental ways that a smart city is different from a traditional city. But how does a city go about achieving smart city status? Is it as

Smart City Transformation Themes

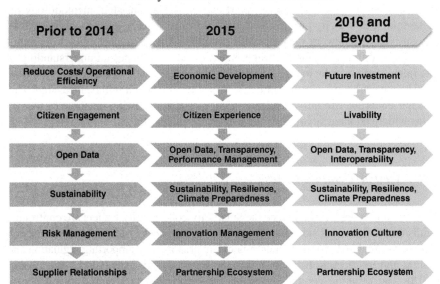

Fig. 1 Evolution of the themes encompassing a smart city © IDC, 2015

simple as just saying, "We're going to be a smart city?" It cannot be, because that would reduce the term to mere marketing, whereas the common understanding among all the various definitions is that smart cities achieve specific, beneficial outcomes for their residents. That leads to the importance of developing frameworks for assessing growth and measuring success.

The Why, What, and How of Smart City Measurement

As one can see from the definitions described above, not only do they vary in meaning and details, but they also use high-level and broad terms, such as "improve quality of life", "effective integration," and "sustainability." While these give city leaders an idea of smart city goals and outcomes, they don't help much in determining which cities are actually "smart," or the process by which a city would be able to define and measure achievement of these outcomes.

With more cities adopting the "smart city" designation, the lack of consistent definitions and goals becomes more problematic. Most cities use the term to indicate that they are investing in specific technology solutions, or that they embrace the smart city ideals around innovation, resident engagement, and sustainability. The types of projects undertaken under the smart city umbrella range widely, however, encompassing open data portals, public WiFi, water sensors to detect leaks, and much more. Just as with the variation in definitions, there is wide variation in priorities and projects that cities point to when stating that they are becoming "smart." Without a more consistent view of what a smart city is, and a consistent methodology for determining how a city progresses to be "smart," measuring success isn't possible. A consistent framework develops a common language, enables cities to be compared and contrasted using the same metrics, and coordinates an understanding of the future path. In order to measure smart cities, one must first be able to define what is to be measured, why it is important to measure, and how it will be measured. This chapter undertakes to answer those critical questions, drawing on some of today's most widely adopted smart city measurement frameworks.

Why Measure Smart Cities?

As more and more cities embrace the smart city concept, city leaders are confronted with complexity on all sides—in their IT and operational systems, in the connection between digital and physical environments, in creating the supporting regulation and policy, and in effecting behavior change to meet desired goals (Clarke and Brooks 2015). The resulting complexity and change management required to test a new approach to managing and growing a city can be a daunting task for city leaders, especially as they try to manage their risk and effectively use limited resources, like money and staffing. Having a framework by which to deconstruct this broad Smart City movement can reduce risk and provide a focused approach to managing change.

Measuring smart cities projects and their success or failure provides the following benefits:

- A common definition of terms so that everyone involved, from department heads, to the mayor, to citizen groups, to technology suppliers, is speaking the same language when discussing complex topics.
- The ability for cities to take a baseline, define where they want to go, and understand the gap between the two.
- To be able to quantify goals and outcomes. For example, how is sustainability as a goal measured? Once a measurement is determined, like a reduction in CO_2 emissions or harmful particulates in the air, then success or failure can be measured.
- Assessment and measurement allow cities to benchmark and compare themselves against their peers, or even from department to department within one city. This helps cities reduce their investment risk as they can follow the best practices and measures of other successful city initiatives.

Ultimately, measurement is a form of assessment that can help cities and those who manage them to get from Point A to Point B. Determining the specific measurements is itself a fundamental step in setting the direction; what smart cities decide to measure will impact what they invest in, how they develop solutions, and what is counted as a success. The outcomes a city decides to measure impacts the entire project, which means that in order for cities to call themselves "smart cities," some level of standardization should be in place in terms of measurements.

Current Models for Assessment: What and How Are We Measuring?

Three types of assessment tools are described below. Each one strives to take the complexity of a city and develop a framework that is broad enough to apply to any city — small, large, developed or emerging — while also being thorough enough to be useful. Frameworks need to be broad enough to leave room for some interpretation, to not be overly prescriptive given that cities have their unique issues. There is a balance between being thorough and detailed, but not overly complicated and hard to use. Similarly, frameworks for assessment cannot reduce complex topics to concepts and steps that are too simplistic. As stated on the British Standards Institute (BSI) website, "cities and their delivery partners face complex choices about what type of future they are seeking to create in order to meet aspirations of their citizens" (BSI 2016).

The British Standards Institute Maturity Model

The British Standards Institute is a highly respected, accredited standards organization, officially recognized by the British government for issuing national standards, as well as internationally recognized for standards that range from products standards (i.e., seat belts, copper wire) to quality and management standards (air pollution monitoring, occupational health and safety standards). The UK Department for Business Innovation and Skills commissioned BSI to develop smart city standards for the UK and BSI. The BSI has developed several Publicly Available Specifications (PAS) related to smart cities, including:

- Standards on smart city terminology (PAS 180): This is a comprehensive list of key smart city vocabulary and their definitions.
- Standards for Smart city frameworks and strategies standard (PAS 181): PAS 181 is a framework of repeatable patterns, taken from best practices, to help city leaders develop their smart cities strategies. Its focus is on the processes by which cities can use technology and data to create a whole-city approach.
- The development of a Data concept model for smart cities (PAS 182): PAS 182 provides a model for data interoperability so that data from many sources can be classified, discovered, and combined to uncover insights about the needs and behaviors of a city's residents and businesses.

The BSI's work is founded in its overarching goals of standards in general. The assumption of the group is that standards will enable cities to reduce risks, costs, and effort in implementing and managing smart cities.

The BSI Smart City Maturity Assessment, depicted in Fig. 2, is a method to determine the level of development of a city from seven dimensions, ranging from the Leadership Environment to Performance Management. Each of the seven components is described, via its characteristics, in five levels of maturity. The levels are

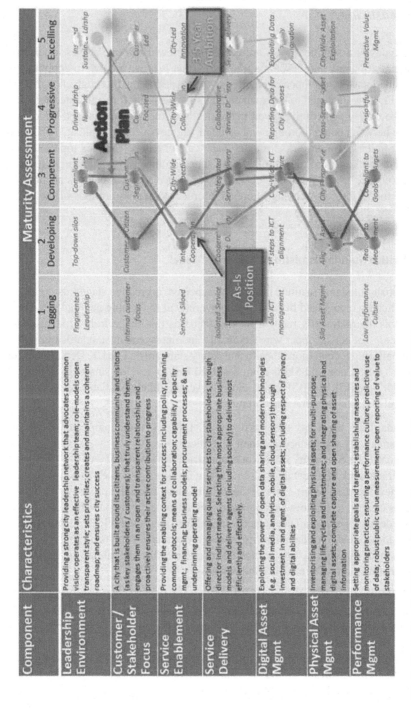

Fig. 2 Illustration of a BSI smart city maturity assessment (Source: UrbanDNA)

progressive stages that show a city's progress—the lowest level being "Lagging" and the highest, "Excelling."

The BSI model has a broad, strategic focus on the process of transformation and innovation of cities, therefore providing a valuable input for the analysis of stakeholder interaction models, governance patterns, and overall policy issues. A city can assess itself along each of the seven components to determine its "As-Is Position" relative to its 3–5 year Ambition. This then sets the groundwork for how to achieve the Ambition state.

The BSI framework offers both an assessment and a process by which to get to the outcomes a city wants by having cities collect and review the information on their current and desired status and ensuring the engagement of multiple stakeholders in the process.

ISO 37120: Sustainable Development of Communities—Standard Indicators for City Services and Quality of Life

The International Standards Organization is a global, independent, nongovernmental organization that develops international standards through its members. ISO members include 161 standards bodies that work together to develop standards across a wide swath of topics (BSI is an ISO member); ISO has published more than 21,000 international standards. These standards are what make products interoperable and ensure quality and safety. ISO solely develops standards; it does not provide certifications of compliance with its standards or conformity assessments. These are provided by separate certification organizations.

ISO 37120, Standard Indicators for City Services and Quality of Life, was published in early 2014 as the first international standard of measurement for city data. ISO 37120 used research from the Global City Indicators Facility, which has a network of 255 global cities on which these indicators were tested. The Global City Indicators Facility is hosted by the Global Cities Institute, which is part of the University of Toronto in Canada. The ISO standard has 17 themes:

1. Economy
2. Education
3. Energy
4. Environment
5. Finance
6. Fire and Emergency Response
7. Governance
8. Health
9. Recreation
10. Safety
11. Shelter
12. Solid Waste
13. Telecommunications and Innovation

14. Transportation
15. Urban Planning
16. Waste Water
17. Water and Sanitation

The standard contains 46 core indicators and 54 supporting indicators across the 17 themes. This work strives to ensure that cities are measuring and reporting the same data, with consistent definitions and methodologies, so that cities can compare and benchmark themselves in a meaningful way.

Due to differences in cultures and values between cities around the world, the ISO 37120 standard does not offer a rating system or value to benchmark on how a city scores in any area. For example, in the Education theme, a core indicator is the percentage of female school-aged population enrolled in school. The standard provides the method by which this should be measured—"the number of female school-aged population enrolled at primary and secondary levels in public and private schools (numerator) divided by the total number of female school-aged population (denominator). The result shall then be multiplied by 100 and expressed as a percentage" (The standard provides definitions of primary and secondary schools) (ISO 2014). The standard, however, does not indicate what a good or poor score might be—some cities may score at 95 % and some at 30 %. Certification organizations that do certify cities also tend to shy away from these values, certifying cities based on how many indicators they measure but not on their qualitative results.

IDC's Smart City MaturityScape

International Data Corporation (IDC) is an experienced global provider of market intelligence, advisory services, and events for the information technology, telecommunications, and consumer technology markets. More than 1100 IDC analysts provide global, regional, and local expertise on technology and industry opportunities and trends in over 110 countries worldwide. In 2011, IDC launched a dedicated Smart Cities program as part of its Government Insights practice.

IDC's Smart City maturity model, called a MaturityScape, was developed on the belief that successful deployment of Smart City initiatives depends on a multifaceted approach guided by a strategy that accounts not just for technology, but also for human and capital resources, organizational culture, business and IT processes, and the data smart city systems generate. IDC Smart City MaturityScape is a structured way for cities to identify their current level of maturity, and the gap between where they are and where they want to be, and is a way to reduce the friction of change, to make more precise investments, and to identify the details of governance, process, technology, organization, and other factors that can derail the best-laid technology initiative.

The IDC Smart City MaturityScape provides a framework of stages, measure, actions, and outcomes required for organizations to effectively transform, enabling a city or a department to:

- Assess its Smart City competency and maturity.
- Prioritize Smart City technology investments, data policies, governance structures, and other related decisions.
- Uncover maturity gaps among business units and between business and IT groups.

Based on extensive primary and secondary research, IDC has identified common stages that cities go through as they mature as smart cities, and key best practices area that make them successful. IDC's Smart City MaturityScape includes five stages (Ad Hoc, Opportunistic, Repeatable, Managed, and Optimized) and five key success dimensions (Vision, Culture, Process, Technology, and Data). Each stage builds on the capabilities of the one before it. Each of the dimensions has indicators that define the key success factors within in each dimension and provide a way to measure maturity. There are 19 such indicators, and each indicator is defined within each stage of maturity (Clarke and Brooks 2015). For example, in the Data dimension, three of the indicators are Citizen Data Protection, Data Sharing and Data Discovery, and Analysis Examples. As illustrated in Fig. 3, the goals and outcomes are described for each indicator depending on the stage of maturity.

IDC has conducted a series of MaturityScape Benchmarks in which cities and state are surveyed to determine the overall maturity of a region or country. Benchmarks have been conducted in the USA, Canada, and Western Europe, allowing cities within those regions to compare themselves to their geographic peers.

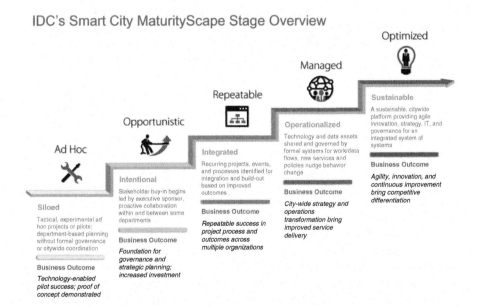

Fig. 3 IDC's smart MaturityScape © IDC, 2015

Comparison of the Three Models

The three models of assessment summarized in this chapter are complementary to each other in many ways and could be effectively used together for a more complete picture of a smart city. The ISO standard provides a level of quantitative measures that neither BSI nor IDC's models have; the ISO is focused on the main activity of accurate and consistent measurement, whereas the BSI and IDC models are focused on the process of change and meeting specific outcomes. These two models do, in essence, assign inherent values to certain behaviors. For example, in the BSI, a Lagging Leadership Performance is indicated by fragmented leadership, whereas a more mature behavior is a Driven Leadership Network. Using the models in concert could take As-Is measures of ISO core indicators and couple them with an aspirational state for cities and a process by which to achieve that aspiration via the BSI or IDC models.

In addition, BSI and IDC look at areas that are hard to quantify but have been proven to be essential to successful smart city initiatives. For example, IDC describes the stages of maturity around data use and analysis, acknowledging that most data in municipalities is not fully analyzed or used for improved understanding and decision-making. Measuring the level of data analysis in a quantitative way is difficult. Instead, IDC relies on the self-reporting of cities to describe their systems and behaviors.

All three models rely on the self-reporting of cities, though with the concrete ways to measure from the ISO standard, and the required independent audit of cities for certification, the ISO process is less susceptible to bias in reporting. In IDC's benchmarks, for example, analysts have found that survey respondents tend to overestimate their competency even when asked very specific and structured questions on specific tasks. In all cases, what is measured reveals a belief system. Even without an inherent value by the ISO standards on core indicator results, the very fact that it considers school enrollment of the female population as a core indicator sets forth an opinion.

In summary, ISO 37120 focuses on the quantitative "what" of a smart city while the BSI and IDC focuses more on the framework for "how." ISO leaves out many soft factors that are essential to this how, like leadership, funding models, and a culture of innovation. Between the BSI and IDC, IDC is focused on technology and data in depth, though it covers best practices for areas within Vision, Process and Culture, BSI goes into depth in its framework in terms of models of smart city structures and enabling factors. The two frameworks have several common elements, specifically in the identification of the main factors driving the development of smart cities, but they are also complementary.

The goal of these assessments is to help cities achieve their loftier societal goals including digital inclusion, community engagement, equal access to services, and equitable and environmentally sustainable development. These factors play a varying role in the definition of smart cities; many cities have developed their own construct, such as New York City's Smart+Equitable City. How these assessments can flex to meet the needs of each city is important. The ISO measures certainly establish a baseline for analyzing inclusion and access to basic services like water or education, while IDC's model, for example, includes aspects of resident engagement and sustainability in its best practices. It is a true challenge to provide frameworks that can be used consistently to improve quality of life across widely different cultures globally while remaining in synch with the foundational tenets of the smart city movement.

Challenges to Smart City Assessments

Smart city assessments and the field of smart cities in general is a developing area still in its early years. Cities are complex ecosystems and the challenge is to create assessment models that are not burdensome to cities, which already do a lot of performance tracking and measurement, often at the behest of higher levels of government at the state/ province or national levels. Following are some key considerations.

Ecosystem Players Have Different Motivations: Even as cities and their support-ers attempt to assess themselves to develop their roadmaps for smart city growth, there are sometimes conflicting motivations between key stakeholder groups and even within departments. For example, thinking about sustainability and quality of life often leads to a discussion about traffic, especially for commuters on highways. Many cities would want to shift cars to arterial roads in cases of high highway con-gestion, though if a highway is a toll road, the highway department may want to keep traffic flowing through its tollbooths in order to collect tolls. Consistent mea-surements do not necessarily solve this, though strong leadership and explicitly stated goals may help. A structured process to engage stakeholders may also help bring these conflicting motivations into the open so they can be managed.

Understanding Standards and Common Language Requires Time, Staff, Resources, and Money: Reading through the multiple reports from BSI and ISO on vocabulary definitions and standards takes time. These documents are thorough and can be long. City officials also have to read through many other forms of documen-tation, for example, public safety standard operating procedures or other operating standards developed at higher levels of government. Finding the staff resources to take time for such things may be difficult, especially for smaller sized cities where staff may have multiple roles and be even more stretched. Becoming certified or having an assessment also requires money, another limited resource.

Investment in Smart Cities May Require Money to be Reallocated: Not many cities have line items in their budgets for smart city assessments. This means that they have to find funds for the projects, often by taking money away from another initiative. Assessments need to be affordable. For suppliers, this means they have to be able to offer repeatable services so that they also remain viable. IDC manages this by conducting online assessments or engaging with national entities for a multi-city approach.

The Results Are Just In: Because of the newness of many smart city projects, there haven't, to date, been an abundance of examples that show positive results or return on investment. Cities are risk-averse and tend to want to follow in the successful footsteps of other cities; this has proved a challenge since metrics for success, cost savings, and other benefits are just starting to be publicized by early adopters.

Processes Can Take Longer than Elected Officials Have in Office: Cities do not necessarily move quickly and require time to procure, pilot, and adopt new strategies and initiatives. As initiatives are often driven by a mayoral agenda, projects can often be delayed mid-stream if there is a change in leadership. Elected officials might also wait for their second terms or just before they leave office to start pushing for innovations when they feel more able to take risks and want to leave a legacy.

Strategic Next Steps for Smart City Leaders

So, in light of the opportunities and challenges that smart cities hold, what are key steps cities can take that are lower cost and lower risk but that still move them forward in adopting new technologies and becoming a smarter city?

- **Create a City-Wide Inclusive Smart City Strategy**: An explicit city-wide Smart City vision and strategy is almost a city's own standard for assessing itself and creating a common language across departments. Creating an inclusive city-wide strategy requires that leaders gather stakeholders to provide their input, align departments around a common vision, prioritize the goals of the city, focus the discussion on specific challenges, and differentiate each city in its approach to becoming smarter. By including input from key stakeholders early on, the strategy gains local buy-in and legitimacy, and increases the likelihood for support of related initiatives.
- **Embed a Culture of Innovation within the Strategy**: Oftentimes in both the public and private sector there is a real fear of failure around the higher risk of using new business models and technologies. However, tackling age-old problems requires innovative solutions and that can only happen via the managed trial and error of new ideas. There are many ways to manage risk, however. Co-developing solutions with suppliers can mean that cities don't use taxpayer dollars and as such failure is less politically and economically risky. Separating innovation into a distinct organization can offer cities experts in iteration and innovation (as Boston does with its Office of New Urban Mechanics) as well as distancing departments from failure. Creating innovation districts and test beds can also help cities test new solutions on a smaller scale, to allow them to evaluate more solutions, while engaging new innovative organizations in the process.
- **Leverage Expertise From the Smart City Ecosystem**: There are many events and organizations—from technology suppliers, to foundations, to research organizations

that have expertise and best practices in urban environments. An example of this is MetroMatch, a program from the Global City Indicators Facility that pairs municipalities so that they can share information on how to improve their performance relative to ISO 37120 indicators. Similarly, the World Council on City Data has a data portal where cities can share data. Many cities have Open Data platforms and are working to make sharing data across cities easier.

• **Determine Top Priority Services Areas that Deliver Publicly Noticeable and Concretely Measurable Results**: Look across the all city divisions to key areas where it is easy to see value. Transportation, lighting, and public safety may be areas where small adjustments or projects would produce results that residents notice quickly. Projects are noticeable when their implementation results in clear benefits to residents that they can experience on a daily basis, and concretely measurable means that the before and after can be quantified. These two factors are extremely important in building the business case for smart city investment.

Conclusion

Smart City implementation remains in the early stages. According to IDC's benchmarking of American, Canadian, and Western European cities, the vast majority are still in the first two stages of development, Ad Hoc and Opportunistic, per the IDC Smart City MaturityScape (Fig. 3). At this point, however, leading cities do have several years of experimentation under their belts, meaning that a larger number of cities are prepared to learn from them and invest with less risk. It is expected that this will result in high growth in smart city programs and an increased interest in self-assessment, gap analysis, and strategic road maps.

Given that most smart city projects require the involvement of a broad group of technology suppliers, utilities, and city departments, a common understanding of issues and definition of terms will continue to be very important. Even with cities defining their smart city strategy differently, agreement on the foundational issues—sustainability, technology innovation, community engagement—must be in place for the term "Smart City" to have real meaning and not just be used as a marketing term. And, it will become increasingly clear that cities need a central organizing group to bring together various configurations of people for effective smart city project design and implementation, including measurements for successful outcomes.

For the future, assessments and certifications will only be adopted if they are affordable and easy to carry out, which means they must be available to cities both as non-custom, repeatable tools as well as more personalized services. In addition, what cities decide to measure and how they measure it is crucial for implementing smart city projects for maximum impact and sustainability, and an area where current measurement frameworks offer a strong place to start.

References

BCN Smart City (n.d.) BCN smart city home page. http://smartcity.bcn.cat/en/bcn-smart-city.html. Accessed 28 June 2016

BSI (2016) Smart cities. http://www.bsigroup.com/en-GB/smart-cities. Accessed 28 June 2016

Clarke RY, Brooks A (2015) IDC MaturityScape: smart city. International Data Corporation. IDC Doc #US40814315

Comstock M (2012) What is a smart city and how can a city boost its IQ? Sustainable Cities. http://blogs.worldbank.org/sustainablecities/what-is-a-smart-city-and-how-can-a-city-boost-its-iq. Accessed 28 June 2016

European Commission (2013) European innovation partnership on smart cities and communities strategic implementation plan. http://ec.europa.eu/eip/smartcities/files/sip_final_en.pdf. Accessed 28 June 2016

European Commission (2015) Smart Cities. https://ec.europa.eu/digital-single-market/en/smart-cities. Accessed 28 June 2016

Infocomm Development Authority of Singapore (2014) Smart national platform. https://www.ida.gov.sg/~/media/Files/About%20Us/Newsroom/Media%20Releases/2014/0617_smartnation/AnnexA_sn.pdf. Accessed 28 June 2016

ISO (2014) ISO 37120 Sustainable development of communities—indicators for city services and quality of life. http://www.iso.org/iso/catalogue_detail?csnumber=62436. Accessed 28 June 2016

Juvara M (2015) Smart city: can it lead to smart planning? UrbanSilence. http://www.urbansilenceltd.com/smart-planning/item/smart-city-can-it-lead-to-smart-planning.html. Accessed 28 June 2016

Sims R (2009) Cities, towns and renewable energy: yes in my front yard. International Energy Agency. http://www.iea.org/publications/freepublications/publication/cities2009.pdf. Accessed 28 June 2016

Smart Cities Council (2015) Smart Cities Readiness Guide. Smart Cities Council, Redmond

The World Bank (2016) Urban development—overview. http://www.worldbank.org/en/topic/urbandevelopment/overview. Accessed 29 June 2016

UN Department of Economic and Social Affairs (2014) 2014 revision of world urbanization prospects. http://www.un.org/en/development/desa/publications/2014-revision-world-urbanization-prospects.html. Accessed 28 June 2016

Wang G, Alberto JD, Munindra M, Bangah S, Chang S, Ditton E et al. (2016) IDC FutureScape: worldwide smart city 2016 predictions. International Data Corporation. IDC Doc #259907

Measuring Your Company's Impact: How to Make the Most of Sustainability Reporting Frameworks

Jen Anderson and Jessica Abensour

Abstract The world's leading companies are looking beyond their financial performance to more holistically understand their impact. Through the many tools of corporate sustainability reporting, more and more companies are measuring, managing, and reporting on their environmental, social, and governance performance. As corporate sustainability reporting has grown, it has also evolved. It is moving beyond a company's four walls and looking to better understand the organization's entire value chain map, and its full impact on the economic, social, and environmental factors that are relevant to multiple corporate stakeholders.

This chapter explores the evolution of corporate sustainability and social impact measurement, starting with the foundations of reporting. It examines tools that companies and other organizations can use to measure and manage their impact better, with a focus on the Global Reporting Initiative (GRI). Ultimately, it will provide companies and organizations with a path for how to measure and manage social and environmental impact so that they are well equipped to address the associated risks, and to identify strategic opportunities for positive social impact.

Keywords Corporate impact measurement • Global Reporting Initiative (GRI) • Sustainability reporting

Introduction

The world's leading companies are looking beyond their financial performance to more holistically understand their impact. Through the many tools of corporate sustainability reporting, more and more companies are measuring, managing, and reporting on their environmental, social, and governance performance.

In 2010, only about 20 % of the Standard and Poor's 500 companies had published regular sustainability reports. By 2015, that number had jumped to 75 % (Facilitiesnet 2015). As corporate sustainability reporting has grown, it has also

J. Anderson (✉) • J. Abensour
VOX Global, 1615 L St NW #1110, Washington, DC 20036, USA
e-mail: janderson@voxglobal.com; jabensour@voxglobal.com

© Springer International Publishing Switzerland 2017   255
M.J. Cronin, T.C. Dearing (eds.), *Managing for Social Impact*,
Management for Professionals, DOI 10.1007/978-3-319-46021-5_15

evolved. It is moving beyond a company's four walls and looking to better understand the organization's entire value chain map, and its full impact on the economic, social, and environmental factors that are relevant to multiple corporate stakeholders.

Reporting is evolving because companies' role in society is evolving. Consumers are more skeptical of traditional advertising at the same time that social media gives individuals a platform to quickly disseminate information—whether positive or negative—about what companies are up to. With this level of transparency and movement of information, nongovernmental organizations and advocacy groups are better able to hold companies accountable for their impact. In addition, expectations have shifted so that stakeholders including customers, advocacy groups, community members, and government entities are looking to business to help solve societal problems.

This chapter explores this evolution, starting with the foundations of reporting. It examines tools that companies and other organizations can use to measure and manage their impact better, with a focus on the Global Reporting Initiative (GRI). Ultimately, it provides companies and organizations with a path for how to measure and manage social and environmental impact so that they are well equipped to address the associated risks, and to identify strategic opportunities for positive social impact.

Evolution of Corporate ESG Reporting

The first corporate sustainability reports were issued in the 1980s and 1990s by companies that were recieving pressure from outside groups to account for their environmental impact. Primarily these were companies whose products directly affected ecosystems, like mining and chemical companies. Since then, companies in nearly all industries are looking at their environmental and social impact. Several reporting frameworks have emerged in an attempt to guide companies on the path to corporate sustainability reporting. Corporate sustainability reporting goes by many names: corporate responsibility reporting, triple-bottom-line reporting (people, planet, profit), and ESG reporting (environmental, social, governance). There are also multiple frameworks and tools that companies use to measure their ESG performance.

Today, the GRI is the most widely used sustainability reporting framework. Other initiatives include the UN Global Compact, the Sustainability Accounting Board Standards, and, more recently, the UN Sustainable Development Goals (SDGs). It's important to note that none of these frameworks are in direct competition with each other, and several have issued linkage documents to help reporters understand the role and interconnectivity of each. That said companies frequently call for more consolidated reporting requests and probably wouldn't mind if one framework were to emerge to rule the rest. The SDGs is the most recent guidance to be published. While companies are not the primary audience for these goals and targets, they are encouraged to support them and link reporting to them. This represents a significant move from output to outcome reporting. Exemplified by efforts like the SDGs, a new discussion has emerged recently around not just a company's social and environmental performance (input and output), but also the broader social and environmental impact and outcome of its performance over time. Stakeholders are asking for increased disclosure around how a company's actions are impacting, or being impacted by, significant global issues—human rights, climate change, poverty, and the well-being of communities.

There are several motivating factors for this. One is simply the natural evolution of measurement. Once companies start collecting and reporting core ESG data, stakeholders want to fully understand its impact and interconnectivity with other data. Another factor is an emerging expectation that companies have a role to play in tackling significant environmental and social topics, whether that's preserving natural habitats, providing vaccines, or developing job training for unemployed youth. The notion is that it's not sufficient for companies simply to reduce their negative impacts. Stakeholders now look to the corporate sector for innovative programs that will help solve social problems.

Consider the 2015 United Nations Climate Change negotiations (COP21) in Paris, France. Nearly 200 nations gathered to create a historic framework through which to tackle global climate change. What was also notable about this conference, the 21st of its kind, was the unprecedented corporate presence—both in the sheer number of company executives who were present and in the substance of their contributions. Before and during the Paris gathering, corporations worked with policy makers to frame the issues and develop workable solutions. The International Chamber of Commerce reflects this perspective on sustainability as a corporate priority. The business group stated that "Private sector innovation, investment and expertise will be vital if we are to successfully tackle climate change and promote sustainable and inclusive growth. That's why we are advocating for an ambitious global agreement which works with business to speed emissions reductions and build climate resilience" (International Chamber of Commerce 2015).

Overview of Reporting Frameworks

Global Reporting Initiative

In 1997, Ceres, an environmental NGO, and the Tellus Institute created an organization called the Global Reporting Initiative (GRI) (GRI 2016b). The GRI's mission was to create a framework that would guide corporate sustainability reporting. After a thorough stakeholder engagement process, the GRI issued the first set of guidelines in June 2000 (van der Molen 2015). Since then, the GRI has issued four iterations of these guidelines, most recently the GRI G4. Today, 93 % of the world's largest 250 companies report on their sustainability performance and 82 % align reporting with the GRI (GRI 2016a).

The most recent transition from the GRI G3 guidelines to the G4 guidelines saw a transition from quantity to quality. While the G3 incentivized companies to report on as many indicators as possible, the G4 encourages companies to dig deeper on their most material topics.

The GRI's strength is that it provides a clear and comparable framework. What it currently lacks is the ability to translate the data that a company reports into an overall expression of the company's broad social impact. The GRI itself has acknowledged this and recently announced some updates that will transition the GRI G4 from guidance to a standard. Most changes focus on the format and presentation—the main content, concepts, and disclosures from G4 will carry through to the GRI Standards (GRI 2016d). This will include three primary changes: (1) a new digital format with multiple information sources; (2) new content requests focused on overall impacts to society and natural resources; and (3) a new role for stakeholders with increased access. According to the GRI (2016c):

> Sustainability disclosures and related data will provide a clear overview of business contributions to climate change, to eliminate contamination, to protect ecosystems and to the regional management of natural resources. The data will also reveal contributions to the quality of life—access to food and water, education, health services and civil rights—of all those individuals and communities involved in the business' extended value chain/operations.

The new GRI Standard was announced in the Fall of 2016. Companies will adjust their reporting to align with it it over the next year.

To fill the current gap in holistic impact assessment, new measurement tools have been developed to look more fully at impact and outcomes, not just output. None appear nearly as well defined as the GRI, but various alternative and complementary ESG frameworks are taking hold.

Other Frameworks

Additional popular frameworks worth noting include the UN Global Compact, the Sustainability Accounting Standards Board, and Integrated Reporting.

UN Global Compact

The UN Global Compact consists of ten principles that aligning companies are expected to fulfill. More than 8000 business participants and 4000 nonbusiness participants align with the UNGC and report their performance against it.

These principles are outlined in Table 1.

Sustainability Accounting Standards Board

For many companies, ESG information still exists separately from financial reporting (annual reports, 10-Ks, etc.). Some large socially responsible investors (SRIs) and advocacy groups are advocating for integration of the numbers through movements such as Integrated Reporting and the Sustainability Accounting Standards Board (SASB).

Table 1 The ten principles of the UN Global Compact (Source: UN Global Compact 2016)

Human rights	Principle 1: businesses should support and respect the protection of internationally proclaimed human rights
	Principle 2: make sure that they are not complicit in human rights abuses
Labor	Principle 3: businesses should uphold the freedom of association and the effective recognition of the right to collective bargaining
	Principle 4: the elimination of all forms of forced and compulsory labor;
	Principle 5: the effective abolition of child labor
	Principle 6: the elimination of discrimination in respect of employment and occupation
Environment	Principle 7: businesses should support a precautionary approach to environmental challenges
	Principle 8: undertake initiatives to promote greater environmental responsibility
	Principle 9: encourage the development and diffusion of environmentally friendly technologies
Anticorruption	Principle 10: businesses should work against corruption in all its forms, including extortion and bribery

The Sustainability Accounting Standards Board (SASB) was conceived in 2011 in an effort to incorporate material ESG topics more formally into a company's financial filings. Material topics are defined by the SEC as those that have "a substantial likelihood that the disclosure of the omitted fact would have been viewed by the reasonable investor as having significantly altered the 'total mix' of information made available" (SASB 2016). A product of the recession of 2008, the intention of SASB is to provide investors with a more holistic view of the company's environmental, social, and governance performance. SASB's 2016 goals were to publish industry-tailored standards for 80 industries in 10 sectors. These standards list specific indicators deemed most material to companies in each industry.

Adoption of the SASB standards has been slow. As of 2016, only Bloomberg has issued any reporting based on the SASB guidance. The incentive for others to follow is unclear and the next few years will tell us if mainstream investors are truly looking for this ESG information to be included in financial filings, or if they prefer to receive the data through another vehicle—like a GRI report.

In the meantime, many companies are using the standards as an internal tool to understand better what social impacts its shareholders and investors are likely to be asking about.

Integrated Reporting

Integrated Reporting goes beyond SASB, in an effort to promote full merging of financial and ESG data. The International Integrated Reporting Council (IIRC) is a group of regulators, investors, companies, and advocacy groups that promotes the value of integrated reporting. IIRC has created and published an integrated reporting framework, <IR>, which gives companies a roadmap for combined reporting. <IR> does not prescribe specific data points to report. Instead, it is a process for combining information about an organization's "strategy, governance, performance and prospects in the context of its external environment" (IR 2016). So far, companies have been slow to adopt truly integrated reporting. As is the case with SASB, time will tell if this form of merged financial reporting and ESG reporting is valuable.

New Tools in Reporting for Impact

Social Impact Measurement

In the meantime, as reporting frameworks evolve and adapt, companies are looking for other ways to measure social and environmental impact. The first rule of measuring social value is that no set of fixed rules applies to every company, at least, not any widely accepted standards or norms that cut across various industries. Just as companies develop a social or environmental program focus that tends to be a unique reflection of their businesses, decisions about the best impact measurement strategy should be grounded in the specific corporate, industry sector, and stakeholder context.

A Conference Board study, *Framing Social Impact Measurement*, explores various frameworks and cites three emerging organizations developing measurement methodology: LBG, True Impact, and Mission Measurement. The trend that is emerging with these, as well as others, is a movement away from measuring inputs.

A growing number of businesses are using these new methods of reporting to calculate their societal impact. In fact, 76 % of companies are measuring the societal impact of their philanthropic and other corporate social responsibility (CSR) programs. However, only 18 % of those have been doing so for five or more years, signifying an incredibly fast pace of change (The Conference Board 2014). Later in this chapter, we'll discuss some specific elements of the most popular frameworks that might be helpful to companies and organizations in measuring social impact.

Net Positive

In addition to measuring the social impact of philanthropic or CSR programs, there's a movement afoot called Net Positive that seeks to quantify the total social or economic benefit a company and its products have. This movement is being driven by organizations such as Business for Social Responsibility, Harvard's SHINE project, and Forum for the Future. According to the Forum for the Future, "Net Positive is a way of doing business which puts back more into society, the environmental and the global economy than it takes out" (Bent et al. n.d.). Such groups are looking to help establish methodologies through which companies might measure their overall impact. Companies involved in this effort include AT&T,[1] BT, Dell, IKEA, and Unilever. It's still early days for this movement, and there are many more questions than answers.

Some of the lingering questions about the general trend toward measuring corporate impact include the following:

- How should a company define its impact? What are the boundaries?
- Should a company's "net impact" be broken down by issue (e.g., carbon emissions), or measured as an overall company impact?
- How should positive and negative impacts be measured and compared? How should companies account for trade-offs?

UN Sustainable Development Goals

Another relevant framework for this conversation is the UN Sustainable Development Goals (SDGs), which the UN launched in September 2015 as part of the global organization's 2030 Agenda for Sustainable Development (UN 2015). These goals are updates to the UN Millennium Development Goals (MDGs) announced in 2000. They reflect far-reaching global aspirations for social justice and sustainable economic development through 2030. While the goals are intended for nation-states, they call companies to engage on the most significant global challenges of our time and play their role. The goals include objectives like "end poverty in all its forms everywhere," and "end hunger, achieve food security and improved nutrition and promote stainable agriculture."

The United Nations, World Business Council for Sustainable Development, and the GRI have developed a tool called "SDG Compass: The guide for business action on the SDGs," to help companies understand how they should interact with the SDGs (2015). Their five steps are:

1. Understand SDGs
2. Define priorities
3. Set goals
4. Integrate into business
5. Align with reporting and communications

For now, we're seeing early adopters demonstrate how various corporate social impact initiatives already align with specifics goals. Several partnerships are emerging as well that will bring together the public and the private sector in looking to tackle these significant goals together. For example, Champions 12.3 is a coalition of executives from governments, businesses, international organizations, research institutions, farmer groups, and civil society dedicated to driving action to achieve SDG Target 12.3. That target is to, "by 2030, halve per capita global food waste at

---

[1] AT&T is a VOX Global client.

the retail and consumer levels and reduce food losses along production and supply chains, including post-harvest losses." Company members include executives from Tesco, Kellogg Company, Nestle, Rabobank, Sodexo, and Unilever (Champions 12.3 2016).

Deep Dive: Tools to Measure Impact

With the overarching background of reporting frameworks in mind, it's helpful to look at some specific examples. This section dives into two: the Global Reporting Initiative and CSR impact measurement. As noted earlier, the GRI is one of the most widely used frameworks for capturing and reporting a company's ESG data.

GRI: Using GRI G4 as a Tool for Understanding and Measuring Impact

GRI Basics

The GRI asks a company to disclose specific data and information about its governance, economic, environmental, and social performance. There are two categories of data: (1) general standard disclosures and (2) topic-specific performance indicators.

1. General standard disclosures are to be completed by all organizations. They ask companies to complete data about the company, financials, employees, stakeholder engagement, and governance.
2. Topic-specific performance indicators have three categories: economic, environmental, and social. Under each category are a collection of *Aspects*, or topics. A company is required to report on specific data points under each of the Aspects that are deemed "material," to the company. Companies use a materiality assessment process to determine these topics. It's important to note that this definition of materiality that the GRI uses is not the same as the SEC definition discussed previously.

Completing a GRI report has many nuances and requires specialized terminology. Before embarking on formal GRI reporting, it is helpful for managers who will implement the reporting to receive training in the framework, or work with a partner that has received this training. The general GRI reporting approach, however, can be roughly summarized in seven steps:

1. Identify stakeholders.
2. Ask your stakeholders which economic, environmental, and social topics are most important to the company.
3. Ask internal leaders which economic, environmental, and social topics are most important to the company.

4. Using the feedback, systematically create a list of the most important ESG topics.
5. In a GRI table, disclose prescribed data for each topic that is considered most important.
6. In the same form, disclose additional data required by the general standard disclosures.
7. Many companies also write an additional narrative that brings the data to life, and highlight important milestones for the company in the reporting year. The GRI data and narrative combined comprises a company's Corporate Social Responsibility Report.

Specific Tools

When the GRI G4 framework was announced in 2013, it introduced some especially useful tools for companies. These include materiality assessment and stakeholder mapping, as well as value chain mapping.

Materiality Assessment and Stakeholder Mapping and Engagement

The GRI requires companies to conduct a materiality assessment. Simply put, through a materiality assessment companies reach out to both internal and external stakeholders and ask them to rank the environmental, social, and governance topics that are most relevant to their business. The result is a matrix that plots topics based on rank along two axes: importance to external stakeholders and importance to business (ranked by internal stakeholders).

A materiality assessment is not just a requirement of GRI reporting. It's a valuable tool for companies to understand where their most significant impacts are. Organizations are then able to prioritize resources accordingly. Before completing a materiality assessment, companies should conduct a stakeholder mapping exercise to identify which stakeholders are most important to their company and therefore which to reach out to in the assessment. Categories to consider are employees—current and future, policymakers/regulators, advocacy groups, general consumers, business customers, supply chain, and academics.

Value Chain Mapping

Another valuable tool from the GRI is value chain mapping. Through this exercise, companies are asked to map their organization's entire impact—from raw materials to disposal. In the process, companies develop a deeper understanding of what their value chain looks like and can also indicate where their most material topics exist.

Metrics

An important strength of the GRI is that it offers companies a well-defined framework of metrics through which they can better understand their impact within specific topics, such as energy, biodiversity, occupational health and safety, and supplier human rights. Measurement leads to better understanding and equips companies to take action accordingly.

Measuring Impact

While the GRI and its tools can be incredibly useful in helping companies understand their full performance and reach, the GRI indicators don't yet naturally translate into measuring outcomes and impacts. Rather, they focus on outputs. This is where using an impact framework is helpful.

Measuring impact over outputs empowers companies to better understand their impact and communicate it to key audiences. For example, instead of a pharmaceutical company announcing its intention to donate money to combat malaria, imagine that same company announcing that it had cured or dramatically reduced the incidence of malaria in a certain location. This positive outcome would be a much more powerful story. The social impact of curing a debilitating and chronic disease would itself be an enormously positive step toward achieving the UN's Sustainable Development Goals. Such a breakthrough would garner widespread media coverage and resonate with policy officials, consumers, or whatever key audience is most important to that company. But, in order to tell that story in an authentic way, companies must be in a position to track the return on their investment all the way through to outcomes and impacts.

Principles of CSR Impact Measurement

One area where we're seeing steps toward tangible impact measurement is in company Corporate Social Responsibility and philanthropy programs. The demand for such measurement is being driven by both internal and external factors, such as the proliferation of "watchdog" nongovernmental organizations (NGOs), the desire of business to prove return on investment (ROI) on every dollar spent, and the higher expectations consumers and employees have of businesses' role in society.

Measurement can be applied to CSR programs whether they focus on societal issues (education, hunger, homelessness, etc.) or environmental issues (emissions reductions, alternative fuel vehicles programs, internal recycling programs, etc.). In order to be effective, CSR impact measurement should follow a set of key principles and quantifiable metrics that will help companies to track program progress.

Here are five key principles for CSR measurement.

1. **Involve others**: Don't go it alone. Ask internal and external stakeholders to help along the way.
2. **Start with objectives**: Identify the social and business objectives first. Use those objectives to help make decisions about what can be measured.
3. **Focus on what the program can truly impact**: Don't spread the program too thin.
4. **Be transparent**: Transparency brings credibility. If a CSR program is not driving the impact expected, be up front, find out why and change course.
5. **Have others substantiate**: Ensure partners and/or independent third parties validate results.

Tracking Progress from Inputs and Outputs to Outcomes and Impacts

While there's no set framework, Fig. 1 distills several impact measurement frameworks into a four-step process. Keeping in mind the five principles of CSR measurement listed above, companies can measure the impact of their CSR program through these steps.

1. **Identify Societal Objectives**

Start with societal objectives: What are the social, community, or environmental challenges the CSR program will address? Examples can be as straightforward and high level as improving education, job skills, nutrition, or even water quality for a certain population or geographic area. However, the more focused and specific the objectives are, the clearer the path to measuring impact.

MEASURING IN FOUR STEPS

IDENTIFY SOCIETAL OBJECTIVES
What social, community or environmental issue do you want to address?

MAKE THE BUSINESS CASE
What business objectives can your CR initiative help move the needle on?

SET SPECIFIC GOALS
With your objectives in mind, what are the specific goals for your program?

DEVELOP METRICS
Identify the inputs, outputs and outcomes that you will track

Fig. 1 A four-step process for impact measurement (Source: VOX Global)

2. Make the Business Connection

With for-profit companies, it's also critical to have an eye on the bottom line. Decades ago, it was seen as poor form to publicly connect philanthropy to business strategy. A firewall existed between business and philanthropy functions. Today, while companies are expected to "do good" and play a role in addressing social problems, it is also widely recognized that doing good can and should be good for business.

Setting business objectives related to CSR, however, is not always as straightforward as identifying a company's societal objectives. Companies often struggle to define business ROI from social impact programs beyond improving reputation. According to a KPMG survey of 4100 companies around the world (KPMG 2013), the top five business opportunities most often cited for engaging in CSR activities are to:

1. Innovate new products and services
2. Strengthen brands and corporate reputation
3. Improve market position/growing market share
4. Drive cost saving
5. Improve employee motivation

The "Creating Shared Value" section of this chapter provides examples of companies that have implemented a shared value model for integrating CSR efforts with clear business ROI.

3. Set Specific Program Goals

Once societal and business objectives are identified, integrate goals into the CSR measurement strategy. Integrating goal setting helps ensure that the goals are measurable and that what is being measured is aligned with what the CSR program aims to accomplish. Over half of Fortune 500 companies have goal platforms, and the more ambitious the goals, the more they can set companies apart for their CSR leadership.

Elements of strong CSR goals include the following:

- **Concrete**: Set tangible, actionable deliverables derived from societal and business objectives.
- **Long Term**: Multiyear goal platforms demonstrate future vision and a sustainable direction for the company.
- **Transparent**: A company must be confident publicly sharing the goals and reporting progress toward reaching them.
- **Measureable**: It's not enough to be qualitative with results; show quantifiable results using absolute figures and data over general statements.

4. Develop Metrics

After societal and business objectives are set and goals are identified and incorporated, it's time to track progress using an impact framework that includes the following categories:

- **Inputs**: Money, time, and in-kind giving you bring to the table.
- **Outputs**: Direct result from an activity; usually answers the question "how many."

- **Outcomes**: Changes that result from an activity; often in # or % increase/decrease.
- **Impacts**: Determine both societal and business impacts using third-party data and research.

Table 2 presents a worksheet developed by VOX Global to illustrate the factors that should be considered in executing this four-step measurement process

Success in achieving societal goals should ultimately be measured by the impact that a company's CSR program has, not by the amount of money the company donates to causes, the number of hours that its employees volunteer, or in-kind products it donates to a cause. Using an impact framework will help the company identify and track the data points it will need to understand its full impact and to tell a compelling and credible impact story.

In its recent corporate social responsibility report, Nike summed up this strategy nicely, stating: "We recognize that lasting change requires more than investment. It requires results. That's why we aim to measure the social impact of our community investments. We aim to move away from measuring inputs and outputs alone" (Nike 2015).

Table 2 A sample worksheet for the four-step measurement process (Source: VOX Global)

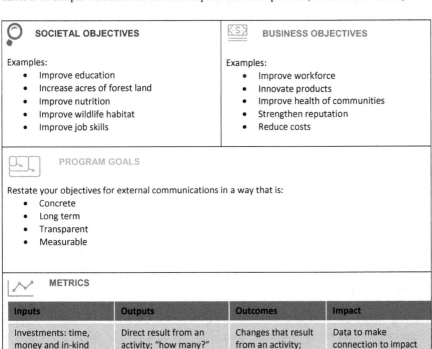

SOCIETAL OBJECTIVES	BUSINESS OBJECTIVES
Examples: • Improve education • Increase acres of forest land • Improve nutrition • Improve wildlife habitat • Improve job skills	Examples: • Improve workforce • Innovate products • Improve health of communities • Strengthen reputation • Reduce costs

PROGRAM GOALS

Restate your objectives for external communications in a way that is:
- Concrete
- Long term
- Transparent
- Measurable

METRICS

Inputs	Outputs	Outcomes	Impact
Investments: time, money and in-kind	Direct result from an activity; "how many?"	Changes that result from an activity; often in # or %	Data to make connection to impact on society or business

Creating Shared Value

FORTUNE recently announced its inaugural "Change the World" list (Fortune 2016). The 51 companies on the list were recognized not based on their overall "goodness," but for *"doing good as part of their profit-making strategy."* Examples like these put a finer point on the evolution of philanthropy and CSR towards a shared value model, where value to both society *and for the business* is realized simultaneously through CSR and broader company efforts. To be a key driver of positive reputation, CSR needs to be authentically aligned to business strategy as well as to the goals of corporate stakeholders.

There are several ways companies can connect these elements. For example, Cisco's Networking Academy utilizes Cisco's products and services to boost technical skills and career training opportunities for people and organizations around the globe (Netacad 2016).

Companies like chocolate manufacturers and coffee retailers, with supply chain needs in developing countries, have a growing interest in serving communities where their products are sourced. This includes providing community education and training, minimizing their environmental footprint, and other responsible sourcing supports and initiatives, often in developing countries.

Tech companies, such as AT&T, Apple, and Microsoft, have more than one reason to commit support to the Obama Administration's ConnectED initiative (ConnectEd 2016). They have the opportunity to work with the White House to reach the meaningful and business-aligned goal of bringing broadband connectivity to 99 % of American students within 5 years. They also have the opportunity to work directly with school districts, teachers, and school technology officers on developing new products and services, ultimately leading to innovation and market growth as those new products and services are brought to market.

Business Benefits

In summary, there are many benefits for companies that commit to measuring and reporting their environmental and social impact. The measurement frameworks and tools discussed in this chapter can support business growth in the following ways:

Resource Allocation

The materiality assessment and stakeholder engagement tools are valuable for helping companies allot resources to addresss their ESG performance. The value chain map can help a company see more clearly its entire environmental and social performance and impact.

Stakeholder Expectations

Stakeholders are expecting companies to account for the environmental and social impact and performance. This is no longer a competitive advantage for top companies, but a necessity. Consider how institutional investment Blackrock issued a climate disclosure guidance for companies to follow (Fleming 2015). They understand that a company doesn't do business in isolation, but is interconnected to macro global trends.

Reputation

It's no surprise that social and environmental factors, like citizenship and how a company treats its employees, are having a growing impact on corporate reputation. In fact, according to the Reputation Institute, corporate social responsibility-related topics make up over 40 % of consumers' perception of a company's reputation. Of the seven factors their RepTrak Pulse score factors into reputation, three—citizenship, governance, and workplace—are considered CSR factors. So while product and service are vital, if a company doesn't have strong corporate social responsibility initiatives, its reputation is likely suffering (Reputation Institute 2014).

Employees

Companies are leveraging environmental and social initiatives to strengthen employee engagement. Engaged employees have a stronger emotional commitment to their company. They work for more than a paycheck; they work on behalf of furthering their company's goals, and they use extra, discretionary effort to do so.

In short, they are more committed, and employees who are most committed to their organization put in 57 % more effort and are 87 % less likely to leave than employees who feel disengaged. In contrast, a company will lose $13,000 annually for each employee who is disengaged, whether they remain with the company or they leave (Kruse 2012).

Elements of Effective Employee Engagement
Engaging employees effectively through CSR initiatives, such as volunteer activities aligned to strategic philanthropic gifts or utilizing employees' expertise to help solve a societal challenge, does not happen organically. It requires a deliberate and well-executed strategy that starts with identifying the right messages and best communications channels to reach the employees most likely to participate. As a result, a business may find that text messaging is more effective than e-mail, or posters in break rooms and elevators are more effective than announcements from management.

Although it may be counterintuitive at first, it is important that employee engagement opportunities are clearly aligned to business goals. Making it matter to the business will provide incentive, beyond just doing good, to participate.

Lastly, recognize and incentivize employee participation. Measure results, collect and share stories, and use rewards as appropriate to recognize the work being done, encourage more employees to participate in the future, and make it fun.

While research finds that social impact is valued by employees of all experience levels and generations, it particularly drives Millennial's engagement and satisfaction with employers. Three out of four want to work for a company that cares about how it impacts and contributes to society. Among Millennials already in the workforce, 65 % say that their employer's social/environmental activities make them feel loyal to their company (Cone Communications 2009).

In addition to recruitment and retention, employees who are engaged are more likely to advocate on behalf of their companies when a crisis occurs, such as a data breach or an impending legislative vote that will have negative consequences to the business. And, as mentioned previously in this chapter, how a company treats its employees influences its reputation, ultimately affecting its bottom line.

Conclusion

Corporate sustainability reporting is growing and evolving. Stakeholders are seeking to understand a company's full impact—economic, social, and environmental—and companies can use several reporting tools to help provide the answer. The benefits of corporate reporting and measuring for impact are broad and companies that start now will be at a competitive advantage as this trend continues into the future.

References

Bent D, Uren S, Le Grand Z (n.d.) The net positive project. https://www.forumforthefuture.org/project/net-positive-project/overview. Accessed 29 June 2016
Champions 12.3 (2016) Champions 12.3—about. https://champions123.org/about/. Accessed 28 June 2016
Cone Communications (2009) Past. Present. Future. The 25th anniversary of cause marketing. http://www.conecomm.com/research-blog/past-present-future-the-25th-anniversary-of-cause-marketing. Accessed 19 July 2016

ConnectEd (2016) ConnectEd home page. https://www.whitehouse.gov/issues/education/k-12/connected. Accessed 28 June 2016

Facilitiesnet (2015) Sustainably dashboard: growth of sustainability reporting reflects growth of green, social, and environmental issues. http://www.facilitiesnet.com/site/pressreleases/Sustainably-Dashboard-Growth-of-Sustainability-Reporting-Reflects-Growth-of-Green-Social-and-Environmental-Issues--36324. Accessed 28 June 2016

Fleming P (2015) BlackRock, Ceres launch investor guide on US corporate engagement. Ceres. http://www.ceres.org/press/press-releases/blackrock-ceres-launch-investor-guide-on-us-corporate-engagement. Accessed 28 June 2016

Fortune (2016) Change the world list. http://beta.fortune.com/change-the-world/. Accessed 28 June 2016

GRI (2016a) GRI at a glance. https://www.globalreporting.org/information/news-and-press-center/press-resources/Pages/default.aspx. Accessed 28 June 2016

GRI (2016b) GRI's history. https://www.globalreporting.org/information/about-gri/gri-history/Pages/GRI's%20history.aspx. Accessed 28 June 2016

GRI (2016c) The next era of corporate disclosure. https://www.globalreporting.org/resourcelibrary/The-Next-Era-of-Corporate-Disclosure.pdf. Accessed 28 June 2016

GRI (2016d) Transition to standards. https://www.globalreporting.org/standards/transition-to-standards/Pages/default.aspx. Accessed 28 June 2016

Integrated Reporting (2016) IIRC home page. http://integratedreporting.org/the-iirc-2/. Accessed 28 June 2016

International Chamber of Commerce (2015) ICC home page. http://cop21.iccwbo.org/. Accessed 28 June 2016

KPMG (2013) The KPMG survey of corporate responsibility reporting 2013. http://www.kpmg.com/Global/en/IssuesAndInsights/ArticlesPublications/corporate-responsibility/Documents/corporate-responsibility-reporting-survey-2013.pdf. Accessed 28 June 2016

Kruse K (2012) What is employee engagement? Forbes

Netacad (2016) Netacad home page. https://www.netacad.com/. Accessed 28 June 2016

Nike (2015) Our ambition: double our business, with half the impact. http://about.nike.com/pages/our-ambition. Accessed 28 June 2016

Reputation Institute (2014) What drives reputation in the U.S. communications industry in 2014? http://www.reputationinstitute.com/getattachment/9a6839b1-afc8-47ca-a356-bb52fdfe55cd/Industry-Reputation-Drivers-Brief-US-Communications-05Nov14-ZK.pdf.aspx;;?ext=.pdf. Accessed 5 July 2016

SASB (2016) Materiality—why is it important?. http://www.sasb.org/materiality/important/. Accessed 28 June 2016

SDG Compass (2015) SDG Compass home page. http://sdgcompass.org/. Accessed 28 June 2016

The Conference Board (2014) Framing social impact measurement. https://www.conference-board.org/publications/publicationdetail.cfm?publicationid=2861. Accessed 28 June 2016

United Nations (2015) A new sustainable development agenda. http://www.undp.org/content/undp/en/home/sdgoverview/. Accessed 28 June 2016

United Nations Global Compact (2016) The ten principles of the UN global compact. https://www.unglobalcompact.org/what-is-gc/mission/principles. Accessed 28 June 2016

van der Molen F (2015) Behind the first 15 years of GRI sustainability reporting (trans: Azaria, A.). Greenbiz. https://www.greenbiz.com/article/behind-first-15-years-gri-sustainability-reporting. Accessed 28 June 2016

Index

© Springer International Publishing Switzerland 2017
M.J. Cronin, T.C. Dearing (eds.), *Managing for Social Impact*,
Management for Professionals, DOI 10.1007/978-3-319-46021-5

CPSIA information can be obtained
at www.ICGtesting.com
Printed in the USA
LVOW05*2052040118
561827LV00001B/15/P

9 783319 460208